POPULATING THE NOVEL

POPULATING
THE NOVEL

LITERARY FORM AND THE
POLITICS OF SURPLUS LIFE

EMILY STEINLIGHT

CORNELL UNIVERSITY PRESS
Ithaca and London

First published 2018 by Cornell University Press

Library of Congress Cataloging-in-Publication Data

Librarians: A CIP catalog record for this book is available from the Library of Congress.

LCCN: 2017027639

Cornell University Press strives to use environmentally responsible suppliers and materials to the fullest extent possible in the publishing of its books. Such materials include vegetable-based, low-VOC inks and acid-free papers that are recycled, totally chlorine-free, or partly composed of nonwood fibers. For further information, visit our website at cornellpress.cornell.edu.

For D.S.H.

CONTENTS

Acknowledgments

This book is the product of four cities, four universities, and a population of interlocutors, colleagues, friends, and mentors whose conversation has sharpened it and whose support has buoyed me through its completion. I am especially grateful to Jed Esty, Heather Keenleyside, Jacques Khalip, Anna Kornbluh, and Benjamin Morgan for offering invaluable feedback on chapter drafts over the past year. Each chapter is substantially stronger for their having read it. It was an immeasurable privilege to work with Nancy Armstrong, Kevin McLaughlin, and William Keach on the earliest version of this project at Brown University. I owe a great deal to the expertise, judicious guidance, and kind encouragement of all three, as well as to the example of their own scholarship. Nancy was and is both the most exacting critic and the most generous mentor possible. She will always be a decisive voice in my head.

Elements of this work developed in new directions thanks to engaging responses from audiences at the Cogut Center for the Humanities at Brown, the University of Chicago Society of Fellows Symposium and Weissbourd Conference, the Eighteenth- and Nineteenth-Century Cultures Workshop at the University of Chicago, the Global Nineteenth Century Workshop at the University of Pennsylvania, the Rutgers British Studies Center, and various ACLA seminars. My cohort in the Society of Fellows was a consistently exhilarating source of intellectual energy and solidarity; I hope they will see signs of their combined influence throughout these pages. Along the way, some of the most thrilling moments in my working life have been spent with the students I've had the good fortune to teach at the University of Chicago, Trinity University, and Penn.

I benefited from material as well as intellectual support from the English Department and the Cogut Center at Brown, from the Humanities Division at the University of Chicago for a Harper-Schmidt Fellowship, from Trinity University's English Department, and from the English Department and the School of Arts and Sciences at the University of Pennsylvania. I also thank the donors of the Roland G. D. Richardson Fellowship at Brown and of the Mr. and Mrs. Patrick H. Swearingen Faculty Fellowship at Trinity. I owe special thanks to the Stephen M. Gorn Family for their generous contribution to my research at Penn.

At Cornell University Press this book found an ideal home, and I greatly appreciate the dedication of everyone there who worked on it with me. For his confidence in the project and for guiding it so conscientiously through the review process, I am grateful to Mahinder Kingra. I am also indebted to the insight of two phenomenal readers whose illuminating and attentive reports gave me the direction I needed at the final stage. Many thanks are due to Martin Schneider for copyediting the manuscript with exceptional precision and care, to Karen Laun for deftly conducting it through the stages of publication, and to Kevin Joel Berland for preparing the index.

The good company of friends and colleagues over the years made the work of writing almost bearable. I hope Jed Esty, Paul Saint-Amour, and Michael Gamer know how thankful I am to them for giving me the very best advice at crucial moments, and I thank Nancy Bentley, Jean-Christophe Cloutier, Amy Kaplan, Josephine Park, Melissa Sanchez, and Salamishah Tillet for their conversation and support in many things. I am grateful to the entire Penn English Department for fostering such a lively and welcoming intellectual community. For indispensable suggestions and inspiration, I heartily thank David Kurnick, extraordinary critic and generous interlocutor. I am better for knowing and exchanging ideas with Katie Chenoweth, Nicholas Gaskill, Wendy Allison Lee, Rob Lehman, Ben McKean, Nasser Mufti, Sam Solomon, Audrey Wasser, and Danny Wright. Anna Kornbluh has been as brilliant an interlocutor and as faithful a friend as I could hope to find. Ritu Sen's friendship has been one of the best things in my life for nearly twenty years.

I surely would not be where I am without my parents' constant encouragement and love, and I'm lucky to be able to rely on the perspicacity, humor, and loyalty of my incomparable sister, Alexandra Steinlight, whose instincts I trust more than my own. I will not try to enumerate what Dave, my first and last audience and partner in all things, has contributed to my work. I owe this book, and much else, to him.

University Press. A version of chapter 4, "Why Novels Are Redundant," was first published in *ELH* 79.2 (Summer 2012), 501–535. Copyright © 2012 The Johns Hopkins University Press. Reprinted by permission of The Johns Hopkins University Press. Some material from chapter 5 previously appeared in a substantially different form and context within an essay titled "Hardy's Unnecessary Lives: The Novel as Surplus," in *Novel* 47.2, 224–41. Copyright 2014, Novel Inc. All rights reserved. Republished by permission of the copyright holder, and the publisher, Duke University Press.

POPULATING THE NOVEL

Introduction

The Biopolitical Imagination

Prefacing his life story with an apology for the excesses he is about to describe, Thomas De Quincey paraphrases Terence to explain the philosophy of an opium eater such as himself: *"Humani nihil à se alienum putat"* (7). His transient existence in London, his friendship with a prostitute, his drug experiments and exotic visions may be unusual, he owns, but they form part of the range of human experience—and nothing that is human is alien to him. Yet his confession narrates a process quite at odds with this sentiment. He loses, by measures, the capacity to recognize anything other than the overwhelming strangeness of his species. Having once ecstatically sought out East London's most crowded zones in order to sympathize with the English masses on as large a scale as possible, the opium eater is later consumed by fear and loathing of the multitudes that populate his nightmares of foreign continents "swarming with human life" (81). Solitude offers the former connoisseur of crowds no solace from what he can only describe as "the tyranny of the human face" (80). Echoed in hallucinatory dreams of endlessly reproducing global hordes that undercut his cosmopolitan ideals and nullify his humanist credo, De Quincey's memories of immersing himself in the element of mass humanity are shot through with "perplexities moral and intellectual" (54). To put it plainly: everything that is human becomes alien to him.

For all the solipsism of this text, the story it tells is one that connects a range of nineteenth-century narratives. *Confessions of an English Opium Eater*

recounts an experiential shift that disrupts the urban spectator's most elemental conception of his fellow creatures, making it imaginatively necessary
for him to lose himself among them and yet difficult to emerge unscathed.
This story finds a key precedent in William Wordsworth's poetic recollections of London in the 1790s. Though the poet ultimately recovers his "love
and reverence / Of human nature" in the tranquility of the Lake District,
Book VII of *The Prelude* portrays the city's human density as profoundly
destabilizing. Individuals, reduced to a series of stimuli, lose any distinct perceptual character for the spectator; the "weary throng" presents merely a
repetitive sequence of non-encounters, "face to face / Face after face . . ."
(172–73). In stark contrast with Joseph Addison's *Spectator*, whose journalistic persona delighted in mingling anonymously with the heterogeneous
multitudes of early eighteenth-century London, or with John Stow's cheery
Elizabethan-era appraisal of that proto-panoptic city where the felt gaze of
so many strangers ensures justice and good conduct, Wordsworth senses
in the crowd and in himself a sudden dissolution of "all stays, / All laws of
acting, thinking, speaking man" (605–6).[1] Friedrich Engels was compelled to
begin his later diagnosis of the condition of the working class in a similar
vein. He describes London's crowds in a Wordsworthian idiom of affective
alienation and sensory oppression. Amid the "human turmoil" of the streets,
the observer experiences "something repulsive, something against which
human nature rebels" (*The Condition of the Working Class* 68). What surfaces
almost explicitly in such responses to the city is a contradiction within the
category of the human. "Human nature" is repulsed by "human turmoil";
some qualitative human essence recoils from the sheer quantitative excess
of human beings pressing against each other. Rather than dramatizing a
conventionally Romantic tension between internal self and external society,
these and other nineteenth-century texts radically rearticulate what it means
to belong to a human aggregate.

Three related problems emerge from these representations of urban
experience: first, the social meaning of masses and crowds; second, the philosophical coherence of humanity and the perceived value of human life;
and third, the role of literary form itself in making a new approach to the
human aggregate into the basis for imagining a habitable world. The mass
assumes its unique status in cultural modernity as a paradoxical unbinding
of community through its own concentration; sociality takes on a dissocia-
tive and implicitly agonistic character with the increased proximity of bodies
in a common environment. A sudden destabilization or even repudiation of
humanity appears to follow from writers' encounters with this concentrated
human multitude. Though the causal link between these two phenomena

is less self-evident than it thus appears, the question of the masses and that of the human do share a source. Both arise not simply from the palpable pressure of human aggregation but also from a seismic shift in political thought—one that accorded new importance to population. Literature did more than document this transformation as it submerged its subject in what Wordsworth called the "great tide of human life." Romantic and Victorian writing provided the aesthetic conditions that enabled an expanding readership to conceive of population not only as a perceptual object but also as the horizon of all social action.

This book begins with a fairly obvious premise: that the social worlds assembled in nineteenth-century literature are phenomenally crowded, crammed far beyond their capacity with living human beings. From this premise, it draws some less obvious conclusions. What we glimpse in De Quincey's imperial nightmares of global overpopulation—no less than in Wordsworth's dizzying impressions of London's "overflowing streets"—is not simply a reflection of demographic growth in England but a distinctive political paradigm in the making, one that centered on the natural life of the human species and that relied, paradoxically, on demographic excess. To forge that new paradigm, these and other texts animate a vast and heterogeneous human aggregate that contractual models of society could no longer govern. It stalks forth in Mary Shelley's tale of terror, a nameless mass of miscellaneous flesh that can neither be granted the rights of an individual nor assimilated into the existing body politic. It assumes new forms in Elizabeth Gaskell's textile mills, Charles Dickens's teeming slums, and Mary Braddon's curiously overcrowded genteel households, all of which create a gross quantitative imbalance between biological life and the social order newly tasked with managing it. Rather than working to restore balance, these writers' literary techniques are organized around the formal principle of producing population in excess of material constraints. The surplus of humanity that Thomas Malthus imagined pressing against the limits of society thus unexpectedly became an enabling condition for literary narrative—and indeed, as the following chapters suggest, for modern political thought. In revealing the accumulation of life perpetually surpassing society proper, fiction gave form to what can now be called the biopolitical imagination.

To understand how Romantic and Victorian writing shapes a politics of collective human life requires some historical elaboration. Population acquires its importance as the outcome of three distinct developments: the material impact of industrial capitalism, the rise of the life sciences, and the political realignments that followed from the French Revolution. With regard to the first, the masses that pervade so many nineteenth-century narratives can be seen in an obvious sense as the demographic correlate of sweeping changes in British society, including urbanization, mass migration to cities and factory towns, proletarianization, and a complex of economic, medical, and social causes yielding a decline in mortality and, by some accounts, a series of spikes in fertility rates.[2] The more than tripling of England's population over the course of the century (from about 8.9 million in 1801 to 32.5 million in 1901) appears as both a cause and an effect of the shift from a primarily agrarian to a manufacturing-centered economy. Privately owned heavy industry relied on and profited from a constant surplus of human labor power—in Karl Marx's terms, "a disposable industrial reserve army" necessarily in excess of employment.

Though these demographic trends are well documented, the significance they take on from the Malthusian moment onward is not transparent in census returns. In fact, there was no general census in Great Britain before 1801; population had previously been estimated based on samplings of the local baptismal and burial records kept by parishes. And while statistical analysis had gained prestige over the course of the eighteenth century, neither aggregate data nor calculations concerning the birth rate automatically led to the conclusions Malthus reached, namely that human reproduction naturally outpaces the agricultural production of sustenance, resulting in a "redundant population" bound to suffer poverty and demanding checks to prevent broader casualties.[3] What Zygmunt Bauman would reframe in the twentieth century as the "inevitable outcome of modernization"—the irony that the accumulation of wealth in capitalist societies is accompanied by the global mass production of "'human waste,' or more correctly, wasted humans" (5)—had not seemed inevitable to economic thinkers or natural philosophers who witnessed the first fifty years of industrial expansion. The theory of redundant population in fact marks a break with classical political economy, which up to the end of the eighteenth century did not generally assume a scarcity of resources or impose limits on demographic growth.

On the contrary, increasing human numbers prior to *An Essay on the Principle of Population* were routinely equated with the wellbeing of the body politic.[4] Adam Smith treats population as a measure of national strength and prosperity. In *The Wealth of Nations*, the triad of "agriculture, industry, and population" appear and flourish together as wealth's principal sources; Smith repeatedly suggests that what is favorable to one benefits all three. Political economists throughout much of the eighteenth century, even in the midst of bread riots, did not fear the prospect of too many mouths to feed. In fact, they more often worried that mortality rates were on the rise and fertility in need of bolstering.[5] David Hume's *Of the Populousness of Ancient Nations*

(1752) goes so far as to propose that "a wise legislature" would do well to identify and remove any constraints to the unlimited "desire and power of generation" he attributes to all human beings (376). Robert Wallace, while disputing Hume's historical claim that modern nations are more populous than ancient empires, shares his basic premise that the best policies as well as the best social norms are those that promote population, and Benjamin Franklin similarly reasons in 1755 that the wisdom of any economic policy can be judged by its impact on the birth rate.[6] These and other sources bear out Frances Ferguson's suggestion that an eighteenth-century writer could credibly certify the virtue of any program by linking it to demographic growth and decry vice in anything that could be blamed for reducing fertility (117). This was not solely the position of empiricists and proto-utilitarians; Edmund Burke, no admirer of the "calculators" of his day, refused to think ill of any institution "found to contain a principle favourable . . . to the increase of mankind" (66, 113). Though not wishing to flatter "the contrivances of man" for the abundance of life he attributes principally to Providence, he held as late as 1790 that "no country in which population flourishes . . . can be under a very mischievous government" (112). Not until the very end of the century was it conceivable to treat population growth as anything other than a natural wellspring of capital and an obvious social good—much less to claim, in the interest of curtailing widespread misery, that restraints to procreation were needed.

If population took on new political weight at this moment, its altered status coincides not only with a shift in economic thought but also with the emergence of biological life as a key object of knowledge. The start of the nineteenth century saw the birth of a field that redirected natural history's attention from the characteristics of organisms to the study of "life," defined by the French anatomist Xavier Bichat as "the set of functions that resist death" and constituting the common principle of being from man to microorganism (*Physiological Researches* 21). Biology quickly became a master discourse of the modern era, providing a new vocabulary and new objectives for government. In concert with the quantitative social sciences, it came to anchor a political model focused on the vital functions and developmental capacities of human groups. Statistics, notably, made knowledge of vital phenomena available to far-reaching analysis; as Ian Hacking and Alain Desrosières have shown, the science of probability transformed what had once looked like random events (bad harvests, cholera outbreaks, spikes in infant mortality) into more or less predictable and thus potentially governable tendencies in bodies and environments. Demography thus emerged out of the application of statistical methods to biological and social knowledge, forming an essential technology by which changes in populations could be measured. Auguste Comte's grandiose dream of a "final Biocracy" that would harness all the ecological "forces of the living world" and minister to the species on a global scale finds corresponding realities in governing policies concerned with public health, sanitation, and the regulation of fertility (500). Such policies, which Michel Foucault would identify as those of biopower, approach life as the purpose of social organization rather than its precondition.

The particularity of modern biopower, by Foucault's account, is that it transforms the old sovereign right "to take life and let live" into a new systematic impetus "to make live and to let die," thus resituating life as the strategic end rather than a tactical means of power (*"Society Must Be Defended"* 241). If power over life had once meant the right of the king either to impose the death penalty or to grant pardon, it took on different positive and negative meanings from the eighteenth century onward. Death no longer figured as the omnipresent specter of sovereign punishment or divine judgment. Indeed, life and death in the age of biology cease to be simple opposites. Bichat's definition of life as the set of functions that resist death transmutes the very idea of death from life's fated end, its annihilating antithesis, into a plurality of risks to which life is constantly exposed and against which it can be strengthened.[7] To secure life became the goal of the modern polity, which made itself responsible on the one hand for averting famine and epidemic, increasing longevity, maximizing bodies' capacity for labor, and improving environmental conditions, while on the other hand allowing (infamously, with the end of outdoor relief under the New Poor Law) a certain number of people to die in order to prevent widespread scarcity. What is distinctive about the political objectives of making live and letting die is, first, that they shifted focus from individual to population, and second, that they redefined the object of governance in biological terms. Epistemologically speaking, as Foucault suggests, "the population as a collection of subjects is replaced by the population as a set of natural phenomena" by the early nineteenth century (*Security, Territory, Population* 352). In a period often equated with the rise of the individual and (thanks in part to Foucault's own work on discipline) with the institutional regulation of individual conduct, quite another set of governing strategies targeted the ecological conditions and biological functions of the human species at large.

What motivated such a recalibration of the relationship between society and species, polity and population, power and life? One familiar answer is that the natural sciences yielded a revised conception of humanity, no longer ontologically set apart from other animals or sovereign over created nature, and that this in turn necessitated a revised model of governance. In a sense, this is true. The universal man of earlier social contract theory became quite a different animal once he could no longer leave the state of nature. If *Homo sapiens* were subject, as Malthus surmised, to the same basic "physical laws" and bodily needs that determine the behavior of other species, then human society would need to understand itself as continuous with rather than opposed to the creaturely conditions of existence. Institutions would need to be designed around the newly salient problem (more accurately, the newly decisive value) of natural life. Moreover, biological crises would be imaginatively necessary to these institutions, giving sanction to a form of government that pledges to shield populations from risk and make them thrive. Such government aims at different ends than those advanced by social contract models of the state. Laws addressed to the rational individual and directed at the protection of property would be of little use against the pandemic Mary Shelley wrote into the hypothetical future of *The Last Man*—a novel that draws implicitly on Georges Cuvier's discovery of the fossils of past species to raise the specter of human extinction. For the very reason that existing institutions were powerless against such a crisis, Shelley uses it to imagine a new geopolitical system. Even when, as in *The Last Man*, no system or state can actually ensure the survival of the species, a new basis for evaluating the success or failure of government is evident: promoting life has become the ultimate political program.

The developments in biology and geology that shape such stories are unquestionably transformative, yet they do not occur in a vacuum. They are also intensified expressions of new forms of secular historical consciousness that can likewise be seen in Constantin François de Volney's *Ruins, or Mediation on the Revolutions of Empires*, which spread out a landscape on which the impermanence of every present regime could be read in the skeletal remains of the past. As such, scientific theories of the forces at work in the creation and destruction of life forms do not simply inform politics; they are themselves political. The sciences could no more avoid framing natural processes in political metaphors (as is clear in Georges Cuvier's description of earthquakes and volcanic eruptions as "revolutions" or, later, Charles Darwin's analysis of the "laws" governing the "polity of nature" or Ernst Haeckel's image of cells as "citizens" of the body) than political philosophy could avoid speaking of the state as an organism or of mass uprising as an epidemic. Rather than thinking of politics as importing a biological vocabulary in order to naturalize power, we might follow Georges Canguilhem's suggestion that politics "borrows from biology what it has already lent to it" (*Knowledge of Life* 72). Life surfaced as a paramount concern of science in part because it was already becoming a paramount concern—and the definitive authorization—of politics.

Though Foucault's seminal 1976–78 lectures at the Collège de France do not fully explain the historical impetus behind this biopolitical turn, Malthus himself offers a hint. He opens his argument concerning the necessity of regulatory checks to human reproduction with an ambivalent reference to "that tremendous phenomenon in the political horizon, the French Revolution," an event that inaugurated "a period big with the most important changes . . . that would in some measure be decisive of the future fate of mankind" (67). What is striking here is not just Malthus's intimation that the revolutionary mob is a natural outgrowth of surplus population. While his concern to limit the birth rate of the poor has a definite political subtext, his rhetoric also reveals—even at the level of metaphor—a conception of governance already irreversibly altered by the Revolution. The symbolic and practical consequences of this event cannot be understood solely as the passage of absolute power out of the body of the sovereign and into the disembodied realm of modern institutions.[8] The dramatic replacement of monarchical succession with the principle of popular sovereignty, as Eric Santner has argued, also required a substantial reformulation of the body politic. This imaginative necessity is written into the figural dimensions of Malthus's argument, over and above the logic of his claims. As the *Essay on Population* suggests, implicitly equating revolutionary transformation with the image of the reproductive body ("big with . . . changes"), the political future could only be understood as a new incarnation of power in an insistently fleshly form.

The new importance of organic life, in other words, must be understood at least partly in terms of the necessity of investing power in an embodied populace.[9] If it was clear even to so conservative a commentator as Thomas Carlyle that "dealing with [the] masses" in the wake of the Revolution and in the era of wage labor would henceforth be "the sole point and problem of Government," it was equally clear that these masses were not just an inert object to be acted upon; Carlyle endows the people with "sinews and indignation" (*French Revolution* 30). Like the "filthy mass" of muscular flesh assembled by Frankenstein only to make demands that its creator refuses to meet, the specter of popular uprising simultaneously appears as an energetic body and as a collective subject asserting new political agency. Such imaginative incarnations of the populace shape something more substantial than the projected target of a regime of social control. To account for their impact, one might turn to Santner's analysis of modern political theology, which provides a crucial supplement to Foucault in demonstrating that sovereignty does not disappear at the moment when discipline and biopower emerge.[10] What is most urgently at stake in the intensities surrounding biopolitics, as Santner suggests, "is not simply the biological life or health of populations but the 'sublime' life-substance of the People, who, at least in principle, become the bearers of sovereignty" (*Royal Remains* xi–xii).[11] This process of creating a new popular body seems obviously connected to the rise of nationalism—and in some respects, it is. Yet, in practice, by situating the field of political action in mass life, it yielded collectivities that necessarily exceeded national identity. Rather than producing a quantity of "merely human" life denuded of political subjectivity, it extended the scope of political meaning beyond those who claim what Hannah Arendt would call "the right to have rights" (296). It is for this reason that the peculiar excessiveness of humanity came to constitute not only the essential problem on which states were founded and societies organized but also the basis for contesting their organization.

There is thus a double process at work in the politics of population. On the one hand, the social dangers attributed to surplus population promoted imperial expansion as a release valve for demographic pressures in the metropole, creating "blank spaces" on the world map where, as Bauman puts it, "local congestion can be globally unloaded" (35). On the other, the imaginative construction of a global mass of humanity in such texts as Joseph Conrad's *Heart of Darkness* also produced forms of transnational affect (often, affects quite incompatible with liberal-humanist sympathy) that challenged imperialism. On the one hand, the scientific analysis of populations is clearly tied to the rise of biological theories of race and to overt and covert forms of state racism. On the other, it also facilitated an evolutionary paradigm of human development through which race loses ontological permanence and, at least theoretically, becomes untethered from nationality. The accumulation of life in excess of its means indeed provided the basis for most of the theories of organic and historical transformation for which the nineteenth century is known, from natural selection to class struggle. There is a fine irony in the fact that Darwin was able to deduce the origin of new life forms and the mechanism behind their development from the very problem that, in Malthus's view, made progress impossible. The theory of natural selection, premised on a constant disproportion between population and subsistence, identified the process by which every species gradually approaches perfection in the fatal ratio that, for Malthus, implied the imperfection of the human condition. A similar irony makes demographic pressure, for Marx and Engels, into a catalyst for new forms of political solidarity that arise dialectically out of the haphazard massing together of so many living bodies in the service of capital. In fiction, too, it provides an impetus to nearly every plot and grants the novel new political agency—so much so that the industrialist W. R. Greg, attempting to explain the pull of Chartism, socialism, and communism, was also compelled to account for "a new class of novels, of which 'Oliver Twist' and 'Mary Barton' are the type," novels that turn social insufficiency and struggle into history's conditions (*Enigmas of Life* 35). The ambiguously defined surplus of humanity assumed its importance—scientifically, politically, and not least aesthetically—for the very reason that it challenged both the primacy of the individual and the establishment of a coherent body politic.

It is above all through narrative and aesthetic forms that the biology of species, mass politics, and literature come together around this dual challenge. Literature, not coincidentally, acquired its current meaning—no longer a term for gentlemanly knowledge of classics but a broad descriptor for the modern art of writing, with the novel occupying a prominent position—and asserted its own social urgency at the moment when population politics came to the fore.[12] There are several reasons for turning to nineteenth-century literature, and to the novel in particular, to consider how this new biopolitical imagination took shape. For one, fiction over the course of the century takes on a dual character, both mass media and serious art. This status situates the novel as a material effect and medium of the mass population through which it circulates (disseminated more widely than ever, thanks to cheaper modes of publication and distribution, especially in the case of serial fiction) and, at the same time, as a prestigious and socially consequential form—cited by journalists and social scientists on matters concerning the organization of collective life. In fact, the simultaneous surge of state-sponsored demographic, sociological, and medical studies, as Oz Frankel has shown, relied on a notably literary supplement to the "avalanche of printed numbers" Ian Hacking describes; such studies borrowed fiction's material and formal strategies, from serialization to free indirect discourse, to give numbers meaning and to cultivate a readership for the publications of a newly prolific government.[13] Literature and criticism, in turn, announce their aims in conversation with statistics, with George Eliot famously championing art as the higher mode of social knowledge, more attuned to the forms of human aggregation indicated by such terms as *the masses*. Comparing the two in "The Natural History of German Life," she favors realist art, wagering its legitimacy on its proximity to the "the life of the people" and its promise to make mass life affectively graspable.[14] At the most basic level, literature's self-definition, its claims to autonomy and to political engagement, and its concrete formal strategies can be seen as establishing and responding to the new significance of population. Moreover, in mediating population and giving the concept aesthetic force and narrative consequence, it mobilizes a new political logic strangely energized by the contradictions within it.

If population management produces the problem it has to manage, then literary form, by yielding a constant excess of life, helps make that problem into the organizing principle of political thought. And if there is, as I have been suggesting, a double process at work in the politics of population, so too is an aesthetic double process operative even in the crisis of perception dramatized in Wordsworth's and De Quincey's reflections on the city. On the one hand, as we saw at the outset, the representation of urban modernity produced narratives in which human aggregation brings about a collapse of distinctions. The quantity and diversity of social stimuli paradoxically yield an impression of overwhelming homogeneity: thousands upon thousands of people and things appear "melted and reduced," as if by the heat of industrial blast furnaces, "To one identity, by differences / That have no law, no meaning and no end" (*The Prelude* 703–5). On the other hand, the demand to accommodate human life on an expanding scale called forth new efforts—at once poetic and political—to give constituency to the flux and heterogeneity of collective existence. If Wordsworth and De Quincey endured the difficulty of restoring "the endless stream of men and moving things" to their proper proportions, their very failure to do so registers a new aesthetic project. The art of writing found fresh purpose in generating a flood of human and cultural material that no existing subject, family, institution, or state—indeed, nothing other than literature itself—could contain. Reacting to a sense of aesthetic or figural excess, nineteenth-century criticism establishes an implicit association between literary and demographic surplus. (Indeed, it is worth considering how much of critical practice, then and now, has been tacitly conditioned by the axiom of redundant population.) The common complaint that novels were oversaturating their plots and their prose with unnecessary figures, trivial details, and valueless lives attests to Malthusian premises. The conception of an overpopulated world shaped fiction's reception such that the excessive qualities of literary forms and styles effectively came to be experienced as crowding. This reaction is ideological, but it mediates something real. In overpopulating the forms on which it relied, literature not only developed alternative modes of perception and narration but also made it possible to imagine collective life in radically revised terms.

Mass Aesthetics and the Stakes of Literary Demography

The strategic overcrowding of narrative space necessarily alters literature at the level of form. The bildungsroman could no longer tell the story of an individual's development without exposing that individual to an unending struggle for existence, beginning—as the opening of *Oliver Twist* suggests—at the moment of birth. Domestic fiction could no longer test the sexual morality of a character like Samuel Richardson's Pamela and then reward her with marriage and social mobility. The sensation novels of the 1860s turned the marriage plot's solution into a problem; as Wilkie Collins, Mary Braddon, and Ellen Wood demonstrated in their shocking tales of bigamy and multiple identities proliferating at the heart of the domestic sphere, the sexual contract and the household offered no plausible refuge from the systemic stresses of a populous world. What Malthus termed redundant population thus provided the precondition for a range of new genres, including the city novel, industrial realism, sensation fiction, and naturalism, all of which developed uniquely literary strategies for managing the novel's own demography.

This book will show that nineteenth-century literary texts at once presuppose and challenge the principle of population. To begin with, they dynamize social existence around the pressures of aggregation and the production of human redundancy. While Gaskell earnestly laments the uneven distribution of the means of life in *Mary Barton*, her heroine's story can commence only at the moment when the Barton household is no longer sufficient to sustain its inhabitants. And while Dickens mocks the father of population science in *Hard Times* by naming one of Gradgrind's sons Malthus, his plots nonetheless hinge on the general problem of human reproduction outstripping its material resources. Indeed, the protagonists of virtually every Dickens novel enter the world as surplus lives: Oliver, whose birth in the workhouse represents "a new burden imposed on the parish" (*Oliver Twist* 2); Esther Summerson, raised to feel "sensible of filling a place . . . which ought to have been empty" (*Bleak House* 31); Pip, treated by his authoritarian sister "as if [he] had insisted on being born" and failed to join his parents and five brothers in the churchyard (*Great Expectations* 23). Their stories do not solve the problem by granting each character a place she or he had formerly been denied. The human surplus from which they spring continuously overpopulates the novel. For every Oliver rescued from the workhouse, there is inevitably a hapless fellow orphan who dies off the page; for every Esther who finds a home, a homeless urchin Jo singled out only as a casualty of a citywide epidemic—an arbitrary instance of mass death. The absence of a ready-made solution appears at once an insurmountable dilemma and the condition for imagining the future of common existence: a social state prepared to serve unmet human demands. In setting itself this task—seeking to overcome the vast gap between the given and the possible—fiction began to plot conflicts on an entirely different scale from the routinely described antagonism between self and society.

Attending to the novel's part in rethinking the relationship between the biological functions of the species and the organization of political communities entails some revision of critical models. In the first place, it changes fiction's subject. Novel theory since Georg Lukács and sociological accounts of novel history since Ian Watt have understandably read the genre as centered on the modern individual in society; my claim, by contrast, is that Victorian fiction's narratives ultimately concern themselves with a population projected to exceed the scope of society as such. Then, at a theoretical and historical level, this shift in emphasis entails a revised understanding of the era's governing techniques; at the level of literary criticism, it entails reassessing how fiction interacts with such techniques. New historicist scholarship famously turned to Foucault's *Discipline and Punish* to make the case that Victorian fiction carried the mission of surveillance into the realm of popular entertainment. The novel, according to such critics as D. A. Miller and Nancy Armstrong, was complicit in a disciplinary system directed toward creating individual subjects and training them to regulate their own conduct within domestic space. Even as it assisted in assembling a social body, Mary Poovey likewise reasoned, Victorian serial fiction was best understood as one among many "individualizing technologies" (*Making* 22). Such critical approaches had the advantage of denaturalizing the private individual at the heart of liberalism from a different perspective than Marxist criticism had done. They also importantly questioned the separateness of the household and family from politics and from the realm of institutions. Insofar as this tradition cast the novel as an instrument of social control, though, critics including Amanda Anderson and Lauren Goodlad (and, from a different angle, more recent advocates of postcritique) found reason to challenge the new historicist view of the genre; Goodlad, for instance, notably cites Foucault's lectures on governmentality and liberal statecraft as a more pertinent framework than panopticism for analyzing Victorian literature and politics. Yet such responses, where they recur to classically liberal assumptions about freedom from bureaucratic regulation (or, in the case of postcritique, exempt fiction from politics altogether), risk restating the problem by substituting one version of liberal individualism with another. To treat the novel either as a disciplinary apparatus or as a defense against power's incursion is to miss the defining formal challenge that Dickens, for example, writes into the unique split narrative of *Bleak House*—one side speaking in the first-person voice of Esther, who evaluates each character she meets as a unique individual, the other side dealing impersonally (or transpersonally) with life as a statistical aggregate.

Rather than perform the fictional equivalent of surveillance or resist it in the name of personal freedom, this impersonal narration attests to another form of power equally pertinent to the history of liberalism: one defined less by a concern to maintain norms than by relative indifference to most of what it sees. For all that *Bleak House* satirizes Mrs. Jellyby's disastrous colonial scheme to settle a "superabundant home population" in coffee plantations along the Niger, Dickens is only half joking when he dismisses the novel's entire populace in free indirect discourse as "supernumeraries" and proceeds to dispose of masses of characters. In overcrowding its narratives to such an extent, Victorian fiction creates a problem discipline cannot solve—one that indeed finds no immediate solution other than that of natural death. This technique more closely resembles what Foucault would characterize as the logic of laissez-faire that governs population. While Foucault will eventually encompass both discipline and biopolitics under the rubric of governmentality, the two systems serve disparate objectives. In contrast with a disciplinary system that seeks to regulate every individual body, as his 1976 lectures suggest, biopower's techniques work in part by "letting things happen" on a broad statistical scale. They structure a political economy of life according to which a certain number of people can be allowed to die.

Taking stock of this aspect of population management shows that there is some truth on both sides of the debate as to whether liberalism in practice meant governing more or governing less. One need not choose between Miller's argument that what looks like freedom from power has masked the regulation of whole areas of human action (sexuality in particular) not previously of political concern and Goodlad's counterargument that Victorian society was liberal specifically in its resistance to centralized state institutions and its faith in self-governance. These seemingly opposed perspectives are actually complementary. It was tenable for liberal advocates of the Contagious Diseases Acts of the 1860s, for example, to view prostitution as a necessary evil while calling for centralized policing of female bodies to check its attendant public health risks, just as it was tenable for Josephine Butler to oppose these laws on liberal grounds, arguing that their administration (the mere suspicion of prostitution authorizing police to impose mandatory pelvic examinations) is a violent assault on the freedom of "every individual English woman" (6). That the Sanitary Commission in the 1840s sent doctors and bureaucrats to examine how many bodies occupied a bed or what they did with their waste shows an unprecedented effort to regulate life. That members of the same official body, notably Edwin Chadwick, recommended cutting off longstanding forms of welfare in order to let the laws of political economy run their course attests to the liberal fantasy of governing less. On one side, the call to manage biological processes and ecological conditions opens up a broader arena of administrative intervention; on the other, it reveals that power may also be passively enacted through systematic neglect. From either angle, though, the same governing principle is at work: that the success or failure of any policy or institution can be best assessed by its impact on life in the aggregate. This new governing principle is both established and tested in the novel's imaginative experiments. To examine how fictional narratives confronted problems on the scale of the species, this book shifts critical focus from a micropolitics of the individual subject to a macropolitcs of population—a politics for which the individual is no longer the basic integer and social integration no longer the telos.

In turning to the novel, long assumed to focus on the individual and to negotiate that subject's relation to social totality, this book recharacterizes the genre's essential human material and its narrative project. It finds fiction's point of departure in a surplus of humanity that does not initially appear as a subject at all and its political stakes in the management of mass life. If one maintains, with Fredric Jameson, that every narrative is a "symbolic meditation on the destiny of community," this entails recognizing that vitality, health, and biological reproduction are elemental to the ways in which political community came to understand its own problems and possible futures through nineteenth-century narrative (70). But this alignment of species life with political futurity also means that the fate of an individual cannot in itself fulfill "the destiny of community" and thus, contra Jameson, cannot be the sole bearer of narrative significance. So too does it suggest that fiction's imaginary resolutions to social contradictions remain partial at best. Indeed, I part with Jameson (and with Franco Moretti, who similarly treats the novel as a project in social reconciliation that affirms the new status quo ushered in by the bourgeois revolution) in stressing how nineteenth-century fiction overruns and overwhelms the socioeconomic order it presents.[15]

While these earlier theorizations of the novel remain indispensable, it now seems feasible to approach fiction from a wider angle that brings into view problems of number and superfluity. This is evident in a range of critical interventions concerned with different scales of analysis, attention, and subject matter, from John Plotz's literary-historical study of crowds and Alex Woloch's formalist analysis of fiction's multitudes of minor characters to Caroline Levine's thinking about networks to Catherine Gallagher's consideration of bioeconomics and Maureen McLane's analysis of key questions of species that preoccupied Romantic and Victorian writers.[16] At the level of method, some of these projects bespeak a growing interest across fields in scalar thinking itself, from new applications of world systems theory to experiments in distant reading to literary histories situated in deep time.[17] At the level of political theory and historiography, recent critical attention to population and adjacent concepts likely also owes at least in part to the translation history of Foucault's seminars of the late 1970s and early 1980s, which began appearing in English starting in the early 2000s. It will already be clear that the lectures published under the titles *"Society Must Be Defended"* and *Security, Territory, Population* in particular inform my own analysis. These and subsequent lectures have been crucial not only in extending the brief account of biopower offered in *The History of Sexuality* but also in historicizing liberalism—a pressing project for critics engaged in assessing the continuities and discontinuities of a neoliberal present with a longer history of capitalism, and a topic of longstanding interest to Victorianists concerned with the political life of the novel.

What would a history of the present entail for readings of the politics of Victorian fiction? On this count, my gambit is not to replace discipline with biopower as the novel's dominant modality of policing and otherwise to assume fiction's general complicity. If one took literary narrative either to originate or simply to mirror social regulation, the resulting criticism might thematically equate the novel's demographic experiments with a suite of policies extending from the Malthusian New Poor Law to Francis Galton's proposals for selective human breeding. But fiction, far from turning itself into a crowd control device or a eugenic justification for weeding out unfit organisms, changes the politics of population management. Rather than contain and classify life, optimize its value, or discipline each body, the novel calls attention to what exceeds the established categories of class, race, nation, gender, and personal identity. The plague Dickens lets loose in *Bleak House*, for example, does not just check London's transient slum population; indifferent to the divide between the novel's main character and masses of anonymous others, it disfigures the heroine beyond recognition, eroding the ideological meanings written on bodies. And *Lady Audley's Secret* does not just police sexual norms by expelling its deviant antiheroine from the English household. Far from marking her as an abnormal specimen, Braddon makes her impossible to isolate from the novel's population by showing how easily she can change places with a potentially infinite series of others. In collapsing the distinction between individual and crowd, these novels also collapse all socially codified distinctions between fit and unfit organisms, productive and wasted lives. The result is a collective subject that necessarily exceeds itself, multiplied by plots that at once confront the calculated management of life and turn that process against the economic imperatives and sciences of statecraft that set it in motion.

The literary excess these novels generate thus serves other purposes than the forms of statistical excess tabulated by social science. Literature, I am suggesting, finds its authorization not in any quasi-scientific claim to reflect the concrete totality of society but in the potential to give aesthetic expression to the scope of what its represented world has yet to accommodate. On this score, I approach the literary in terms similar to those of Jacques Rancière, who links it to a new "distribution of the sensible," or a reapportioning of space and time that changes who or what is perceptible; rather than represent and grant a proper place to new subjects, literature generates excesses of figures and signs that throw representation into question and confound the administrative ordering of subjects, bodies, and spaces.[18] Since the aesthetic revolution Rancière identifies dates to a Romantic and post-Romantic moment, and since such a conception of literature, as I have suggested, appeared together with the new significance of population and with a politics hinged on demographic surplus, I would add that what may sound like transhistorical claims for literature's uses of figural and aesthetic excess here prove historically specific.

Even in noting that the exceptional status literature claims for itself is a product of its historically contingent relation to population, this book— unlike new historicist scholarship—takes seriously the particularity of literature and its divergence from other types of discourse. It does so most basically by stressing the point that fiction, in contrast with bureaucratic forms of social representation (Blue Books, census forms, police maps, and the like) to which Victorian novels have been compared, may put forth what surpasses officially established sums of persons. This holds true for the deceptively simple reason that the genre claims an inventive rather than a documentary relationship to lives and social formations. While realist fiction may play for significance on referential grounds by making plot coincide with historical events, mapping the movements of fictional personae on actual city streets or subjecting fictional populations to government policies or sociologically described circumstances, fictionality as such—as Gallagher has suggested— changes the conditions of reference.[19] Even where a figure all but announces itself as standing for an entire class, it necessarily remains a figure added to any prior totality of actually existing persons rather than a direct mimetic representation of a particular individual or set. In this sense, the literariness of literature arguably consists in its tendency to generate figures in excess of human and social referents. As against social-scientific discourse, where figural excess risks compromising what is calculable about groups and jeopardizing the referential practices necessary to positivist inquiry, fiction authorizes forms of excess that activate rather than inhibit narrative. This is not to say that the novel paints an actually existing utopia in which excess conduces directly to redistribution, and everyone gets an equal share. As Rancière's reading of *Madame Bovary* attests, lives that exceed the recognized count or seek other kinds of experience than their status allots them rarely end happily.[20] But even when fiction demands Emma Bovary's grisly suicide, drowns Maggie Tulliver, raises the black flag for Tess Durbeyfield, and lets Little Father Time hang himself and his siblings, the very introduction of these figures disturbs the hierarchy of lives worth preserving over those that can be unceremoniously disposed of without mention. In dealing with such figures, novelists were implicitly dealing with masses.

These cases invite some reconsideration of aggregation and the function of character. On both scores, my project takes a page from Victorian critics who evidently knew that mass life rather than individuals or society had become fiction's main concern. John Ruskin, in "Fiction, Fair and Foul," found no subject in modern novels other than "the hot fermentation . . . of the population crowded into large cities" and the "trampling pressure and electric friction of town life" (269). Excoriating "Cockney literature" for its attraction to disease, decay, and data, he offers a sort of actuarial table for *Bleak House*. His aim is to demonstrate that such novels have no higher aim than to reflect urban mortality rates—making fiction less a source of wisdom than an outpost of the Registrar General's office, indifferently adding births and deaths to the ledger. His own list of the dead, however, inadvertently reveals that counting characters (difficult in itself) will not convey the scalar and aesthetic shift to which he objects, perhaps because the form's "trampling pressure" has subsumed and altered the category of character. Ruskin counts nine casualties, not including "the baby" (Jenny's), which is mentioned as an afterthought (272). Fair enough: though Dickens could hardly wring more pathos out of the scene of infant mortality at the brickmaker's cottage, the nameless newborn cannot quite be called a character. Neckett (a.k.a. Coavinses) and the unfortunate Gridley, however, are also omitted and Miss Flite mistakenly declared dead. To quibble about the list of names or the sum seems oddly beside the point, though, since the novel's massive scope extends beyond any nameable set of persons. Its pervasive morbidity consists less in nine or ten dead characters than in the deaths glimpsed in passing or not at all: an infected corpse carried down the street, or the ominously swelling ground of the churchyard where Nemo is laid to rest. One might tabulate the known fatalities in *Our Mutual Friend* and yield a lower number, but what of all those unidentified bodies in the river?

It quickly becomes clear why no census could reckon what E. M. Forster facetiously calls "the population of noveldom" (52). The sense of crowding that pulsates throughout the city novel owes not just to hundreds of characters but also to the suggestion of countless unindividuated others. Even to enumerate a novel's definite inhabitants, one would first have to define the unit that character is. Named figures who repeatedly appear in the story's diegetic time and space may be confidently counted even if they rank as minor, but is there a point at which one reaches the minimum of specificity? How to register, for example, the unnamed two out of four identical human "buffers" seated at the Veneerings' table in the second chapter of *Our Mutual Friend* and later conflated (perhaps an oversight on Dickens's part) into a single character named Buffer? Such cases resist any easy alignment of character with those aspects of narrative that call for qualitative evaluation (psychological interiority, personality, ethics, aesthetics) and against impersonal forms of quantification (mortality tables, occupational statistics, demographic heat maps) that still fail to capture them. Even in the realm of prominent minor characters, Jo's death is worth narrating in *Bleak House* because there is nothing qualitatively unique about it or about him; the climax of the scene is its generalizing claim, "dying thus around us every day."

To account for the force of such claims, the chapters that follow stress the ways in which nineteenth-century literature made masses and crowds not just perceptible but elemental to narrative. Here, the current project joins the efforts of Plotz, Woloch, and Nicholas Daly, among others, to take stock of the social density of the century's texts. This density can take forms other than literal representations of crowds, as is clear in Woloch's attention to the division of character space or in the tableaux of volcanic eruption that Daly reads as images of demographic explosion. From most critical perspectives, though, the process of literary crowding (to the extent that it is treated as something other than a reflection of demographic facts) still looks like part of a strategy of individuation. The crowd has often been understood as providing a backdrop for the fashioning of personal identity and the catalyst for a retreat into a private sphere that finds its objective form in the household and its subjective form in psychological interiority.[21] And the mass, with its more pejorative connotations, has been relegated to the phantasmagoria of class ideology: culture's projected enemy, per Raymond Williams; a site of simultaneous erotic desire and abjection—the bourgeois body's unmentionable yet perennially mentioned lower half—per Stallybrass and White; a falsely aggregated target of sociomedical control per Poovey. In contrast with such approaches, my readings demonstrate that mass life is not a phobic object but a constitutive political phenomenon, and that fiction, instead of seizing on population as an already existing entity or problem to be represented, makes it appear, strategically exacerbates the conditions of crowding and superfluity, and turns these conditions into sources of narrative energy.

These readings show how literary form, whether at the level of narration, figuration, quantification, or metonymy, at once mediates and contests the social structures of an emerging biopolitical order. At times, this demands peculiar modes of narrative discourse that play on the inadequacy of the established forms they modify: an impossible first person in *The Last Man* to witness crises on a planetary scale, for instance, or the dual narration *Bleak House* requires to plot life and death in the city. Most chapters attend closely to the structural operations of plot as they bear on the making of life and its political conditions. Tracking, for example, the uses of the "redundant woman" plot in sensation fiction shows that redundancy is not a theme or an attribute of character but a form. In such cases, narrative process suspends emphasis on character or makes it into something more provisional than the fictional equivalent of the individual. In others, it treats individuation itself as a socially prevalent form of excess, such that the very characteristics that differentiate a protagonist like Thomas Hardy's Jude Fawley from his milieu paradoxically render him a statistic.

The narrative handling of such figures attests that masses, crowds, and populations are never merely the opposite or the omnipresent outside of the individual and that character, in turn, can operate in other ways than as the individual's counterpart.[22] At times, character proves a fragile container for the aesthetic and formal process of populating narrative space and multiplying political demands. Even *Jane Eyre*, for all its individualism and its comparatively small number of characters, voices its heroine's seemingly singular protest as that of anonymous "millions . . . in silent revolt against their lot," counting her struggle among uncounted "rebellions ferment[ing] in the masses of life which people earth" (129). In other texts, large numbers shed their abstract, propositional status and come forth diegetically, and the membrane of subjectivity and particularity separating characters from masses becomes more permeable. To speak of a narrative hierarchy of major over minor characters (per Woloch's ingenious paradigm), then, might not explain the novel's engagement with mass life both through and beyond the level of characterization. It would yield limited insight into *Our Mutual Friend*, which has no protagonist, or *Jude the Obscure*, in which no extent of individualizing focus can save the protagonist from being relegated to the statistical category of "unnecessary life." Woloch's analysis forcefully illuminates structural inequalities that are indeed refracted in the novel's form, yet I reach different conclusions about how the dynamics of character and human numbers mediate such inequalities. Where he focuses on asymmetries of attention and characterological complexity that distinguish protagonists from everyone else, my approach to fiction's populations shows a systematic emplotment of superfluity undermining such distinctions: it shows, for example, that *Mary Barton*, in subjecting its population to the instabilities of the labor market, makes the role of protagonist into a job one can lose, or that Hardy's and Gissing's novels turn the fact of being a novel's central figure into a death sentence. Characters in these novels appear as products of (rather than alternatives to) demographic processes and, at times, as remainders of demographic categories. Hardy's Tess emerges as central because she is neither a "child of the soil" nor the "exhausted seedling of an effete aristocracy," as Angel Clare alternately misperceives her, but a resolutely modern figure expelled from every existing social category. It is just this non-belonging that enables her to express what Hardy treats as the collective experience of the age: the "ache of modernism." At the various levels of plot, narration, and characterization, Victorian fiction charts the instability of boundaries between the one and the many.

To name "the many" at all may sound dubious, since such a term describes the perceived effects of aggregation—subjective phenomena rather than any verifiable social entity. Wordsworth, after all, is no more isolable from London's "many-headed mass" than his fellow pedestrians who appear to constitute this monstrous body. No one inherently belongs to or stands apart from "the millions" whose tastes worried Margaret Oliphant, "the masses" whose interests William Gladstone vowed to champion in Parliament, or the "crowds" in which Gustave Le Bon glimpsed a composite image of hysteria. What is notable about all of these terms is that they forgo description in favor of an imprecise gesture toward quantity. Whether they connote class, populace, or everyone who happens to occupy the same environment at a particular moment, they designate fluctuating constellations of undifferentiated people rather than permanent categories of identity.

For this reason, Victorian writers themselves were sometimes inclined to treat the masses as a misperception: a socially symptomatic failure to distinguish among individuals. Dickens assumes this perspective in *Hard Times* when he describes the middle-class Louisa Gradgrind's visit to the factory worker Stephen Blackpool's home as her first encounter with "anything like individuality" among the multitudes of "Hands"—a population she had understood to exist theoretically "by hundreds and by thousands" as a totalized quantity of labor power and empirically "in crowds passing to and from their nests" (155). But the lesson extracted from this personal encounter is oversimplified. In a novel urgently concerned with transpersonal truths and populated with human creatures as much "like one another" in their circumstances as the identical brick buildings into which they are packed, the primacy of individuals cannot be taken for granted (27). Stephen's fate is not personal; the pit into which the isolated worker falls, as he himself recognizes, has already "cost . . . hundreds and hundreds o' men's lives" (263). *Hard Times*, despite its facile anti-union polemics, attests that there are structural reasons why it is accurate to perceive industrial Coketown's population as masses. The language of aggregation springs from palpably real social processes, and the novel makes it possible to recognize this even while acknowledging that the explanatory power of such terms as *masses* and *crowds* is limited.[23] These versions of the human aggregate operate alternately as expressions of uniformity and multiplicity, totality and excess, empirical reality and Gothic spectrality. Yet their semantic incoherence, indeed their very interruption of the sociological categories ready to receive them, makes them perceptible as aesthetic phenomena rather than scientific objects or historical referents.

It is in their aesthetic rather than referential sense, then, that I will invoke these terms. Instead of positing "the masses" as a repository of new social subject matter waiting to be mimetically assimilated into the novel's representational universe, I will propose that the mass operates in literature—much as Ernesto Laclau argues of "the people" in populist discourse—as an empty signifier in an affirmative sense.[24] It calls for a constituency where there are no recognized terms of common identity, a collective subject that has no proper embodiment or predetermined mode of representation. This rhetorical strategy similarly enabled Abbé Sieyès's definition of the Third Estate: a quantum of everything that is currently ranked as nothing and demands to become something. Pervasively present as form, such demographic figures produce real effects not despite but because of their emptiness of ontological content. Rather than denoting a category, they compose what Rancière would call the "part of those who have no part." Insofar as fiction discovers the mass of humanity as perpetually arising from within rather than outside social formations and narrative forms, its presence can never finally be written off. Even where it eludes any positive definition, it persistently reappears as a necessary premise of modern politics and a decisive stimulus for writing: subject and audience, problem and constituent, medium and message of literature.

"Life Itself"? Uses and Disadvantages of Biopolitics for Literature

Literary mass aesthetics and mass politics, I am suggesting, are decisively linked to the nineteenth century's emerging concern to govern the life of the human species: a concern that defines what we now call biopolitics. In making this claim, I want to distinguish my own usage of Foucault's term from the connotations it takes on for some of his interlocutors. From a certain theoretical standpoint, the masses that take shape in Romantic and Victorian writing are liable to look like the product of a totalizing system through which power seizes hold of "life itself." In addition to challenging the assumptions behind this formulation and defining politics as something other than the exercise of power, my readings point toward a different outcome. In its poetry and prose of population, nineteenth-century literature obsessively figures a living mass far larger than the society that seeks to contain it. It does so not in order to dispose of a demographic surplus, to impose rigid norms on bodies and lives, or to justify economic inequality by appeal to natural law. On the contrary, the very moment when population control would appear to reach its literary consummation—the brutal "done because we are too menny" in *Jude the Obscure*—reveals the extraordinary inadequacy of the existing social order. Fiction thus redefines what counts as political precisely in narrativizing that which exceeds the capacities of the polity.

For the purposes of this book, biopolitics furnishes a valuable descriptive paradigm insofar as it identifies population as the central object and datum of modern politics. The administrative techniques Foucault describes for managing life in the aggregate can indeed be seen at work throughout the nineteenth century, whether in Henry Mayhew's taxonomy of casual labor, Chadwick's sanitary mapping of cities, William Acton's medico-social survey of prostitutes in Great Britain, or Engels's analysis of workers' living conditions. They are likewise evident in the technology of the census, decennially administered in England, Scotland, and Wales after the 1800 Census Act, centralized under the Registrar General by the Population Act of 1840, and extended to the British colonies in 1861. Such efforts to make human life, its health and reproduction, and its global dispersion administratively measurable reveal a biopolitical logic too readily occluded by accounts of Victorian liberalism that treat politics as a negotiation between the state and the individual citizen-subject. Historiographically speaking, Foucault's analysis is therefore crucial to an understanding of modern power's naturalization via the production of biological knowledge and via the computation of human numbers. Insofar as population continues to anchor economic and political order and to delimit existing social formations, insofar as the Malthusian rhetoric of redundancy continues to sanction calls for the corresponding austerity measures, and insofar as state racism continually resurfaces in new forms, a genealogy of biopower and an analysis of biopolitical narratives remains vital to critique. Accordingly, Foucault's lectures have prompted alternative theorizations of power and life—most prominently, by Giorgio

Agamben and Roberto Esposito, both of whom, to differing effect, refer life to sovereignty in ways that Foucault does not.[25] Agamben extrapolates a less historically situated account from the Roman legal figure of *homo sacer*—the person whose life is placed outside the law, unprotected by the state but detained within it and secretly lodged at sovereignty's symbolic center; taking biopower as a mode of domination for which "only bare life is essentially political," he identifies the Nazi concentration camp as the logical extension of all of modern politics (*Homo Sacer* 106). Esposito posits an immunitary paradigm of sovereignty that seeks to protect life from itself by exposing it to death, yielding a thanatopolitics that an affirmative biopolitics is called on to counter. Apprehended in these various ways, however, biopower retains some ambiguity. The term bears the weight of ambiguous definitions of life and of power as well as conflicting assumptions about what linkage should or does exist between the two.

The phenomenon of life, in the first place, is conceptually vague. Its frequent qualification by various adjectives (biological, natural, social, bare, mere, organic, creaturely, animal, surplus, and so forth) generates incompatible meanings while highlighting the term's insufficiency. *Mere* and *bare* in particular make qualification ironically necessary to describe a lack of qualification—a state of being without characteristics or life suspended in its exposure to death, which Agamben holds central to biopower but often conflates with the concept of natural life.[26] What also remains equivocal, in the work of both Foucault and Agamben, is whether life should be understood as a political construct or as a material fact that is then acted upon and remade by certain political strategies. While Foucault argues in *The Order of Things* that "life itself" was invented by biology around 1800, his account of how power seizes hold of life in *The History of Sexuality* seems to give substance to what is otherwise a discursive construction. In Agamben's analysis, the concept of life long predates the modern sciences and can be deduced from the distinction Aristotle draws between the general fact of animate existence (*zōē*) and specific forms of life that characterize individuals and groups (*bíos*)—though the notion of being alive in Aristotle's basic sense differs markedly from Bichat's conception of life as a coordinated system of organic functions resisting death; as Catherine Mills observes, Agamben's treatment of *zōē* as synonymous with biological life is anachronistic (96). His looser genealogy frames what Walter Benjamin first called "bare life" at one moment as a category of being invented by political discourse and then actualized in the treatment of bodies and at the next moment as an object that precedes the law to which it is subjected. Consequently, it is not always clear what becomes of life when it is "politicized" or what becomes of politics when "life" names its goal.[27] For Agamben, who casts bare life as the foundational exclusion that grounds politics from the moment of Aristotle's city-state, biopolitics has effectively replaced politics proper in the modern era. For Foucault, by contrast, politics is already an object of suspicion; his use of the term often makes it synonymous with the deployment of power.[28]

From either perspective, it is difficult to say whether the goal of exposing a regime of biopower is to rescue life from the captivity of politics or to cure politics of its obsession with life. When, for example, the political philosophers Laura Bazzicalupo and Clarissa Clò assert that "every day we see politics exerting power over life directly without mediation," it remains to be seen how, or by what agency, something called "politics" assumes command over something called "life" (109). At what point, one wonders, was there a concretely existing entity called "life" that was not yet subject to law or to economic control? And is the problem with biopower really, as they suggest, that "we are ruled by necessity and survival, which is neither human nor politically free" (112), or is this neo-Aristotelian distinction between mere life and the good life precisely what modern states' techniques for managing health and improving living conditions perpetually aim to overcome?[29] Moreover, what remains of politics when life is subtracted from its concerns? On this count, a biopolitical theory of modernity becomes tenuous if it suggests that natural life can be meaningfully separated from political life. This separation owes in part to the legacy of social contract theory, which hypothesized a primal state of nature in which solitary man exists outside of any political community. Marx's early writings, in addition to discrediting the liberal notion that human existence precedes social formations, arguably provide a basis for viewing the specter of bare life as a symptom of human self-alienation: the distance between the individual and a common consciousness of species-being. From this standpoint, the perceived monstrosity of the "merely human"—the Malthusian nightmare of continents "swarming with human life" in De Quincey's opium visions—would appear as the misrecognition attending an economic system in which man competes against all others and against himself for the means of life and in which life presents itself solely as the means of producing value.

Whether or not one approaches the problem of the human in these terms, there is room for some skepticism toward attempts to theorize natural life as extricable from or prior to sociopolitical life. Jacques Derrida and Laurent Dubreuil are among those who reject the categorical distinction between *bíos* and *zōē* that Agamben claims to find in *The Politics*. Nor are they wrong to note that Aristotle's characterization of man as a *zōon politikon* admits of no such distinction. While Agamben takes this adjectival construction to mean that "'political' is not an attribute of the living being as such, but rather a specific difference that determines the genus *zōon*" (*Homo Sacer* 2), its syntax actually implies little more than that Aristotle may not have viewed mollusks as city-dwelling creatures. For the human species that the phrase positively defines, however, its meaning is clear: politics is the nature of the beast. If man is essentially "zoo-political," then it follows quite plainly, as Derrida puts it, that "what is proper to man is politics; what is proper to the living being that man is, is politics" (*The Beast and the Sovereign* 348–49). And if "human life is *by nature* political" for Aristotle, there is little sense in differentiating, as Dubreuil reasons, "between political practice and the course of life" (83).[30] While this may not entirely account for the separation Aristotle implies between the necessity of "mere life" from which the polis begins and the higher goal of "the good life" for which it continues to exist, or between the fact of existence and the ethical character of human existence, it is nonetheless true that the adjective *political* is ontologically substantive and not merely descriptive. It cannot be added to or subtracted from the being of the human creature. Indeed, while these responses to Agamben center on the definition of the human, it bears remarking that *The Politics* does not restrict political life to man. Aristotle's distinction between human and animal is a distinction not of type but of degree; his claim is simply that man is *more* political "than bees or other gregarious animals" (1253[a]7). Consequently, the attribute of political nature in itself does not separate either humanity or the city from the larger realm of creaturely life.

To insist on "life as such" might be courting abstraction, since, in practice, the fact of being alive cannot present itself independently of the forms of life, its embodiment (even at the cellular level) in specific organisms, and its social and historical coordinates. It is, however, conceivable to approach the phenomena of animate existence without opposing life to form—as Herbert Spencer, for example, does in defining life as "the co-ordination of actions," thus giving it the status of a systematizing drive, or as Canguilhem more recently does in maintaining, against a mechanistic conception of the organism, that "life is the formation of forms" (*Knowledge of Life* xix). It is through Canguilhem, notably, that Foucault eventually redefines biological life as "that which is capable of error": an outcome of sheer chance detached from the subject, and thus, in the context of human existence, "something like a disturbance in the informative system, something like a mistake" ("Life" 476).[31] This element of chance, of error, and of resistance to subjectivization, for Elizabeth Grosz, too, makes a Darwinian conception of biological life worth maintaining. Life, from this vantage point, does not refer to being but to becoming: It is "the ongoing exploration of and experimentation with

the forms of bodily activity that living things are capable of undertaking"
(*Becoming Undone* 21). Such an understanding holds out the possibility of
political and aesthetic transformation as against essentialism, so that "instead
of ensuring that life conforms to existing social categories," it allows for
ontological openness and variation (Grosz, *The Nick of Time* 1). Rather than
placing a reified and dematerialized life principle at odds with specific forms
of life, splitting apart *zōē* from *bíos*, one might thus understand life as the
potential for new forms to emerge.

That definition might afford an approach to biopolitics that is particularly
apt to the literary forms with which this book is concerned. The term, rather
than naming either the omnipresence of power or some messianic dream of
resurrection, might be taken to encompass a complex of struggles to recon-
figure the relationship between creaturely life—birth, death, eating, sleep,
growth, motion, sex, procreation, aging, interaction with environments—
and the social structures within which all aspects of living take place. The
very contingency of natural and social life, as fictional narratives attest, make
humanity an irreducibly political subject rather than (per Arendt's critique
of human rights) the abstraction that slips between the cracks of the polity and falls into permanent abjection when sundered from the nation-state.
Even in its most depersonalized figurations, from *The Last Man*'s nameless
plague victims to the human "bundles of acute angles" used up and left to
die in Conrad's geometrically abstract vision of forced labor in the Congo,
the living flesh that appears at the limits of social recognition is not a mere
cipher of life bereft of social character and held in a permanent state of
exception but a provocative testament to the expansiveness of politicity and
its resistance to closure.

It is this resistance to closure, this sense of the contingency of life, politicity, and form, that the nineteenth-century novel is distinctively impelled to
narrate. Perhaps this is why contemporary philosophers and theorists often
turn to fiction to illuminate their claims about the substance of the political—
why the scene of suspended animation in *Our Mutual Friend* captures the
strangely depersonalized life that Deleuze celebrates and Agamben problematizes; why *Madame Bovary*, in blurring the line between life and art, defines
democracy for Rancière; why *Dracula* figures the multitude for Hardt and
Negri and explains the autoimmunitary mechanisms of modern sovereignty
for Esposito. In so doing, they imply what my own project seeks to make
explicit, that politics is a matter of form—of the ordering and disordering
of a common world and the mode of its presentation. The political may be
productively understood, in Levine's terms, as "the jostling of incommensu-
rable forms of order" rather than the establishment of a single order (639).[32]

It is a question, in other words, of the distribution not only of means but also of meaning, of attention, interest, and perceptibility and thus (as Rancière reminds us) is intimately bound up with aesthetics.

Literature, as it took on its current definition in the nineteenth century, seems to have found much of its dynamism in a capacity to lend unexpected form to life and unexpected life to form. From Percy Shelley's call for a "poetry of life" to Thomas Hardy's prognosis of a "coming universal wish not to live," the texts for which the century is known shape a politics that begins rather than ends with the excessiveness of species life to its existing social frame. The following five chapters aim to show how five key genres— Romantic confession, industrial realism, the city novel, sensation fiction, and the naturalist anti-bildungsroman—thus reinvent politics out of the process of human aggregation. The sheer proliferation of genres that engage population should in itself illustrate the generative force of this concept for literary production. While the texts I examine are certainly not alone in bending their strategies to the task of imagining life in excess of its recognized limits, they represent what I regard as some of the boldest narrative experiments in modern political thought.

Populating Literary History

Taking a long view of the mutually defining relationship between modern literature and biopolitics, this book extends roughly from the era of the French Revolution through the end of the nineteenth century, with a brief conclusion looking ahead to the altered aesthetic and political terrain of the First World War and toward the present. The chapters are ordered more or less chronologically, though their focus is generic rather than episodic; they treat literary history's unfolding relationship with population as a form-giving process rather than a series of events. Chapter 1 shows modern biopolitics taking its first recognizable shape in the late eighteenth century, coming to the fore in a prolonged clash between Malthus and two generations of Romantic writers. Wordsworth, Coleridge, Godwin, Percy Shelley, and William Hazlitt were among those who disputed the principle of population. Their responses, as McLane and Gallagher have suggested, helped consolidate literature's ethical as well as aesthetic importance. Poets and philosophers enlisted the art of writing in defense of human exceptionalism, accusing Malthus of demoting man to the level of animal on the one hand and statistical abstraction on the other. Yet their affirmations of humanity reveal striking ambivalence about what political claims can be made on behalf of the species and about the universalism they purport to embrace—sometimes upholding Malthus's view of the compulsory nature of reproduction and of the attendant threats of scarcity and violence.

Frankenstein puts just these claims to the test. In this respect, Shelley's Gothic romance of life-production can be understood as a timely experiment in Romantic political theory rather than a cautionary tale about the dangers of science. The heterogeneous mass of flesh assembled by her protagonist grants ambiguously human form to the nineteenth century's revised conception of the populace. Shelley carries to its limits the Malthusian logic of Frankenstein's anxiety to prevent this creature from procreating—an anxiety echoed in De Quincey's imperial nightmares of endlessly self-multiplying global hordes. The global scope of Romanticism's concern with the relation between power and life is still more evident in *The Last Man*. Here, Shelley lends new metaphoric expression to an imagined danger internal to humanity by refiguring that danger as an infectious disease. The pandemic that ultimately wipes out the species in this novel's millennial future becomes the basis for a new geopolitical order whose sole purpose is to stave off the threat of extinction. Disconnecting the ancient trope of plague from any notion of divine judgment, *The Last Man* equates it instead with revolutionary transformation. In the mode of confession, Shelley and De Quincey animate a multitude incompatible with the idea of man as individual and exceeding the boundaries of the nation-state. Yet they incarnate the principle of popular sovereignty even in what seem like phobic images of mass life: monsters, crowds, contagious diseases. My readings of *Frankenstein, Confessions of an English Opium Eater,* and *The Last Man* find a new political subject coming into being in literature and transmuting the older metaphor of the body politic into something massive, uncontainable, and startlingly alive.

Moving into the early Victorian era and focusing on the city as a key site for the administration of mass life, chapter 2 takes up the relation between population and class. Writers so opposed as Edwin Chadwick and Friedrich Engels, as they set out to document proletarian living conditions in the 1830s and 1840s, together advanced a theory best characterized as a natural history of class struggle. Their studies of creaturely life in the city at times conceived of the proletariat as a new race emerging from within and becoming differentiated from a given national population in consequence of ecological conditions, not least of all crowding. Yet the natural-historical model also made demographic excess (contra Malthus) favorable to the progress of the species and of society. Even as scientific studies and realist novels warned that degradation, disease, and unrest would inevitably follow from urban overcrowding, their stories recast the pressures of population as the precondition for all historical change. Between Mayhew's ominous images of a disposable human residuum and Marx's redefinition of relative surplus population as a systemic requirement of capitalist accumulation, the reproduction of surplus life variously appears as an irremediable problem, part of the inevitable *faux frais* of production, and the basis for a radical mass politics.

Contra the cliché that fiction personalizes while social science aggregates, this chapter finds industrial fiction contributing to a mode of mass writing that proliferated alongside quantitative population analysis. Reading Gaskell's *Mary Barton* together with the reportage of Mayhew, Engels, and others demonstrates a formal problem in demography to which all three variously responded: Counting and classifying the human aggregate yields a quantity in excess of category. The production of remainders yields a narrative of its own, one at odds with attempts to naturalize class or to place it in a stable relation to work; the argument of chapter 2 suggests that the industrial novel narrates a process of *déclassement* that occupational statistics fail to capture. Gaskell's novel shows how class and character alike lose their grounding in the routine circumstance of unemployment. It singles out its initial working-class protagonist only to eject him from the workforce and gradually unmake him. If its explicit purpose is to offer up John Barton as a representative specimen of the English working class, its plot implicitly calls representativeness into question as it sidelines the character and empties him of his defining characteristics. Attending to this process both in fiction and in social science as they confront a category labeled on the 1841 census as "unemployed persons and women," I contend that the industrial novel's aim is ultimately not to construct a fixed national class of workers but to reveal a residuum constantly being ejected from it.

The Dickensian city novel, perhaps more than any other genre, works toward forging alternative modes of sociality out of the human surplus. Chapter 3 considers the political stakes of Dickens's refusal to solve the problem his narratives so spectacularly create: the incapacity of all existing institutions—the state, the factory, the workhouse, the prison, and above all the family—to sustain the quantity of life they produce. Such sprawling serial novels as *Bleak House, Little Dorrit,* and *Our Mutual Friend* can consequently be read as intentionally failed experiments in population management. This chapter resists the new historicist tendency to equate Dickens's narrative techniques with surveillance and preventive policing, emphasizing instead how his fiction shows power operating primarily through neglect rather than active intervention or the omnipresent gaze of the law. Such a reading likewise challenges the critical tradition that treats these texts as the product of a quintessentially liberal vision, a perspective that separates the one from the many, defends personal autonomy and private property in the body and the home, and bolsters the comforts of the hearth against the inhumanity of institutions. *Bleak House* lets an epidemic erode the boundaries separating characters, households, and social strata in order to deform and reshape the social body. Even in killing off scores of city dwellers while proliferating still more, Dickens extends the novel's scope beyond the parameters set by British society. Rather than try to represent the unrepresented or count the uncounted, *Bleak House* reconstitutes its social world as a total always in excess of itself. The pervasive presence of such "supernumeraries" as Jo, the homeless crossing-sweeper, give malleable form to an unspecified quantity of human life over and above the recognized totality of society. The disease Jo spreads as he is "moved on" throughout the city figuratively conveys not simply a generalized risk to the survival of a population but also the otherwise imperceptible interdependencies and metonymic linkages of common existence.

This metonymic process extends the phenomenon of urban social aggregation beyond the geographical space of the city. Chapter 4 follows the narrative logic of biopolitics into the English countryside, where similar pressures turn out to be covertly at work. The sensation novels of the 1860s became notorious for enclosing the infectious qualities of the crowd within a female body and allowing that body to infiltrate the apparently protected sphere of domestic fiction. To explain the outrage provoked by such bestsellers as *Lady Audley's Secret* and *East Lynne*, I attribute their distinctive plot twists to the Victorian demographic theory of "redundant women": a female population exceeding the national demand for wives and mothers. Sensation novels overpopulated households with a small army of *femmes fatales* whose very existence imperiled domestic norms, yielding countless tales of bigamy and fraud. The redundant woman becomes one of the most provocative devices of a genre whose female characters prove irreconcilable with the conjugal family and yet impossible either to domesticate or to expel from British society. By raising the specter of women invading the nation from within and by sheer force of numbers, the novels of Mary Braddon and Ellen Wood made their antiheroines all but synonymous with mass population, mass culture, and systems of industrial mass production.

Their critics inadvertently echoed these novels' plots even in deploring the genre as a profusion of mass-produced feminine material with which serious literature could not compete for popular appeal. Further, in worrying that readers could no more readily distinguish healthy from dangerous novels than sensation fiction's characters could distinguish fit spouses from madwomen and criminals, they turned what Darwin termed sexual selection into a literary-critical problem. Reviews of sensation novels and essays on the social mission of criticism in the 1860s conceive of literature itself as a population. This conception would shape F. R. Leavis's national canon-building project in the early twentieth century (and, more recently, Moretti's seemingly antithetical effort to apply quantitative methods to the transnational analysis of genres and to characterize literary history as a story of ruthless competition within a crowded ecosystem of texts). For Leavis, the critic's calling was to aid in the selection of texts worthy of survival and cultural reproduction, but the line between high art and popular trash was never as bright as he and his Victorian predecessors wished. While reviewers held up George Eliot's high moral seriousness as a counterpoint to the cheap thrills supplied by Braddon, Eliot's canonical novels incorporate and rely on recognizably sensational plot elements. To wit, as this chapter suggests, the narrative problem of redundant women lived on in *Daniel Deronda* after sensation fiction had all but disappeared. Leavis's frustration with that novel, culminating in his failed editorial attempt to perfect it by deleting Daniel and making Gwendolen Harleth its sole focus, shows that realism did not outlast or absorb the deviant subgenre but was substantially altered by it.

One need only look to the late Victorian fiction of Hardy and Gissing to see how spectacularly failed were the norms of domestic fiction by the century's end. Much as sensation fiction threw the marriage plot into question, naturalist fiction removes all developmental purpose from the bildungsroman and casts still more fundamental doubt on the protocols of a society organized around heterosexual desire and the conjugal family. Chapter 5 examines what happens to the novel at a notably post-Darwinian moment. If earlier novels of formation set their protagonists apart from masses of others who do not adapt and survive, *The Odd Women*, *New Grub Street*, *The Mayor of Casterbridge*, and *Jude the Obscure* explicitly mark their main characters as disposable lives. Telling tales of blocked generational mobility, depleted vital instinct, and failed procreation, these late Victorian texts dealt a forceful blow to the reproductive future that fiction had once promised.

To carry out their assault on the logic of development, Hardy's and Gissing's novels at once rely on and resist two contemporaneous discourses: Emile Durkheim's sociology of anomie and August Weismann's germ plasm theory of heredity. The two theories offered opposing accounts of what impedes character development and curtails social mobility: from one angle, the weakening of social norms, and from the other, biological degeneracy that resists social remediation. They compete for determinacy in *Jude the Obscure* in particular, yet neither ultimately suffices to explain the suicidal impulses that propel the novel's plot. The shocking self-destruction of Jude Fawley's and Sue Bridehead's children, often misread as validating Malthus, proves incompatible with any familiar principle of demographic, sociological, or biological necessity. Rather than pathologize its characters' failure to thrive, Hardy's anti-bildungsroman universalizes the peculiar will toward dissolution that Freud would term the death drive. In so doing, it divests fiction from the project of promoting life. Little Father Time's suicide note further instantiates a break between intention and its formal expression, between meaning and event, word and world, that would all but define literary modernism.

In questioning the force of conscious personal intention in governing life, Hardy's last novel points toward the more explicitly globalized concerns that shape Conrad's fiction. In *Heart of Darkness*, civilization and the death drive indeed prove inseparable. It is apt that Kurtz's betrothed, a ghostly figure for the empty ideals of Europe's purported civilizing mission, has no other name than his "Intended" in a novel in which neither Kurtz's nor Marlow's motivations for venturing into the heart of imperial darkness are transparent even to themselves (34). Yet for all Conrad's emphasis on the mysteries of the psyche and his encoding of the voyage outward as a voyage inward, the population dynamics that spurred imperial expansion are still at work in his fiction. His characters, named and unnamed, bear out Arendt's insight that the European powers' rabid Scramble for Africa relied on an endless supply of "superfluous men" (189).

It will perhaps seem fitting, as this book begins with De Quincey's initially inexplicable revulsion toward humanity, that it ends with a text whose narrator famously experiences a *frisson* of recognition that the Congolese people "were not inhuman": that across a chasm of difference, "what thrilled you was just the thought of their humanity—like yours" (36). Yet the conceptual distance between the two texts is vast. *Heart of Darkness* exposes human excessiveness and the fragility of social constraints as psychological rather than biological conditions. Taking stock of this psychologizing turn, a brief conclusion considers how proto-modernist fiction reconfigures the literary landscape and reimagines population by venturing into the mystified realm of interiority. If population in De Quincey's *Confessions* subsumed the individual, it projects itself in Conrad's imperial romance as a half-buried trace of the primal horde at the core of the individual psyche. In imagining a global mob within the self, *Heart of Darkness* shares a strategy with Robert Louis Stevenson's *Dr. Jekyll and Mr. Hyde*: both are stories in which internal and external pressures on the subject become reversible, and the crowd outside reappears as the crowd within. These novellas, widely though they differ in setting and genre, take a similar approach to the felt excessiveness of human life by resituating the masses within the unconscious, thus intersecting with contemporaneous theories of crowd behavior, which prove foundational to the story Freud would later tell about the formation of the ego. Marlow's tale translates its unsettling images of African multitudes from a beguiling external force of otherness into what was being theorized (not least of all by Freud) as an internal Africa. With the modernist turn, the mass reappeared at once as a means of describing psychological resistance to social integration and as the uncanny remainder of collectivity. Conrad and Stevenson, however, did not take the individual psyche as prior or alternative to sociality. Instead of fetishizing the secret springs of personality, their narratives individualize impersonality itself. These tales thus plot their own peculiar efforts to imagine how a society might incorporate the larger mass of humanity with which it is simultaneously interdependent and radically at odds.

CHAPTER 1

Populating Solitude

Malthus, the Masses, and the Romantic Subject

> O ye numberless,
> Whom foul oppression's ruffian gluttony
> Drives from life's plenteous feast! O thou poor wretch
> Who nursed in darkness and made wild by want,
> Roamest for prey, yea thy unnatural hand
> Dost lift to deeds of blood!
>
> —Samuel Taylor Coleridge, "Religious Musings"

In the summer and fall of 1798, two anonymous publications caught the attention of English critics: William Wordsworth and Samuel Taylor Coleridge's *Lyrical Ballads*, which introduced what Wordsworth called a "new species of poetry" and charted a bold course for its future, and the Reverend Thomas Robert Malthus's *Essay on the Principle of Population*, which advanced a troubling hypothesis about the future of the human species. Apart from the mixed reviews both initially received, there would seem to be little common ground between the experimental volume of poetry later credited as a foundational document of British Romanticism and the ominous pamphlet on political economy later acclaimed as a foundational work in population science. Understandably, it is customary to align these texts and their authors with antithetical worldviews: Wordsworth and Coleridge, idealistic young poets committed to human perfectibility and inspired by nature's benevolence, and Malthus, an anti-utopian who projected the grim statistical inevitability of poverty, violence, and epidemic as natural checks to human population.[1] The revised 1802 Preface to the third edition of *Lyrical Ballads* suggests this very antithesis when it places "the Poet" in opposition to "the Man of Science." The poet, Wordsworth argues, "is the rock of defence of human nature; an upholder and preserver"—his polemical formulation implying that human nature is susceptible to violation and in need of reinforcement.

Heated responses to the *Essay on Population* from Coleridge, Robert Southey, William Hazlitt, Percy Shelley, William Cobbett, and William Godwin affirm an antagonism between Malthusian theory and the humanistic ideals of modern poetry. Hazlitt's 1807 *Reply to the Essay on Population* actually attributes the text's shortcomings to its author's antipoetic sensibility: "If he had been a man of sanguine or poetical feelings," Hazlitt speculates, Malthus might have felt that any increase in the world's human population would be attended by a proportionate increase in human happiness. The sentiments one ought to feel about population evidently demand poetic expression, as suggested by the paraphrase of Wordsworth and quotation from Milton that follow: this prospect of so many new births should have "made his heart leap up with a lively joy—to see 'fast by hanging in a golden chain this pendant world,' &c." (86–87). Poetry is repeatedly held up analogically as a gauge of the *Essay's* faults. Hazlitt, remarking on Malthus's attempt to reconcile his argument for "moral restraint" with an account of human nature that contradicts it, compares him to "a bad poet who to get rid of a false concord alters the ending of his first line, and forgets that he has spoiled his rhyme in the second" (74). Godwin, too, finds occasion to contrast the prose of such an "uninspired writer" unfavorably against the language of psalmists (*Of Population* 106). Poetry itself, accordingly, provides a privileged space for debate with Malthus. Wordsworth's *Prelude* implicitly takes issue with his physiological determinism, disputing the premise that human advancement is impeded by mere "animal wants and the necessities / Which they impose" (12:94–95), and Shelley, Byron, and other second-generation Romantics spare no opportunity to vilify Malthus and parody his theorem as a non-satirical sequel to Swift's *Modest Proposal*—at best an absurd delusion, at worst a genocidal plot against the poor.[2]

While Romantic poetry and the principle of population are less opposed than they appear, it is no coincidence that this clash with Malthus erupts at such a transformative moment in literary history. The first two decades of the nineteenth century, which witnessed the rise of the life sciences and of statistical social analysis (the start of that "avalanche of printed numbers" Ian Hacking describes), also saw *literature* emerge as keyword: a descriptor not just for a set of texts but also for a subjective orientation toward the world. It is around the time of the *Essay on Population* that literature began making universalizing claims for its own ethical value—often, as Maureen McLane has emphasized, in the language of philosophical anthropology.[3] Shelley held that poetry, defined as the expression of the imaginative faculty, "is connate with the origin of man" (*A Defence of Poetry* 511). Godwin similarly identifies literature in its broadest sense as the ultimate evidence of human exceptionalism: "the grand line of demarcation between the human and the animal kingdoms" (*The Enquirer* 31). In making this assertion, Godwin does not just echo Aristotle's claim that poetry arises out of an innate mimetic tendency in the species.[4] He also joins Kant in equating artistic production with human autonomy, distinguishing creative activity from the natural world's productive processes according to an opposition—elemental to Romanticism—between freedom and necessity.[5] Such an account of poetic work offered a domain of experience free from physiological or mechanical compulsion and unbound to any systemic teleology. It helped shore up a particular version of humanism against the functional imperatives of natural history on the one hand and political economy on the other. Ironically, though, it hinged its claims for human creativity on the very term that risked compromising humanity's uniqueness: "we want the poetry of *life*," wrote Shelley in his impassioned *Defence of Poetry*: "our calculations have outrun conception; we have eaten more than we can digest" (530).

The Romantic-era texts considered in this chapter all share this basic problematic. They aim to vindicate humanity against some force that threatens it, whether in the form of political violence, statistical abstraction, animalization, or biological and ecological risk. In so doing, their appeal to natural life reveals that "human" has become an ontologically unstable category, often with the result that it appears an empty or even suspect term. This is one of the less obvious outcomes of the Malthusian shift in British political thought (whose most direct policy consequences included the mandate for a decennial national census after the 1800 Census Act and, later, the dismantling of most nonpunitive forms of welfare under the New Poor Law of 1834), but it accounts for Malthus's persistent presence in literature and his place alongside Wordsworth and Byron in Hazlitt's *Spirit of the Age*. The dilemma is readable in *Frankenstein*'s project in life production, Thomas De Quincey's opium visions of an overcrowded globe, and *The Last Man*'s romance of extinction. These narratives describe experiments—scientific, personal, and political—motivated by an interest in humanity yet haunted by an unforeseen terror of human life, which seems to yield monstrous bodies, mobs, and contagious diseases that violate distinctions among individuals. Such figures attest to a biopolitical drive in Romantic writing—a defining interest in animacy and population and the struggles both entail—but they are not just ideological symptoms or tragic images of bare life. They also embody a new conception of collectivity that relied on literary expression.

It found expression in what seems like the most individualizing of all genres: confession, broadly construed here as including poetic and fictional autobiography as well as nonfiction memoir in the tradition of Jean-Jacques Rousseau. The confessional texts discussed here diverge from a version of Romanticism that privileges a solitary self, isolated from the banality of the social world by poetic consciousness. They describe limit experiences that confront the individual with heterogeneous global masses that threaten the very distinctions on which the self/society dualism is founded. At the level of form, they deploy a sort of impossible first person that strains the unity of its speaking subject by obliging it to witness and narrate global biological processes on a transhuman scale. In staging such encounters, they present not only alternative approaches to population but also experiments in redefining literature's human subject as something other than the private individual.

The miscellaneous creature assembled in *Frankenstein* bodies forth all the aesthetic volatility, political conflict, and philosophical contradictions that arise from the effort to reconstitute power in the object of population. Here, it is worth revisiting McLane's illuminating reading, which masterfully connects *Frankenstein* to the Godwin-Malthus controversy and to a discourse of species: for McLane, Shelley's novel is ultimately "a critique of the anthropological and anthropomorphic foundations of all human knowing" (87), with Malthusian thought serving to displace the humanities, biologize the concept of humanity, and enable Victor Frankenstein to claim a monopoly on its application. My claim, by contrast, is that the biopolitical turn opens up a fissure within the category of the human such that anti-Malthusians who professed to speak on humanity's behalf could rarely avoid provincializing the concept themselves, resisting the universality of biological species nature, or implying that human is precisely what they wish not to be. Further, even as it destabilizes the human in Victor's attempts to champion that abstraction, *Frankenstein*'s overarching project is to mobilize and give flesh to a new conception of mass humanity poised to assert itself as a political subject. This walking, speaking aggregate appears monstrous less because of its essential otherness than because it overwhelms the existing political categories that rise to meet it: the private individual, the nuclear family, and the body politic. Victor's confession gives form to the imagined nonequivalence of humanity with a social body it at once comprises and exceeds. To assess the political stakes of this nonequivalence—or, put differently, to assess how a distinctly new type of politics came to hinge on this nonequivalence—requires us to consider why, and to what effect, the task first fell to novelists and poets to demonstrate the peculiar excessiveness of human life.

The Passion of Thomas Malthus

> For what purpose were the passions implanted?
> That man by struggling with them might attain a
> degree of knowledge denied to the brutes, whispers
> Experience.
>
> —Mary Wollstonecraft, *A Vindication of the
> Rights of Woman*

In the decades-long debates the *Essay* sparked, there is one consistent refrain: Malthusian theory is an assault on humanity itself. Opponents across the political spectrum charged Malthus with a scandalous indifference to culture and a willingness to subordinate human intellect to the brute forces of instinct, the pressures of environment, and the undiscriminating laws of probability. Where Enlightenment philosophy dignified humans from animals in their capacity to exert mental control over bodily impulses, Malthus thought it likely that "the body has more effect upon the mind than the mind upon the body" (153). If neither individual self-interest nor agricultural development nor political reform could compensate for the "natural inequality of the two powers of population and of production in the earth" and no constitution could rewrite "the great law of our nature which must constantly keep their effects equal" (72), what claims could be made for the rights of man or the contractual protections of the state? If the "passion between the sexes" were merely an involuntary and statistically generalizable drive and the resulting propagation of human life ceased to be a good in itself, what then would distinguish love from the mating of other species?

The debate, in other words, centered on human exceptionalism. And critics were not altogether wrong to charge the *Essay* with a libel against humanity in its honorific sense. Malthus strongly implied that such exalted characteristics as reason, language, sentiment, and political capacity were superseded by basic physiological needs and creaturely instincts. "Elevated as man is above all other animals by his intellectual faculties," he argues, "it is not to be supposed that the physical laws to which he is subjected should be essentially different from those which are observed to prevail in other parts of animated nature" (225). If the divide between humans and other animals already looked less categorical from the vantage point of natural history, Malthusian thought gave human biology its most bluntly formulated political consequences. His adversaries, in response, set out to refute his claims by defending the uniqueness of their species.

Yet what these debates also demonstrate is that humanity's exceptional status is not really undone by the subsumption of the human within the category of creaturely life. On the contrary, it is substantially reinforced both by the elevation of the species to the level of a political object and by the subjective fear of human reducibility to the animal.[6] In the eighteenth century in particular, natural history no less than metaphysics had contributed to shoring up a distinctly modern version of human difference paradoxically based on man's unique concern that no such difference exists. Such a conception of humanity takes shape in the theoretical compromise between logical abstraction and biological materialism that Buffon named *Homo duplex*. Man, Buffon argues, consists of two equal and opposite principles, spiritual and animal, that are perpetually at war.[7] This story of human nature's war against itself—a war within the subject, per Buffon, but often recast as a struggle between population groups, races, or classes—provides a narrative framework for the conflicts through which biopolitics emerges. Romantic literature, as the following sections suggest, adapts this biopolitical narrative of the species' war against its own nature in order to reveal its tortuous logic: notably, in Victor Frankenstein's war with the body whose reproductive capacity he regards as a threat to humanity, in De Quincey's visions of armies marching toward an epic battle for "human nature" against the swirling anarchy of planetary species life, and in the Last Man's reckoning with an internal human enemy recast as contagious disease (85). To understand the preoccupations of their narrators (whose agitation contrasts sharply with the composure of Malthus, for whom humanity's danger to itself was its own solution thanks to the perpetual feedback mechanism of checks to population), it is necessary to assess the altered situation of the human subject in whose tremulous voice they spoke. The principle of population made humanity exceptional in its demand for institutionalized protection from the very material facts that sustained its existence: the need for food and an inevitable—and inevitably procreative—sexual impulse.

Sexuality, more than almost any other element of the argument, was a sticking point in the anthropological controversy that greeted the *Essay on Population*. Notorious though Malthus became for his own modest proposal that the poor might be deterred from breeding or else allowed to starve to death to prevent general scarcity, critics seeking to defend humanity reserved their harshest criticism for the Malthusian account of desire and copulation as instinctive biological functions. Refuting this theory of sexual impulse was a goal that crossed political divides. Southey, though not wishing to align himself with Godwin (and lamenting in his 1803 review of the *Essay* that the debate concerning man's future hopes had been left to two such thinkers), denounced as nothing less than sacrilege the proposition that human "lust and hunger are alike passions of physical necessity . . . independent of the reason and the will" (296).[8] Hazlitt, writing from a liberal perspective, was less apt to argue in theological terms, yet his objection was much the same: "Mr. Malthus's whole book," he charged, "rests on a malicious supposition, that all mankind . . . are like so many animals *in season*" (127). The radical Godwin, pilloried in the *Essay* for suggesting that desire, marriage, and procreation might decline with the advancement of human reason, returned fire by accusing Malthus of subordinating the intellect to the sex drive.[9] In his long-delayed 1820 response to the fifth edition, he takes exception to the idea that "we shall in practice always blindly obey our appetites, and that . . . no future generation of men will ever conduct themselves with more virtue and discretion than the past" (Godwin, *Of Population* 512).[10] The *Essay*'s account of sexuality, as he read it, represented a backlash against Enlightenment and an insult to human understanding. This premise was well established in Enlightenment philosophy. As Kant's lectures on ethics assert, the sexual impulse in and of itself is "a degradation of human nature" ("Duties towards the Body in Respect of Sexual Impulse" 163). Yet Kant, unlike Godwin, sees no choice but to acknowledge that "without it a man would be incomplete; he would rightly believe that he lacked the necessary organs, and this would make him imperfect as a human being" (164). Because desire's object "is not human nature but sex," entailing no distinction between human behavior and "animal nature," he concludes, "[s]exuality, therefore, exposes man to the danger of equality with the beasts" (164).[11] At once elemental to man as an animal species and incompatible with a human nature defined by the capacity for moral judgment, self-mastery, and political self-determination, the small matter of "sex" poses a formidable philosophical problem.

The inevitability with which Malthus biologizes sexuality and links it to reproduction meets with surprisingly inconsistent counterarguments. It places Percy Shelley at odds with Godwin, as Catherine Gallagher shrewdly observes.[12] Shelley seems to take his father-in-law's part when he condemns the *Essay on Population* as an authoritarian assault on human freedom "calculated to lull the oppressors of mankind into a security of everlasting triumph" (*The Revolt of Islam* 34). While the two agree that the *Essay*'s argument is predicated on its author's clear "contempt for human nature" (Godwin, *Of Population* 512), their accounts of what is most odious in Malthus and what is most natural in human nature are covertly opposed. In stark contrast to Godwin's characterization, the Malthus vilified by Shelley is no crude sensualist; he is an asexual and anti-sexual figure, an enemy of love. He appears in *A Philosophical View of Reform* as a grotesquely cold-blooded clergyman: "a priest of course, for his doctrines are those of a eunuch and a tyrant" (51).[13]

Godwin and Shelley, despite their diverging views on sexuality, confronted a similar argumentative dilemma. Neither could successfully oppose

Malthus on familiar ethical terrain. Godwin, who had once posited in Benthamite terms that morality was "nothing else but a calculation of consequences" (*An Enquiry concerning Political Justice* 1:342), would sound almost Burkean in exclaiming of Malthus's proposals against parish relief, "What havock do these few maxims make with the old received notions of morality!" (*Of Population* 622). The same Godwin, denounced by Burke for his strident atheism, would contend that "Mr. Malthus's is not the religion of the Bible" and—defending Christianity as "a religion of charity and love"—would assert that "if we embrace the creed of Mr. Malthus, we must not only have a new religion, but a new God" (623). Much as Godwin felt compelled to assume the alien perspective of upholding moral absolutes to argue with a thinker whose utilitarianism rivaled his own, Shelley wound up championing the institution of marriage he otherwise opposed in order to argue with a man for whom it was a sacrament and one of the "fundamental laws of society" (Malthus 142). Against the *Essay*'s proposed deterrents to marriage among the poor, the proponent of free love mounts an uncharacteristic defense of the conjugal family as the natural form of human community. By Malthus's decree, Shelley charges, the poor are "required to abstain from marrying under penalty of starvation," and thus, in effect,

> the one thing which made it impossible to degrade them below the beasts, which amid all their crimes and miseries yet separated a cynical and unmanly contamination, an anti-social cruelty, from all the soothing, elevating and harmonious gentleness of sexual intercourse and the humanizing charities of domestic life which are its appendages . . . this is to be obliterated. (*A Philosophical View of Reform* 52)

Where Hazlitt, like Southey, charged the *Essay* with an overemphasis on sexuality that effectively reduced men to lower animals, Shelley attributes the same effect to the opposite cause: humanity is bestialized not by sex but by abstinence.[14] Byron, along similar lines, satirizes the religious overtones of the *Essay on Population* and the putative asexuality of its author in *Don Juan* when he sardonically speculates whether his Adeline's amorous desires might have been informed by Malthus's "eleventh commandment, / Which says, 'thou shalt not marry', unless well" (15:38). Though playfully professing ignorance of Malthus's book, the speaker of this libidinally charged comic epic closes the stanza with a provocatively loaded couplet: "But certes it conducts to lives ascetic, / Or turning marriage into arithmetic" (38).

For all the cleverness of this jibe, however, Byron's outspoken assertion of sexuality actually aligns him with Malthus. For him, as for Malthus, the body has greater sway over the mind than the mind over the body. This materialist viewpoint is elemental to his humor when, narrating his hero's upbringing, he describes young Juan's education by his erudite mother: "Arts, sciences; no branch was made a mystery / To Juan's eyes, excepting natural history" (1:39). Byron mocks the overbearing Donna Inez for seeing to it that her son reads nothing that "hints continuation of the species" (1:56). Such prudence, as the worldly-wise poetic speaker suggests in his winking insinuations regarding the advantages of college and what one really learns there, is no match for the force of instinct. Human sexual coupling is as inevitable as rhyme. When Juan goes into the forest to reflect on the universe, among other things, his "Longings sublime and mediations high"—mixed with passion for his first love, Julia—are inseparable from his animal nature: "If you think 'twas philosophy that this did," Byron quips, "I can't help thinking puberty assisted" (1:93). *Don Juan*'s speaker thus inadvertently joins the *Essay on Population* in privileging the libido over philosophy. The victory of physiology and instinct in this scene is the punch line of his joke at the expense of Wordsworth's and Coleridge's more metaphysical notions of nature and solitude. In mocking the Lake Poets' idealism in favor of sensuousness, Byron implicitly takes the same view of sexuality for which Godwin and Hazlitt faulted Malthus.[15] The story of his youthful hero's erotic adventures upholds the Malthusian thesis that species nature trumps all forms of training and socialization.

Despite Malthus's blunt treatment of "the passion between the sexes" as a law of nature, the Shelleyan charge of asexuality persists among later commentators. Even Marx cannot resist the temptation to comment on Malthus's personal life as a context for his theory. "Let us note incidentally," he wryly observes in a footnote in *Capital*, "that although Malthus was a parson of the Church of England he had taken the monastic vow of celibacy"; in this, he quips, the man was at least consistent with his principles (766n).[16] In pointing suggestively to this (apocryphal) bit of biographical trivia, Marx hints that the principle of population was symptomatic of some personal irregularity or deficiency in its author. This story finds its complement in another biographical myth published as fact in Michael P. Fogarty's 1958 introduction to the Everyman edition of the *Essay*, which erroneously claimed that its author had "practiced the principle of population to the extent of eleven daughters."[17] Whether as an asexual or an over-fertile hypocrite (worse still, one who begat female children only), Malthus menacingly personifies human excess and icy inhumanity by turns. As Hazlitt imagines him, he is at one moment a sort of lothario ("the glimpse of a petticoat throws him into a flame," Hazlitt speculates; if "Mr. M.'s passions are too much for him," he would do better to "give vent to them in writing love-songs; not in treatises of philosophy") and at the next, a hard-hearted creature of "ill-nature" and "sickly constitution" who cannot "be moved . . . by common feelings" (20, 68). Marx's favorite adjective for Malthus's reasoning is "schoolboyish" or "child-ish,"[18] and he is ridiculed in the *Grundrisse* as a "baboon" (606).

Given the dire policy implications of the *Essay on Population*, its oppo-nents' preoccupation with sexuality may surprise later readers. What is at stake in the population debates, however, has much to do with what is (less obviously) not subject to debate. Out of the conflict between Malthus and his antagonists emerges an unspoken consensus that not only defines, reifies, and establishes procreative "sex" as a universal norm but also establishes this norm as a problem. On this point, Malthus implicitly departs from Robert Wallace, for whom it was evident in the mid-eighteenth century that mar-riage and fertility served as measures of a society's moral health as well as its prosperity. He similarly departs from another of his key sources, Benjamin Franklin, whose 1755 pamphlet on population treated procreation as virtu-ally synonymous with the work ethic, attributing the high fertility rates of certain families to "examples of Industry . . . and industrious Education" (10–11). Had the views of Wallace and Franklin remained unquestioned, they might support Henry Abelove's conjecture that the reproductive imper-ative of modern heterosexuality and the productive imperative of industrial capitalism belong to one and the same disciplinary regime (128). Yet the theory of economically necessary "preventive checks" to population reveals another element in the normalization of what came to be called sex. It is on the basis of this Malthusian disjunction that John Stuart Mill would later maintain the necessity of self-imposed checks (including birth control, which Malthus rejects as an abomination). "One of the most binding of all obliga-tions," insists Mill in 1848, is "that of not bringing children into the world unless they can be maintained in comfort during childhood, and brought up with a likelihood of supporting themselves when of full age" (*Principles of Political Economy* 31). So too would Matthew Arnold, leery though he was of political economy, arrive at the increasingly uncontroversial conclusion in the 1860s that "to bring people into the world, when one cannot afford to keep them and oneself decently," is a "violation of reason's law" (*Culture and Anarchy* 176).

All of this might suggest that the concept of human and social futurity at the heart of post-Romantic political discourse is driven by other agendas than what Lee Edelman terms "reproductive futurism"—the cult of the child as inviolable emblem of a society's future. The legacy of Malthus at the very least required British writers to respond to a conflicting demand: a contra-ceptive imperative to preserve the fragile economy of social life and prevent the peril of scarcity. The Malthusian moment introduces an extraordinary complication into any historical narrative that automatically equates demography with prosperity or reproduction with generational social progress. As the *Essay on Population* everywhere implies, procreation is both systematically necessary to the continuation of the species and (in the absence of sufficient checks) inimical to its existence.

Contraceptive Futurism

> When one thinks, for example, what . . . innumerable Virtualities not yet got to be Actualities are become and becoming,—one sees Organisms enough in the dim huge Future . . . and much, even in these years, struggling to be born!
>
> —Thomas Carlyle, *Past and Present*

Of all the Romantic reactions to the project of bringing population under strategic social control, the one that most provocatively captures this ambivalent relation to reproduction arguably comes from Mary Shelley. Though its remote setting betrays no explicit link to the Malthusian controversy, the mythmaking first novel of the teenage daughter of Godwin and Mary Wollstonecraft tells a tale centered on the collapse of abstract humanism, the paradox of species nature, and the fear of the masses that converged in the population debates.[19] *Frankenstein* consequently sets forth the conditions of the biopolitical imagination, confronting modern politics with the mutually alien objects it had produced: human consciousness and animal life. The simultaneous demands to optimize life and to prevent the reproduction of some dangerous element within it preoccupy the agonized confession of the man who has, according to the inevitable formulation, created a monster—but more accurately, has achieved his goal of making a man. Victor Frankenstein's experiments deal with a population of one, yet the mass of reanimated human flesh is always simultaneously an individual in the most absolute sense (unlike any other, and forcibly isolated from all others) and an avatar of the multitude of which it is composed. All decisions regarding its life, body, and reproductive potential are made by reference to life in the aggregate.

Frankenstein's dilemma, from his own perspective, is that of deciding what kind of life can safely be permitted to live—and the novel's reception as a myth of hubris turns the lesson he claims to have learned too late ("how dangerous is the acquirement of knowledge" [35]) into the unambiguous moral of the story. What is framed as universal and transhistorical in the text, ironically, is the historically new problem of managing biological processes and protecting the human species from global risks to its survival. The standard reading exemplified in so many stage and screen adaptations that deprive the creature of speech may owe in part to the moralism Shelley herself injects into her preface to the 1831 edition. Though it sits awkwardly with a novel in which God exists solely as a character the creature reads about in *Paradise Lost*, this preface offers an easier settling of accounts with theology than the story suggests: "supremely frightful would be the effect of any human endeavour to mock the stupendous mechanism of the Creator of the world," the novelist affirms; "His success would terrify the artist," who would naturally flee from "his odious handiwork." While readers have often taken such warnings as the text's own earnest message, Shelley's early critics, however hostile, may have been right to find in *Frankenstein* no straightforward didactic purpose. "We need scarcely say," protested a reviewer in the *British Critic*, that "these volumes have neither principle, object, nor moral" (438), and the *Quarterly Review* agreed that *Frankenstein* "inculcates no lesson of conduct, manners, or morality" (385). To accept that this novel is a cautionary tale generally entails assuming, with Victor, that the creature should never have been given life in the first place. This assumption follows a logic that can be called (with apologies to Edelman) contraceptive futurism. It presupposes the need to prevent the reproduction of bodies deemed antagonistic to society's vital interests. Read against such a tendentious assumption, Shelley's novel looks less like a plodding morality tale and more like a timely Gothic experiment in political thought. It does not endorse but problematizes the foregone conclusion its nameless creature has been taken to represent.

To reconsider *Frankenstein* in this light requires putting together two seemingly disparate modes of interpretation: on the one hand, reading the story as engaged with biological questions of speciation and life as they bear on philosophical anthropology, and on the other, treating its plot as a political allegory in which the anomalous life-form functions metaphorically. If these approaches appear contrary, the concept of population makes them indissociable. Biology and political transformation directly converge in the population debates, the key premises of which Shelley writes into Victor Frankenstein's uneasy efforts to impose order on life. The young student's project is shaped by a utopian belief in human perfectibility: the dream of Condorcet and of Godwin (to whom the novel is dedicated). His solitary search for the elusive vital principle—driven by an ambition to be useful to his species—bears as much resemblance to their philosophical speculations on the future of the species as to the debates on galvanism at London's Royal College of Surgeons. His fantasy of "banish[ing] disease from the human frame, and render[ing] man invulnerable to any but a violent death" (23) echoes Condorcet's treatise on the *Progress of the Human Mind*, which argued for the "organic perfectibility" of the human race and its unlimited capacity for progress (including the extension of the human lifespan). "Would it be absurd now to suppose," Condorcet had asked, "that a time will come when death would result only from extraordinary accidents or the more and more gradual wearing out of vitality, and that, finally, the duration of the average interval between birth and wearing out has itself no specific limit whatso-ever?" To this rhetorical question, Malthus had replied in the affirmative; his lengthy refutation, however, treats the theory of organic perfectibility as sufficiently influential to warrant counterargument. Frankenstein's research also recalls Godwin's suggestions (similarly dismissed by Malthus) regard-ing the "total extirpation of the infirmities of our nature," the extension of human longevity, and the diminution of sexual desire in the future. In producing a human being without recourse to the "commerce of the sexes," Shelley tries out the hypotheses of her own famous parents. The experi-ment, which forms an adult man without an intervening period of depen-dent childhood (and without the interference of that "parental affection" that Wollstonecraft had called "despotic" [264]), implicitly tests Godwin's utopian speculation that the future race of "men . . . whom we are supposing to exist, when the earth shall refuse itself to a more extended population, will probably cease to propagate," thereby becoming "a people of men, and not of children" (*Political Justice* 2:528).

Ironically, or so it seems, Frankenstein circumvents sexual reproduction only to discover that his progeny desires a companion of "another sex." The meaning of this request is immediately overdetermined. Though Franken-stein himself is in no rush to marry, he treats his creature's demand more or less as confirmation of the Malthusian axiom that heterosexual desire is "a given quantity" (Malthus 48).[20] Speculating, per the terms of the population debates, that the union of male and female would naturally yield offspring, he anticipates fearsome consequences: "a race of devils would be propagated upon the earth, who might make the very existence of the species of man a condition precarious and full of terror" (138). In his counterfactual fear of a possible future, Shelley's character extends his thought to a biopolitical scale. Every decision he makes with regard to a seemingly singular life may have implications at the level of the species. At the moment when Fran-kenstein creates a mandate to protect humankind from the imagined terror of a coming race, we can perhaps take the force of Foucault's claim that "a society's 'threshold of modernity' has been reached when the life of the species is wagered on its political strategies" (*The History of Sexuality,*

Volume 1 143). The danger Frankenstein fears is one of the key imaginative mechanisms of biopower: the fiction of perpetual war between a "super-race" and a degraded "subrace" that is constantly "infiltrating the social body" from within (Foucault, *"Society Must Be Defended"* 61).[21] Yet the threat of a "race of devils" only points back to the problem represented by a creature simultaneously at odds with and equal to humanity. Behind this threat lurks the Malthusian paradox that the mass reproduction of human life at once enables and imperils the survival of the species.

In finally refusing to provide his creature with a mate, Frankenstein carries the logic of the preventive check to a new level. Whereas for Malthus, anything like a programmatic effort at selective human breeding was unimaginable because it would entail "condemning all the bad specimens to celibacy" (63), Mary Shelley's narrator mandates that his creature remain, as Percy Shelley suggestively put it, "an abortion and an anomaly" ("On *Frankenstein*" 186). For Frankenstein himself, it entails choosing perpetual violence over procreation. The male creature might kill if denied all social ties, but the female might bear offspring. New births represent a more monstrous threat, from his implicitly Malthusian standpoint, than the loss of existing lives.

The outcome of this ban on reproduction, however, applies to the creator as much as to the creature whose social demands he refuses to recognize. Neither one can have a mate; each destroys the other's designated female counterpart. Nor can either claim a place in any political community. Both are consigned to solitary struggle for survival at the unpopulated ends of the earth—as if confirming Kant's speculation that inhospitable regions like the Arctic could only have become inhabited as a result of forced human migrations occasioned by war.[22] Having intended (like Godwin) to perfect human life and having then tried and failed to protect it (like Malthus) from the vital forces he unleashed in so doing, Frankenstein is condemned not to die but to live. Life, once his supreme scientific object, becomes hateful to him. The novel thus looks less like a critique of social engineering than an indication of its futility. In attempting to master the monster, Frankenstein only proves that what looks like the exception is really the rule. If the creature is not exempt from the social needs his creator denies, the creator himself is no more exempt from the biological regulations he attempts to impose. He cannot occupy a sovereign position of command outside the body to which he gave life; nor can he shield his own body, life, and kin from risk.

The fragility of his personal dreams of sovereignty over his body and over other lives dramatizes an implicitly political problem. Sovereignty, far from evaporating with the advent of modern government, is centrally at stake in

Frankenstein. It shapes the novel's attention to the life of human and social bodies, revealing the connection between the population controversy and its revolutionary backdrop. The human form Shelley assembles revives an early modern political trope whose significance is dramatically rewritten in the wake of the French Revolution. This undead amalgam of parts, literalizing the organic metaphor of the body politic as singular personification of the multitude, is an unmistakable echo of Thomas Hobbes's classic conceit. Like "that great Leviathan called a Common-wealth, or State," Frankenstein's fearsome creation is "but an Artificiall Man; though of greater stature and strength than the Naturall" (Hobbes 81). The creature's own language underscores Shelley's implicit allusion to Hobbes's giant figure of the man-made yet organically embodied sovereign: "thou hast made me more powerful than thyself," he reminds his creator; "my height is superior to thine, my joints more supple" (*Frankenstein* 77). Its anatomy, pieced together from scraps of human tissue and organs gathered from graveyards, is a Gothic version of Hobbes's glorious body politic, in whom "[a] Multitude of men, are made *One* Person" (220). In adopting this metaphor, Shelley's novel contorts its unifying logic. For Hobbes (that eternal optimist of political philosophy), it was a matter of course that the multiplicity of man produces, and can never exceed, a functional body politic. Indeed, the multitude is an enabling condition for the exercise of sovereignty: "The Greatest of humane Powers, is that which is compounded of the Powers of the most men" (150), he reasons, "[a]nd be there never so great a multitude, yet if their actions be directed according to their particular judgements . . . they can expect thereby no defence, nor protection" (224). In *Frankenstein*, that great multitude, in becoming one, becomes one too many. The creature incarnates precisely that which cannot be assimilated into the polity. What was once an ideal model of the state thus becomes a specter of lawless violence; far from safeguarding society from the war of all against all, the creature brings the state of nature into the social realm and declares "everlasting war against the species" (111). The novel thus demonstrates the disparity between the body politic and a jarringly distinct version of the human aggregate.

Shelley did not need to turn as far back as the English Civil War, however, to locate this organic conceit. She had a more recent frame of reference in Burke's outraged response to the French Revolution. Burke championed the polity's power of self-revivification in Hobbesian terms by glorifying it as "a permanent body composed of transitory parts . . . molding together the great mysterious incorporation of the human race" (30). Yet his rhetoric gave this image of monarchy a strange twin. To demonize popular uprising, Burke conceived of the Revolution itself as a massive and unkillable body of parts. His description of the anarchic spirit of vice to which he attributes the Revolution transfers the vitality of the sovereign body to the debased flesh of the mob. If there is corruption in one form of power, he argues, it does not evaporate with a change of institutions but is reborn in another form, so that "[t]he very same vice assumes a new body. The spirit transmigrates and, far from losing its principle of life by the change of its appearance, it is renovated in its new organs with a fresh vigor of a juvenile activity. It walks abroad, it continues its ravages, whilst you are gibbeting the carcass or demolishing the tomb" (125). Shelley's own walking carcass incarnates both figures at once: the glorious body that molds together "the human race" and the uncontrollable vigor of the multitude. Her story is the definitive literary appropriation of what was already a familiar Gothic metaphor in political discourse, which made the crowd, as Ian Duncan notes, "an infamous monster of the modern political imagination" (17). The miscellaneous anatomy of the creature and its namelessness attest to its status as a figure of the popular body out of control.

Identifying Shelley's figural vocabulary with Burke's often leads to the conclusion that her novel is reactionary.[23] Yet the rhetoric of monstrous flesh coming to life was not exclusively a conservative conceit. It is shared by Malthus, for whom revolutionary uprising found a different explanation; Malthus frames the need to control popular unrest in liberal terms rather than in the name of traditional authority. "A mob, which is generally the growth of a redundant population goaded by resentment for real sufferings, but totally ignorant of the quarter from which they originate, is of all monsters the most fatal to freedom," he argued in the second edition to his *Essay* in response to the charge that his system promoted state oppression. Malthus renders this monster horrific, notably, by giving it the characteristics of a fertile female body: it "engenders" tyranny and sometimes seems "to devour its unsightly offspring; yet no sooner is the horrid deed committed, than, however unwilling it may be to propagate such a breed, it immediately groans with a new birth" (472). Pregnancy takes on a distinct ideological meaning in such imagery. Malthus's figure of the cannibalistic mother bearing offspring condenses political violence with procreation in ways that signal a substantially revised relation between the state and natural life.

In incarnating this metaphor, Shelley's novel suggests that there is no separating the specter of popular unrest from that of unmanageable biological processes. Even Sandra Gilbert and Susan Gubar's classic reading of the creature's monstrosity as covertly female accrues different historical meaning in relation to the revolutionary potential ascribed to a new mass body. Maternity itself now threatened a deviation from (rather than the reproduction of) traditional forms of authority. This concern is surprisingly pervasive: when Burke, for example, vilifies Jacobin philosophers—including Godwin, who dreamed of doing away with death and making new births unnecessary—for dethroning God, he figures their atheism as monstrous offspring born of a decayed maternal corpse: "the brood of that putrid carcase, that mother of all evil, the French Revolution" (qtd. in Nicoll 70). It is this image of the dead mother bringing forth new life that Frankenstein will come to fear as a still greater threat to human safety than her male counterpart—indeed, that he has always tacitly feared, hence his goal of making life without recourse to the female body. Shelley perfectly distills this terror in the dream that disturbs Frankenstein's sleep the night he succeeds in animating his male progeny: a nightmare in which the act of kissing his cousin Elizabeth transforms her into his own dead mother, her corpse wrapped in a shroud with "grave-worms crawling in the folds of the flannel" (39). If this looks like oedipal anxiety in its purest form, it is an anxiety that gains new potency after Malthus, who made sexuality into a recipe for mass death and the mother's body into the object most in need of regulation. This female mass body, whose reproductive power Frankenstein fears, poses such a grave theoretical danger that it must be destroyed as soon as he fashions it.

What system of governance could assuage such fears? The perils to survival formerly associated with the state of nature can no longer be averted by social contract; the very thought of the female, not yet bound by a prior "compact" made with the male creature, seems to Frankenstein to imply infinite potential for anarchic violence. Shelley's novel here unearths the buried conundrum Carole Pateman would identify in social contract theory's gendering of the political subject: if women are not direct parties to a contract with the state, they are implicitly not bound by its laws.[24] Even before Frankenstein himself violates the terms he has agreed to, his narrative casts doubt on the paradigm of a social contract predicated on the prior natural rights of isolated individuals that may be voluntarily given over in exchange for protection. Rousseau's hypothesis of a solitary natural man finds an obvious analogue in the monster, who enjoys no freedom outside society and yet cannot join it. As McLane, Gayatri Spivak, and David Marshall among others have noted, Frankenstein's self-introduction, "I am by birth a Genevese," is an emphatic nod to Rousseau, who begins his *Second Discourse* with a dedication to the Republic of Geneva from a loyal citizen.[25] But as such, it raises a question: what then is the monster, who was never born at all in the ordinary sense? Cut off from reproductive kinship, this creature cannot claim the constitutional rights of the citizen that attach to the condition of birth—those political rights that ambiguously subtend, even while purporting to follow from, the corollary Rights of Man.[26]

If even natural rights do not exist for the creature, the rights of the citizen prove inadequate to his creator's demands for protection against him. Frankenstein's confidence in the "republican institutions of [his] country" is undermined by the failure of justice that follows from the creature's first crime. The murder of his brother William results in the execution of the innocent servant Justine (perhaps recasting Rousseau's guilty childhood memory, in his *Confessions*, of falsely accusing a domestic servant of a petty theft that he himself committed).[27] This judgment makes the entire community complicit in a second act of violence. Elizabeth, who believes Justine to be innocent, comes to dread the possibility that the rule of law gives sanction to mass bloodshed. The deaths of William and Justine, though perpetrated by different hands, take on an equivalent status for her; she describes both not as murdered but as "assassinated" (72). Human beings, even when they act in the name of order, consequently appear to her as "monsters thirsting for each other's blood" (71). Rather than administering a regime of justice that distinguishes human society from the state of nature, the law belies any moral distinction between the creature and those who punish another for his crime.

Shelley's nameless life form tests the limits of virtually every familiar account of human nature, the principles of society, and the origins of law and government. The liberal model represented by Smithian political economy is ironized when the De Lacys, as the creature puts it, find their store of wood "always replenished by an invisible hand" (90). The hand that provides, as Shelley's repurposing of Adam Smith's metaphor suggests, is not the providential hand of the free market directing self-interested actions to serve the common good; it is the hand of the creature, which soon turns in violence against the idyllic cottage and the family its anonymous labor had served. Never having been the autonomous private individual that Smith's system requires, the creature at this moment plays *Homo economicus* in a state of barbarism, at war with the domestic interests he had set out to benefit. The creature has already learned, from eavesdropping on Felix's instruction of Safie, "of the division of property, of immense wealth and squalid poverty" (96). He knows that the absence either of wealth or of title condemns one to the status of "a vagabond and slave, doomed to waste his powers for the profit of the chosen few" (96). There is good reason for him to apply this abstract social knowledge to himself. While his unseen work for the De Lacys is of the most traditional sort, he is a virtual embodiment of a growing industrial proletariat: concealed from view in a "hovel," performing invisible labor whose products are heralded as magic, and exiled from the society whose demands he has served.[28] The language of Shelley's 1831 preface reinforces this reading by emphasizing the mechanical production of the body, describing how she first imagined its "component parts . . . might be manufactured" and then set in motion by "the working of some powerful engine." No wonder this figure—engendered by machinery and endowed, like Thomas Carlyle's image of the people, with "sinews and indignation"— would lend itself so readily to an allegory of class formation in Elizabeth Gaskell's *Mary Barton*.

If *The Wealth of Nations* provides a dubious frame for integrating individual actions into social structures, neither can Smith's *Theory of Moral Sentiments* reconcile the feeling and suffering monster to a social order based on sympathy. Since sympathy is necessarily a relation between individuals, it does not apply to a subject denied individuation. Frankenstein, hearing the pleas of his creature for a companion who might provide "the interchange of those sympathies necessary for [his] being" (118), finds his own sympathy turned into fear and loathing. "I compassionated him, and sometimes felt a wish to console him," he observes, "but when I looked upon him, when I saw the filthy mass that moved and talked, my heart sickened, and my feelings were altered to those of horror and hatred" (121). The creature's apparent otherness undoes the effect of his words. His literary education affords him access to reservoirs of compassion without any promise of reciprocation.

Literature itself marks the horizon of a strained universalism here, and the creature's exceptional status is reflected not only in its figuration but also in the text's own confessional form. He offers a narrative of his life that is at once recognizable, like Victor's, as a version of the bildungsroman and yet built on modes of first-person articulation that do not unify him as a subject. Further, his speech enacts the verbal analog of his physiology: a bricolage of quotations issues from the amalgamated body of parts, his human language and anthropomorphic form composed of fragments of other subjects. His manifold character and impersonally human being consequently appear as symptoms of literacy itself. Accordingly, in the subplot of his initiation into European letters via his reading of *Paradise Lost*, *The Sorrows of Young Werther*, Plutarch's *Lives*, and Volney's *Ruins*, it is plausible to see, as McLane does, a justified cynicism toward the promises of humanist education, which transforms the creature's consciousness without altering his status.[29] From that standpoint, Godwin's and Wollstonecraft's claims for the emancipatory power of education and of the "literature by which prejudice is superseded" ring hollow (*Political Justice* 3:241). The attainments of literacy, historical knowledge, and sensibility cannot neutralize the creature's perceived monstrosity from the standpoint of the society that repudiates him.

Nor can such an alien figure be assimilated to the cosmopolitan world order Kant envisions in "Toward Perpetual Peace." When he enters the home of the transnational De Lacy family (in exile themselves) to request friendship and protection, the refugee's open appeal to the "universal laws of hospitality" is met with violence.[30] He is likewise rebuffed by his similarly cosmopolitan creator, who declares, "There can be no community between you and me; we are enemies" (78)—further casting into doubt what Kant stipulates as the necessary universal right of visit on which peace depends. Wars of extermination, Kant argues, will cease only with the recognition of "the right of an alien not to be treated as an enemy upon his arrival in another's country" (*Toward Perpetual Peace* 118).[31] Frankenstein himself assumes he enjoys this right, hence his shock at being arrested when he washes up on the shores of Ireland; unsure of his location and unaware that he stands accused of murdering his friend Clerval, he protests that "surely it is not the custom of Englishmen to receive strangers so inhospitably" (145). The creature, by contrast, learns from bitter experience to expect universal aggression. "To me, hated and despised," he reasons, "every country must be equally horrible" (114).

Banned from the polity, rightless from the start, disqualified from kinship and even friendship, the nameless creature might seem to embody the obscure figure Agamben identifies as *homo sacer*: a depersonalized image of bare life whose liminal existence is the inverted form and the basis for sovereign power. Yet such a theory cannot explain the exceptional status of Shelley's character, who proves impervious to the law precisely because he cannot be hailed as a political subject. When Frankenstein calls on a Genevan magistrate to detain his enemy and bring him to justice for his crimes, invoking the juridical power of the state in defense of society as such, he is told that the law can exert no authority over such a creature. In effect, Frankenstein's successful "creation of a human being" calls into question the very object it presupposes—rendering alien the foundational category of virtually every major document of political philosophy (31). All forms of government, from the arbitrary power of absolute monarchy to the administrative devices of modern discipline, fail to accommodate this specter of multiplicity whose uncanny otherness is not that of the inhuman but that of the all-too-human.

The Tyranny of the Human Face

> If we want to be consistent, we must admit that the earth was already overpopulated when only one man existed.
>
> —Friedrich Engels, "Outlines of a Critique of Political Economy"

The terror of too much humanity haunts Romantic confession, fictional and otherwise, from *Frankenstein* to De Quincey's *Confessions of an English Opium*

Eater. These studies in self-disclosure, far from cordoning off their subjects in a realm of private thought, estrange their own narrative form in requiring it to mediate the gap between an approach to social organization centered on the individual and one centered on life in the aggregate. The uncanny excessiveness of human life *en masse* furnishes the Gothic element in De Quincey's autobiographical account of the psychic price he paid for a youthful curiosity that drew him into the heart of the metropolitan crowd. While his tale purports to be a treatise on opium, its narrator is no less addicted to crowds than to the drug under whose influence he experiences them. He too, like Frankenstein and Walton, plays the explorer entering forbidden realms: not the profane vaults where the mysteries of "generation and life" lie hidden (*Frankenstein* 34) but the supposedly unmarked geographical zone of proletarian life—"*terrae incognitae,*" as he calls the working-class slums of East London (53). He attributes his urge to explore this populous no-man's land, as well as his subsequent psychotropic visions of faraway places and peoples, to his love of humanity. "*Humani nihil à se alienum putat*" is his declared motto: he finds nothing that is human foreign to himself. For the opium eater, as for Frankenstein, however, this philosophical stance is unsettled by the aftershocks of his proximity to a multitude of human bodies. Having once spent his Saturday nights mixing with the masses "[f]or the sake of witnessing, on as large a scale as possible, a spectacle with which my sympathy was so entire" (52), he later finds himself transformed from agoraphiliac to agoraphobe and from compassionate humanitarian to paranoid misanthrope. It is not amid the crowd, notably, that this aversion develops but in the pastoral solitude of Dove Cottage—Wordsworth's former home and the tranquil scene where that earlier wanderer in London found refuge from urban chaos. If this quintessentially Romantic locus gave Wordsworth space to realize in retrospect that he had seen and felt "the unity of man" even in the city streets, the change of scenery affects this inhabitant rather differently. The opium eater's recollections of London's crowds torment his dreams in the country, and he is menaced by visions of myriads of human faces and vast continents "swarming with human life" (81).

Rendered in a strikingly disjointed and strained first person, De Quincey's hallucinations chronicle the subjective process by which their narrator runs up against the absolute limits of moral sentiment. For all his professed cosmopolitan curiosity, the self-described Orientalist is gripped by an unexplained yet boundless loathing of a "ferocious-looking Malay" who unaccountably comes knocking at the door of his cottage in Grasmere. In keeping, he claims, with the universal "laws of hospitality," he hands the weary traveler what is surely a lethal dose of laudanum and sends him on his way (91). This gift—a sort of spontaneous condensation of the British imperial trade circuit that flooded China with opium—is instantly consumed. What becomes of its recipient remains unknown, but the man proceeds to haunt the Eastern phantasmagoria of the narrator's opium visions long after his departure. De Quincey's uneasy memory of this unlikely visitor to the Lake District is multiplied into a series of figures and tableaux composing an Orient extending from Egypt and Turkey through India to China and the Malay Peninsula. His dreams produce a stock of incongruous clichés. They catalog the exotic stuff, variously monumental and collectible, of an imprecisely defined East: Hindu gods and Egyptian mummies; pyramids, pagodas, and Chinese cane tables; crocodiles and monkeys; the Ganges and the Euphrates. What unifies this jumble of images and objects is the sense of quantitative excess, disproportion, and inadvertence that characterizes their appearance in De Quincey's mind. Every image is endowed with strange powers of vivification and infinite generation: commodities appear "instinct with life" (82); architecture tends toward "endless growth and self-reproduction" (78); and creatures are "multiplied into a thousand repetitions" (82). These qualities correspond above all to the prevailing figure of excess: a flood of people. Seized by a murderous—indeed, genocidal—hatred for the multitudes that populate his "oriental dreams," he observes of Southern Asia (source of the British East India Company's and likely his own opium supply), "Man is a weed in those regions," and of China (main recipient of British-traded opium), "I am terrified by the modes of life, by the manners, and the barrier of utter abhorrence, and want of sympathy, placed between us by deeper feelings than I can analyse" (81).[32]

The xenophobia panic expressed here is so emphatic as to seem incontestable. Yet its very exaggeration encodes an attempt—not quite successful, since De Quincey is always on the brink of recognizing it as such—to place at a distance something eerily familiar. While he insists on the utter foreignness of the hallucinated racial masses that plague him, his narration simultaneously evokes the crowded *terrae incognitae* of working-class London that these "Asiatic scenes" and swarms of humanity recall (80). The association between East London and these imagined further Easts is nearly explicit even as he transposes the crowd onto foreign geography.[33] "Perhaps," he muses, "some part of my London life might be answerable" for his sublime nightmares of a sea "paved with innumerable faces" that "surged upward by thousands, by myriads, by generations" (80).[34] The reappearance of his lost friend Ann, the prostitute who once saved his life in Oxford Street, amid his visions of the East suggests that the dreamer's terror is not founded in anything so straightforward as a fear of otherness. Cultural identity and

difference seem almost to evaporate in the epic battle he describes as the climax of these visions; all that is perceptible is "tempest and human faces; and
at last, with the sense that all was lost, female forms" (85). Even the oriental-
ized scenery of his dreams loses the specificity that marks it out as foreign
in the process of being described: the uncannily lifelike objects, creatures,
and populations appear disconcertingly interchangeable even as they multiply. While the opium eater affects to tremble at the thought of "the mystic
sublimity of *castes* that have flowed apart, and refused to mix" throughout
history, his visions adduce a contrary source of terror: the sublimity of signs
that mix indiscriminately and bodies unregulated by any cultural norm (81).
De Quincey's opium reveries are the nightmares of Malthus. What he sees
are specters of endless reproduction and of appetitive masses of humanity
engaged in a ceaseless struggle for life.

The "barrier of utter abhorrence" he erects between himself and the alien
world he imagines is thus not so much an explanation as an alibi: an attempt
to remove himself from the scenes into which his guilty consciousness drags
him. He is alternately cast as agent and patient in the syntax of his dreams,
performing extraordinary feats and then passively submitting to abjection. He
acts with godlike power ("I brought together all creatures, birds, beasts . . . and
assembled them together in China or Indostan") and exerts sovereign imperial
authority ("I soon brought Egypt and all her gods under the same law") only
to become subject to the mockery even of animals ("I was stared at, hooted at,
grinned at, chattered at, by monkeys, by paroquets, by cockatoos"). There is
a consistent structure to these seemingly chaotic dreams: the dreamer's symbolic status is constantly inverted. He is alternately the giver of sacred law and
the body on which it is enacted: "I was worshipped; I was sacrificed" (81). This
dizzying sequence of symbolic inversions has a recognizable logic. Through
it, De Quincey choreographs the vital dualism of sovereignty through which
the abject and the divine—the dying human body and the transcendent body
politic—appear as counterparts.

The logic of sovereignty, as we saw in *Frankenstein*'s play on the familiar trope of the organically embodied state, is both challenged and reacti-
vated by the altered political status of human life. Where Frankenstein was
compelled to construct a new body as his experimental subject, the opium
eater's *corpus vile* is himself. In fantasies forged by his fascination with coun-
sels, legislative bodies, and historical figures "who embody in their own
persons the collective majesty of a great people" (77), De Quincey's drug
experiments allow him to embody the mutable forms of collective being
he once sought in the crowd. No longer the urban spectator who sees mass

population from some external vantage point, he himself becomes a body politic overwhelmed by the unruly masses that constitute it. No longer the curious student of an East that unfolds before him in *The Arabian Nights* and British Museum exhibitions, he incarnates an empire extending across spatial boundaries while shrinking from its own violence.

De Quincey's hallucinations collapse the distance between subject and object—and thus, here too, first-person narration becomes a formal expression of its own impossibility. The speaking subject is compelled to narrate, from an individual perspective, processes surpassing the scale of human perception. Indeed, opium provides the only means of subjectively confronting the sublime terror of mass life and of mediating between exceptionalism and explosion. De Quincey's opium-addled consciousness, far from guaranteeing the empire of reason over the body that theoretically sets man apart from other animals, operates repetitively and compulsively regardless of his will. While he shudders to recall the contrast between the "unutterable monsters and abortions of [his] dreams" and the actual "sight of innocent *human* natures and of infancy" as his children appear by his bedside (82–83), the monstrosity from which he, like Frankenstein, recoils is nothing other than human nature and its endless generation of offspring. The "unutterable" specter masked as categorically foreign turns out to be the qualitatively unspecified human (82). "Man is a weed": constant biological self-proliferation is the only characteristic ascribed to humanity.

It is striking, then, that his hallucinations culminate in the scene of "a vast march . . . of . . . innumerable armies" at a moment of crisis "for human nature, then suffering some mysterious eclipse, and laboring in some dread extremity" (112). Human nature as he envisions it seems hardly worth fighting for, whatever that might mean. De Quincey's visions of a war for humanity place him in a paradoxical position—and not just because, as Carl Schmitt reasons, "[h]umanity as such cannot wage war because it has no enemy," even though "wars are waged in the name of humanity" on a regular basis (54). Like Wordsworth casting the poet as human nature's defender, the opium eater exposes the conceptual instability of the human in the act of championing it. Indeed, he inhabits his own humanity somewhat conditionally. A writer plagued by such unnamable guilt, he apologizes in a preface anticipating his readers' lack of sympathy, may need to sequester himself even after death "from the general population of the churchyard, as if declining to claim a fellowship with the great family of man" (29). The human family seems potentially to exclude him, yet to belong to it is never wholly desirable. While De Quincey recalls with affection a homely little girl with whom he led a transient existence in London, declaring that "plain human nature" was sufficient to guarantee his bond with this first "partner in wretchedness," it is precisely plain human nature that he seeks to escape through opium (23). He claims to favor his drug of choice over alcohol because the latter "calls up into supremacy the merely human, too often the brutal, part of [a man's] nature" (47). The secret of opium—its pleasurable pains and painful pleasures—consists in a strange disavowal; it enables De Quincey to project the degradation of being "merely human" onto others, with the result that he must refuse to be human himself.

The opium eater's visions of planetary life, idiosyncratic though they are, register a broader geopolitical problem—one that De Quincey's narration exposes in its appeal to a theoretical humanism that refuses, in practice, to recognize its own object. Western cosmopolitanism and philosophical universalism are defamiliarized here even in their iteration, since they meet with the contrary universalism of species nature. The difficulty of reckoning with this recalibration of philosophical anthropology finds more direct expression in Hazlitt's dyspeptic response to the *Essay on Population*. While Hazlitt outwardly criticizes Malthus for devaluing human life, he also implicitly criticizes him for giving it equivalent value in all contexts—hence the ease of comparing the conditions of life in England to other parts of the world. He devotes a lengthy note to a series of chapters in which Malthus outlines the dietary, marital, and reproductive practices of the peoples of nearly all continents and provides evidence of the checks to which they are subject. Hazlitt objects in particular to the secondhand anthropological summary of Tierra del Fuego, whose inhabitants are ranked in the 1803 edition of the *Essay* as occupying "the lowest stage of human society," and of Van Diemen's Land (claimed as a British penal colony the same year) and New Holland, whose populations are described—on the authority of Captain Cook—as "half-starved . . . shivering with cold, and covered with filth and vermin" (Malthus 29). Here, he notes, Malthus seems to take grim satisfaction in showcasing bodily signs of deprivation. The dispassionate tone in which the *Essay* vividly details the abjection of fellow creatures, he remarks, "does not lead to compassion, but to hatred" (100). And this, he concludes, is just the point. Hazlitt's reading of these passages is in some respects quite apt; he may not be wrong in suspecting that Malthus's account of "the grossness and inconvenience of the savage state" is born of antipathy and calculated to produce the same sentiment in its audience. It is difficult, at any rate, not to detect an unacknowledged sadism masquerading as disinterested reasoning in a theory that prescribes the suffering of others. For Hazlitt, there is no other explanation for taking readers on a worldwide tour of hunger and disease, no less craven motive than to "ransack . . . all quarters of the globe" and "eagerly grope . . . into every hole and corner of wretchedness to collect evidence in support of his grand misery scheme" (101).

At the same time, the misanthropy he blames Malthus for arousing is not solely based on these crude ethnographic sketches. Hazlitt's objection is also to the *Essay*'s logic of cultural comparison, bespeaking a desire for difference to be so absolute as to preclude comparisons between "savages" and Englishmen. While he accuses Malthus of enjoying the contrast between his own quality of life and that of the Australian populations he describes as "neither tall nor well made" and subsisting on "large grubs which are found in the body of the dwarf gum tree" (Malthus 32), Hazlitt's own discomfort with these details is evident:

> We strive to get rid of our uneasiness, by hardening ourselves towards the objects which occasion it, and lose the passive feelings of disgust excited in us by others in the active desires to inflict pain upon them. Aversion too easily turns into malice. Mr. Malthus seems fond of indulging this feeling against all those who have not the same advantages as himself. With a pious gratitude he seems fond of repeating to himself, "I am not as this poor Hottentot." He then gives you his bill of fare, which is none of the most delicate, without omitting a single article, and by shrugging up his shoulders . . . excites in you the same loathing and abhorrence of this poor creature, that he takes delight in feeling himself. . . . He triumphs over the calamities and degradation of his fellow-creatures. (100–101n)

Here, Hazlitt implicates himself in the schadenfreude he attributes to Malthus. His own "loathing and abhorrence" of the "poor creature" parallels Frankenstein's racialized hatred of his creature as well as De Quincey's antipathy toward the Asian hordes who people his dreams. Further, if he rightly perceives in the *Essay* a certain theoretical indifference to culture, his response to this fallacy turns into a torrent of patriotic zeal. That he finds such patriotism necessary reveals what is surprisingly radical in the principle of population: Malthus's formula makes the fact of being human more consequential than the fact of being English. While its governing proposals are restricted to the nation-state, the *Essay*—even in the global data from which it extrapolates—renders national distinctions largely irrelevant.[35] If Joseph De Maistre could sardonically dismiss Rousseau's "Man" as a person he had never met, Hazlitt's complaint with Malthus is that he seems to be acquainted with nobody but man—shorn of all idealism, to be sure, yet no less universalized.

Anti-Malthusian thinkers thus had to face the limits of their own defensive humanism, which did not allow them to appeal to a universal concept of humanity. Condemning the sangfroid with which Malthus equates England's people with other nations and cultures, Hazlitt enumerates the triumphs of English literature, science, industry, military might, liberty, and law, finally concluding,

> And shall we wish to degrade this queen of nations, this mistress of the world once more into a horde of fierce barbarians, treading back our steps, and resigning this splendid profusion of all that can adorn and gladden human life, this gay variety, this happy union of all that is useful and ornamental, . . . the beautiful distinctions of artificial society, and the solid advantages derived from our constitution in church and state, for the groveling dispositions, the brutal ignorance, the disgusting poverty, the dried skins and miserable huts of the inhabitants of Tierra del Fuego, or New Holland? Yet this it seems from the doctrine of Mr. Malthus is our only safe policy. (104–5)

This outpouring of cultural chauvinism does not make for a very compelling argument, even on its own terms. Its rhetoric converts what are meant to be essential differences into decorative elements superadded to nature: culture can "adorn," supplement life with the delicate beauty of social artifice, without which the "mistress of the world" would be abandoned to "disgusting poverty." The guiding assumption seems to be that if one strips away the ornamental trappings of British culture, a "barbarian" lies beneath. Even while reproaching Malthus for underestimating the difference culture makes, Hazlitt tacitly affirms that culture's hold on the species is fragile.

This concern has a broader political scope than the *Essay on Population*. One hears in Hazlitt's vindication of the "queen of nations" an odd echo of Burke's denunciation of the French Revolution as an indecent exposure of the sovereign body. The generalized propositions of human nature and natural rights, by Burke's description, tear off "the decent drapery of life," leaving a king nothing "but a man, a queen . . . but a woman," and "a woman . . . but an animal, and an animal not of the highest order" (67). What is notable in this outraged reaction is that it tacitly accepts the premises it rails against. In framing the imagined spectacle of monarchy denuded of its dignity and reduced to a merely mortal and creaturely state, Burke was compelled to reconsider the very basis of politics in terms to which he claimed to be hostile. Law, custom, religion, morality, and all the conservative principles on which civic order relies, he suggests, are born of the demand to "cover the defects of our naked, shivering nature" (67). At the back of this defense of the old regime against popular sovereignty is a new biopolitical reason of state grounded in something still less grand than the rights of man: as his language implies, power takes its sanction from the generalized needs of the species. Even as he bemoans the end of chivalry in the treatment of Marie Antoinette, the image of outraged majesty he puts forth here bears a striking resemblance to the new incarnation of the polity he wished to reject: a vulnerable human body that shares its "naked, shivering nature" with all others—sacred in its very violation and need of protection, if no longer royal. Hazlitt, however different his politics, quails before a similar specter as he reads Malthus, whose book "lays open all the sores and blotches of humanity with the same calmness and alacrity as a hospital surgeon does those of a diseased body" (105). The diseased body, central to the rhetoric of political crisis, here becomes a trope for the species whose biological nature and suffering are exposed to view. For good reason, this would become the key figure of Mary Shelley's *The Last Man*, which uses an epidemic to plot the mortality of the state en route to the extinction of the species.

Mortal States

> Solitary ruins, sacred tombs, ye mouldering and silent walls, all hail! To you I address my invocation. . . . Mixing the dust of the proudest kings with that of the meanest slaves, you called upon us to contemplate this example of Equality.
>
> —Comte de Volney, *Ruins, or Mediations on the Revolutions of Empires*

The idea of modern England's subjection to the same physiological necessities and accidents that afflict the species in general was, in Hazlitt's view, clearly fallacious. To reach the bleak conclusions Malthus drew about the human condition entailed reading history backwards. If Hazlitt refused to entertain this possibility, though, a number of his contemporaries did—among them Mary Shelley, who obliges her audience to read history backwards in *The Last Man* by writing a millennial future recalled by the lone witness to human extinction. Published in 1826, contemporaneously with the sixth and final edition of the *Essay on Population*, Shelley's novel imagines a world advanced to much the same state Hazlitt envisioned as civilization's troublingly irrepressible past: "a barren island supporting a few wandering half-starved ignorant savages, such as England might have been once" (Hazlitt 102). Pandemic—transmitted to every corner of the earth by military campaigns and mass migrations from west to east and east to west—devours the world's population at the end of the twenty-first century, and England is by no means exempt; London, the "overgrown metropolis, the great heart of mighty Britain" is soon left "pulseless" (261). The novel's

English narrator, Lionel Verney, attests that "an uninhabited rock in the wide Pacific, which had remained since the creation uninhabited, unnamed, unmarked, would be of as much account in the world's future history, as desert England" (378).[36] Closing the volume of the British Empire's "tale of power and liberty" (324), his ostensibly readerless confession bids farewell to his country, to all the cultural "adornments of humanity" (322), and finally, to humanity itself.

Shelley's was not the first Last Man, nor would he be the last. Her novel, alongside Jean-Baptiste Cousin de Grainville's Le dernier homme, Thomas Campbell's poem "The Last Man," and Byron's "Darkness," follows a trend of literary catastrophism that spawned a large population of solitary survivors. While The Last Man initially drew harsh criticism for coming late to the end of history, Shelley's project diverges in at least one key respect from the works it was accused of copying. Hers is not an apocalyptic vision. The heavens do not darken, as they do in Byron's poem; the dead do not rise, as in Grainville's novel; the planet goes on spinning, indifferent to human extinction. Her speculative future, in other words, is not anthropocentric; the human species has no special place in the order of created things. Oxen graze unharmed in the wilderness that remains of cities, and Verney, wandering alone past a Roman aqueduct, perceives "[s]avage, ungrateful nature . . . protruding her easily renewed, and fragile growth of wild flowers and parasite plants around [man's] eternal edifices" (458). Such images of imperial grandeur in decay notably recall Volney's Ruins, in which a personified spirit of the tombs—a voice of historical wisdom borrowed from mortality—delivers nature's admonition to humanity that "the world wherein I placed thee was not made for thee." The plague in this novel, like the creature in Shelley's first, shapes a threat to the species that necessarily eludes the control of any polity even as it couples biological danger with political struggle. Both narratives begin and end with the same problem, that of creaturely life exceeding or outlasting a social order mobilized to protect humanity from the risks of its own animal nature. In raising this problem and making the survival of the human species on a planetary scale the explicit horizon of its plot, The Last Man takes its place in an extended Romantic debate on the contingency of power and life. Offering a different version of the experimental reckoning with humanity that Frankenstein and De Quincey's Confessions attempted, and restaging the consequent failure of universalism in the face of species life, it transmutes an internal threat to the body politic from a self-multiplying anthropomorphic enemy into the nonhuman form of contagious disease.

Shelley's novel, by constructing a speculative future vantage point from which to assess the prospects of the species, confronts the impasse between two familiar hypotheses concerning natural and social advancement. God-win had put his faith in humanity's potential to overcome current physi-ological and intellectual limitations, predicting that the need for government would give way to the "unforced concurrence of all in promoting the general welfare" (*Political Justice* 1:238).[37] Malthus had placed the animal nature of the species and "the grinding law of necessity, misery, and the fear of misery" at odds with all theories of organic perfectibility and social equality (133). Between the two, the "future fate of mankind" hung suspended in the gap separating natural and political life (67). The *Essay on Population* had framed the question of the future in the wake of the French Revolution, speculating whether such a transformative political moment was liable "to inspire with fresh life and vigour, or to scorch up and destroy the shrinking inhabitants of the earth" (67). As if in response, Shelley's plot demonstrates that the answer might be both. Together with Godwin, she imagines the erosion of traditional political institutions as a natural process simultaneous with social advancement in a new millennium: England's last king abdicates in 2073, and the nation declares itself a Republic. This future society easily solves the Malthusian problem of scarcity; Verney boasts of an era in which "[t]he arts of life, and the discoveries of science had augmented in a ratio which left all calculation behind," and "food sprung up, so to say, spontaneously" (106). Yet the march of scientific progress does not preclude the spread of pestilence. Thus, together with Malthus, Shelley's plot submits historical processes to the determinacy of nature. Even in a more perfect social state, the species appears subject to what Verney, sounding much like Malthus, calls "the unchangeable laws of Necessity" (399). Her tale of extinction, how-ever, brings back the dreaded "positive check" (as Malthus had termed such population-reducing phenomena as disease, famine, and violence) once it can no longer be ascribed any systemic purpose. Allowing these opposed theories of progress and stasis to coincide, she synthesizes a future without a future, through the principle of depopulation, as it were.

From the standpoint of Shelley's narrator, pandemic spells the end of politics. By the close of the twenty-first century, Verney reports, "the nations are no longer" (321). Since no state is immune to the plague, borders become irrelevant and citizenship and all other markers of political status obsolete. British institutions deteriorate, and statesmen abdicate; "Death and disease level all men," proclaims the Lord Protector Ryland as he resigns his post, "I neither pretend to protect nor govern an hospital—such as England will quickly become" (244). By the terms of Aristotle's *Politics*, this crisis erodes the very definition of the human as political animal; once collective life has no goal beyond life, humanity loses its distinctiveness from "merely living" animals.[38] Social bodies are bound together, ironically, by nothing but the biological risk human bodies pose to each other. Yet Shelley's futureless future is by no means postpolitical. The plague reveals its ascendency at a site of imperial war in Constantinople (a war so strikingly identical to the Greek War of Independence against the Ottoman Empire that Shelley uses the names of actual Greek generals from the 1820s), and the novel's back-story is the abolition of the British monarchy and aristocracy, followed by another transfer of power after the plague hits England. The surviving popu-lace then unanimously submits to the sovereign global law of Verney's friend Adrian, former Earl of Windsor, who assumes responsibility for human life in general—content to govern a hospital as large as the planet.

Rather than mark the end of politics, Shelley's romance of pandemic explicitly narrates a transition to biopolitics. Its exceptional future ushers in what was really an emerging norm in the nineteenth century, especially in the wake of Malthus: a mode of governance centered on managing popu-lation and authorized by the premise that humanity is an endangered spe-cies. What seems so minimal and debased an objective to Verney serves as the catchword for a sweeping political agenda: "life—life—the continuation of our animal mechanism—was the Alpha and Omega of the desires, the prayers, the prostrate ambitions of the human race" (294). By theoretically removing all goals but survival—or by politicizing "bare life," as Agamben would say—The Last Man reveals the rationale that enabled far broader gov-erning mandates articulated in the name of defending humanity, whether against epidemic, ecological scarcity, terrorism, or the nebulous danger Fran-kenstein had imagined as a new race attacking the population from within.

Though it takes on new resonance in The Last Man, the pestilence that emerges as the central actor in Shelley's plot is a familiar conceit in the dis-course of the body politic. There is a kind of obviousness surrounding the outbreak narrative as allegory of political crisis: proof of the fragility or cor-ruption of a state no longer able to govern itself after the demise of sover-eignty. Romantic-era reviews of the novel, almost all scathing, read Shelley's premise of the foundation of a republic along these lines. Such a transition to popular governance, for one incredulous critic, was "an indication suf-ficiently ominous of the approaching dissolution of the world" (Panoramic Miscellany review 381). "Can we wonder," the review opines, "at the plague that was to follow, and sweep off all the inhabitants of the earth? The holy salt of royalty removed, what was to preserve the mass from corruption?" (381). For some more recent critics, Shelley's narrative hints at this etiology even in its timeline. Since the virus surfaces in 2092, exactly three hundred years after the start of the Terror, there is some basis for treating this novel as a Burkean reaction to the now-dead Jacobin legacy.[39] Shelley indeed plays on the figure of the state as ailing body—though perhaps without any firm wish to restore its health or ensure its immortality. In bringing forward the poetical and formerly radical Adrian (widely taken as a figure for Percy Shelley) as the acknowledged legislator of the world, her plot in fact reinstates the man who would have been king, only to have him declare that "to stay in England would be to enchain ourselves to a corpse" (326). Whereas in *Frankenstein*, Shelley compromises the Hobbesian or Burkean figure of the immortal body politic by equating its self-perpetuation with uncontrolled mass reproduction, here she reworks the afflicted body politic by declining to sanctify it or defend its sovereign boundaries. *The Last Man* makes the nation-state not just mortal but permeable during the course of its existence by a multitude of bodies that seem to belong outside it.

Further, the old trope of affliction does not automatically carry negative connotations. Mary Wollstonecraft had praised the French Revolution as a purgative that would enhance the health of the body politic, and Godwin used metaphors of plague to describe its transformative potential.[40] It was just such rhetoric that Burke was countering when he wrote, "If it be a panacea, we do not want it. . . . If it be a plague, it is such a plague that the precautions of the most severe quarantine ought to be established against it" (78). For the very reason Burke could never recall "that plague-spot in the history of mankind without shuddering," pandemic remained a potent revolutionary metaphor.[41] Friedrich Engels would later describe England as a patient afflicted with an acute "social disease" from which it must recover renewed; until then, in the service of a necessary upheaval, he rejoices "over everything which accelerates the course of the disease" (*The Condition of the Working Class* 149).[42]

For all the political conflict *The Last Man* stages, what leads up to and follows from the plague is less a rejection of collective struggle than a rearticulation of the terms of common existence. This is why, oddly enough, the terror of extinction in *The Last Man* is attended by utopian promise: universal peace, internationalism, the end of inequality and class hegemony, a life without distinction. What was never quite accomplished through political reform is carried out by the plague itself. "We were all equal now," Verney repeatedly insists, "one living beggar had become of more worth than a national peerage of dead lords" (317, 293). Verney's narrative makes the universal susceptibility of human bodies to the same biological danger into the foundation of an egalitarian global order in which everyone "felt a kindred fraternal nature with all who bore the stamp of humanity" (293). In place of those abstract natural rights of man that Hannah Arendt would view as unenforceable, Shelley mobilizes contagion as the paradoxical expression of a common humanity that surpasses the particularities and privileges of political status.

To be sure, the novel conspicuously fails to make good on its belated political promise. Cosmopolitanism easily dovetails with imperialism: "every country shall be England to me," the former princess Idris tearfully reassures her husband Verney on departing their kingdom; so it is, in effect, since the sun never sets on her brother Adrian's domain even as the nation-state recedes into dusk. And even under conditions that supposedly eclipse nationality, race, class, kinship, and other differential forms of sociopolitical identity, universalist ideals often remain hypothetical. Shelley quietly reveals how her narrator's actions contradict his claims concerning the equality of the living. At every turn, we find him reintroducing distinctions of race and class, praising patriarchy, reimagining the internal threat of social war, and encountering human others he cannot accept as kin. From an Arendtian perspective, this is liable to look like the test case for a crisis that becomes most obvious in the fate of the stateless in the twentieth century: that humanity in itself carries no meaning or protection outside of political identity. Whatever is said in principle of human rights, in practice "the world found nothing sacred in the abstract nakedness of being human" (Arendt 299). Yet *The Last Man* is not a tragic tale of merely human (or bare) life shorn of all social particularity and thus all dignity, nor a vision of politics suspended in a permanent state of exception, per Agamben's model, from the moment power and life converge. Rather, Shelley's plot pivots on the demand to change the scope of political community, unbinding it from nationality, blood lineage, or territory. Even in bringing a theoretically boundless totality of human life into collision with something still outside it, *The Last Man*'s story points beyond itself to a collectivity that is necessarily incomplete—necessarily contagious and self-propagating—because it exceeds itself by definition.

This, indeed, is the form in which politics outlasts its established institutional grounding: it subsists in the contradictions Shelley writes into Verney's narrative, occupying the gap between what is declared true of life in general and what evades that declaration. After the devastations of disease and the leveling effects of depopulation, Verney reports that class distinctions no longer exist—or perhaps, he suggests, the poor claim an advantage, being used to "attending to mere animal wants" (309). Equality, once the Republican dream of the novel's most idealistic characters, now looks more like Hans Holbein's images of the *danse macabre*, in which skeletons join the hands of kings, popes, and serfs, all united by their common fate: "near at hand was an equality still more levelling. . . . We had no station among us . . . no distinction save between the living and the dead" (317). These extreme circumstances, however, apparently do not prevent the formerly wealthy from retaining domestic servants, coachmen, and private property. Indeed, under Adrian's regime, "while the decree of population was abrogated, property continued sacred," and material inequalities persist (304). *The Last Man's* global order is in this sense less a brave new world than the sequel to an old story. The national community of equals declared by the Republic before the plague was, it seems, a fiction, and so it remains after all differences of status are again declared moot—thus replaying, in a supposedly postnational context, the problem Marx would pinpoint in his early critique of constitutional law. When a state proclaims every citizen an "equal partner in popular sovereignty" regardless of class, race, occupation, education, and so forth, Marx reasons, this formal equality does not alter the lived reality of such distinctions but renders them private and leaves them "to act after their own fashion," thus keeping de facto inequality in force while declaring that it has no de jure existence.[43] Accordingly, so too do the traces of class identity remain perceptible to Shelley's narrator. Verney describes the followers of a messianic cult as "mostly drawn from that which, when such distinctions existed, was denominated the lower rank of society" (387). Undercutting Adrian's cosmopolitan decree of perpetual peace among all peoples, this religious sect—even on "an earth whose diminished population a child's arithmetic might number"—constitutes a "a tumultuous crowd," a menacing (and predominantly female) "multitude" (385, 401). The security of the new world administration is threatened by the antagonism of this unruly mass, which defies individuation and violently resists the sovereign law of the Protector.

These recurring specters of the masses are not the only challenge to the coherence of the surviving human community. A certain estrangement from the living human species ironically attends this political order centered on protecting it. Verney's narration illuminates a peculiar doubling of "life" that might be understood, in Roberto Esposito's terms, as an effect of modern sovereignty's immunitary logic—a logic nowhere more pointedly captured and tested than in Shelley's contagion plot. The governing biopolitical paradigm of immunity, Esposito suggests, writes self-destructive forces into the very condition of animacy, so that, "in order to save itself, life needs to step out from itself and constitute a transcendental point from which it receives order and shelter" (58). This splitting apart of life from its own biological dangers is the paradoxical foundation of that universalism to which Shelley's narrator appeals: a universalism hinged on humanity's demand to defend itself against an enemy it carries within itself.

Perhaps this is one reason why Verney—despite his avowals of mutual love for a global human family finally united by the threat of extinction—frequently recoils from his fellow creatures. Though he moralizes about the necessity of tending to any and all of the sick regardless of the risk of transmission, he perceives with "mixed horror and impatience" the prone body of "a negro half clad, writhing under the agony of disease" on the floor of his house (336). Violently repulsing the grip of the dying stranger who reaches out for his help, Verney falls on top of him and becomes infected. He immediately senses within himself the contaminating trace of the other with whose human suffering he does not sympathize but whose biological capacity to infect him with the universal human plague becomes the hallmark of the two men's commonality: a shared nature indifferent to the difference Verney sees. The spread of disease takes on added potency as a political metaphor at this moment because the conditions that enable it are so literal. The contact between human bodies hurled into global circulation by empire, war, the transatlantic slave trade, and the mass migrations and deterritorialization brought about by capital guarantees the impossibility of keeping the body politic bounded.[44] Verney's antipathy toward a concretely embodied instance of the species to which he swears allegiance in the abstract thus not only sets human life at odds with itself; it also places him in the position of policing boundaries that have already been breached.

Shelley's novel gives unique consequences to this chance encounter between bodies. The Last Man's fate—his lone survival, and thus the epic tale he has to tell—owes to his collision with the unidentified "negro." In perhaps the most intimate exchange portrayed in his narrative, Verney succumbs to the "convulsive grasp" of the stranger who "wound his naked festering arms around me, his face close to mine, and his breath, death-laden, entered my vitals. For a moment I was overcome" (336–37). This erotically charged embrace of abjection makes exposure to the other's death (indeed, to the death of all others) into an unexpected means of immunity: a life-giving supplement produced by the threat to life, inoculating the individual against the uncontainable communal disease he thereby contracts.[45] The Last Man thus makes contagion rather than reproduction the operative model for the body politic's internal dangers and enabling conditions—or, from a different standpoint, contagion functions as an alternative form of reproduction. The entire story, in effect, is the remainder of the narrator's failed struggle to shield himself from contact—ironizing that perverse process by which the individual defends its sovereign status and private territory by fending off the threat of community, misrecognized as something alien to his own newly privatized life.[46]

The racist terror that undercuts (or gives the measure of) Verney's humanitarian sentiments seems almost calculated to reveal the true face of a politics that claims the species as its object: an ethnocentric and nationalist agenda operating under cover of a sham universalism. And this scenario indeed unearths all the buried contradictions of biopower on which recent political philosophers have seized: the transformation of a biological threat lodged within and transmitted by bodies into a racially differentiated human enemy, barred from a supposedly universal humanity; the thanatopolitical undercurrent of campaigns to protect human life; the immunitary defense of health—of the porous boundaries of the state, home, and body—via a death unleashed on masses of others. In following this biopolitical struggle to its unsettling conclusion, however, the novel makes Verney's immunity an accursed gift rather than a guarantee of sovereignty or security. The individual health he recovers ultimately consigns him to an extreme version of that solitude to which De Quincey's opium eater and Shelley's own Frankenstein were abandoned as they, too, fled in terror from the species they once wished to embrace. His survival leaves him alone to contemplate humanity—monumentalized in poetic epigraphs and artifacts of imperial history but disconcertingly alien to solitary reflection.

If the Last Man feels compelled to memorialize his species in writing, he also yearns to forget it. Having recoiled from the touch of a human being he perceived as an invader, he recoils, in the end, from his own humanity. Recasting the uncanny anomaly that bodies forth in *Frankenstein*, his confession figures monstrosity in the state of exception that constitutes the human. "My person, with its human powers and features," the Last Man observes with horror, "seem to me a monstrous excrescence of nature" (467). If he once prided himself in having crossed "that sacred boundary which divides the intellectual and moral nature of man from that which characterizes animals" under Adrian's benevolent influence, his return to solitude leaves him longing to escape his studiously cultivated humanity (29). "Why could I not forget myself like one of those animals?" Verney laments. Addressing the creatures that surround him, he reasons, "I am not much unlike to you. Nerves, pulse, brain, joint, and flesh, of such am I composed, and ye are organized by the same laws" (459). His organic existence is materially much the same as that of any mammal. "I have something beyond this," he owns, "but I will call it a defect, not an endowment" (459).[47]

The Last Man at this moment is uniquely able to grasp the otherwise unthinkable fact of humanity: that indefinite "something beyond this," which operates by a recursive logic of recognition. To be human is to be conscious of consciousness—no longer in the Cartesian sense but in a distinct sense shaped by the knowledge that one is an animal. Being aware of oneself as human means being aware of precisely this fact: an exceptional awareness of being unexceptional. The paradox is written into Linnaeus's substitution of the imperative *"Nosce te ipsum"* for an inventory of anatomical characteristics that would differentiate the genus *Homo* from the rest of the order of *Anthropomorpha* in his 1735 *Systema Naturae*. This gesture of replacing taxonomic specification with an appeal to self-knowledge, as Agamben reads it, leaves us with the tautology that "man is the animal that must recognize itself as human to be human" (*The Open* 26).[48] But this definition, however tautological, is not as empty as Agamben finds it. It implies that to recognize oneself as human hinges on comparability; man belongs to the order of "manlike" animals, understandable in its resemblance to others. Human consciousness, from this angle, is not a truth to be discovered in solitude (as in the story of the *cogito*) but a social phenomenon. The Last Man, lacking any homology to link him to an existing species, is the name given to an impossibility. As soon as he is last, he is no longer man.

Alive alongside other living creatures yet no longer part of a species, the writer reduced to absolute individuality does not return to the brute state from which he ostensibly began. In the beginning, the wild Cumberland shepherd boy grows up in primal solitude: "My life was like that of an animal," he recalls, and it is only through friendship with Adrian that he "began to be human" (18, 29). In the end, he is something else, plagued by the memory of having been human and unable to forget himself. Like the poetic speaker in Keats's "Ode to a Nightingale," wrenched back into the misery of consciousness by his own words, he makes writing the medium of this agonizing failure to forget.[49] The ultimate dilemma of the Last Man is not that biology reduces him to the level of an animal; ironically, his sad fate is that he cannot become what he perceives animality to mean. The surplus of consciousness that makes writing possible produces a subject that appears monstrous to itself—and writing, so fundamental to Godwin's definition of the human, no longer seems to bear out Verney's earlier reflections on its transcendent power:

> As my authorship increased . . . I found another and a valuable link to enchain me to my fellow-creatures . . . and the inclinations and capacities of all human beings became deeply interesting to me. Kings have been called the fathers of their people. Suddenly I became as it were the father of all mankind. Posterity became my heirs. (157)

Insofar as the novel's conclusion casts doubt on such narratives of sovereign authorial life-giving and textual world-making, *The Last Man* seems a strangely self-canceling work, a study in the futility of Romantic dreams of poetic transcendence. Long after its narrator has declared that "to read were futile—to write, vanity indeed" (308), he is still compelled to write a confession of his life—a text that he assumes no one will ever read.

Transcendence, to be sure, is no longer on the agenda. Caught between the formal circumscription of a first-person perspective and the ambition to narrate a catastrophe that exceeds and outlasts that perspective, Shelley's project not only requires a frame beyond the narration that aims to encompass the end of human experience; even within the confession, it also periodically obliges Verney to report in a quasi-omniscient mode on the details of events he cannot personally have witnessed. On both levels, it thus hails the inadequacy of the very confessional form it adapts and defamiliarizes. But far from proving the futility of writing, Shelley's novel lays out a set of strategically unstable claims about the sources, temporality, and genre of this text. The Last Man's testament presents itself as an eyewitness account of human extinction—a past-tense history of the future end of history, dedicated to "the illustrious dead" (who may or may not be its present audience) with the admonition: "Shadows, arise, and read your fall!" (466). Yet Shelley's preface reframes the text as something quite different. Narrating a trip to Naples with Percy Shelley in 1818, she claims to have discovered the materials for her story in a cave among what turn out to be the prophetic writings of another solitary survivor who likewise had the misfortune to live too long: the Cumaean Sibyl. By her account, she then translated this portion of the Sibylline leaves not from the original English in which she unaccountably found these early Roman artifacts but from "poetic rhapsodies" into a "consistent form"—in other words, from lyric to prose narrative (6). Adding yet another frame to this frame-narrative of her discovery of the Sybil's prophetic framing of the Last Man's last words, Shelley titles this preface "Author's Introduction." In claiming authorship, she stresses the fictionality of her tale of the manuscript's origin. At once future-historical memoir, mythic vision, modern translation of an ancient artifact, and pure fiction, the text's peculiar narrative metalepsis makes it impossible to resolve the three distinct fictional moments of its composition or the three speakers to whom it is attributed.

The confusion this framing creates is no error. The Last Man does not foretell a destiny, much less an end of history. Its narrative frame and apostrophes to past and future readers interrupt historical closure with textual indeterminacy. In this self-interruption and even in its most radical self-negation, writing withstands the catastrophic future that is its own past, as well as the distant past of the Sibyl's prophesy, in order to address an unspecified present. The novel does not know on whose authority it speaks, or to whom it speaks, and it does not need to know. Inscribed to the dead, with its thinly masked portraits of Percy Shelley and Byron and its seemingly inevitable reference to Mary Shelley's own lastness as sole survivor of her circle, Verney's melancholy tale has prompted some critics to read this novel as a valediction to Romanticism.[50] But *The Last Man*—in giving the ostensibly readerless future an audience with the present—produces a quintessentially Romantic formal irony that precludes all lastness. In acknowledging the impossibility of bearing witness to human extinction from a human perspective, Shelley's novel also calls on literature to document the impossibility of transcending what literature itself helped usher into political history: the fact of being human.

CHAPTER 2

Political Animals

*The Victorian City, Demography, and the
Politics of Creaturely Life*

> It is evident that the city [*polis*] belongs to the class of
> things that exist by nature, and that man is by nature a
> political animal.
>
> —Aristotle, *Politics*

Mary Shelley was not the last to imagine man as
an endangered species. The figure of the afflicted social body at the heart of
The Last Man, too, in the 1830s and 1840s became axiomatic to the emerging
social sciences, which sought to organize large societies around the premise
that human life is always potentially at risk: susceptible to contagion, pollution, and degeneration and imperiled by exposure to adverse conditions that
are always partly but never entirely of its own making. The Victorian sciences
of society grounded their epistemology in the knowledge of these biological
risks, as John Stuart Mill's 1843 *System of Logic* attests. The methods Mill held
proper to a "political or social science," whose purpose was to study "the
actions of collective masses of mankind," could be described only by analogy
to medical science—an analogy that immediately ceases to be an analogy,
since Mill implies that medical and social research have the same object. Just
as natural history and general physiology equipped modern medicine with
a systematic grasp of "the laws of nutrition, and of the healthy and morbid
action of the different organs," he submits, so too would an understanding
of "the laws of health" and a firm foundation in social "physiology" enable
political science to "study the pathology and therapeutics of the social body"
(465).[1] In either case, one is dealing with organic life. To ensure its proper
functioning was the mandate of Victorian governance as it turned to the city,
which in a period of industrial expansion as well as working-class resistance

came to figure not only the dangers but also the possibilities of collective life as never before.

The city, then, is the locus of the current chapter. To speak of population is almost inevitably to speak of cities, and vice versa, since modern cities are defined as such by the size and density of their population and since it is in urban space that otherwise abstract statistical indications of human aggregation become empirically perceptible. In that it served to amplify a more general condition of struggle—an undeclared "social war," by Friedrich Engels's account, made manifest in the streets (*The Condition of the Working Class* 69) or a "struggle for existence" intensified by sheer population density, per Benjamin Disraeli's *Sibyl*—urban space proved the most vital of political testing grounds (95). For the same reasons, it became elemental to literary world-making, yielding such new genres as the industrial novel, mysteries of the city, the urban Gothic, and the detective story. Robert Vaughan's *The Age of Great Cities* (1843) identifies literature in general as the consummate "offspring of society as it obtains in cities," arguing that it "derives its character from the state of that society, varying with it in all the stages of social progress" (145). Vaughan would indeed contend that "men possess nothing deserving the name of literature until they begin to build great cities" (145). The magnitude of greatness offered up to evaluation in writing was not architectural or geographical but demographic and measurable in human numbers.

Even as demographic analysis gained new authority in attesting that quantitative changes in the scale of communities have qualitative social effects, population took on an ambivalent status in urban discourse. While overcrowding was regularly blamed for disease, dissipation, unemployment, and sinking wages, it also became the impetus for historical change. Herbert Spencer explicitly credits the foundation of institutions and states to the "pressure of population," holding the species' "excess of fertility" responsible for the origins of agriculture, complex social organization, industrial expansion, and geographical dispersion ("A Theory of Population" 35). Other thinkers, while continuing to presuppose geometric population growth, came to regard fluctuations in birth and mortality rates as social variables rather than biological constants.[2] Marx and Engels, who attribute "relative surplus population" to industry's variable labor demands, treat the consequent "massing together" of workers and potential workers in cities both as systematic requirements for capitalist accumulation and, over time, as dialectical means of bringing about class consciousness and enabling political action. The redundant life that, for Malthus, prevented progress was thus reconceived as fueling organic and social development according to a range of new theories.

While the 1840 Population Act, modifications to the census, and the prolif-eration of urban statistical societies gave decisive weight to numbers, what had changed since the turn of the century was not just the actual demography of industrialized Great Britain and its expanding empire.[3] Social scientists were also in the process of revising, subtly but profoundly, the anthropological premises behind population management. Malthus had taken human needs and instincts as static, suspicious of Jacobin visions of a perfect species living in a perfect social state. His successors, while rarely expecting perfection, understood human life and social formations in far more dynamic terms: William Cooke Taylor, for example, arguing in his 1841 *Natural History of Society* that the "capacity for improvement" is the "essential characteristic of man" and that man's optimal natural environment must therefore be a society that affords "means and oppor-tunities for the development of his improvable capacity" (341). By 1851, it seemed self-evident to Spencer that "humanity is indefinitely variable" over time (*Social Statics* 35). This approach to human and social variability shaped a new concep-tion of city life, one that cast society as an organic form that grows, develops, and adapts to modifications in its environment.[4] In projecting a society's capacity to transform itself via the very processes of crowding, struggle, and internal varia-tion that seemed to threaten its coherence, Victorian writers and theorists made development and social change conceivable under the pressures of aggregation in ways that Malthus could scarcely have imagined.

This concern with aggregation makes realist fiction and social science look like close kin, and it is uncontroversial to say that both seek to capture social totality. Julian Murphet calls nineteenth-century fiction "a cultural technology calibrated to the extinction of social unknowns"; Mary Poovey sees Condition-of-England novels as competing with and offering individual-izing alternatives to economic "calculations about aggregates"; and Benedict Anderson equates the novel with the newspaper and the census as one of the institutional forms through which a nation imagines itself.[5] It is not so clear, though, that social unknowns are banished by fiction or that novels work to include every social integer in a coherent national set. *Mary Barton*, in giving form to large numbers and foregrounding the gender relations that subtend class, exposes deep contradictions within the governing agenda—not least, class reproduction—that made population such a central political object. To understand the narrative project of industrial fiction in terms of population, as Elizabeth Gaskell's novel does, is not to define a closed genealogical group of persons who share physical or cultural traits that suit their assigned class position. It is to conceive of a fluctuating aggregate without any permanent social position, never fully absorbed by the manufacturing system and the work of production with which their very existence is equated.

For this reason, while the present chapter necessarily refers to "the working class" in its readings of Gaskell and Engels, its subject can be more accurately called the proletariat: a term Michael Denning rightly insists on defining "not as a synonym for 'wage laborer' but for dispossession, expropriation, and radical dependence on the market" (81). Neither the specific type nor the general fact of wage work is definitive of proletarian existence or of the socioeconomic structure that gives it the character of a class, since "capitalism begins not with the offer of work, but with the imperative to earn a living" (80). What has defined proletarians from the start, as Jacques Rancière similarly maintains, "is not their identification with a job, nor their popular roots; it is the aleatory character of a situation daily put into question"; structural precarity has always been "the fundamental reality of the proletariat" (qtd. in *Proletarian Nights* xxvii). This unstable existence—enabled by the availability of fungible bodies for labor—accounts for the central paradox of Victorian class ethnography, which drew qualitative distinctions between workers and nonworkers but was always implicitly concerned above all with those who had either fallen out of the wage system or never been integrated into it. Insofar as narratives of urban social formation work at the level of population, they project a different object than that of society or the nation-state: a quantity of life that has to tally with socioeconomic function but never quite does. Figures who personify a surplus of unused or ill-used life were simultaneously understood as products of the existing division of labor and as a threat to it. For that reason, class is both shored up and destabilized by the overlapping concept of the masses.[6]

This chapter takes up a formal problem revealed by realist fiction and social science. With different aims, the two overlap to produce a heterogeneous genre that might be called mass writing. Such writing serves as a heuristic for understanding why population, central as it is, becomes incoherent as a category—why it transmutes not only into other formations, including race, class, nation, and species but also, and above all, into a degraded remainder of itself. The key instances here will be Engels's study of working-class environments, Henry Mayhew's taxonomy of casual labor in London, and Gaskell's classic industrial novel *Mary Barton*. These projects, even as their methods and aims diverge, do similar rhetorical work in narrating the process of aggregation and consequently produce a similar formal as well as conceptual slippage that renders population an absent center. In Engels's case, humanism slides into a kind of scientism, and class analysis loses any recognizable human subject in the effort to document inhuman conditions. In Mayhew's, the dual strategies of classification and personification yield a residuum for which no occupational category can be created and about which no personalized story can be told. In Gaskell's, where the domain of personal experience and the process of characterization seem to take on the greatest value, character in practice falls apart as a means of instantiating a population of workers. What links all three is a shared failure to represent population as a subject.

The formal instability that shapes such narratives of aggregation is variously problematic and generative. For the nascent social sciences, the resulting disintegration of subjects and of demographic groupings ends up undercutting the utility of examples and forestalling the generalization of positive social facts. Fiction, by contrast, is dynamized rather than undone by the instability of its collective subject. In the industrial novel, the project of representing class by individualizing sociological categories ends up stalling out in an overstocked labor market and giving way to a different project arguably more vital to class analysis: that of generating remainders to the very process of classification. In this way, the novel is paradigmatic as a form adequate to making narrative out of an absent center—and population, in turn (to adapt Georg Lukács's maxim), is one of that form's paradigmatic modes of thinking in terms of totality when totality is no longer given.

Press and Danger: Mass Politics, Sexuality, and the Dialectics of Crowding

> The very turmoil of the streets has something repulsive, something against which human nature rebels. The hundreds of thousands of all classes and ranks crowding past each other, are they not all human beings with the same qualities and powers . . . ? And still they crowd by one another as though they had nothing in common. . . . The brutal indifference, the unfeeling isolation of each in his private interest becomes the more repellant and offensive, the more these individuals are crowded together, within a limited space.
>
> —Engels, *The Condition of the Working Class in England*

> All demands for justice and all theories of equality ultimately derive their energy from the actual experience of equality familiar to anyone who has been part of a crowd.
>
> —Elias Canetti, *Crowds and Power*

From occupational demography to government reports on housing to sensational journalism on prostitution, disparate forms of social analysis in the 1840s together forged a new understanding of the relationship between cities and their populations. To study the effects of socioeconomic stratification, urban social observers turned to habitat, demarcating a distinct but iterable terrain called "the slum." This term, which literally denoted a narrow corridor, alley, or back room, entered into metaphoric usage in Victorian writing as a descriptor for an entire milieu.[7] It came to connote a substratum of urban life characterized by destitution, crowding, squalor, disease, sexual transgression, and crime—phenomena that could be synthesized into a generalizable spatial object: "Every great city," explains Engels, "has one or more slums where the working class is crowded together" (*The Condition of the Working Class* 70). By his account, the unifying properties of these milieux may be extrapolated across multiple localities and evaluated through a study of representative cases. Traveling across Great Britain, he surveys streets, enters cottages, and scrutinizes living quarters. From one city to the next, he finds the same deficient infrastructure causing the same hazards: unpaved streets "filled with vegetable and animal refuse, without sewers or gutters," shoddy construction, inadequate ventilation, all made worse by extreme crowding. "[S]ince many human beings here live crowded into a small space," he notes, "the atmosphere that prevails in these working-men's quarters may readily be imagined" (71). Inviting readers to adopt his perspective and vicariously sense the environment he describes, Engels presumes not only a shared class status with his audience but also a shared premise that environments shape the organisms that inhabit them. In this, his assumptions echo those of liberal reformers whose research lay in the same path.

Two ubiquitous terms describe the ecological conditions that such reports consistently linked to pathology: *crowding* and *filth*. Both connoted threats to life and to social order, whether in the form of contagious disease, sexual deviance, or riot. A host of national and regional bureaucracies were created to assess these threats and propose strategies for reducing them—all subsumed under the new governing mission of public health. Summarizing the medical risks of crowding in 1845, J. R. Martin's contribution to the second *Report of the Commissioners for Inquiring into the State of Large Towns and Populous Districts* warns of the dangers of contamination when population density, poverty, and close cohabitation are combined with bad infrastructure:

> [W]hen to this state we add crowding of the sick with each other and with the healthy—crowding of the living and the dead—filth—a noisome and impure air—deficiency in food, clothing and fuel—a deficient and polluted supply of water—defective drainage and sewerage—with ill-constructed, crowded, and ill-arranged habitations and streets;—conditions under which the sensible qualities of the very blood are altered, while the vital powers are wasted and depressed:—in

short, when whole masses of the community are found living in daily neglect alike of the laws of nature and of the means furnished by art; no wonder that disease, immorality, and death—no wonder that epidemic following closely on epidemic—aggravated forms of all those disorders that abridge the term and usefulness of life—should be rife among the poorest classes inhabiting our towns and cities. (111)

The report treats the consequences of filth and crowding as self-evident ("no wonder"), yet the underlying cause of these conditions is not explained, nor is either term defined. Indeed, they seem nearly synonymous as sources of contamination. Martin frames crowding less in terms of numbers of people per house or per square mile than in terms of the violation of symbolic categories: healthy and sick, living and dead. The primary objectives motivating the report, however, are clear in the correlation Martin draws between physiological health and productive potentiality. By the commission's account, a society's imperative is to conserve the "vital powers" of its population and to optimize "the term and usefulness of life." It thus implicitly places life in the service of value production such that the concepts of life and of value become functionally inextricable.

This concern to maintain the supply of useful life explains the sanitary reform movement's obsessive focus on sexuality—and it shows why what is marked as a moral or disciplinary problem is ultimately a biopolitical question. Such is clear even in Martin's choice to sandwich the risk of "immorality" between those of "disease" and "death." William Cooke Taylor propounds a similar and widely shared view when he argues in his *Natural History of Society* that improving "the physical condition of the working classes" is all the more crucial because of the direct "connexion between the physical and moral condition of humanity" (153). "Can we, for instance, doubt," he asks, "that female modesty and female virtue are inevitably perilled in crowded lodgings" or that vice intensifies as a result of insufficient water or bad drainage? (153). Edwin Chadwick's 1842 *Report on the Sanitary Condition of the Labouring Population of Great Britain* likewise stresses the simultaneously social and medical dangers of bodies packed too tightly together and of inadequate ventilation and waste disposal. He contends that populations take on the characteristics of their environments both bodily and behaviorally, such that "their habits soon become 'of a piece' with the dwelling" (194). While private life of the sort that the British and European bourgeoisies had come to take for granted was a recent invention, the *Sanitary Report* assumes that insufficiently private habitations have catastrophic effects on human behavior. The testimonies it quotes from observers in multiple cities correlate the sharing of residential space with every form of sexual transgression. Finding twelve people of various ages and both sexes lodging in a single room in Durham, Dr. William Stephen Gilly, a local official, remarks, "How they . . . can preserve common decency, how unutterable horrors are avoided, is beyond all conception" (191). Riddall Wood, another quoted source, is shocked to observe mothers in Hull and Liverpool sharing beds with their adult children, and, in Manchester, rooms with "two grown up females" in one bed, "two young men, unmarried" in another (192). And a Mr. Baker discovers brothers and sisters in Leeds, together with lodgers of both genders, sleeping in the same room as their parents—an arrangement necessarily resulting, he imagines, in "consequences . . . which humanity shudders to contemplate" (193). The erotic dangers of domestic crowding proceed in both directions: too close contact with kin and exposure to non-kin, resulting in incest in the former case, promiscuity and homosexuality in the latter. Either way, aberration is—a bit paradoxically—the expected outcome, taken to follow inevitably from the proximity of any set of bodies other than a married couple. These prurient expectations show the sexualization of the working class to be a central component of sanitary reform. While the risk of incest and that of sex with strangers suggest different anthropological concerns, both can be understood as part of a single ideological project: class endogamy, or the creation of what Balibar calls a "social heredity," to ensure the continuous reproduction of a population designated for labor.[8] This ideology is evident in programs designed to prevent the counterpart threats of adulteration (sex with strangers entailing the possibility of transnational or cross-class procreation) and internal degeneration through incest—a nightmare outcome of endogamy carried to its extreme.

Crowding, as the *Sanitary Report* illustrates, often defined the dangerous biological and social state of the urban poor—though strategic efforts to reduce its risks were not exclusively oriented toward health and reproductive control. In bringing the unstable character of urban public space into private life, population density in the slum also implied political dangers long associated with crowds. Chadwick's concerns about the amalgamation of bodies indeed make medical pathology and sexual deviation into the symbolic counterparts of a broader fear of mass uprising.[9] Such concerns extend beyond the policy context of sanitary reform. Gladstone, in 1877, would explicitly link the crowding of England's "town populations," which necessarily "dwell in masses closely wedged together," to the risk of revolution: "It is in this state of juxtaposition," he observes, "that political electricity flies from man to man with a violence which displaces judgement from its seat and carries off individual minds in a flood by the resistless rush of sympathy" (qtd. in Jones 151).

For the young Engels and Marx, the conduction of "political electricity" and "resistless rush of sympathy" through the crowd were just what made urbanization vital to social transformation. Engels, responding to earlier versions of Gladstone's commentary, affirms that "our bourgeois is perfectly justified in his fears" of the danger immanent in the crowded conditions of proletarian life (*The Condition of the Working Class* 148). Ironically, he notes, "the massing of population" in manufacturing centers does not just produce wealth. It also has the unintended effect of forcing the "development of the workers more rapidly . . . to feel as a class," since constant enforced contact makes the common experience of oppression evident on a vast scale (148).[10] If capital "masses together in a single place a crowd of people unknown to each other," so too does the resulting condition reveal the need for "combination" and collective action (Marx, *The Poverty of Philosophy* 188). The making of masses thus becomes a precondition for class consciousness even as it threatens the positive identity and coherence of class categories.

The apparently contradictory concepts of mass and class are in this sense interdependent. The mass is at once the symptom of alienation and the means of overcoming it, a crisis of social disjunction and sociality in its most concentrated form. Relative to class, it mediates between what Marx terms a "class in itself" (defined by the functional similarity of workers from the vantage point of production) and a "class for itself" (a self-conscious proletariat unified by shared interests).[11] Insofar as class consciousness is itself provisional—a means of achieving the actual aim, which is the end of class—the mass is not just what precedes class but also what follows it. Anticapitalist struggle consequently relies, positively and negatively, on the process of aggregation.

But for all that Engels hails this "massing together" as a crucial political development, and for all that his agenda opposes that of the Victorian health bureaucracy, his scientific analysis of urban populations often casts proletarian masses and congested spaces in the light of problems of social hygiene. The same sexual dangers imagined in the *Sanitary Report* trouble *The Condition of the Working Class in England*. Engels's revolutionary program, to be sure, clashes with the tutelary schemes of James Kay, Chadwick, and their colleagues, whose work he cites in order to use his ideological enemies' evidence against them—"to defeat the liberal bourgeoisie by casting their own words in their teeth" (31). His ultimate aim is not to reduce vice and disease but to transform the relations of production that cause them. Yet his assessment of the biological effects of social relations and vice versa relies on the same epistemology that informed the sanitary reform movement, and he shares its view of crowding as conducive to a risky intermixture of bodies. In Manchester lodging houses, he reports, the crowding of boarders "mixed indiscriminately" in their sleeping quarters gives rise to practices he treats as both obvious and unspeakable. "What physical and moral atmosphere reigns in these holes I need not state," he notes with a shudder, and the reader is tasked with imagining each one as "the scene of deeds against which human nature revolts" (102). So too does he assume, with his liberal sources, that dirt and crowding at work and at home imperil kinship norms. Under "the demoralizing influence of want, filth, and evil surroundings," he suggests, "family life" becomes sociologically impossible (71, 154). Families whose female members work in factories lose the benefits of maternal nurture: "The employment of the wife dissolves the family utterly and of necessity," he argues, and "this dissolution . . . brings the most demoralizing consequences for parents as well as children" (166). While Engels himself opposed marriage and seems to have had no qualms about maintaining a longstanding relationship with the factory worker Mary Burns (to whom he likely owed much of his contact with the Manchester labor movement), his insistence on separate spheres in *The Condition of the Working Class* is resolute.[12] The text tacitly universalizes bourgeois norms of domesticity, privacy, temperance, and sexual propriety—all of which it links to the reproductive health of generations.

In his ecological analysis too, Engels echoes the Sanitary Commission, which sought to show "how strongly circumstances that are governable," as Chadwick put it, "govern the habits of the population, and in some instances appear almost to breed the species of the population" (164).[13] Engels treats material conditions as a shaping force not only on human habits but also on the process of speciation. Adverse living conditions in manufacturing districts, he argues, do not just cause individual debility but result in "a progressive deterioration in the physique of the working population" (129). Notably, laboring bodies figure as improperly sexed in the very process of being sexualized: the factory system, Engels observes, leaves women "unfit for childbearing" and men emasculated and "enfeebled" (184). Evoking the clinical gaze of the physicians whose reports he cites, he diagnoses female workers with either "abnormally early" puberty brought on by the heat of factories or "retarded development of the female constitution," including "deformities of the pelvis" and "irregular menstruation" due to overwork (180, 179, 181). Male workers, in turn, fall victim to an "unnerved, uncomfortable, hypochondriac state of mind and body" (133). Changes in the gendered division of labor, especially in cases where the family structure is "turned upside down" (meaning that men become the dependents of women and children), are directly reflected in physiological changes (167). The techniques that enabled sanitarians to medicalize the city, sexualize the working class, and manage its reproduction with a view to maintaining a productive workforce and ensuring social order paradoxically subtend Engels's indictment of the social division of labor.

Such scientism reveals the interdependence of class analysis and population analysis. However rigorously Engels denaturalizes the economic system that constitutes it, his description of a proletariat formed and materially transformed by its habitat gives it the secondary status of a biological phenomenon. Environmental conditions materially alter bodies, and these changes are passed down generationally. Class, understood as the product of adaptation to these environments and of reproduction within them, thus takes on a racial rather than strictly socioeconomic character.

Race, Class, and the Human Animal

> Such was the nameless one of whom we speak. We cannot say that he thrived; but he would not die.
>
> —Benjamin Disraeli, *Sybil*

> He is of no order and no place; neither of the beasts, nor of humanity.
>
> —Charles Dickens, *Bleak House*

Engels's attempt to describe the objective conditions of cities and their effects yields a narrative of its own—one that conflicts with his purposes of generalizing class as a social formation and giving it human form and agency. Further, his ethnographic project serves less to define two opposed class categories than to show how the seemingly singular category of the working class multiplies and self-differentiates endlessly, in ways that compromise its human content. It is here that social science merges with the discourse of natural history. A distinctive construction of race—understood more as a process than an essence—underwrites the class concept. Engels uses the term less to index preconstituted and permanently separable identity categories than to denominate an ongoing process of natural-historical development.[14] Two versions of racial difference intersect in his dealings with Irish immigration, which he cites as an "influence of great moment in forming the character of English workers" (149). Here, race simultaneously describes a nature shaped by consanguinity and one made and progressively altered by socioeconomic structures. The two definitions, incompatible though they seem, are not wholly separable. Even when Engels joins Kay and others in identifying Irish immigrants as a racially foreign population infiltrating England's working class, he renders race detachable from national origin and allows it to permeate masses of people who share physical environments. On the one hand, "Irish nature" is taken to connote either an excess of sentiment or a bestial indifference to squalor—both traits marked as alien to Englishness. On the other, Engels maintains that English workers have taken on these traits "in part by a mixture of the races, and in part by the ordinary contact of life" (150). What changes as a result of the intermixture of populations, by his account, includes the habits and manners that constitute culture. He holds the Irish responsible for altering the English diet, for spreading the practice of wearing patched clothing made of "so-called 'Devil's-dust' cloth," and for introducing "the custom previously unknown in England, of going barefoot" (103). Since culture, too, can transform the body by modifying what it wears and eats, cultural "contact" and reproductive "mixture" are accorded the same biological causality over time.

Rather than essentialize national identity, however, Engels deploys race yet again to consolidate a mutable aggregate that diverges from the national population out of which it springs. Due partly to harsh living conditions and partly to "the abundance of hot Irish blood that flows in the veins of the English working class," he claims, the English proletarian has developed a different physiology, temperament, cognitive faculties, and culture from his bourgeois countrymen. In effect, he argues, "English nationality is annihilated in the working man" (223). He thus modifies the conceit by which Alexis de Tocqueville and Disraeli framed the struggle between "the Rich and the Poor" as a civil war between "two nations . . . who are formed by a different breeding, are fed by a different food, are ordered by different manners, and are not governed by the same laws" (*Sybil* 96). Ironically, though, the story Engels tells about the development of the English working class facilitates a sort of internal internationalism. Even as he suggests, with Kay and others, that Irish immigration has lowered English workers' standard of living, Engels recasts the hybridization of English and Irish as potentially advantageous. For the very reason that the presence of the Irish has "degraded the English workers, removed them from civilization, and aggravated the hardship of their lot" by enabling wages to fall, these worsening conditions also serve as a catalyst for revolution (149). Over time, Engels speculates, the transformation of the proletariat into a new race should thus prove "productive only of good," allowing for a necessary estrangement between workers and the English middle class that will make oppositional class consciousness possible and motivate collective action (150). Though class struggle is ultimately an international project, Engels attributes political agency to the proletariat by declaring that it will decide "the future of England" despite its essential non-Englishness (150). The working class thus awakens into world history at once as the national majority of the English people and as "a physically degenerate race, robbed of all humanity" (100)—like Shelley's creature, placed at odds with an ambiguously defined human population.

The threat of reduction to what Giorgio Agamben would term "bare life"—mere biological being, bereft of all qualities beyond the fact of being alive—hangs over *The Condition of the Working Class*. Of the mostly Irish cottage-dwellers in Manchester who live "in measureless filth and stench," Engels remarks, "this race must really have reached the lowest stage of humanity" (98). Despite his hypothesis that Irish immigration might promote class consciousness, Engels echoes Kay's charge that the Irish were demoralizing, barbarizing, even animalizing England's working population. By Kay's argument, Irish workers in England sink below the level of subsistence and yet (*pace* Malthus) survive and multiply—in so doing, influencing English workers to limit their own expectations to mere survival and engendering a reckless indifference that threatens civilization:

> Debased alike by ignorance and pauperism, they have discovered, with the savage, what is the minimum of the means of life, upon which existence may be prolonged. The paucity of the amount of means and comforts *necessary for the mere support of life*, is not known by a civilised population, and this secret has been taught the labourers of this country by the Irish. (6)

This contrasts starkly with the view of labor that Dickens will attribute to industrialists in *Hard Times* when Bounderby the factory-owner equates demands for a living wage or safety regulations with a wish to dine on "turtle soup and venison, with a gold spoon" (72). What Kay fears is not workers' desire for a higher standard of living but, conversely, their lack of desire for any standard of living.[15] While Engels envisioned a radically different solution from that of improving workers' habits, he concurs with Kay on what becomes of a population forced to scrape by on subsistence wages: Engels finds "no cause for surprise if the workers, treated as brutes, actually become such" (142). This reasoning creates an apparent double bind between the biological demands of survival and the valuation of humanity as a qualitative state of being—a state of flourishing—that exceeds survival.

Subsistence, for this reason, represents a different problem for Victorian social science than it did for Malthusian political economy. Where Malthus approached subsistence (like sexuality) as a "fixed quantity" necessary to sustain life, his successors saw potential for fluctuations in human organisms' needs and desires. Such capacity for change in bodily requirements often implied degradation; Tocqueville found no capacity for improvement in a person "reduced to the satisfaction of his most pressing needs" (61). Such a person, he argues, "looks at the future as an animal does. Absorbed in the present and the ignoble and transient pleasures it affords, his brutalized nature is unaware of the determinants of its destiny" (61). Mayhew and Andrew Halliday, at the end of Halliday's contribution to the final volume of *London Labour and the London Poor*, use similar rhetoric to assert that charity is wasted on "a large class of mankind" whose dependency makes them "mere human animals who eat, drink and sleep" 4:448). This emphasis on animal life betrays the interdependence of economic rationality and biopower. The production of surplus value requires British society to reproduce more bodies than it can use at once, resulting in a surplus of biological material that is itself understood to lack value; merely to be alive and to have needs confers a null social status.

Such representations of poverty suggest that the social nullity of "bare life," which Agamben would write into the origin of politics (in the supposed separation of *zōē* from *bíos*), is far more historically specific. It is linked to surplus population and is thus the product as much of capital as of political sovereignty. The working class, nominally praised at times for the social benefits of its labor, does not merely contain a surplus—a separate "industrial reserve army." Rather, as will be agonizingly apparent in *Mary Barton*, the class as a whole is redundant at the level of individual lives. It constitutes a permanent proletarian mass that, as Marx sardonically surmises in *The Poverty of Philosophy*, may perish by thousands when employment is scarce but "will always be numerous enough for the capitalist class to decimate without fear of annihilating it" (222). Life thereby acquires an ironic status for the purposes of production. Industry feeds on human life to produce the means of life (to which capital becomes symbolically equivalent). Yet the living bodies it produces are a means rather than an end, per the general law of capitalist accumulation. Humanity is thus valued as usable life and devalued where it presents itself as "mere life."

While the specter of degraded or merely living humanity is customarily attached to the idea of animality (as in Tocqueville's contempt for the "brutalized nature" of England's poor, Mayhew and Halliday's horror of "mere human animals," and Engels's vision of worker "brutes"), it in fact eludes a simple human/animal binary. The underlying suggestion of all these narratives of degradation is not really that humans are becoming (nonhuman) animals but that they have arrived at some other status, an anomalous creaturely state that is neither one nor the other. This is indeed explicit in Marx's *Economic and Philosophical Manuscripts of 1844*, which describe habituation to "dirt and misery" as a decline in sentience and a consequent loss of species-being. Here is Marx's description of what becomes of humanity under industrial conditions:

> Light, air, etc.—the simplest *animal* cleanliness—ceases to be a need for man. *Dirt*—this stagnation and putrefaction of man—the *sewage of* civilization (speaking quite literally)—comes to be the *element of life* for him. . . . None of his senses exist any longer, and not only in his human fashion, but in an *inhuman* fashion, and therefore not even in an animal fashion. . . . It is not only that man has no human needs—even his *animal* needs are ceasing to exist. (94)

Capitalist production thus does more than reduce human existence to a brute struggle for survival. It so totally instrumentalizes the worker's labor power, by Marx's account, that even the most basic creaturely demands of self-preservation fade from the horizon of activity. Humans forced to live in a state of extreme physical deprivation do not become animals; indeed, they are no longer even animals. Kay draws similar conclusions about the effects of overwork, submitting that the length and intensity of the workday and the monotony of labor in Lancashire's cotton mills demoralize, intellectually stultify, and dehumanize the worker to such an extent that he "disregards the distinguishing appetites and habits of his species" (7). This perception accounts for the frequent contradictions surrounding the fear of dehumanization, which can correspond either to the reduction of the human being to a living body with no aim beyond survival or to the decline of instincts and a reckless indifference to self-preservation. Even in its biological characteristics, the human animal is perpetually in danger of becoming discontinuous with itself.

The need to rescue humanity from such a fate drives *The Condition of the Working Class*. For Engels, the stakes of the class struggle are nothing less than the prevention of "the final destruction of the human being physically as well as mentally" (221). Insofar as the protagonists drafted into this struggle were necessarily those in danger of losing the qualities innate to their species, his theory of revolution makes masses of ambiguously human creatures into a—indeed, *the*—political subject.

Perhaps this is why Engels's human subject seems oddly fugitive. It is striking that, amid so many physiological generalizations, no specific bodies or persons are diegetically encountered in this text. The Manchester through which Engels walks his readers, notable for housing "the manufacturing proletariat . . . in its fullest classic perfection," is a ghost town (83). The notoriously crowded courtyards and cottages entered into are depopulated and silent, their human occupants' presence signaled only metonymically, via a heap of rancid food refuse or the overflow of "a privy without a door" (88). Broad references to "the working man" abound, but virtually no such man appears or speaks; the text's rare human figures flash by as gruesome shadows of undifferentiated life, "a horde of ragged women and children" swarming around a pile of debris, "filthy as the swine that thrive upon the garbage heaps" (98). Personification forms no part of Engels's strategy. The conditions affecting the working class must be assessed above all through structure, through the geography, architecture, infrastructure, and ecology of the built environment, and so these structures constitute the primary object to be represented.

Engels's empirical method, however, accumulates so much observational detail as he moves through the city that the text's political conclusions periodically become subordinate to it. What *The Condition of the Working Class* portrays is not, in the main, a socioeconomic class of workers becoming conscious of their situation but an ecosystem in the process of destroying its mysteriously absent creatures. The description of living conditions does not just furnish examples but generates a type of plot. Its travel narrative—following the conventions of *katabasis* to chronicle a descent into the underworld—links an intimate knowledge of the slum with dissociation and repulsion. At one moment, Engels accords Manchester exemplary status as "the classic type of a modern manufacturing town" (83). He proposes to focus on it for this reason, and also because he "know[s] it as intimately as [his] own native town, more intimately than most of its residents know it" (83). Having claimed such familiarity with the city, the tour guide at the next moment veers down dead-end streets, loses his way, and multiplies horror upon horror, exposing "heaps of débris, refuse, and offal . . . and a stench which alone would make it impossible for a human being in any degree civilized to live in such a district" (90). Streets and interiors paradoxically acquire their typical status only to the degree that they can be framed as extraordinary aberrations. Their representativeness necessitates that they be declared unrepresentable. Variously lurid and euphemistic in depicting cottages and cellar apartments where "[t]he filth and comfortlessness that prevail . . . is impossible to describe" (125), he speaks of families of Irish immigrants "crowded together" in one bed, sharing rooms with pigs and "other disgusting things of the most revolting kind" (101, 102). Such elliptical references to the sources of disgust are essential to his rhetoric. Filth, like crowding, operates as a term for the contamination of categories— much as Mary Douglas would understand dirt ("matter out of place") anthropologically as "the by-product of a systemic ordering and classification" from which a certain object or element has been ejected (36).

The purpose of maintaining categories into which social objects can be placed is to allow for meaningfully generalizable comparison, above all the extreme contrast between the protected domain of private property and the province of rented spaces where the majority live and die. Yet description overwhelms categorization and forestalls conclusion—so much so that Engels repeatedly exclaims "Enough!" to punctuate a section, as if to rein in a compulsion to continue. Even as the descriptions of one set of houses after another seem more than sufficient to convey the conditions of an entire locality, the text perpetually strains to outdo itself. Engels finds the most depressed outer streets of St. Giles in London "nothing in comparison with the dwellings in the narrow courts and alleys . . . between the houses, in which the filth and tottering ruin surpass all description" (71). He identifies the poorest quarters in Dublin, where, again, "the filth, the uninhabitable-ness of the houses and the neglect of the streets, surpass all description," only to insist on drawing further distinctions—even though "the wretched-ness of Dublin is nothing specific, nothing peculiar to Dublin, but something common to all great towns" (76). Walking across Long Millgate in Manchester, Engels calls even the most dilapidated rows of houses "nothing in comparison with the courts and lanes which lie behind," of whose disarray "it is impossible to convey an idea" (87). After discovering alongside the River Irk a hidden court "the filth and horrors of which surpassed all the others by far" (90), the tour guide continues onward to locate "the most horrible spot" in another part of Manchester known as Little Ireland, whose "sickening filth . . . furnishes such a hateful and repulsive spectacle as can hardly be equalled in the worst court on the Irk" (98). This rhetoric of comparison sets up a series of untenable yet progressively intensifying superlatives. Each instance is bound not just to be worse than the last but worse than the worst. Every location, at the moment of encounter, achieves an effect of foulness beyond degree, yet each in turn becomes the standard for the next, which proves still more unimaginable. Rather than drawing a bright line between human and inhuman conditions or even a sliding scale of squalor, the descriptive voice generates unanticipated variations even in repeating the same phrases. We arrive at the ninth circle and then keep going. There is no point at which the accumulation of grotesque spectacles and obscene insinuations (however self-similar) can end—no limit they can exceed.

Gothic excess is part of the text's aesthetic strategy, even as it aims at the most factually precise and concrete exposition of social reality. Though relentlessly driven to represent, the social investigator must encounter at every turn a reality that surpasses representation. Indeed, "on re-reading [his] description" of Manchester's "Old Town," Engels insists that "instead of being exaggerated, it is far from black enough to convey a true impression of the filth, ruin, and uninhabitableness" of this district (92). Readers, to be moved to action, must be left begging the narrator to stop. Yet a peculiar effect of boundlessness emerges as one of the ironies of urban exploration. The texts that establish the slum as a distinct set of spaces inhabited by a distinct population begin by presupposing a single class boundary. They locate the secret world of the poor on the other side of a divide separating it from the accepted norms of the bourgeois milieu that serves as the starting point. Crossing this divide, however, does not yield a determinate referent. Instead, it plots a potentially endless descent, multiplying and subdividing its subject and projecting still lower social strata and ever more degraded conditions of biological existence to which one might sink.

This is not to say that Engels fails to capture the reality of class; he dauntingly captures a central element of class relations, the deprivation and placelessness of masses concentrated in one place, even as he fails to construct an internally consistent class category. Yet the rhetoric of description, as Engels's writing illustrates, has its own distinct stylistic effect in nineteenth-century social analysis. It operates, by a principle of infinite regress, to suggest what exceeds the system of categories it applies. For all the human material that Victorian texts included and classified, the task of description produced still more that eluded evaluation, pointing toward exceptions that called every rule into question. As the accumulation of information exceeds the classifications devised to organize its meanings, urban discourse generates specters of superfluous matter, superfluous life, disintegrating bodies. Assuming a variety of shapes, this residue became crucial to narratives of social formation even in problematizing the coherence of British society.

Social Refuse

> Is anything to be done with them? Can anything be done for them? Or is this million-headed mass to be regarded as offering a problem as insoluble as that of the London sewage, which, feculent and festering, swings heavily up and down the basin of the Thames with the ebb and flow of the tide?
>
> —William Booth, *In Darkest England*

Garbage, filth, and abjection are obviously key signifiers of social crisis; this holds true for Engels as much as for his liberal contemporaries. Yet these signifiers do not refer solely to an environment external to bodies, contaminating them from outside. They also substitute discursively for bodies and populations.[16] The sanitary reform movement's concern to manage sewage in order to protect human life did not mask the (often explicit) claim that human beings are themselves waste products—excreted remains of the system of production. All aspects of existence beyond work appear irrelevant, useless as soon as they cannot be converted into capital. The laboring body is consequently imagined as a machine at work, an animal taking nutriment at home, and a mass of sewage or a rotting carcass when unemployed. If the ideology behind this seems obvious, it is worth recalling that even Marx consistently denigrated the *lumpenproletariat* as "refuse."

This symbolic abjection expresses two related problems: the contradictory economic status of the living human body and the contradictory status of the proletariat when approached as a population. Those classed as workers or potential workers are at once the main object of national population management and not a population at all—not, that is to say, a consistent, temporally continuous, localizable, or externally bounded set. The geographical flux and reflux of capital as well as industry's perennial cycles of expansion and contraction ensure a heterogeneous working class whose sole generalizable characteristic is its reliance on an unreliable employment market. Because the working class, as Balibar notes, is too circumstantially contingent to amount to "a social caste" (212), class boundaries are routinely drawn and redrawn at the levels of citizenship, race, employment, language, family structure, and so forth in order to create the appearance of fixed identity. If these ascribed characteristics allowed social science to totalize a set of bodies and align them biologically and socially with labor, they also served to prevent the proletariat from encompassing such a mass of people that it reveals itself to be larger than the nation-state. Subdividing classes along these various lines allowed Kay to blame Irish immigration for demoralizing English workers. It enabled the architects of the New Poor Law to remove a large number of people from the ranks of the "deserving poor" by casting them as "idle," authorizing liberal thinkers to treat those out of work as morally inferior to those currently engaged in wage work. It allowed Disraeli to vindicate "the people" as heirs to a national bloodline while vilifying "the dangerous classes" as a criminal subpopulation at war with society—a threat made more menacing to Home Office commissioner Jelinger C. Symons because it encompassed not just "criminals" and "paupers" but also "that proximate body of people who are within reach of its contagion" (1). Marx and Engels recognized early that industrial capitalism relies on a "reserve army of the unemployed," yet they too imagine a dangerous class of permanently "unemployable" persons: petty criminals, prostitutes, beggars, a ragged subpopulation blamed for its precarious condition. This mass of social outcasts, which Frantz Fanon would re-characterize as a crucial cohort

in the anticolonial struggles of the twentieth century, represents an inas-
similable threat to class coalition for Marx.[17] Even as *The Communist Manifesto*
hails the proletariat as the universal class, it ejects a residuum of nonworkers
as "social scum" (482). While systematic scarcity and an overstocked labor
market guaranteed the impossibility of universal employment, the Victorian
social sciences broadly assigned those whose means of subsistence is intermittent or not legally sanctioned to a separate order of being. The unemployed
became a heterogeneous human remainder—less a fixed social category
than a concession to the insufficiency of categories.

Such insufficiency, for all that it seems to thwart the taxonomist's dream
of classifying everything, is a feature of the process of classification (as is
clear in the original Linnaean system, which creates a *monstrosus* taxon to
separate out "abnormal people" and "unknown groups" from the four identified races of the genus *Homo*). If Marxism loses the clarity of a strict binary
opposition of bourgeoisie versus proletariat as it consigns prostitutes and
beggars to a status beneath that of the working class proper, more granular
classificatory schemes similarly yield something left over. Mayhew's investigative journalism for *The Morning Chronicle*, later collected as the encyclope-
dic four-volume *London Labour and the London Poor*, perfectly illustrates the
remainder that even the most exhaustive population analyses produce. His
goal is to catalog every occupation of the city's poor, from coal-whipping to
artificial flower-making, and to fit those particulars to global generalizations
about the species. To that end, he painstakingly disaggregates minutely specialized types of casual labor, often qualified by gender, age, ethnicity, and
location and illustrated by exemplary figures: "The Jew Old-Clothes-Man,"
"The Indian Crossing-Sweeper," "Old Sarah, The Well-Known Hurdy Gurdy
Player." All these must ultimately be catalogued under the broad headings of
"Those That Will Work," "Those That Cannot Work," and "Those That Will
Not Work." Individuals who fit one of Mayhew's numerous subcategories,
however socially marginal, can be interviewed, catalogued, and extended
some measure of sympathy via their narratives. Yet the relation between
type and instance generates some friction.

The whole process, indeed, falls apart when the journalist confronts a mass
too large to subdivide and too abject to functionalize. In sketching the "mar-
vellously pathetic scene" of multitudes of homeless people asleep in a shelter
seen from the viewpoint of a generalized middle-class spectator, Mayhew dramatizes a slippage from sympathy to disgust. He begins with the projection of
interiority, as "[t]he sight sets the mind speculating on the beggars' and the outcasts' dreams," only to narrate a second moment at which "the thoughts shift,
and the heart is overcome with a sense of the vast heap of social refuse—the

mere human street-sweepings—the great living mixen—that is destined . . . to be strewn far and near over the land, and to serve as manure to the future crime crops of the country" (3:442). The journalist here encounters the limits of his ambition to showcase "the poor" as individuals with whom he and his readers can identify. Even so, if the following moment finds "the well-to-do visitor" overcoming aversion through an abstract gratitude "that 'he is not as one of these,'" it also compels him to admit that a simple twist of fate could have cast him into the same dustbin. His status, he owns, is the result of birth and privilege, not of any "special virtue" that makes him "different from them" (3:443). Consigning this abject mass of bodies to the status of garbage—that ubiquitous figure for the permeability of cultural boundaries—provides no criterion by which Mayhew can distinguish himself from such "social refuse."

This scene exposes a conflict between two conceptions of humanity: one that is stridently egalitarian (hence the desire to make everyone a potential subject, to give everyone a life story) and one concerned to hierarchize human types and classes (hence the elaborate taxonomy). Perhaps the latter seems to carry the day. Yet the dissonance between the two resurfaces when Mayhew and his co-authors insist that socioeconomic status does not correspond to any intrinsic quality in persons. *London Labour and the London Poor* makes one of its subjects a mouthpiece for this claim in the final volume on "Those That Will Not Work," the heading under which Mayhew and his colleagues Halliday, John Binny, and Bracebridge Hemyng classify vagrants, "professional beggars," swindlers, thieves, and prostitutes. Hemyng's interview with a woman in Fleet Street—an autodidact and occasional prostitute who has worked since age twelve in the printing office of a London daily newspaper—yields the following monologue:

> Birth is the result of accident. It is the merest chance in the world whether you're born a countess or a washerwoman. I'm neither one nor t'other; I'm only a mot who does a little typographing by way of variety. Those who have had . . . the advantages of a sound education, who have a position to lose . . . may be blamed for going on the loose, but I'll be hanged if I think that priest or moralist is to come down on me with the sledge-hammer of their denunciation. You look rather surprised at my talking so well. I know I talk well, but you must remember what a lot has passed through my hands for the last seven years, and what a lot of copy I've set up. There is very little I don't know, I can tell you. (4:256)

This woman's self-justifying speech reiterates Mayhew's reflection that the accident of birth rather than merit raised him above the homeless men he

nonetheless perceives as "human street-sweepings." But in so doing, it belies
the system of categories into which its speaker has just been placed. Even
if one follows Mayhew and Hemyng in treating prostitution as vice rather
than labor, the typesetter plainly does not rank among "Those That Will
Not Work." Her story, on the contrary, suggests that the very page on which
she appears could have been composited by her hands. Yet the insufficiency
of this legitimate employment, in throwing her upon the resource of street-
walking to supplement her meager income, removes her from the category
of those "willing" to work. By taking on additional work, she becomes a
nonworker. If this seems more than a little ironic, the sometime prostitute's
role in the production of print and the circulation of social knowledge makes
this irony foundational to *London Labour and the London Poor*. Her narrative
implicitly provokes readers to imagine the text before them as a print commodity produced by the work of the nonworker it purports to represent—a
set of typologies typeset by a woman who is not of her own type.

This subject is not alone in being "neither one nor t'other." The difficulty
of accounting for those who straddle categories hangs over Mayhew's effort
to systematize his massive collection of data. Prefaced with the assertion that
the world's population is split into "two distinct and broadly marked races,
viz., the wanderers and the settlers—the vagabond and the citizen," *London
Labour* admits to being concerned with those "partaking of the attributes of
both" (1:349). Even as Mayhew turns, in the third volume, to those ranked
categorically as "vagabonds," the category loses the ontological absoluteness
of a "race" when he attributes vagrancy to improper nurture: specifically,
"the non-inculcation of a habit of industry" (3:369). This sociological generalization, too, falls short of accounting for the range of people classed as
"vagrants," since Mayhew acknowledges a subclass of formerly "industrious
workmen" who, having been laid off, went on the road seeking work without finding it for so long that their nomadic state became permanent (3:369).
Stumbling on case after case that swerves from its classification compels the
journalist to note the limits of his system, but its terms stay in place.

Mayhew remains committed to social taxonomy; classification, he contends, is the highest calling in science, and it demands a certain diligence. Yet
his efforts lead him to suspect that even the most valiant attempt to "bring
any number of diverse phenomena within the rules of logical division is . . .
generally unsuccessful" (4:452). Having separated the "Sellers of Dried Fruit"
from the "Sellers of Fresh Fruit" and the "Sellers of Ballads" from the "Sellers
of Long Songs," Mayhew cautions against "drawing distinctions where no
real differences exist" (4:458). Having generated hundreds of classifications,
he argues that the registrar general's occupational data should reflect the

singular class boundary between employers and employed over and above all other distinctions. Indeed, Mayhew is not wrong to detect a category problem there. He aptly criticizes the Occupation Abstract of Great Britain's 1841 Census for conflating factory owners, businessmen, and industrial workers under the broad rubric of "persons engaged in commerce, trade, and manufacture" (4:458). These totals derive from occupational categories as granular as Mayhew's own: Great Britain and Wales, among their total reported population of over eighteen and a half million, tabulate 538 spoon makers (counted separately from the fork makers—both categories returning larger numbers than the ranks of stevedores, mysteriously limited to single digits), 268 salt miners, 167 authors, 41 bombazine manufacturers, 9 artificial eye makers, and 5 ventriloquists. This survey, in categorizing work primarily by its product, is more useful for measuring the scale of various industries than, say, the prevalence of wage work compared with salaried work or casual labor. For that reason, Mayhew takes issue with its methods, and he faults the Irish census for "the same disregard of the great 'economical' divisions of society" (4:459). He makes no remark, however, on the logic by which both surveys absorb what escapes their classifications under the following headings: *"Remainder of population, including women and children"* or *"Residue of population,* not having specified occupations, and including unemployed persons and women" (4:458, 459). This final category on Great Britain's 1841 occupational survey turns out to contain nearly eleven million persons—outnumbering, not surprisingly, the totals counted under nearly all of the identified occupations.

If the dream of the census is to add each human integer to its proper social set, these residues expose a mass of exceptions larger than the rule. Further, the fact that "unemployed persons and women" form a single category illustrates two problems linked by their very incongruity. First, work has become the index of each person's social status, despite its largely temporary and depersonalized character. Second, the demand to classify the whole national population on the basis of formal employment makes women—especially in their normatively prescribed domestic role—into a demographic anomaly. Conflating these asymmetric groupings is strikingly awkward. It places an entire gender (regardless of class) into the same statistical set as unemployed people and those without recognized occupations (regardless of gender). Even on a practical level, calculating unemployment rates must have been tricky if women of the propertied class (or possibly all women and children) were added to the count of the unemployed. The language of the census thus obliquely emulates the very process its occupational survey fails to quantify: the class system is constantly rendering masses of people extraneous to the set of occupations it recognizes, and thus to any fixed category of identity.

Mary Barton and the Residues of Class

> The facts are all in all; for they are facts.
>
> —Charles Kingsley, "Recent Novels"
> (review of *Mary Barton*)

This process of demographic remaindering forms the narrative crux of another genre of urban writing: the industrial novel. *Mary Barton* shows that making remainders, rather than representing a consistent class of workers, is what industrial fiction and social science share. Such an approach to Gaskell's novel and to the genre sounds counterintuitive, since industrial realist fiction has been praised for its fidelity to class identity (if not for the plausibility of its resolutions to class conflict). Novels of factory life in northern England, as Raymond Williams observes, skirt the complexity of London, with all its historic trades and multifarious subclasses, by turning to cities where the class system presents itself as a stark binary.[18] Gaskell's fiction, like Engels's study, brings into view newly urbanized spaces where every aspect of daily existence is choreographed by the demands of production— factories at the center, makeshift cottages proliferating around them in all directions, every built structure reflecting its function. For this reason, the genre has been hailed for reflecting capitalist social reality more nakedly than other forms. Mayhew found almost infinite subtypes of costermongers in London, which did little to demystify the conditions that spawned this mass of data, whereas the Manchester of *Mary Barton* is split along the single axis of "masters and men." Industrial fiction thus positions itself to do what even the census could not, as Mayhew noted, by revealing the definitive socioeconomic divide between "employers" and "employed." But while this divide indeed names the structuring opposition in Gaskell's Lancashire, the state of being employed does not encompass the novel's proletarian mass subject. This is the case for several reasons. For one, the conditions of wage work make employment tenuous as an index of class. In addition, large numbers of impoverished people in factory towns are not directly employed as industrial labor in the first instance. Not least significantly, the dyad of masters and men is destabilized by a third term: women.

Though *Mary Barton* and *North and South* portray female workers employed in factories, garment workshops, and domestic service as well as piecework and care work at home, employment demography tends to chart women's status by kinship rather than occupation.[19] Counted as dependents by the census, they appear statistically bracketed off from socioeconomic categories, and yet their function is central to the biological as well as social reproduction of class.[20] Gaskell writes this problem into her fiction, and her plots show such bracketing in action. Even so, they do not adhere to the gendered division of labor that customarily forms a backdrop to the divide between masters and men. In fact, they operate by taking men out of circulation and putting women to work.

Mary Barton not only makes the need to work into the condition for its heroine's emergence as such; Gaskell's first novel also presents itself as a sort of make-work program for its author. Its preface writes the novelist herself into the dynamics of employment and unrest that structure its story. While Gaskell disavows any knowledge of political economy and identifies workers' "state of feeling" as her sole concern, sentiment adopts the terms of political economy (4). She frames writing as a form of occupation that dissipates suffering by converting grief into anxiety, anxiety into narrative, and narrative into work. The novel, by her account, arose out of two experiences of distress: first, the death of her child (alluded to only as a personal "circumstance") made her "anxious to *employ* [her]*self* in writing a work of fiction"; second, a dawning awareness of crowds passing by her in the streets of Manchester preoccupied her with the hidden distress of others whose lives are structured by the rhythm of "strange alternations between work and want" (3, emphasis added). The more she reflected on class relations, she reports, "the more anxious I became to give some utterance to the agony which, from time to time, convulses this dumb people" (3). Feeling, it turns out, is not a private affair; the preface concludes by hinting that the discontentment of England's working class and the anxiety this discontentment should induce in readers are corroborated by "the events which have so recently occurred among a similar class on the Continent"—that is, the revolutions of 1848 (4). Gaskell thus constructs a direct analogy between the text and its subject by linking states of feeling to states of work. The novelist's "anxiety" to alleviate her own grief by "employing [her]self" in the work of writing is made to mirror a social anxiety to alleviate the widespread misery of unemployment. In the process, however, the novel reveals the paradox on which the genre of industrial fiction pivots: the social fact that defines Gaskell's characters— their relation to work—is the least stable aspect of their existence.

Gaskell's fiction consequently sets out to give class a different ontology, one based on its generational character rather than its functionalization as labor. If this entails a certain emphasis on familial relationships, it also obliges the novel to approach its subject matter from the first as a population. Before introducing John Barton and his family, Gaskell offers a generalizing view of workers exiting a textile mill: "Their faces were not remarkable for beauty," she notes, "indeed, they were below the average," with "sallow complexions and irregular features" (6–7). What identifies them as workers precedes and extends beyond their specific relation to the factory system. Gaskell ascribes to this class a distinct physiology, marking its deviation from a statistical "average." Such ethnographic description encompasses the central characters; even as the novel begins to single Barton out as a subject, his role as protagonist is founded not on particularity but on typicality. He enters the text as a "specimen" of his class, "born of factory workers, and himself bred up in youth, and living in manhood, among the mills"—and Gaskell's narration stamps him with physical and cultural traits described as common to "a manufacturing population," which seems to reproduce itself quite naturally (7). What makes him representative is both genealogical and environmental; class identity has a double status here, at once inherited ("born of factory workers") and acquired through life experience. The population to which Barton belongs is thus defined by the confluence of economic relations, geography, cultural habits, and biological characteristics.

Gaskell's novel at first takes pains to distinguish an ethnographically consistent population of workers from a subpopulation that is constantly falling out of the bottom of that category—much as Kay aimed to distinguish between English and Irish, Disraeli between the people and "the dangerous classes," and Mayhew between those who would and would not work. Two gendered figures incarnate this human remainder: the debilitated, unemployed man and the prostitute, both of whom are essential in shaping the novel's collective subject. They demarcate the working class externally by appearing to lack the positive traits assigned to it: strength, sexual propriety, and the dignity of labor.[21] Insofar as Gaskell's main characters are held up against these figures, the story seems to center on a conflict between the social reproduction of the working class proper and the degeneration threatened by those set apart from it. In practice, however, the separation between the two categories is undone rather than upheld by *Mary Barton*'s plot. What is remarkable about this novel is that, in contrasting these demographic categories, it ends up totally denaturalizing them.

John Barton's story, indeed, runs counter to the logic of natural-historical development that makes him such a "thorough specimen" of his class. The novel turns its representative man into a feared anomaly through a series of crises that are—as is clear from the start—built into the ordinary experience of proletarian life, with its predictably unpredictable cycles of "work and want" (3). His family is virtually annihilated by the conditions that formed it; his wife and son die, and a depression leaves him short of work and then out of work. Gaskell treats his zeal for Chartist politics and union organizing at once as a natural response to misery and as a self-evident source of crime, culminating in the murder of Harry Carson, the mill owner's son (who, unbeknownst to him, was scheming to seduce his daughter). While the process of criminalizing Barton and the union is perhaps the most ideological aspect of this novel, it also allows the exemplary character's story to unsettle the official distinction between the working class and the so-called dangerous classes. Barton sinks, along with a relative surplus of workers, from the census category of those "engaged in . . . manufacture" to that large non-category reserved for the "residue of population, including unemployed persons and women." In so doing, he is brought into parallel with his outcast sister-in-law Esther, whose fall into prostitution serves to elevate the respectable working poor to the status of "that happy class to which she could never, never more belong" (236). Gaskell forcefully drives home the analogy when she finally buries the two figures of devalued mass life in the same unmarked grave.

Lest we take his destruction and death as punishment for his political sins, Barton's descent into the residuum is in the works long before he pulls the trigger. This is clear even in an early scene that seems to contrast his masculine self-sufficiency against the abject state of an unemployed former power loom weaver named Ben Davenport, who "had sunk lower and lower, and pawned thing after thing" after losing his means of subsistence and whose family now lies starving on the floor of a cellar flooded with sewage (59). The narrator's imaginative entry into the interior spaces of working-class Manchester via "many half-finished streets, all so like one another, that you might have easily been bewildered and lost your way," is thus followed by further passages inward and downward on the part of her characters (14). Barton and his friend George Wilson, who gingerly make their way down overflowing alleys to call on the Davenports, are shocked by the conditions they find there. The home they enter is defenseless against (or rather, is part of) its toxic surrounding environment: "stagnant, filthy moisture of the street ooz[ing] up" through the floor on which an indeterminate number of children sleep (60)—the ooze from below and pig droppings from above implying, as Poovey observes, that "the homes of the poor can never be private in the sense that they cannot exclude the literal refuse from the streets" (144). Here, we are made to compare the impeccable tidiness of the Bartons' home with the squalor of the slum, the energetic hero with his enervated counterpart. Barton rushes to the aid of the family, exerting himself to restore some semblance of domestic order. Gaskell sets his practical capacity in relief against the dependent state of the man reduced to "a worn skeleton of a body" lying half-clothed on straw; her narration shows the protagonist making a small fire, cooking gruel, and feeding the children "with the useful skill of a working man" (62). Yet the contrast between the well-kept home and the oozing slum is not durable, nor is the contrast between the industrious, sturdy Barton and the depleted, starving Davenport. All the modest signs of respectability that dignify the Barton household as we are first welcomed into it (the checkered curtains that keep it private, adequate furniture, almost enough crockery to serve everyone tea) will soon be at the pawnshop.[22]

The difference between the two families is illusory from the start, relying as it does on Barton's ascribed identity as "a good, steady workman, and, as such, pretty certain of steady employment" to supply the household's needs (24). That little "as such" quietly distills the novel's bitter situational irony, as the subsequent economic downturn belies any correlation between steadiness of character and steadiness of employment. Barton and thousands of others out of work in the still worse years to come will soon find themselves likewise "sinking under the pressure of want and despair into a premature grave" (85). Personal reliability and occupational competence offer no assurance of work and thus no promise of survival, since precarity is a structural condition of wage labor. In this regard—contrary to its narrator's implausible claim that workers' interests are aligned with those of the factory owners who are forcing down their wages—*Mary Barton*'s plot reveals an understanding of the labor market not altogether different from Engels's. "Who guarantees that willingness to work shall suffice to obtain work," asks Engels, or "that uprightness, industry, thrift, and the rest of the virtues recommended by the bourgeoisie, are really [a worker's] road to happiness?" All that is certain, if an employed worker "has something today," is that "it does not depend on himself whether he shall have something tomorrow" (70). Gaskell likewise reveals such conduct lessons as hollow, invalidating W. R. Greg's objection, in his 1849 review of *Mary Barton*, that Barton's poverty owes to his improvidence and that the "want" of the proletariat is "moral, not material" ("Mary Barton" 139). The novel's supremely dependable and principled workman, from the vantage point of capital, has always been expendable.

Not despite but because the industrial novel recognizes the irony around which its plot is structured—that character (however central to fiction) is irrelevant to employment, and employment erratic as a class marker—it resorts to unmaking and sidelining the character who epitomizes his class. The eminently "useful" man, despite his contempt for the ruined sister-in-law who abandoned "that happy class," is consigned to a similar status:

both are absorbed into an imagined criminal subpopulation. Contra the distinctions the Poor Law drew between the deserving and the undeserving poor, between the productive working class and the degraded remainder, or between, as Mayhew put it, "the *energetic* and the *an-energetic* . . . the hardworking and the nonworking" (4:3), Gaskell's plot reveals that the fluctuations of the market are constantly ejecting masses of people from the workforce—creating, in so doing, the conditions that incite Barton and others to organize.[23] The story's causal logic was so unsettling that critics who feared its political repercussions could only censure Gaskell either for making her character behave uncharacteristically or for treating Barton as typical and thus generalizing unrest. Greg's review did both, protesting that the hero's "conduct is radically inconsistent with his qualities and character" while also rejecting him as a "fair representative" of his class (127, 125). The animosity voiced in *Mary Barton*, Greg asserts, is "exceptional, not general . . . and certainly not entertained by the working population at large"; he confines it to the ranks of "irregular, dissolute, and discontented *ex*-workmen" (125). Since the novel shows that any member of "the working population" can—indeed, will—wind up an "ex-workman," Greg's attempt to draw moral distinctions between employed and unemployed fails to explain away the grievance that drives Gaskell's plot.

Character itself is subject to unemployment in this novel. Barton is displaced by his daughter, receding into the story's margins. Perhaps Mary seems a safer protagonist, love a surer prospect than labor. Gaskell consequently takes quite a bit of flak from later critics for abandoning her radical working-class hero, transforming him into an opium addict and murderer, and shifting focus to a romantic plot. The common charge, by Raymond Williams and others, is that Mary's story distracts from class struggle with a melodrama of attempted seduction, romantic rivalry, and murder, which can then close with the happy resolution of marriage. By this account, the novel ceases to be about class when it starts to be about women. Yet the subordination of one plot to the other is less a detour from politics than a reframing of class, which too easily congeals into a demographic object (or, as we have seen, a race). Having turned its representative working man into a social exception and having created a crisis it can only conceive of handling through charity, the industrial novel is faced with a double challenge: that of quelling political resistance under conditions that make it inevitable, and that of ensuring the reproducibility of a population defined by its lack of social stability. Capitalism's essential task, which Balibar places at the origin of neo-racism, "is to keep 'in their place,' from generation to generation, those who have no fixed place" (213). We have already seen how advocates of sanitary reform approached the problem by targeting errant sexuality and seeking to regulate reproduction. Gaskell's transfer of attention from John Barton to his daughter may be read as a provisional attempt to solve this problem by similar means.

The turn to Mary's story, widely dismissed as a distraction from socioeconomic conflict and a detour from politics, is anything but.[24] It may be true, as is often noted, that the apparently comforting resolution of the courtship plot was a concession to editorial pressure to soften the novel's edge; Gaskell's letters suggest as much.[25] But the novel does not disengage from the dynamics of class in switching to a female protagonist and shifting the burden of the plot to sexual and familial conflicts. In the first place, the father's and daughter's plots are rendered inseparable by Gaskell's choice to make Mary's attempted seducer the very same person as the class enemy on whom the union avenges itself; Harry Carson's dually oppressive role, as Hilary Schor and Kate Flint have argued, makes sexual exploitation analogous to labor exploitation.[26] So too does Gaskell's story unsettle the gendered separation between the private sphere of kinship relations and the public sphere of the factory, the market, and the state—all suffused by the slow violence of expropriation. Further, the marriage plot, rescued from a fallen woman tragedy, entails another crucial contrast between norm and exception that does not quite hold. This is why Mary's aunt Esther plays an increasingly pivotal role in the story from which she was ejected before it began.

Mary's promotion to the position of heroine relies not just on her father's fall out of the workforce and into the statistical "remainder" but also on her aunt's prior fall out of the family and into the street. Read as prelude to a conclusion that strains to naturalize class through marriage, the backstory of Esther's transformation into an "abandoned and polluted outcast" looks like a cautionary tale of domestic norms gone awry (235). Yet the prostitute, instead of personifying those vices that must be kept out of the household, reveals in practice what feeble protection it offers. Rather than an aberrant figure, she iterates the larger problem of the gendering of work. As is evident in Gaskell's novel, female labor outside the factory is often casualized or uncompensated—and women dependent on men's wages are hardly shielded from precarity. "Father does not like girls to work in factories," Mary remarks to her widowed family friend Jane Wilson (a former mill worker herself prior to her marriage), who agrees that wage work leaves no time for housework, making homes so inhospitable as to drive husbands to drink (121).[27] Tellingly, the street scene that follows shows the consequences of this division of labor once the sexual contract and the support of male kin disappear. It finds John Barton angrily shoving aside a woman "of no doubtful profession," who turns out to be his disowned sister-in-law (124). As Esther's case illustrates, sexual danger is contained in the familial economy that promises to prevent it. History gets ready to repeat itself here: like the aunt who ran off with a man she hoped would marry her, Mary's conditioned belief that marriage is the best way to support herself prompts her to welcome the attentions of a rich man who plans to use and discard her. It is not moral laxity but her will to win the job of wife that puts her on track to end up a prostitute.

For this reason, the aunt's loss of self-possession is not simply an error to be avoided, a sad counterexample to the heroine's learned self-control. Both characters are actuated by the same demands, and the heroine gains her status as such not by resisting the temptation to leave home but by being pushed out into the world of nondomestic work by economic necessity. The fragility of the nuclear family and the material inadequacy of the domestic sphere paradoxically prompt her to supervise herself as she ventures into the streets. If Mary passes the test her aunt failed, earning her place as protagonist by claiming the property in herself that the prostitute is presumed to lack, her ability to do so owes more to Esther's intervention than to any essential difference between the two. Both share the freedom as well as the danger that make the city a peculiarly feminine symbolic space, one where prostitution, bound up with the definitive urban act of walking the streets, is such a pervasive trope not just for commodification but for exchanges with strangers and dislocation from familial roles that, as Elizabeth Wilson remarks in her study of urban discourse, "it almost seems as though to be a woman . . . in the city, is to become a prostitute—a public woman" (8).

Gaskell of course saves Mary from this fate, marrying her to Jem Wilson, the workman and family friend reserved for her from the novel's first chapter—a match that looks calculated to ensure class endogamy. In this respect, her plot confirms that the relations of "masters and men" were mediated from the start by women, who sustain the generational continuity of both. But insofar as the novel tries to constitute a manageable population of workers, it confronts a dilemma that the class system itself struggles to resolve: as Balibar puts it, how "to mark with generic signs populations which are collectively destined for capitalist exploitation—or which have been held in reserve for it—at the very moment when the economic process is tearing them away from the direct control of the system" (213). This problem circumscribes the stories of both John Barton, the consummate worker out of work, and Esther, the woman who sells sex when she has no other means of subsistence. It thus reveals a real linkage between the falsely conflated census categories of "women and unemployed persons." At the end of the day,

Mary Barton cannot shore up class identity against the political and sexual forces that threaten it because those forces are internal to it.

Gaskell's narrative thus reveals why population remains a political problem rather than just a neat ideological solution. First, the effort to reduce unstable elements within the class system proves that the exception is the product of the norm. It proves, moreover, that the industrial novel's subject is never finally the reified national working class it claims to represent; instead, it is the indefinite human remainder that is constantly being displaced and dissociated from that set. Invested as *Mary Barton* seems to be in the process of class formation—in nationalizing, racializing, and culturalizing the working class, personifying it in a male hero, and aligning it with manual labor in order to naturalize its status as such—Gaskell's plot belies any real distinction between workers and nonworkers. The vagaries of employment, the heterogeneity of the proletariat, the prevalence of casual labor and of reproductive labor (not recognized as work) all make it impossible to treat the working class as a fixed or self-enclosed population. For this very reason, the novel's emphasis on the remainder, and on "women and unemployed persons," is not a turn away from class but, ironically, a turn toward it—toward disclosing the relations that constitute class rather than the identarian qualities ascribed to English workers. As *Mary Barton* brutally illustrates, the non-category demarcated "residue of population" (difficult to count especially in the case of those, like Esther, without fixed habitations) in fact comes closer to capturing the essential dynamic of proletarian experience than any occupation, cultural characteristic, demographic set, or representative figure.

Further, even the effort to perpetuate class endogamy has two potential outcomes. It furnishes the biological component of what Louis Althusser would call the reproduction of the relations of production (so easily taken for granted that Althusser himself largely ignores procreation). Yet it also allows for the very circumstance bourgeois social reformers aimed to prevent: the political mobilization made possible by intensified class affinity and growing proletarian numbers. In this regard, the politics of realist fiction may not be contained in the liberal wish to resolve socioeconomic conflict through individual sympathy, to rationalize political economy's measures of value, or to incorporate mass life into a unified social body. Realism's project, as it sets its sights on the city, may lie in larger quantities than the existing social order is ready to count.

Fiction indeed has its own techniques for recasting the stories Victorian government told about its aims, limitations, and the problems that necessitated it. These techniques required biopower's organizing tropes to take on oppositional political meaning, such that overcrowding and even illness could signify resistance and transformation rather than crises to be remedied by the state. Dickens's notoriously crowded tales of city life put the figurative strategies of population management to use in order to contest rather than affirm the existing political order, as the next chapter will show. *Bleak House* in particular startlingly demonstrates, by spreading a disease throughout the city that physically transforms its protagonist, how the modern social body constitutes itself via exposure to the very forces that appear to endanger its survival. Yet it also relentlessly tests, at the levels of narrative form and of character, the perceived limits of this social formation even in the process of mapping its features onto a series of obscurely connected bodies. In peculiar fashion, the city novel alters the politics of life production by carrying it to a quantitative extreme. The tension between these two processes is the essential narrative dynamic through which nineteenth-century writing shaped the city. It places all risks to collective survival at the heart of a stalled dialectic of development, oscillating between the promise of a radical mass politics and the constantly changing imperatives of population control.

CHAPTER 3

Dickens's Supernumeraries

> The rise of Dickens is like the rising of a vast mob.
> This is not only because his tales are indeed as
> crowded and populous as towns: for truly it was not
> so much that Dickens appeared as that a hundred
> Dickens characters appeared. It is also because he
> was the sort of man who has the impersonal impetus
> of a mob.
>
> —G. K. Chesterton, *The Victorian Age*

In a classic Dickensian moment, the third-person narrator of *Bleak House* paraphrases the ominous political speculations of Sir Leicester Dedlock's distinguished guests at Chesney Wold, all of whom are agreed on at least one point: that in matters of state, "nobody is in question" but themselves.

> A people there are, no doubt—a certain large number of supernumeraries, who are to be occasionally addressed, and relied upon for shouts and choruses, as on the theatrical stage; but Boodle and Buffy, their followers and families, their heirs, executors, administrators, and assigns, are the born first-actors, managers, and leaders, and no others can appear on the scene for ever and ever. (191)

Juxtaposed against the previous chapter's scenes of poverty, death, and the horrors of an overcrowded churchyard, this glimpse of the *beau monde* seems to contain an obvious commentary on the fatal consequences of such indifference to the populace. This is a familiar theme for Dickens. He returns to it in *Hard Times*, satirizing a legislature that recognizes "no duty to an abstraction called a People" (286), and again in *Little Dorrit*, which offers a similar parody of political reason among the ruling class:

> It was agreed that the country (another word for the Barnacles and Stiltstalkings) wanted preserving, but how it came to want preserving

was not so clear. It was only clear that the question was all about John
Barnacle, Augustus Stiltstalking, William Barnacle and Tudor Stiltstalking, Tom, Dick, or Harry Barnacle or Stiltstalking, because there
was nobody else but mob. (333)

Everybody else, in number, has become "nobody else" in social meaning
and political voice; so pervasive is this problem that it can be no surprise
that Arthur Clennam, witnessing this reported conversation, finds it futile to
intervene, "bethinking himself that mob was used to it." It thus falls to the
narrator to do what his characters cannot: to say something "on the part of
mob" (334).

While such rhetorical performances moved Anthony Trollope to satirize
him as "Mr. Popular Sentiment" in *The Warden*, Dickens has more often—
and for the same reasons—been acclaimed as a champion of the people so
readily dismissed by the Boodles and Buffys, Bounderbys, and Barnacles of
the world.[1] George Gissing, despite his own ambivalence toward populism
and democracy, hails the Dickensian novel as a radical event in social history:
from the moment *The Pickwick Papers* appeared, its author had "opened the
new era of democracy in letters" (*The Immortal Dickens* 48). Dickens's chosen subject matter and setting, his project of "embodying the essentials of
popular life in the capital city," and the ethical thrust of his writing were
all, in Gissing's view, "purely democratic" (48, 107). It is with approbation
that G. K. Chesterton dubs his favorite novelist "not only the democrat but
even the demagogue of fiction" (*Criticisms and Appreciations* 212), celebrating Dickens's achievement not just as a spectacularly successful producer of
"mass literature" but in every sense a phenomenon of the mass: the authorial
personification of "a mob in revolt" (*The Victorian Age in Literature* 81). This
revolutionary potential had not been lost on Marx, who famously praised
the author of *Bleak House* as one of those great novelists "whose graphic and
eloquent pages have issued to the world more political and social truths than
have been uttered by all the professional politicians, publicists and moralists
put together" ("The English Middle Class" 106). Other debates aside, critics
have rarely failed to recognize in Dickens's work a profound commitment to
the representation of the urban masses. Read in light of this commitment,
the political import of that scene in *Bleak House* looks obvious. The vague
perception of the people, among Sir Leicester's circle, as "a certain large
number of supernumeraries" would seem to be the target of self-evident
moral outrage—much the same outrage provoked by Gradgrind's settling
of social questions in the abstract without a glance at "the teeming myriads
of human beings around him" (*Hard Times* 95), or Podsnap's chauvinistic

refusal to hear of residents dying of starvation in the streets of his great metropolis (*Our Mutual Friend* 143–44), or Scrooge's Malthusian attitude toward a "surplus population" in need of decreasing (*A Christmas Carol* 39). In *Bleak House*, however, the implicit verbal irony of the narrator's description strains toward the further irony of an unlikely narrative truth. For all its strident populism, the novel generates larger numbers than its own domestic and political economies can accommodate.

Nor is it only the muddy streets and labyrinthine underworld that Dickens populates beyond their capacity. *Bleak House* as a whole is a world teeming with life, from the numberless children of the middle-class Jellybys to the inhabitants of the ancestral home of Sir Leicester—and the novel registers, with the sensitivity of a pressure gauge, the felt density of its population within the limited space of these human environments. For all the tumult of its London chapters, Dickens similarly crowds the estate in Lincolnshire with an unspecified number of persons who apparently cannot be accounted for. Even the ranks of Boodle and Buffy—though they regard themselves as "the great actors for whom the stage is reserved"—denote, for the purposes of this novel, an unfixed quantity of trivialities. Contrary to Lord Boodle's insistence on the impossibility of reassigning administrative agency, "giving the Home Department . . . to Joodle, the Exchequer to Koodle, the Colonies to Loodle, and the Foreign Office to Moodle, what are you to do with Noodle?" (190), Dickens's rhyming alphabetic designations plainly belie, in their arbitrariness, all qualitative distinctions among these variables. Like the "Everybodys" and "Nobodys" among Sir Leicester's seemingly innumerable cousins (446, 447), parasitically swarming Chesney Wold and appearing "quite as much at a loss how to dispose of themselves, as anybody else can be how to dispose of them" (448), the MPs are themselves supernumeraries.

To be sure, the burden of that "*something over* that nobody knows what to do with" represented by the dependent Dedlock cousins—much like Boodle's proposition that "the country is shipwrecked . . . because you can't provide for Noodle"—resonates ironically with the dire situation of multitudes struggling to survive in the disease-ridden slums of Tom-all-Alone's (446, 190, emphasis added). At the same time, the persistent recurrence of such formulations, satirical or otherwise, underscores a problem of remainders that the narrative is perpetually compelled to restage. Despite Dickens's commitment to "systematically . . . turn[ing] Fiction to the good account of showing the preventable wretchedness and misery in which the mass of the people dwell," his novels give no indication that misery is preventable by any existing means ("To Working Men" 227). In *Bleak House*, where Parliamentary politics is a sham and "telescopic philanthropy," local pastorship, and familial relations alike prove more destructive than beneficial, all professions of humanitarian sympathy and attempts at intervention only set into stark relief the seemingly inevitable failure of any individual or institution either to "provide for" or to "dispose of" an overwhelming surplus of human life.

How, then, does the novel resolve this contradiction? The argument of this chapter is that it doesn't, and that Dickens's fiction instead performs a series of deliberately failed experiments in population management. To understand the stakes of these experiments requires some reconsideration of the politics of Victorian fiction. The Victorian novel is perhaps too hastily read either as a crypto-bureaucratic "technology of individuation" or as a reflection of cultural anxieties about the fate of individuals in a homogenizing and bureaucratized mass society. By contrast with both approaches, I suggest that Dickens, rather than undertaking either to discipline individuals or to free them, gives narrative form to the virtually unthinkable problem suggested by the term "supernumeraries": the paradox of a total in excess of the total.

In this respect, his multiplot city novels share some ground with industrial novels like *Mary Barton*. Gaskell's plot, as the previous chapter showed, turned out to be geared less toward the representation of a fixed class of "working men" than toward the making of statistical remainders—"unemployed persons and women," per that large, awkwardly conflated category on the 1841 Census, into which John Barton inevitably falls. *Bleak House*, by giving fleeting personification and aesthetic density to demographic excess, brings to the analysis of the state what Gaskell brought to class and employment: it reveals the potential for statistical analysis to produce its own exception. What Nikolas Rose identifies as liberalism's project of "governing by numbers," as these novels illustrate, is perpetually challenged by the surplus life it presupposes and requires.[2] The demographic scope of Dickensian London is of course far broader than Gaskell's Manchester, and its excess more palpable. The human heterogeneity of his bustling city novels, indeed, is often taken as a sign of their author's liberal-democratic will to include the excluded. Yet Dickens resists such platitudes in allowing the totality of the people to be dismissed as supernumeraries. This term, which often describes nonspeaking parts in the theater, also more basically names "extras" to any identified set. *Bleak House* does not try to make each person count (as national citizen-subject, character, or demographic unit). To the contrary, it reintroduces the prospect of equality by subsuming the entire population within the null set of the quantitatively uncounted and qualitatively discounted.

More than perhaps any novel of its time, *Bleak House* hinges all the contingencies of its plot on the biological and social processes that both constitute and alter its population. This text is thus a touchstone of my claim that population, rather than the individual or society, is Victorian fiction's principal subject. Though Dickens's novel has been read as a vindication of individual agency against a faceless system and, alternatively, as a study in the individualizing processes of disciplinary power that covertly serve that system where they seem to oppose it, the causal centrality of *Bleak House's* outbreak plot—elemental to its concern with the management of life—suggests that biopolitics rather than discipline is the primary mode of governance with which its narrative engages. The disease Dickens unleashes on his fictional population, infecting and transforming the protagonist, merges her with the mass from which her first-person narrative would seem to distinguish her. So too does it reveal, via Jo and scores of others exposed to all the hazards of city life without the protections of citizens, a problem unsolved by those disciplinary techniques of surveillance and normalization that new historicist criticism famously saw at work in *Bleak House*. On these points, the current chapter responds not only to D. A. Miller and his critics but also to a tradition of reading—variously new historicist and Freudian—that aligns Dickens's novel with the perspective of sanitary reform and treats filth, abjection, and pathology as the objects of a generalized fear of contamination. Where Peter Stallybrass and Allon White, Robert Lougy, Pamela Gilbert and others understand city novels like *Bleak House* as narrating a fantasy of hygiene and social control, I suggest that this novel embraces the power of epidemic to belie apparent distinctions between individual and mass and among classed bodies and spaces.[3] Turning to the phenomenon of the police—so prominent in the plot, yet always either too late or simply unconcerned to intervene—this chapter further finds in Dickens's fiction a redefinition of the aims of policing. Here, if one wishes to consult Foucault, as Miller famously did, his lectures on the macropolitics of "security" (uninterested in individual subjects) turn out to be far more germane than his account of a micropolitics of surveillance. By persistently exposing what policing ignores, *Bleak House* produces forms of resistance made possible, paradoxically, by overpopulation.

Supernumeraries

> The mother, her husband, the prying solicitor, the French maid, and the whole Dedlock set might be eliminated from the book. . . . Even then, a comprehensive etcetera would be needed for supernumeraries. So crowded is the canvas which Mr. Dickens has stretched . . . that a daguerreotype of Fleet Street at noon-day would be the aptest symbol to be found for

> it; though the daguerreotype would have the advantage in accuracy of representation.
>
> —George Brimley, review of *Bleak House*

The idea that Dickens's novels are structured around the premise of surplus population may sound odd. Crowded though his fiction is, Dickens's antagonism to political economy makes it difficult to imagine his fiction affirming the Malthusian account of necessary checks. Statistical rhetoric certainly does not fare well in *Hard Times*, with its blistering satire of an industrial regime of quantitative reason concerning population, labor power, and utility that aims to supplant all qualitative judgment concerning good and evil; British society, the narrator suggests, would do better to "govern these awful unknown quantities by other means" (71). And the novelist's perspective is explicitly anti-Malthusian at the level of policy. In fiction, journalism, and public life, Dickens railed against the New Poor Law of 1834—the most directly observable national policy shaped by the *Essay on Population*. Dickensian characters who voice the problem of surplus population are usually vilified or ridiculed in his novels: Gradgrind's scheming model pupil Bitzer, who contends that Coketown's workers owe their poverty to their "improvidence" in having families and that they would be better off saying, "While my hat covers my family . . . I have only one to feed, and that's the person I most like to feed" (*Hard Times* 118), or Mrs. Jellyby, who promotes her farming venture in Borrioboola-Gha as a means of spurring emigration and thus relieving the pressure of England's "superabundant home population" (*Bleak House* 49–50). But for all that *Bleak House* satirizes Mrs. Jellyby's disastrous colonial scheme for "the general cultivation of the coffee berry—*and* the natives" (49), Dickens does not in practice dismiss the idea of overpopulation. In fact, it is the central dynamic of his novels. The question is whether this superabundance of life, and the economic scarcity that Malthus identified as its basis, is the consequence of natural law or social conditions.

Dickens's novels overwhelmingly favor the latter explanation, even while provocatively suggesting that none of the existing institutions designed to check population actually serve this function. The workhouse system portrayed in *Oliver Twist*, though it splits up married couples with the goal of lowering fertility rates, sees an extraordinary number of illegitimate births such as Oliver's. The debtor's prison, as *Little Dorrit* attests, hardly deters its inmates from reproducing: "Children? Why, we swarm with 'em," exclaims the turnkey of the Marshalsea (74). Jaggers, in *Great Expectations*, avows from the vantage point of criminal law that "all he saw of children, was, their being generated in great numbers for certain destruction" (413). The market and the factory system, while providing limited employment, rely on redundant population: the manufacturing town in *Hard Times* boasts "a considerable population of babies" reared by schools that resemble and feed into factories, all of the city's human inhabitants "shouldering, and trampling, and pressing one another to death" (53, 66). Virtually every institution depicted in Dickens's fiction, from charities to schools to prisons to the city itself, seems to multiply human population at an astonishing rate while failing to provide proportionate material support for so many bodies.

To critics, the sprawl of these chaotic public worlds and mismanaged institutions often looks like the necessary antithesis to an orderly domestic sphere where everyone finds his or her proper place. D. A. Miller, notably, argues that Dickens's narratives call attention to the incoherence of the socio-institutional world (the Court of Chancery standing as its icon) only to relocate power within a private sphere onto which the liberal fantasy of freedom from carceral authority is projected. He is certainly right that the success of a novel like *Bleak House* depends on the conspicuous administrative failures it stages; the novel's plot, however, makes the domestic order inextricable from these failures. Like other institutions, the family is implicated in the phenomenon of overcrowding. Mrs. Jellyby's own masses of children attest that, despite their mother's theoretical commitment to reducing surplus population, the household is not just subject to external pressures but internally overrun even by the normative logic of reproductive kinship.

This notion of an excess of human life proliferating within as well as beyond the domestic sphere raises political questions that the prevailing interpretive models do not confront. Critics who read Dickens's fiction (or Victorian fiction in general) as a vehicle for domestic ideology are generally compelled to sidestep the issue of population. For all the moral certainty that domesticity has been taken to represent in Victorian culture, the Dickensian household stands on a remarkably precarious foundation. Set up in theory as a model for good governance, the household in practice becomes a figure of monumental inefficacy and general scarcity. In *Our Mutual Friend*, for example, it seems clear enough at first that Dickens can muster more sympathy for the petit-bourgeois domestic economy of the House of Wilfer than for the political economy that prevails in the House of Podsnap. Introducing the meek R. Wilfer as a man possessed of "a limited salary and an unlimited family," the narrative seems to favor the shabby drugstore clerk's "mental arithmetic" concerning his household over his wife's proposal to take in two boarding pupils as an additional source of income (40). It grants him the point that the family cannot house even two "young ladies of the highest respectability"; regardless of class, by Wilfer's reasoning, these ladies amount to "the same thing" in number as any two other "fellow creatures" for whom there is no space (43). In accepting this egalitarian premise, however, the novel implicitly extends the argument to those far greater numbers who likewise cannot be accommodated "from a fellow-creature point of view" (43). Such calculations—the ratio of too many bodies to too little space (and too scarce resources)—seem entirely reasonable in Wilfer's sympathetic construction. To add more dependents would be multiplying human need beyond the means of the household. Yet these calculations nonetheless lay the ground for Podsnap's more overtly Malthusian response to the reports of deaths in the street that he finds distasteful as a topic of after-dinner conversation: "You know what the population of London is, I suppose" (144).

To approach the question of resources and their distribution from a "fellow-creature point of view," then, is not necessarily to proceed with the compassion of common need but often with the acknowledgment of common scarcity. Despite Dickens's declamation against the Poor Law, the workhouse, and their effects on such a "fellow-creature" as Betty Higden, among so many "other fellow-creatures" (324), the shared humanity implied in this formulation is itself the name of a problem. While Mrs. Wilfer's prospective pupils seem comparatively unlikely to starve, the domestic economies of Dickens's novels are determined by the same logic of equilibrium that governs the human population at large. A similar impasse presents itself in *Bleak House*. Despite the narrator's memorable tirade on behalf of London's neglected homeless children who, like Jo, are "dying thus around us, every day" (734), even the compassionate doctor Woodcourt is permitted to marvel at the "strange fact" that, while Jo lives, "this creature in human form should be more difficult to dispose of than an unowned dog" (719). And the novel, for all its outrage, knows of only one way to dispose of such a creature. Nor is there any clear answer, within the existing frameworks of legislation, private charity, or moral sentiment, to the unnamed brickmaker's declaration to the self-appointed home visitor Mrs. Pardiggle that the deaths of his "five dirty and onwholesome children" were "so much the better for them, and for us besides" (132). Even for the middle-class Jellybys' brood of "Wild Indians," as Mr. Jellyby calls them, the eldest daughter Caddy cannot dismiss her father's alarming pronouncement that "the best thing that could happen to them was, their being all Tomahawked together" (475). And the novel, notwithstanding Ada's and Esther's horror at this macabre joke, does not seem altogether prepared to dispute Mr. Jellyby's reasoning.

Madame Defarge herself would struggle to keep count of the number of characters the novelist kills off in *Bleak House*. Ruskin puts the novel's body count at nine in a review essay condemning "Cockney literature" and its audiences for a collective lust for crime, pathology, and morbidity;

modern fiction, he charges, can give and get entertainment only in the variety of reported deaths. His objection to *Bleak House* is not really a question of numbers, however. Walter Scott's novels, Ruskin admits, feature as many fatalities, but these rise to the level of tragedy or serve some edifying purpose. The deaths of Dickens's characters, by contrast, serve only as "the further enlivenment of a narrative intended to be amusing; and as a properly representative average of the statistics of civilian mortality in the centre of London" (272). While the reference to vital statistics and their "properly representative" character might tie the novel to a particular version of realism, Ruskin's claim is that the novel's statistical representativeness reflects a false doctrine rather than a body of meaningful social-scientific facts. The untimely deaths of so many personae, from the street sweeper to Richard Carstone to Lady Dedlock, merely "illustrate the modern theology that the appointed destiny of a large average of our population is to die like rats in a drain" (272). The phrasing of this critique is suggestive: he objects to the extermination not of a proportion of the population but of a "large average" thereof. Instead of marking a specific subset of individuals for death, the average sweeps across a broad distribution to include even those whom Ruskin classes as "respectable persons" (272). As he reads it, this novel treats human beings as aggregate data, which might just as readily be represented as dots on a census diagram indicating number of inhabitants per hundred acres.

Ruskin is half right. Though Dickens no more believes premature death to be the "destiny" of Londoners than Jonathan Swift believed Irish babies to be destined for the stew pot, there is indeed a sense in which his fiction is consummately statistical. Readers of *Hard Times* may be expected to balk at Gradgrind's suggestion that his daughter Louisa base her acceptance or rejection of Bounderby's marriage proposal on actuarial calculations concerning the median ages of spouses and "the average duration of human life" (99), yet the novel's conclusion, which projects its characters' futures in terms of mortality and fertility, bears out the hard facts Gradgrind teaches. Though Louisa objects that the issue at hand is her own life and not averages, and though the narrative suggests that her statistically minded father must be taught a painful lesson through his children about the incalculability of human experience, Gradgrind is right after all that Louisa's life is "governed by the laws which govern lives in the aggregate" (99). Everyone falls somewhere on the curve of mortality; all characters can be assumed to die at some point, though only some die on the page. Dickens's novels, as Ruskin perceives, leave no one exempt from the probabilities to which human existence in general is subject. It is telling that Ruskin registers his opposition to this rough handling of characters by linking the cruelty of abstraction ("a large average") to the horror of animalization ("like rats in a drain"). His reaction to this combined fate bespeaks a distinct premise, which he in fact shares with the novelist: freedom from the doom of being caught either in a drain or in an average relies on the sacredness of human life.

Dickens, contra Ruskin's criticism, writes just this premise into all of his novels. It is most evident in the famous scene of suspended animation in *Our Mutual Friend*—a key reference point for Gilles Deleuze's, Giorgio Agamben's, and Roberto Esposito's analyses of biopower—where a crowd of bystanders exert themselves to save the life of the universally despised Rogue Riderhood, simply "because it *is* life, and they are living and must die" (443). This impersonal thing called life is just what is ultimately at stake on the political terrain of Dickensian fiction. Biological existence and the means by which it is preserved or expended have become more elemental to the work of the novel than any other object, *telos*, or metric. If such readers as Ruskin were shocked by the intimation that life was being systematically devalued either in the actual world or in Dickens's distorted image of that world, their reactions owe to the seemingly contradictory fact that life was being systematically valued in the very process by which certain bodies and lives came to appear disposable.

In this regard, Dickens's city novels do more than thematize national debates on the New Poor Law and sanitary reform. Their plots set forth the logic of a system of governance and urban planning whose aim was the management of biological life. While Dickens often satirizes the emptiness of political rhetoric, his critiques of bureaucratic inefficacy and of the state's indifference to human life are rhetorically consistent with the statements of government agencies themselves. Dr. Charles Wilson's remarks on a survey of sanitary conditions in Kelso, quoted in Edwin Chadwick's *Sanitary Report*, echo Dickens in looking forward to a day "when governments shall be induced to consider the preservation of a nation's health an object as important as the promotion of its commerce or the maintenance of its conquests" (410). Even in pointing to the need for such a change of priorities, these reports illustrate a major shift that has already taken place both in political discourse and in the practice of governance.

That the preservation of life should be paramount among the interests of the Victorian state is an article of faith that cuts across what seem like unbridgeable political divides. Even the cultural commentator John Eagles, who criticized both sanitary reform and the 1851 Census as violations of privacy by a "great Gargantuan Busybody," saw the results of the census as evidence of a crisis that demanded state intervention (319). In an 1854 essay on the census in *Blackwood's*, Eagles expresses dismay at the infant mortality rate and low life expectancy of children in England's manufacturing towns. Citing the finding of the Registrar General's 7th Report that in Manchester, more than half of all children born will be dead within six years, he concludes that wealth cannot justifiably be accumulated at "such a cost of human life" (356). Wary though he is of meddlesome state apparatuses demanding to know, for example, the marital status of each person and how each is related to the head of household (two new questions added to the 1851 Census), he contends that Parliament must act to prevent the "massacre of childhood" reflected in mortality statistics (356). "From whatever state of things this great evil arises," Eagles reasons, "it ought not to be, and surely the people as one man should look to the Legislature to provide proper sanitary and other means to check a national cruelty" (356). Dickens's novels likewise treat the preservation of life as the ultimate aim of government. Consequently, they produce narratives in which the success or failure of the political order plays out at the level of population.

Despite the biopolitical dimensions of fictional narratives, debates about the politics of Victorian fiction since the 1980s have tended to focus on disciplinary power. From the standpoint of new historicist critics influenced by Foucault's *Discipline and Punish*, the novel trained readers not just to imagine themselves under constant surveillance and thus to internalize the normalizing strictures of discipline but also to enjoy each extended lesson in how to be normal. *The Novel and the Police* found in *Bleak House* the classic case of a narrative that outwardly disavows the panoptic gaze of modern institutions like the metropolitan police in the process of installing that gaze, through narrative itself, in a private realm that appears autonomous from policing. Miller's move toward making fiction complicit in an institutionalizing regime marked a shift from liberal criticism that linked the Victorian novel to an affirmative individualism and read Dickens's fiction as a critique of political institutions; so too did it diverge both from a Marxist investment in social contradiction within narrative and from a poststructuralist celebration of indeterminacy.[4] Critics of new historicism, aiming to historicize Victorian liberalism and British policy debates in more nationally specific terms than Foucault's genealogy of discipline might allow, countered that Dickens was mistrustful of centralized administrative power and that Victorian fiction was broadly committed to personal autonomy.[5] (One almost hears Podsnap, in *Our Mutual Friend*, rebuffing what he calls "centralization": "Not English!" [144].) Such criticism tends to take for granted the assumptions Miller and Nancy Armstrong, among others, had sought to problematize: that the self-governing individual, the domestic sphere, and the family exist prior to and remain independent of the sociopolitical sphere, compensating for the inadequacies of a crowded external world and furnishing a haven from the clash of its ignorant armies.[6] Underlying most interpretive debate is a consensus that the Victorian novel is necessarily, for better or for worse, a liberal project—invested in the idea of separate private and public spheres (whether that separation is an ideological fantasy or a historical reality) and committed to individualism (whether fiction produces the individual as an effect of power or defends its inherent autonomy). On balance, readings that treat the novel as a defense against modern power rather than an instrument thereof tend to take as a given the process new historicism only forestalled by prescribing it as fiction's *telos*: the making of the liberal subject.[7] The disagreement is thus little more than a question of primacy. Whether it precedes the novel or is invented by its form, the private individual—as critics from Watt to Jameson to Armstrong maintain—seems unquestionably to give fiction its reason for being.

Without declaring individualism irrelevant either to the novel or to politics, it is possible to trace a different governing logic in Victorian fiction that lays stress elsewhere. Foucault himself would in fact take a step beyond the epistemic shift described in *Discipline and Punish*, attesting in his lectures at the Collège de France in the mid- to late 1970s that the history of modern power in the West does not end with the rise of discipline and the invention of the liberal subject. Building on the concept of biopower introduced in 1976, the 1977–78 lectures extend that new paradigm to a broad analysis of the modern "society of security" (*Security, Territory, Population* 11). Setting discipline aside, Foucault proposes that the larger trajectory from the end of the eighteenth century to the present is toward governmentality: a system that has "population as its target, political economy as its major form of knowledge, and apparatuses of security as its essential technical instrument" (108).[8] Such governing techniques differ from a "juridical-disciplinary system" in that their object is neither the control of individual bodies nor the self-mastery of subjects but the management of population in the aggregate (37). The individual becomes a means rather than an end, little more than "the instrument, relay, or condition for obtaining something at the level of the population" (42).

While Foucault later suggests that discipline and population management complement each other, it bears remarking that the two aim at distinct objectives that at times bring them into tension. The former seeks to produce individuals capable of regulating themselves, whereas the latter yields a statistically generalizable population from which certain subsets can be devalued and eliminated. This tension is present at the levels of character and plot in virtually every Dickens novel. In fact, it is written into the anomalous form of *Bleak House*. The novel's divided narrative structure—one side recalled in the past tense by a character who encounters a series of eccentric personae and evaluates each one as an individual, the other relayed in the present by an impersonal narrative system that spans the city and speaks in many voices— attests both to the interdependency and the difficulty of reconciling the dual systems that simultaneously individualize and aggregate human life.[9]

Dickens's evocation of the supernumerary expresses just this tension between individuation and the calculus of population management. The term, though it corresponds to no identifiable referent, is thus far from nugatory. Doubly ironized by the narrative, this figure of negated excess operates as a double negative; the novel unexpectedly affirms its positivity even where it withdraws from representation. Rather than simply embodying the statistical object of population and confirming census data by supplying the correct number of bodies, the multitude that materializes in Dickens's fiction yields what Rancière would call a "count of the uncounted—or the part of those who have no part." It claims no ontological substance, no unifying principle by which to classify bodies or lives. The supernumerary at once designates a sum exceeding the maximum allowable quantity (thus the number of units in excess of the total) and something in excess of number as such. It marks as a category the unquantified mass of life that exceeds categorization, rendering inclusion and exclusion equally impossible.

The concept of the supernumerary is elemental to the novel's effort to mediate a social order in which containment strategies govern the city. The fate of those consigned to this status compels us to reconsider what it might mean to praise, as Chesterton does, Dickens's extraordinary literary "faculty of managing a crowd" (*Criticisms and Appreciations* 212). As *Bleak House* demonstrates, the crowd is not merely the hazy backdrop against which character takes shape, nor a literary attempt to represent what cannot represent itself and must be represented. Disrupting the logic of reference on which realist representation is taken to depend, the crowding of narrative space exerts a metonymic force that refigures collective life in moments of collision, breach, immersion, explosion, and contagion.

The "Tough Subject"

> Their identification is next to impossible, for they are like each other as apples in a sieve, or peas in one pod. Moreover, to tell their numbers is out of the question. It is as incomprehensible as is their nature. They swarm as bees do, and arduous indeed would be the task of the individual who undertook to reckon

up the small fry of a single alley of the hundreds that
abound in Squalor's regions.

—James Greenwood, *The Seven Curses of London*

Unaccountable though they are to the heedless MPs and public adminis-
trators who conceive of them in the abstract, Dickens's supernumeraries
at times take fleshly form in *Bleak House*—notably, in the figure of Jo, who
appears virtually inseparable from "the general crowd" in which he trav-
els and the physical environment to which he belongs (163). Metonymically
connected to the mud he sweeps from the streets, Jo himself is part of "that
kindred mystery . . . which is made of nobody knows what, and collects
about us nobody knows whence or how: we only knowing in general that
when there is too much of it, we find it necessary to shovel it away" (163).
Like the sediment that accumulates and begrimes everything in the city, the
vagrant crossing-sweeper's fleeting presence leaves traces of ineradicable
problems and contingencies of which the novel's world cannot be cleansed.
Constantly ordered by the police to "move on" from one end of the city to
the other, he resurfaces everywhere, encounters everyone, sees everything,
and yet knows, per his own refrain, "nothink." He likewise remains unknow-
able to the legal system when it addresses him and even to the narrator who
monitors his movements only to show him, among the "other lower animals,
get[ting] on in the unintelligible mess as they can" (258).

In a novel that seems to invite critical debates wherein a totalizing institutional power structure and the conflicting possibility of individual agency
are the only options, Jo is difficult to pin down. Though entirely lacking
autonomy, un-free without question, he proves remarkably impervious both
to the mechanisms of discipline and to carceral authority. Despite his propensity to turn up again and again like a bad penny, he can scarcely be located
even in his own temporary dwelling. Inspector Bucket and Snagsby, inquiring
after him in Tom-all-Alone's, discover that the "Jo" they seek could be anyone: "Carrots, or the Colonel, or Gallows, or Young Chisel, or Terrier Tip,
or Lanky, or the Brick" (359). Emerging from an environment in which—as a
superintendent of police, quoted in Chadwick's *Sanitary Report*, had incredu-
lously related—there might be some "thousand children who have no names
whatever, or only nicknames, like dogs" (199), Jo turns out to be, as his nick-
name suggests, a "Tough Subject" indeed (359). The intelligence he produces
in an inquest regarding the death of the pseudonymous "Nemo" cannot even
be recorded in the official report. Finding him unable to respond to basic
questions that would identify either himself or the deceased as juridical subjects, the coroner cannot "receive his evidence" and—declaring Jo's statements "terrible depravity"—orders that the boy be "put aside" (177). With no

fixed address, surname, family, legally recognized occupation, or legitimate social function and only the most aleatory associations, Jo is less an individual subject than a walking synecdoche for the crowd. Unless dragged bodily by Bucket, the narrator relates, "neither the Tough Subject nor any other subject could be professionally conducted to Lincoln's Inn Fields" for legal questioning (362). Even when apprehended, his proximity proves inimical to everyone with whom he comes into contact.

Devalued and abjected though he is, and interchangeable though he may be with any other child of Tom-all-Alone's, Jo brings to the novel something beyond the specter of a social danger to be prevented. Indeed, what takes place in *Bleak House* is impossible without him. Transforming everything he touches, Jo's circulation throughout the novel's metropolitan geography fuses Dickens's impersonal narrative to Esther Summerson's first-person narrative and drives the plot inexorably forward.[10] While Esther seems the obvious protagonist of the novel, her apologies for "always writing about myself," "as if this narrative were the narrative of *my* life" are perhaps too readily taken with a grain of salt (137, 40). As if in answer to this self-effacing rhetoric, Dickens's counterpart narrative not only formally interrupts the autobiographical mode but also calls into question whether *Bleak House* really is, or can be, primarily Esther's story. Like the painted figure of Allegory on the ceiling pointing "obtrusively toward the window" to that muddy world outside where Tulkinghorn refuses to look (259), the impersonal narrator insistently points to something just outside of the frame that the novel struggles to impress upon the reader's attention:

> Dirty, ugly, disagreeable to all the senses, in body a common creature of the common streets, only in soul a heathen. Homely filth begrimes him, homely parasites devour him, homely sores are in him, homely rags are on him: native ignorance, the growth of English soil and climate, sinks his immortal nature lower than the beasts that perish. Stand forth, Jo, in uncompromising colours! From the sole of thy foot to the crown of thy head, there is nothing interesting about thee. (724)

Jo is rendered alien because, ironically, his poverty is all too prosaic and familiar. He thus appears not merely as the bad conscience of domestic fiction but as the avatar of a more general condition that no house or nation can hold at bay. His "wonderfully strange" state of existence both unsettles and connects the world of *Bleak House* because it is coextensive with the institutions that seek either to contain or to shield against his bodily presence (258). His futile labor of sweeping the city streets collapses all distinctions between sanitation and filth, work and idleness. His vagrancy is not the opposite of domesticity; it carries with it the homelessness of home itself. Further, in a genre that typically sets a high premium on the interiority of its principal characters, Jo presents a surface that not only resists interiorization (knowing "nothink") but also compromises the distinctiveness of those who rise to the level of subjectivity.

The presence of such figures in the novel effectively destabilizes any hierarchy of major and minor characters. Though Jo's role in the story seems obviously subordinate to Esther's, readers have rarely failed to note that the phenomenal imaginative energy of Dickens's novels does not center on his protagonists. E. M. Forster famously remarks on the almost galvanic illusion of vitality and "roundness" sustained by Dickensian characters who are, without exception, actually "flat" (71–72). Terry Eagleton marvels at Dickens's "bizarre, perverse creations," observing that "Woodcourt is admirable, but Krook is magnificent. We may pity Oliver . . . but we delight in Fagin. The pious little Nell . . . is an intolerable bore, whereas Quilp . . . is hideously fascinating" (Preface vii). It was likewise evident to Dickens's fellow novelists that, as Trollope put it, his "great attraction [was] his second-rate characters" who (unlike his idealized protagonists) "live among our friends a rattling, lively, life" (135). These odd creatures serve as more than an entertaining quirk of Dickensian fiction; for Alex Woloch, they are part of an extraordinary democratizing effort to "make more of minor characters," even while their prominence reveals a more profound asymmetry of major and minor (35).[11] Woloch compares the distribution of human complexity among characters to the division of labor among classes. Dickens's "character-system," by his account, reduces minor characters to the functional role of repeating certain gestures and phrases, thus symptomatically enacting their secondary status. The same narrow functionalism might apply to the dramatis personae of any genre (the folktale, for example, per Vladimir Propp's formalist analysis, in which characters serve as "donors," "helpers," "dispatchers," and so forth rather than as free human agents). Yet Woloch finds a "distortion" in figures like Krook and Quilp that is distinctively Dickensian; such characters, for all the noise they make, remain "trapped in their minorness" (156). While his analysis of character space yields illuminating insight into novelistic form, Woloch's argument seems to proceed on the assumption that every fictional persona is a potential protagonist, artificially hemmed in and stunted by being relegated to a minor role. Such an assumption has the effect of naturalizing the literary conventions of characterization surrounding novel protagonists as though they were the features of real individuals. It implies that to be a Nell Trent, a Florence Dombey, an Esther Summerson, or an Arthur Clennam is to enjoy a quality of human freedom denied to the majority of other characters; in practice, the presumptive depth and agency of these protagonists is no less constructed than the exteriority and compulsive self-repetition of their counterparts.

To be a protagonist, further, is not to be exempt from the fate that befalls Dickens's "second-rate characters," as Trollope called them. While Woloch finds fiction isolating "the one" from "the many," such illegitimate children as Esther and Arthur are no more secure in their status as distinctive individuals than such oddities as Grandfather Smallweed or Mr. Turveydrop can be equated with an anonymous "many." Such memorably named and consistently grotesque figures in fact stand out in starker relief against the "roaring streets" into which Arthur and Amy disappear together at the end of *Little Dorrit* (859). This image of individuals vanishing into the crowd is the exact counterpart of what takes place aesthetically when Jo is made to "stand forth" from a multitude of others—all of them, from a statistical point of view, superfluous. These two devices show why major and minor characters cannot be ontologically separate; from both directions, Dickens's novels undermine even their own apparent distinctions between the one and the many.

Attending to the function of supernumeraries reveals that Dickens's fiction performs its most vital work through what might almost be called its third-rate characters: those who are so inseparable from their milieu that they often remain nameless, susceptible to being confused with, substituted for, or merged with others, virtually ceasing to be characters at all.[12] Circulating infectiously through narratives in which they have no evident function other than to live and die in incomprehensibly large numbers, they give form to the novel's urban Gothic ecosystem, evincing a strange capacity to collapse all distinctions between "round" and "flat," subject and object. Their multiplicity resolves into an uncontainable yet positively charged non-identity, thus lending unexpected credence to the otherwise dubious condition described as "nobody's state of mind" (*Little Dorrit* 325–38). While such formulations as "Nobody's Fault," in *Little Dorrit* and elsewhere, seem freighted with bitter satire in their disavowal of personal agency, Esther's frequent references to herself as "Somebody" in *Bleak House* simultaneously point in the direction of particularity and anonymity. As the indefinite pronoun inevitably implies, Somebody might, for all intents and purposes, be Anybody. Like her unknown father, whose moniker of "Nemo" is Latin for "no one" and who earns, in death, "his pretensions to that name" (166, 167), the novel's heroine proves no exception to the principle of impersonality.

Critics have credited Esther's character with a unique status in the novel that seems to exempt her from the limitations placed on every other character. She benefits, in the view of Pam Morris, from a capacity to "bridge . . . without collapsing public and private interests, subjective and objective perspectives, individual and aggregate realities" (131). Viewed in this light, Esther appears exemplary of the Victorian ethos of personal responsibility: an ethos expressed in the accusatory voice of Gridley, the enraged Chancery litigant who demands to confront the individual agents behind an impersonal legal system "face to face" before dying (252). Yet the outcome of Esther's close contact with Jo inverts the logic of individual accountability implied in the prospect of such a face-to-face encounter. The disease she contracts from the young transient disfigures her, so radically altering her features as to render her unrecognizable; as Bruce Robbins has observed, her personal effort to confront the impersonal forces at work in the city ironically leaves her faceless (224). As if merging with the anonymous crowd from which Jo materialized and to which he exposed her, Esther loses, as she puts it, her "old face"—and in the throes of delirium, "all [her] experiences" dissolve into nothing (555). Even she, despite her relative prominence in the story, is not immune to losing the very characteristics (from her physical features to her memories) that would externally or internally separate her from the rest of London's population. In a novel whose personae can, like Mr. Smallweed, unexpectedly "collapse into a shapeless bundle," restored to life only by vigorous poking and violent shaking (427), or, like Krook, spontaneously combust, anyone and everyone may become, as George Rouncewell describes himself, a "self-unmade" man (845).

The Sickness unto Life

> The course of the social disease from which England is suffering is the same as the course of a physical disease; it develops, according to certain laws, has its own crisis, the last and most violent of which determines the fate of the patient. And as the English nation cannot succumb under the final crisis, but must come forth from it, born again, rejuvenated, we can but rejoice over everything which accelerates the course of the disease.
>
> —Friedrich Engels, *The Condition of the Working Class in England*

It is neither as a character nor even as representative of a class but above all as the means of contagion that Jo fulfills his transformative function in the novel. He illustrates, in an obvious sense, one of the public health risks that reformers of the 1840s and 50s aimed to avert through improved sanitation infrastructure, including ventilation and drainage. And Dickens certainly maintained that sanitary reform "must precede all other reforms; and . . . without it all other reforms must fail" ("To Working Men" 227). Yet the plot of *Bleak House* relies on the propagation of infection rather than the containment or prevention of illness. The purpose of this outbreak narrative is not so much to warn of the need for disease prevention as to dramatize the permeability of class boundaries. While typhoid, cholera, smallpox, and other viral and bacterial illnesses all too evidently flourish in the city's most crowded quarters and disproportionately kill the poor, their potential for transmissibility is unlimited. It is possible to read this cynically as implying that infectious diseases are a problem only insofar as they affect a larger social body that includes the middle class, or else simply as equating poverty with pathology—a false medicalization of social inequality. Both of these perspectives indeed shed some light on the governing agenda that motivated the Sanitary Commission, as the previous chapter suggested. But for Dickens, the invisible presence of a disease that passes from one stratum of society to another is at times the only means of materially expressing otherwise occluded commonalities among socioeconomically segregated bodies.

This is just the purport of the morality fable "Nobody's Story," a Christmas tale in which Dickens narrates the spread of a pestilence that seems to originate in the squalid and overcrowded quarters of a laborer called Nobody but quickly decimates his master's family and an entire community without regard to class. The depersonalized protagonist of this allegory, when questioned by the aggrieved master, speculates that while "most calamities will come from us, as this one did, . . . none will stop at our poor doors" (65). The plague in this story follows a Christian apocalyptic schema of divine justice that levels worldly distinctions. It recalls Mary Shelley's *The Last Man*, which (as noted in chapter 1) similarly revived the old plague trope of the *danse macabre* in imagining the brutal equality of mass death. Sickness and mortality are plainly not dealt out with an even hand under all but the most exceptional circumstances, as Dickens recognized, nor is political attention evenly distributed. The ranks of Nobody—like Jo in *Bleak House*—are "little likely to be heard of . . . except when there is some trouble," as Nobody himself acknowledges; yet he goes on to insist in a monologue to his master that such trouble "never begins with me, and it never can end with me. As sure as Death, it comes down to me, and it goes up from me" (65). In this story, as in *Bleak House*, the class structure is so ideologically and materially entrenched that there is no way to unsettle the hierarchy it ensures other than by letting loose a biological hazard indifferent to class identity. The truth that crosses social boundaries in these narratives is simply the common species character revealed through exposure to illness. To have human physiology is to be vulnerable.

Dickens is not alone in recognizing the significance of this fact. In Charles Kingsley's Christian socialist tract "Cheap Clothes and Nasty," the clothes produced by sweatshop labor turn out to be "tainted"—not only morally, as Thomas Hood's dolorous ballad of an overworked seamstress in "The Song of the Shirt" had suggested, but also quite literally,

> for it comes out now that diseases numberless are carried home in these same garments from the miserable abodes where they are made. . . . These wretched creatures, when they have pawned their own clothes and bedding, will use as substitutes the very garments they are making. So Lord ——'s coat has been seen covering a group of children blotched with small pox. The Rev. D—— finds himself suddenly unpresentable from a cutaneous disease, which it is not polite to mention on the south of Tweed, little dreaming that the shivering dirty being who made his coat has been sitting with his arms in the sleeves for warmth while he stitched at the tails. The charming Miss C—— is swept off by typhus or scarlatina, and her parents talk about "God's heavy judgement and visitation"—had they tracked the girl's new riding habit back to the stifling undrained hovel where it served as a blanket to the fever-stricken slop worker, they would have seen why God had visited them. (xii–xiii)

The scenario Kingsley describes might be read not simply as an anticipation of but as an unexpected counternarrative to Marx's classic account of commodity fetishism. Whereas the commodity in *Capital* (famously exemplified in Marx's hypothetical coat) is the great concealer of the secret source of surplus value's extortion, "Lord ——'s coat" ironically mediates the material conditions of production that its very form would seem to obscure.[13] Of course it cannot, as a commodity in exchange, represent the reified social relations or the specific human labor that is its provenance. Yet at the precise moment when it realizes its use-value, it becomes an accidental substrate for an unexpressed relation between bodies that manifests itself as contagion. Conveying the absent presence of the "wretched creatures" who sewed it through the mysterious agency of the diseases they carry, the garment forcibly transmits misery and death from the sphere of production to the sphere of consumption.

Here, metonymy is not simply a rhetorical device but the figural expression of a material truth that eludes the logic of exchange: the environmental contiguity of bodies and things and the contingency of their very matter. In *Bleak House*, Jo becomes both the medium and the substance of this truth.

Through the vehicle of his diseased body, "Tom" (the personification of Tom-all-Alone's) "has his revenge" on the society that begat him:

> There is not a drop of Tom's corrupted blood but propagates infection and contagion somewhere. It shall pollute, this very night, the choice stream . . . of a Norman house, and his Grace shall not be able to say Nay to the infamous alliance. There is not an atom of Tom's slime, not a cubic inch of any pestilential gas in which he lives, not one obscenity or degradation about him . . . but shall work its retribution, through every order of society. (710)

Like those tainted articles of clothing by means of which infection permeates class boundaries and indiscriminately enters houses and bodies, Jo serves as a relay for "infection and contagion" (and thus, "retribution") even as he notably disappears from description. He is metonymic in the most absolute sense—a sense not captured by a critical tradition that equates metonymy with the figural logic of realist reference.[14] Resisting metaphorization, with its suspension of substance and substitution of signs, he is not a referential bearer of deferred meaning—not the index of mimetic realism's absent real—but a site of contact among multiple bodies, objects, and identities. If "Tom" metaphorically embodies, personifies, *represents* the "crowd of foul existence" inhabiting Tom-all-Alone's (256), Jo is simply *of* it: an arbitrary instance of its uncontainability.

The narrator's allegorization of epidemic as retribution accords with Dickens's charge in *Household Words* that public indifference to pestilence and health hazards among "the dwellings of the poor" is tantamount to "wholesale murder" ("To Working Men" 226). Even in identifying the crime, however, the novel's sanitary plot resists holding any individual accountable for a problem that so obviously exceeds the scope of individual agency. Though Esther is appalled by Skimpole's callous suggestion that the suffering child be turned away, his reasoning that such a contagious body is "not safe" proves no less sound than Bucket's avoidance of a procession carrying a corpse that he perceives only as "the fever coming up the street" (493, 358). By contrast, Esther's unflagging dedication to the principle of individual responsibility does more harm than good. Her voluntarism not only fails to save the dying boy but also infects Charley and herself with the disease. Further, her contact with Jo sets into motion a series of events leading to Tulkinghorn's discovery of the scandal of her birth, her mother's subsequent flight and ignoble death, and the fall of the House of Dedlock.

This is not to say that the plot punishes Esther individually for ministering to the needs of another individual. Quite the contrary: in allowing the ravages of disease rather than the force of personal intention to determine the course of events, the novel projects a transpersonal field of power—an epidemiology of power, one might almost say—that does not recognize an individuated subject. The population of *Bleak House* is brought into communication through the agency of an epidemic that violates established distinctions between bodies and among the stratified spaces of the city; "When the East End sneezes," as Eagleton puts it, "the West End catches a cold, if not something altogether more lethal" (Preface ix). It is through the infection of Esther via Charley, as much as through Jo, that Tom's revenge on "every order of society" finds expression. The outcome, though, is not simply revenge but a curious reordering of those separate milieux. The protagonist's illness becomes a link in the fateful "chain of circumstances" connecting her to her unknown parents, rich and poor, whom Jo unwittingly reunites in death (468).[15] It indirectly reveals and conceals the secret of her identity and the original "infamous alliance" through which she was conceived: the prior sexual transgression "polluting" the noble family. Sickness at once brings her into contact with her concerned mother and affirms her own self-effacing drive quite literally, its scarring symptoms masking the resemblance between mother and daughter by rendering Esther nearly unidentifiable. Noticing on recovery that Charley has removed her mirror and quickly guessing why, Esther refers to her face not as disfigured but as absent: "I hope I can do without my old face very well," she reassures the young maidservant and fellow orphan who strangely resembles her (558). This suggestion of a pure lack of characteristics, a blank rather than a change, persists when Esther takes courage to confront her reflection: "I had expected nothing definite," she recalls, "and I dare say anything definite would have surprised me"; whatever she had before, "it was all gone now" (572). In losing her distinguishing external characteristics, the character whose tale has been read as "a true liberal story of individualism" becomes nearly indistinguishable from the mass.[16]

Disease transmission in *Bleak House* thus operates as the organizing principle of an otherwise obscurely connected social body. It alternatively reveals and substitutes for other suppressed social relationships that are likewise transacted in the contact between bodies—notably, illicit sexuality and secret consanguinity. In this novel, as in *The Last Man*, disease invisibly occupies and effectively closes the imagined space between classed bodies, expanding the scope of community on the basis of mere susceptibility to the conditions of city life. It thus bears out Ernesto Laclau's insight that the sociopolitical metaphor of contagion (phobic though it may seem, for example, in Gustave Le Bon's account of crowd psychology) does not necessarily point toward pathology but may instead serve as "the expression of a common feature shared by a group of people, one which is difficult to verbalize in a direct way, and can be expressed only by some form of symbolic representation" (28).

Given that Esther survives the disease that kills Jo, it would be easy enough to read her recovery as part of an effort to consolidate a healthy middle-class body as the national norm: a body tested and proven fit to survive the risks afflicting less healthy forms of life (the extremes of the enervated aristocracy and the sickly underclass).[17] Yet the heroine's survival does not simply restore her to her former state. Though her life is spared, the transformative effects of her encounter with a child of the streets also leave their disfiguring mark in more ways than one. Even after she becomes "useful . . . and attached to life again" (557) and convinces herself that she "could not have been intended to die, or [she] would never have lived" (586), no affirmation of her individual utility can shield her from the "crowding reflections" that continue to beset her (791). This psychic crowding extends one of the defining sensations she experienced in her feverish state: "a curious sense of fullness, as if [she] were becoming too large altogether" (502). Esther's sense of exceeding the physical confines of her body merges her psychologically as well as physiologically with a heterogeneous crowd that subsumes her particularity.

This state is not just a delusion. It is an expressive form of resistance to the privatization of life. Esther's sensory experience breaks through what Esposito would theorize as "the artificial vacuum created around [and constituting] every individual"—the immunitary structure by which the individual is apparently "protected from the negative border that makes him himself and not another" (61). A similar symptom afflicts Stephen Blackpool in *Hard Times*: the uneasy factory worker wanders the streets of Coketown plagued by thoughts about the circumstances of his life that give him "an unwholesome sense of growing larger, of being placed in some new and diseased relation towards the objects among which he passed" (82). This shared sensation of bodily enlargement cements the connection between Esther, typically regarded as an ideally self-contained individual, and characters who seem designed to personify unruly masses. Both figures are in this respect linked to the superhuman largeness and multifariousness of Frankenstein's creature. They thus share in the aesthetic and sensory trope of Gothic aggregation—easily associated with monstrosity but more meaningfully connected, as suggested in chapter 1, with popular sovereignty. Stephen and Esther, far from being set apart from the crowd other than in being singled out as characters, demonstrate that anyone may embody, haphazardly and temporarily, the life of the *demos*.

This is the case even when direct connections to collective existence remain hidden or interrupted. Indeed, all of Esther's symptoms express something unmistakably real that surpasses the particularity of her medical condition. Her every sensation is articulated in the language of political processes that Dickens and his characters alike are apt to describe as natural phenomena. In addition to the feeling of growing larger, she experiences a sensation that "great water-gates seemed to be opening and closing in [her] head, or in the air" (913). This imagery pointedly echoes the figural language of two sets of metaphors that prove directly connected: first, Sir Leicester Dedlock's dread of the ends of aristocratic privilege as an "opening of floodgates" (450), and second, the impersonal narrator's conceit of the "polluted stream" of the old Norman house tainted by "Tom's" blood (a conceit that equates Jo, the child of Tom-all-Alone's, with Esther, bastard child of Lady Dedlock). These fluvial and oceanic figures, connected to the circulation of blood through the anatomy of society, belong to a vocabulary of terms describing the crowd that "flow[s] . . . in two streams" through London's streets and floods the space of the story (315, 359). They reinforce the suggestion that it is none other than the docile Esther who, after Jo's death, comes to embody the feared opening of floodgates. Unbeknownst to her, Esther herself is the specter that reputedly haunts Chesney Wold; her existence confirms the legend of the Ghost's Walk, associated from the start with revolutionary forces surfacing from within the very order of the family. The sound of footsteps attributed to the ghost of a former Lady Dedlock who took the Parliamentarian side (against her husband) in the English Civil War portend doom to the noble family whenever they are heard. The current Lady Dedlock hears the insistent step of the ghost, thinking, "what step does it most resemble? A man's? A woman's? The pattering of a little child's feet, ever coming on—on—on?" (457). Esther's altered body emerges on the other side of illness as a corporeal form of mass life—a veiled, faceless figure who uncannily takes on the characteristics of the dead as well as the living, incarnating at once the social body in all its largeness and the remainder that still exceeds it. As if in consequence of the survival of a life that had no proper place in the social order from the start, the narrative hurtles with increasing force toward a conclusion that decimates "the great old Dedlock family" and levels a moribund aristocratic order.

Dickens writes this social process into his descriptions of environmental conditions as well as bodies. The incursion of some unsettling element that appears external to privileged bodies and private homes is perceptible even in the dampness from the steady "drip, drip, drip" outside the estate in Lincolnshire (21). Moisture permeates the interior spaces of Chesney Wold, where the historic Dedlock portraits seem to "vanish into the damp walls in mere lowness of spirits" (21). Like the downpour that is at once outside and inside, rotting the very images of the aristocratic family's enduring legacy, the sea traversed by Sir Leicester and Lady Dedlock on their return from the Continent "has no appreciation of great men, but knocks them about like the small fry" (184), internally unsettling the baronet's sensitive constitution. Turning his face green with seasickness, the element of water affects "a dismal revolution" in his "aristocratic system" (184). The hydrophobic Sir Leicester has good reason to fear his defenselessness against what he experiences as "the Radical of Nature" (184). Yet he fails to apprehend that the floodgates are already open and that the tide has been steadily rising from the beginning. In the first scene in which the estate appears, a driving rain has turned the "low-lying ground" of the land to which his family claims title into a "stagnant river" (20); returning by a gradual but inevitable process, "the cold and damp steal into Chesney Wold . . . and eke into Sir Leicester's bones" (446). What seeps through his skin, and through the walls and floors of every home from the Dedlock estate to Tom-all-Alone's and from the brickmaker's dank cottage to Bleak House itself, is in fact a threat to more than the entrenched class interests of the hereditary aristocracy. This leveling force that renders bodies indistinguishable points toward the end of all sociopolitical distinction. In simulating the exposure of a population to itself via Jo's circulation, the epidemiology of *Bleak House* leaves the social body radically open and ultimately unbound by individual subjectivity.

Population, Policing, and the Limits of Discipline

> A clerk enters in a thick ledger the name, age, trade, and place of birth of the applicants [to the Asylum for the Houseless Poor of London], as well as where they slept the night before.
>
> As the eye glances down the column of the register, indicating where each applicant has passed the previous night, it is startled to find how often the clerk has had to write down, "in the streets"; so that "ditto," "ditto," continually repeated under the same head, sounded as an ideal chorus of want in the mind's ear.
>
> —Henry Mayhew, *London Labour and the London Poor*

If the problem Jo instantiates cannot be contained by domesticity, neither is it dismissed by killing him off. The Malthusian "positive check" no longer seems plausible as nature's last resort for curtailing population growth. This element of demographic analysis, as the previous chapter noted, was contested and revised during Dickens's lifetime. Chadwick, in the 1840s, rejected

Malthus's account of positive checks as a "dreadful fallacy" and calculated that in the poorest districts, where the mortality rate was highest, the birth rate was still far higher (270). While accepting the basic Malthusian premise that population multiplies beyond its means if left unregulated, the *Sanitary Report* offers evidence to support Chadwick's counterargument that "the ravages of epidemics and other diseases," contra Malthus, "do not diminish but tend to increase the pressure of population" (423). As James Greenwood, reporting on London's "street children," likewise grimly speculates, "Should death tomorrow morning make a clean sweep of the unsightly little scavengers who grovel for a meal amongst the market offal heaps, next day would see the said heaps just as industriously surrounded" (12). Death offers no solution, but neither does discipline. No lesson in self-regulation can secure the survival of the entire population, by these accounts, nor can it produce the autonomous citizen-subject in whose interest liberal institutions are presumed to operate. From the standpoint of discipline, the inability to normalize all individuals looks like a failure of government; from the standpoint of biopower, however, governance entails deciding when not to intervene.

In his perorations on Jo and his milieu, Dickens joins a wave of Victorian journalism in accusing the public of a murderous—and ultimately suicidal—indifference to a problem at once obvious and unknown: the condition of a "vast deal of life," as envisioned by the journalist John Hollingshead, "that skulks or struggles in London" and "burrows in holes and corners, at the back of busy thoroughfares, where few know of its existence, or care to follow it" (*Ragged London* 7). In the press, this specter is perpetually brought to light only to be declared an even greater mystery than it had seemed. "Here is a country," marvels Hollingshead, "that spends one hundred million pounds sterling a year in universal government, and yet allows hundreds of its children, in the metropolis alone, to be annually starved to death" (189). Greenwood, writing of untold numbers of homeless orphans who subsist on garbage, similarly holds that they are "of as small account in the public estimation as stray street curs, and, like them, it is only where they evince a propensity for barking and biting that their existence is recognised" (12). To the scale of the calamity these journalists describe, perhaps no quantity of information could ever suffice. Even while complaining that "[t]he sweepings of society have seldom been carefully traced back to their hiding places," Hollingshead's "London Horrors" series in the *Morning Post* cynically testifies that certain parts of the city "have been visited by day, inspected by night; have formed the text-books of preachers, the back-bones of sanitary reports, and the building materials of popular authors," all to no effect (13). As he sees no avenue for state intervention and no benefit in "tinkering philanthropy," the purpose of his sensational reportage is not altogether clear.

For all the outrage of journalists and novelists, neither public indifference nor lack of knowledge could be plausibly claimed. The sheer volume of
sociological and medical studies of the working class, occupational surveys
of casual labor, and investigative journalism on homelessness, unemployment, and prostitution published in the 1850s alone is overwhelming.[18] The
popularity of such series as those by Mayhew, Greenwood, and Hollingshead
counters the narrator's allegation in *Bleak House* that his contemporaries find
"nothing interesting" about Jo, who seems almost to have wandered into
the novel from *London Labour and the London Poor* (724). Dickens's portrayal
of the young crossing sweeper is informed by (and accords with) Mayhew's
assessment of the crisis that "street-children" represent for British society:

> [E]very means by which a proper intelligence may be conveyed to their
> minds is either closed or at the least tainted, while every duct by which
> a bad description of knowledge may be infused is sedulously cultivated
> and enlarged. Parental instruction; the comforts of a home, however
> humble—the great moral truths upon which society itself rests;—the
> influence of proper example; the power of education; the effect of
> useful amusement; are all denied to them, or come to them so greatly
> vitiated, that they rather tend to increase, rather than to repress, the
> very evils they were intended to remedy. (I: 479)

This lament sounds a note echoed in social criticism throughout the century.
In his own study of "metropolitan social degradation," Hollingshead con-
curred: "With all our electro-plated sentiment about home and the domestic
virtues, we ought to wince a good deal at the houses of the poor" (v–vi). To
wince, however, is a fairly limited program; beyond this gesture, no subsequent action is recommended. If such analyses of deficient "domestic virtues" enshrine the norms of bourgeois culture and the evaluative apparatuses
of a disciplinary society, they do so not simply in regretting the absence of
such norms and apparatuses but in conceding their inevitable failure.

Bleak House takes a more destabilizing approach to social crisis. It extends
the apparent failure of sanitation, stability, and morality into middle-class
homes that would ordinarily model the qualities found wanting in the
city's slums. Indeed, in Dickens's narrative, the spread of disease effectively
undermines the distinction between Tom-all-Alone's, in its "obscenity or
degradation," and Bleak House, in its apparent safety and middle-class propriety. That the novel was originally titled *Tom-all-Alone's* attests in itself to
the erosion of such distinctions. The process seems to be underway even
in the author's preliminary notes, which explore various permutations
of titles and subtitles. On the one hand, the course of revision and selection that ends with the title "Bleak House" might appear to illustrate—in

anticipation of the plot that kills Jo and saves Esther—the teleology of a
series of substitutions and displacements by which the domestic locus of
Esther's narrative comes to supersede the crowded, homeless world that
might have been its subject. On the other hand, the list of working titles that
includes "The Ruined House," "The Solitary House," "The Ruined Building /
Factory / Mill / House" actually elaborates a set of possibilities within which
the architecture of "Bleak House" is not simply analogous to but continuous
with and constructed from the imaginative materials of "Tom-all-Alone's"
(Appendix 3, *Bleak House*). Accordingly, where Dickens's dual narrative form
seems implicitly to stage an ongoing argument between Esther's sentimental personhood and the forces of impersonality, Jo's crossing from one side
to the other renders the conflict all but irrelevant. His passage between the
novel's two narratives, like his movement through the city, troubles the text's
apparent boundaries between domestic and professional, interior and exte-
rior, individual body and statistical mass. In this way, the continual resurfac-
ing of the supernumerary proves its very excessiveness inalienable from the
social categories that occlude it.

What the house fails to contain seems just as inevitably to escape the
grasp of the carceral institutions that domesticity—according to Miller's
seminal thesis—was constructed to render nearly unnecessary. If Victorian
fiction fetishizes a concept of home that its narratives cannot sustain, its
preoccupation with detection operates to similar effect. The novel allows
policing to work only when it does something quite different from what it
claims. This contradiction is evident in a much-cited report of the inefficacy
of Paris police summoned in 1834 to impose a *cordon sanitaire* during a cholera outbreak and to quell a riot by "mobs of chiffoniers." As the prefect of
police recalls:

> My agents . . . could not be at all points at once, to oppose the fury
> of those crowds of men with naked arms and haggard figures, and
> sinister looks, who are never seen in ordinary times, and who seemed
> on this day to have arisen out of the earth. . . . I had great difficulty in
> getting through these dense masses, scarcely covered with filthy rags;
> no description could convey their hideous aspect, or the sensation of
> terror which the hoarse and ferocious cries created. (Chadwick 163)

This spectacle of abjection, which the report frames in a Gothic idiom of
indescribable horror, seems calculated to justify police intervention even as
it demonstrates how limited the gaze of the law really is. The terror excited
by these "dense masses" is simultaneously medical and political, as the prefect's references to the chiffoniers' "filthy rags" and "ferocious cries" attest.

Such eyewitness testimony can and often did furnish ideological support for campaigns to regulate the city by illuminating its dark corners. One need not look to *Discipline and Punish* for this insight; in *The Holy Family*, Marx and Engels already see the impetus for surveillance in Eugène Sue's popular *Mystères de Paris*. "For Parisians in general and even for the Paris police," they sardonically quip, "the hide-outs of criminals are such a 'mystery' that at this very moment broad light streets are being laid out in the *Cité* to give the police access to them" (77–78). Sensationalizing the so-called dangerous classes and claiming to discover new life forms that threaten the social body's survival, as Marx recognized, was a pretext for policing the city in the service of protecting private property. New historicist scholars have been equally quick to identify, in such accounts of urban crisis, an implicit panoptic scheme by which the "'labouring' and 'dangerous' classes would be transformed . . . once they became visible" (Stallybrass and White 135). Yet there is another side to the process of revealing social danger to scrutiny that is not wholly consistent with aggressive police tactics. Visibility is no guarantee of safety—and throwing up one's hands may indicate a distinct approach to policing rather than a drive to impose order or an inability to do so. *Bleak House* suggests as much in tracking the path of Jo, whose brief existence embodies what Hollingshead would describe as "secrets that no census has ever fully exposed" (7). In a story that has often been read as a case study in surveillance and preventive policing, the mass of humanity remains an open secret that resists detection precisely because it has never been, and cannot be, concealed.

Perhaps the most shocking discovery of *Bleak House* is that even the daily activity of the police reveals the insufficiency not only of disciplinary power in preventing deviance and crime but also of law enforcement itself. Dickens's reportage in *Household Words* on his experiences shadowing Inspector Field (a model for Mr. Bucket) describes quite a different form of power at work in the city. Following the detective and constable on their nightly patrol, Dickens is led into London's "innermost recesses" and immersed in the element of mass life ("On Duty with Inspector Field" 316). Police work in this murky realm, it turns out, has less to do with identifying the suspect and solving the unspecified crime under investigation than with the inspector's command to "clear the street, half a thousand of you!" (309). Inspector Field and Constable Rogers hail individuals (sometimes by name) only to tell them "we don't want you" and to order them to disperse (308–9). They demand that "crowds of sleepers" in lodging-houses show their faces only to declare that "it's not you" whom the law seeks (312, 315). Thus, in effect, the police exercise their authority above all in looking the other way.

Dickens here reveals that the object of modern policing—namely, security—is not achieved by detecting every deviation from disciplinary norms or ferreting out every violator of the law but in deciding what can reasonably be ignored. In contrast with the panoptic techniques of discipline, which by Foucault's account necessarily seek to "regulate everything" and "allow . . . nothing to escape" from surveillance, security's distinctive strategy is that of "let[ting] things happen" (literally, *laisser-faire*) in the interest of a broader equilibrium. A direct extension of political economy, the logic of security consists in "allowing prices to rise, allowing scarcity to develop, and letting people go hungry so as to prevent something else happening, namely the introduction of the general scourge of scarcity" (*Security, Territory, Population* 45). This logic, which dictates that the interests of society are served by a certain degree of neglect, does its police work in *Bleak House* merely in repeatedly ordering Jo to "move on."

By allowing his narratives to be governed according to the principle of security, Dickens's fiction confronts the central ideological dilemma of biopower. Victorian institutions, in their effort to preserve equilibrium, approach population as a more or less predictable statistical entity; however, they routinely encounter the human aggregate as something other than this—a surplus of ungovernable life that exceeds and threatens the coherence of society. Dickens, rather than seeking to contain this projected threat, not only allows the surplus to infiltrate the social body in *Bleak House* but also compromises the distinctions it seems to draw between those who rise to the level of individuals and those relegated to the status of disposable life. The novel demonstrates, if nothing else, that population will always exceed its established economic and cultural parameters—a necessary outcome of the demand to harness infinite quantities of human labor and of the imperial ambition to govern the species on a global scale.

This problem is also a condition of possibility. Much as institutions and governments require that which exceeds their administrative capacities and violates their law in order to exist, so too does the novel find in the unmanageable mass of supernumeraries its own peculiar reason of state. What takes place in *Bleak House* necessitates—to the profound frustration of readers, and designedly so—that Jo and his "swarm of misery" remain a greater problem than "Lord Coodle, and Sir Thomas Doodle . . . and all the fine gentlemen in the office, down to Zoodle, shall set right in five hundred years" (256, 257). In producing the longing for an ending it does not offer, the novel stakes the future of social life on the solution to a problem that modern nation-states and capitalist labor markets are designed to leave unresolved (or indeed, perhaps, to perpetuate). Rather than neatly solve the problem its narrative creates, *Bleak House* relentlessly reproduces life in excess of material support and social regulation. It thus exposes the perverse logic by which liberal governance sustains itself not despite but through its administrative failures and contradictions. In so doing, however, the novel also opens up an empty interval between the collective wish for a better ending and the perpetual nonfulfillment of that wish. This gap between the given and the possible is not simply the space occupied by ideology or a concession to the inevitability of inequality. It is rather the demand, and the already present potential, for a political community that has its basis in the human surplus overrunning the recognized limits of the social body—and for an equality that can be sensed in the very density of the city's crowds.

CHAPTER 4

The Sensation Novel and the Redundant Woman Question

> To common sense there was something lacking, and still more obviously something redundant in the nature of this girl who had drawn him to her.
>
> —Thomas Hardy, *Jude the Obscure*

In an 1862 issue of *The National Review*, essayist William Rathbone Greg alerts readers to a demographic trend he regards as new and alarming: nearly a million unmarried English women who, "not having the natural duties and labours of wives and mothers," are compelled to work for a living and "lead an independent and incomplete existence of their own" (47). His article—titled "Why Are Women Redundant?"—cites anecdotal evidence as well as census data to illustrate a deviation from domestic norms, a tendency spanning the class spectrum and surprisingly prevalent among "the middle and upper classes" (47).[1] Among the likely causes he includes disproportionate emigration of men to the colonies, male promiscuity, and the susceptibility of both sexes to "the morbid luxury of the age" (65). These factors conspire to make marriage either statistically impossible or simply less desirable for a large subset of England's female population.[2] If Greg's definition of feminine nature seems to remove women from the sphere of the market, his analysis yields a determinately economic account of female life: the chief problem is that of supply exceeding demand. His article frames the situation of "redundant women" as a devaluation crisis affecting not just unmarried individuals but the nation at large. He recommends prompt intervention, proposing a large-scale population transfer of women to Australia to address this "besetting problem which, like the sphinx's, society must solve or die" (49).[3]

Though there is every reason to doubt Greg's premises, the implications of his argument are both broader and less obvious than they appear. His expressed concerns about the decline of marriage and a surplus of women resonate strikingly with the claims of critics who were just then reading similar signs of social upheaval in the pages of popular fiction. "There can be no doubt," wrote Margaret Oliphant in *Blackwood's*,

> that a singular change has passed upon our light literature. It is not that its power has failed or its popularity diminished—much the reverse; it is because a new impulse has been given and a new current set in the flood of contemporary storytelling. We will not ask whence or from whom the influence is derived. It has been brought into being by society, and it naturally reacts upon society. ("Novels" 173)

The change to which she was referring was the immense success of what critics called the sensation novel, a new genre whose shock appeal relied on the disclosure of a calamitous surplus at the heart of the domestic sphere. "The acknowledged new element of this order of fiction," wrote a reviewer in *The Christian Remembrancer*, "is the uncertainty given to the marriage relation. Unless we go with the bride and bridegroom to church, and know every antecedent on each side, we cannot be at all sure that there is not some husband or wife lurking in the distance ready to burst upon us" ("Our Female Sensation Novelists" 218). Readers were quickly trained to expect, as Alfred Austin affirmed in *The Temple Bar*, "to meet with an inconvenient number of husbands, and a most perplexing superfluity of wives" (413). Notorious for exposing bigamy, adultery, and false identities in seemingly ordinary and often genteel milieux, the novels of Wilkie Collins, Mary Elizabeth Braddon, Ouida, Ellen Wood, and Rhoda Broughton shifted emphasis from the perils of the marriage market to the sanctuary of the household—revealing marriage itself to be equally crowded and unstable.

Until the obscenity scandals provoked by a modernist avant-garde, the British literary world had seen nothing quite like the critical outcry against sensation fiction. In the view of Oliphant and others, the marriage plot had been a secure prospect and a healthy social influence prior to the present generation.[4] The sensation novel's rise seemed to coincide with and cater to a new audience of presumptively female readers whose literary tastes (and, perhaps, life choices) threatened the domestic foundations of British society. By the argument of the genre's most vehement detractors, the relation between this new generation of nondomestic women and the mass-produced print matter they voraciously consumed was not simply mimetic but causal. Calculated to "preach . . . to the nerves instead of the judgment," as H. L. Mansel famously put it, these lurid tales seemed liable to provide a dangerous stimulus to a rapidly expanding readership (482). Critics feared this new mass audience would respond somatically rather than intellectually to the texts put before them and might even mimic the criminal deviance of Braddon's antiheroine, who fakes her own death, assumes a new identity, commits bigamy, tosses her first husband down a well, and goes on to commit arson and another attempted murder before being confined to a madhouse in Belgium.

The novel form, which had once helped normalize domesticity and heterosexual kinship through the marriage plot, now appeared at odds with marriage. Sensation novels blurred the boundaries fiction itself had drawn between those within and those excluded from the household, making their central characters virtually indistinguishable from a multitude of others. In a genre whose classic heroines, from Pamela to Jane Eyre, had played no small part in inventing the modern individual, a flock of female characters now bodied forth the specter of the crowd. Lady Audley, who abandons the role of wife and mother and runs away to London to "lose [herself] in that great chaos of humanity," brings all the heterogeneity and anonymity of the city with her into the traditional country estate she easily infiltrates (Braddon, *Lady Audley's Secret* 362). If domestic fiction showed, as Nancy Armstrong has argued, that "the modern individual was first and foremost a woman" (*Desire and Domestic Fiction* 8), sensation novels transform this woman into a figure for mass population, for a new mass readership, and for the regime of industrial mass production to which both were linked.[5] To put it simply, the sensation novel raised the question of why women are redundant. Addressing this disconcerting question, as this chapter suggests, gives a new genre of fiction its distinctive form.

What is perhaps most surprising about the female surplus animated by sensation fiction is that redundancy is not confined to single women. In this sense, the novels of Braddon, Collins, and Wood write Greg's dilemma into their plots even while challenging his solution. Against the critical claim (notably, in D. A. Miller's reading of Collins) that sensation fiction dramatizes the violation of norms in order to reinforce them, these novels hardly keep the world safe for marriage. The crowding of the household belies the liberal distinction between the realm of the market and the supposedly extra-economic relations of the hearth. Further, if the concept of female redundancy is founded on the most transparent form of gender ideology, as Mary Poovey has argued, its consequences are far from ideologically consistent with Greg's own claim that only those who "are supported by, and . . . administer to, men" fulfill the "essentials of woman's being" (Greg 74).[6] For all the tendentiousness of Greg's insistence on naturalizing gender difference and defending the cultural imperatives of marriage and domesticity, the very premise of a redundant population effectively decouples sexuality from gender. This decoupling would later make it possible for Edward Carpenter to praise "homogenic love" and argue for the emancipation of sexuality from any procreative mandate on the basis that "not only Man (the male) objects to lower Nature's method of producing superfluous individuals only to kill them off again in the struggle for existence; but Woman objects to being a mere machine for perpetual reproduction" (*Love's Coming of Age* 177–78). Greg's own statistical inference also has the ironic effect of providing a rationale for the independence of women faced with narrowing matrimonial prospects. This rationale is most succinctly articulated thirty years later by Rhoda Nunn, the feminist heroine of George Gissing's *The Odd Women*, who embraces the female surplus as "a great reserve" ready for training to do "the world's work" (41). Arguments for sexual equality earlier in the century had often been backed by demographic claims; to John Stuart Mill, for example, "the industrial and social independence of women" was desirable not least of all because it would result in "a great diminution of the evil of over-population" (*Principles of Political Economy* 139). It is likely that the motive for Victorian writers' interest in the Woman Question, and much of the impetus for feminism itself, emerges from (and remains bound up with) the redundant woman question.[7]

This chapter explains why a particular narrative version of redundancy became paradoxically central to fiction as well as to the sexual and cultural politics of criticism. Here, it is worth recalling this book's larger claims. I have argued thus far that a demographic surplus rather than any individual, group, or social type forms the Victorian novel's most elemental human material, and that this surplus, which fictional narratives aim (not always successfully) to manage at the level of biological life, exposes the inadequacy of existing political structures. As defined by Thomas Malthus, surplus population was an economic fact; insofar as gender entered into his calculus, it did so as a function of sexual instinct and marriage, held responsible for geometric human reproduction. The novels discussed in this chapter, by contrast, disconnect redundancy (at least outwardly) from class and align it with women in ways that destabilize class distinction, denaturalize gender, and reverse the very plot devices that used to offer middle-class heroines an irreversible and irreplaceable social position. To do so, they devise different literary tactics for handling population. First, the paradigm of the redundant woman allowed fiction to incorporate specters of mass population into an ungovernable female body—a figure Gustave Le Bon would later apply to the crowd in his study of mob psychology. "Like women," he remarks, the crowd "goes at once to extremes," producing violent excesses of affect that suspend personal responsibility and make possible "sentiments and acts impossible for the isolated individual" (70). This first move—the incorporation of the multiple into the singular—enables the novel then to expel the living remainder that eludes individual regulation (hence the deaths of fallen women so prevalent in Victorian literature). The removal of this excess reveals one of the stranger forms of the narrative logic by which fiction dealt out life and death to the inhabitants of a crowded social world.

Such crowding is not immediately evident in sensation fiction. In contrast with industrial fiction's riot scenes or the swarming streets of the Dickensian city novel discussed in chapters 2 and 3, Braddon's *Lady Audley's Secret* and Wood's *East Lynne* construct a far quieter and seemingly more restricted sphere: a household, a provincial community, a limited field of characters. They return to the milieu of domestic fiction only to reveal that the pressures of population are active even in the space of the home. While masses and crowds are almost never directly represented in these novels, the narrative dynamics of aggregation nonetheless overcrowd and compromise the domestic sphere. More conventional marriage plots routinely alleviated such pressures by rendering their heroines worthy of marriage while expelling others or allowing them to die. Readers of *Mary Barton*, for example, could scarcely object to the inevitability with which Elizabeth Gaskell's plot sends Mary's aunt Esther to an early grave, not least because the alcoholic prostitute provides a counterexample against which to measure Mary's self-possession and worthiness to rise above the masses. The contrast is still more pronounced in *Bleak House*, where Esther Summerson's ruined mother, Lady Dedlock, must die in the street before the daughter can be suitably married. The sensation genre's plot twists, by contrast, deliberately remove just such qualitative distinctions among characters. Thus, the double strategy of incorporation and abjection fails to rid the novel of the surplus population it generates. This narrative strategy shapes not only recognizably sensational texts but also critically acclaimed novels that do not at first glance appear to observe the new standard it sets—calling into question realism's presumptive separateness from sensationalism.

The unanticipated influence of *Lady Audley's Secret*—one of the bestselling novels of the nineteenth century—is a case in point. Despite critical consensus in the 1860s that Braddon's book was exceptionally bad, it is difficult to find a traditional domestic novel written after its publication. (A glance at Gissing and Hardy, discussed in the next chapter, reveals how unsustainable the marriage plot had become by the 1890s.) The sensation novel's literary conventions provide a formula almost compulsively repeated both in its own shrill reception and in much of the fiction that follows. In the controversy the genre sparked, the connection between the discourse of mass population and that of literary mass culture comes to the fore. This connection may account for the surprisingly long critical afterlife of the short-lived genre. Sensation fiction's own alleged redundancy has a lasting impact on the ambivalent project of national canon-building—illustrating the extent to which criticism itself relies on the conception of an overcrowded literary field in need of regulation.

Strategic claims of redundancy motivate literary criticism well into the twentieth century. When F. R. Leavis declares that "the great English novelists are Jane Austen, George Eliot, Henry James and Joseph Conrad," he defines this national "Great Tradition" specifically against mass culture (1). Victorian criticism had laid out the terms for Leavis's project by positing a surplus of inferior cultural material. As early as the 1860s, what Malthus once called redundant population had come to connote another form of excess: an uncontrollable mass of texts mobbing the literary world. This discourse signals a peculiarly biopolitical turn in criticism; the problem of how to manage surplus population resurfaces here as a metaphor for critical practice. Adopting an evolutionary logic of selection, Victorian critics set themselves the task of ensuring the survival of culturally "fit" texts at the expense of ostensibly weaker forms. Such a model depends on the disposability of most cultural material—just as Leavis's canon depends on a mass of expendable texts, and the sensation plot on a mass of expendable bodies.

Interlopers

> "Give me any name you like," she said; "I have as much right to one as to another."
>
> —Wilkie Collins, *No Name*

To some Victorian writers, the onslaught of trashy fiction described by Oliphant and Mansel was not accidentally related to the female surplus population Greg identified; redundant women were the source of such fiction. Indeed, Greg himself makes this connection, observing that a growing Victorian taste for luxury and entertainment was giving rise to

> a large and increasing call for a supply of literary food, such as many well-educated women find themselves fully able to furnish; and if only those who are really competent to this work were to undertake it, it would keep them in ample independence. Novels are now almost as

indispensable a portion of the food of English life as beef or beer; and no producers are superior to women, either as to delicate handling or abundant fertility. ("Why" 37)

That many who were not "really competent to this work" had nonetheless taken to writing novels was a pervasive complaint in the 1850s and 60s. George Eliot—even as she denies that women possess any special qualification or any inherent disadvantage as writers—had little patience for the growing demographic of "lady novelists" whose work she ridiculed.[8] G. H. Lewes similarly notes an overabundance of authors in his 1865 introduction to the *Fortnightly Review*, describing a literary world "thronged with incompetent aspirants" hoping to make a living. "Still lower in the ranks," he writes, "are those who follow Literature simply because they see no other opening for their incompetence; just as forlorn widows and ignorant old maids thrown suddenly on their own resources open a school—no other means of livelihood seeming to be within their reach" (21). By the logic of his simile, literature plays host to a parasitic mass whose lack of qualification is best conveyed by reference to figures of redundant women.

These accounts of literary overproduction draw on a key trope of sensation novels. Rather than presenting the oversaturation of the market as a condition from which one can find refuge in the family, the novels of Braddon and Wood subject the household to the same forces of mass circulation and devaluation. They allow female characters of unknown origin to drift in and out of the domestic spaces of the novel as effortlessly as pages of newsprint. In introducing the enchanting governess who so quickly won Sir Michael Audley's heart, Braddon's narrative lays great emphasis on the fact that "no one knew anything of her except that she came in answer to an advertisement . . . in the *Times*" (*Lady Audley's Secret* 47). Equating the protagonist's movement with the anonymous circulation of disposable mass media, such novels as *Lady Audley's Secret* and *East Lynne* sweep away all qualitative distinctions based on taste and morality—the very distinctions that, in earlier marriage plots, seemed to promise social mobility to the right sort of woman in order to guarantee a stable basis for English society. Just as sensation novels were disparaged as mass-manufactured "to meet an ephemeral demand, aspiring only to an ephemeral existence," the women who populate their narratives became metonymic of this condition of disposability (Mansel 485). Echoing the paradoxical fascination of such disposable heroines for the male characters who cannot resist their charms, the sensation novel's own unaccountable popularity appeared to call distinction itself into question.

By destabilizing the marriage market, in other words, sensation fiction created a problem at the level of the book market: selecting a worthy spouse or a worthy novel seemed fraught with peril in the face of a surplus and under conditions of mass circulation. In his noted *Quarterly Review* essay on this new disreputable genre, Mansel laments the circumstances under which cheap fiction is bought and sold, describing railway bookstall displays catering to passengers who have no time "for examining the merits of a book before purchasing it" (485). Like Lady Audley herself, the enticing book covers are designed simply to attract and, in so doing, defy any qualitative basis for selection. Mansel's imagined scene in which an unsuspecting reader is automatically drawn to one of these unworthy novels perfectly replicates the scene of fatal attraction in *Lady Audley's Secret*. On seeing the almost child-like blonde beauty who calls herself Lucy Graham, the wealthy baronet in Braddon's novel "could no more resist the tender fascination of those soft and melting blue eyes . . . than he could resist his destiny" and falls prey to "this fever, this longing," sensations he has never known (48). Judging the book by its cover, he immediately proposes marriage—little suspecting the risks of bigamy and fraud. His nephew Robert Audley, the amateur detective who attempts to track down this mysterious woman's hidden identity, seems justified in wondering whether any prospect in life could be less certain than that of marriage: "Who is to say which shall be the one judicious selection out of nine hundred and ninety-nine mistakes? Who shall decide from the first aspect of the slimy creature, which is to be the one eel out of the colossal bag of snakes?" (225).

Almost from the moment she appeared in the *Sixpenny Magazine* in 1862, the enigmatic Lady Audley presented a new kind of heroine and a new kind of problem for the Victorian novel. Rather than a lone woman who has lost her place in the social order (a character, like Jane Eyre, in search of a home), she belongs nowhere by virtue of the fact that she occupies many positions at once. With regard to Greg's thesis—that too many English women do not marry either because male colonial emigration prevents it or because they prefer independence and luxury—Braddon's plot merges both scenarios, reverses their causation, and yet yields the same result. Lady Audley, formerly Helen Talboys, changes her name to Lucy Graham and becomes a governess only after her first husband leaves for Australia in search of work; she then marries Sir Michael under false pretenses in order to secure wealth and comfort. In so doing, she exposes the redundancy of every position defined by domestic fiction, demonstrating that virtually everyone with whom she associates is replaceable: George Talboys, the first husband she no longer needs; Matilda Plowson, the consumptive girl she buries as her proxy; Alicia

Audley, daughter of her second husband, whom Lady Audley displaces as the main object of Alicia's father's affections as well as her cousin Robert's romantic interest. To this string of displacements she adds the population of castoff lives she herself has led.

While Robert Audley's investigation seems to locate the *telos* of the narrative in the discovery of his young aunt's secret identity and hidden past, his findings are less conclusive than they appear. Braddon's novel refuses to confirm that the established facts of an individual's character, bodily appearance, or genealogy contain any fixed meaning or essential truth. The suggestion that Lady Audley may carry the "hereditary taint" of her mother's madness remains dubious in the end as an explanation for her crimes—enough so to make critics complain that her portrayal "leaves the impression, not of an evil woman, or a mad woman, or any definite kind of woman" ("Lady Audley's Secret," *The Spectator* 1197). Finding no textual evidence for the diagnosis of madness, the *Spectator*'s review of the novel objected that its "author should have shown us her mind, painted the struggle with the momentary flashes of insanity, and the remorse which would so certainly have followed them," as though this foreclosure of interiority were accidental (1197). All other known details of this woman's personal history tend to equate her with rather than differentiate her from the rest of the novel's female population. Robert's own misogynistic reveries render the *femme fatale* unexceptional: "How these women take life out of our hands," he marvels, "Helen Maldon, Lady Audley, Clara Talboys, and now Miss Tonks—all womankind from beginning to end" (256).

The very idea of womankind set forth in sensation discourse is in excess of itself almost by definition. Victorian critic E. S. Dallas only reasserts this paradox when he attempts to explain why female novelists create characters that violate the constraints he assigns to femininity:

> It is certainly curious that one of the earliest results of an increased feminine influence in our literature should be a display of what in women is most unfeminine. One is reminded of the famous fact that the first record of feminine conduct in the world's history is unfeminine. Eve is said to have eaten the apple in a masculine lust of power— to be as the gods; Adam in a feminine weakness of affection for the mate who offered it. (*The Gay Science* 298)

In his reading of the narrative of the Fall from Paradise, even before a feminine norm has been established, female nature has already emptied it of any meaning retroactively ascribed to it. The feminine consequently refers to a category that has been abandoned or undone from the beginning; it disappears at the first moment of history and thus can never claim any positive content. Woman, then, is neither a stable essence nor even a performative construction of identity but a role that cannot be fulfilled.

For this reason, despite later critics' view of the detective plots of sensation novels as successful attempts to install a regime of surveillance within the household, Lady Audley's is a secret that is not so much revealed as replicated by detection.[9] The disclosure that she is really Mrs. George Talboys, *née* Helen Maldon (rather than Lady Audley, *née* Lucy Graham) is less a revelation of her true self than a suggestion that all four of these names refer to something provisional. And once the mystery is ostensibly solved, Braddon's narrative can conclude only by adding to the potentially endless series of pseudonyms: when Robert finally commits her to the asylum, "the wretched woman who had borne so many names" is checked in as "Madame Taylor" (434). Removing this supposedly abnormal specimen from the English population and isolating her from society, moreover, can scarcely remedy the larger problem that she instantiates. In effect, as the proliferation of personae suggests, Lady Audley could be anyone—or everyone, perhaps, given the ease with which at least two other characters (her maid Phoebe Marks and Matilda Plowson) pass for her and take her place.[10] The play of likeness and difference among these and other women formulates itself in this novel not merely as a substitution of roles or a doubling of individuals but as a perpetual fugue of arbitrary distinctions.[11] No wonder, then, that the novel's resolution brought no relief to critics who named it the most vile of all modern books. Braddon's narrative does not actually eliminate the threat of redundancy from the novel's world; on the contrary, it erodes the conventional boundary between the self-regulating individual and the unmanageable multitude.

Such a threat was no more easily removed from Ellen Wood's bestselling *East Lynne*; the tale of Isabel Vane's fall likewise begins and ends with the problem of the redundant woman. If *Lady Audley's Secret* proved that the daughter of a poor drunkard could easily shed all traces of her origins and infiltrate the British aristocracy, *East Lynne* proves that the daughter of an earl can just as easily lose her name, face, and claims to family, property, and pedigree. Left impoverished and displaced from her ancestral home upon the death of her father, the dissipated Earl of Mount Severn, Lady Isabel is unexpectedly thrown on the mercy of strangers: "Instead of being a young lady of position, of wealth and rank, she appeared to herself more in the light of an unfortunate pauper; an interloper in the house she was inhabiting" (141). Wood's narrative defends its melodramatic premise, in its own fulsome style, with classically realist truth claims to authenticate and even universalize the perils facing its unfortunate protagonist. "It has been the custom in romance," the narrator remarks, "to represent young ladies, especially if they are handsome and interesting, as being altogether oblivious of everyday cares and necessities, supremely indifferent to the future prospects of poverty—poverty that brings hunger and thirst and cold and nakedness in its train; but, be assured, this apathy never exists in real life" (141). Wood's salient use of the definite article insistently generalizes "the future prospects of poverty," as though this were not her heroine's unique fate but any woman's potential circumstance.

If Lady Isabel's aristocratic title cannot protect the orphaned girl from dispossession, neither can a middle-class marriage to the kindly solicitor Archibald Carlyle restore her to a suitable place in the household. From the first moment, every position in the domestic sphere is already occupied, every function fulfilled. Cornelia Carlyle, the spinster sister-in-law (a relation that would ordinarily put her outside this household), moves into East Lynne—significantly, having been displaced from her own home by her brother's marriage—and serves as mistress of the house. Isabel's husband is perpetually occupied either at work or in private meetings with the unmarried Barbara Hare (whom she suspects to be Carlyle's actual love interest, and who in fact will take her place as Mrs. Carlyle after Isabel is reported dead). Her situation models what George Eliot would later describe as the "gentlewoman's oppressive liberty" (*Middlemarch* 274), with the difference that Wood configures the paradoxical trap of the aristocratic woman's freedom as an outcome of relative overpopulation. With her children cared for by servants and no other prescribed function left for her to serve, Isabel is just one too many in a household already overpopulated with women. Thus, for all the scandal of her seduction by the classic libertine who carries her off to France, her flight from East Lynne is not so much a desertion of her proper place as a concession to her own self-evident redundancy.

To be sure, Wood's narrative scrupulously avoids justifying its fallen heroine's actions. The novel presents itself as the most extreme sort of object lesson in sexual morality: "Oh reader, believe me! Lady—wife—mother!" the narrator expostulates, "should you ever be tempted to abandon your home," a similar fate awaits you (334). But its critics were unconvinced that its declamatory moralism was sincere. The shock that greeted this novel's publication suggests that readers felt a contrary ethical pull, perhaps because the act for which Isabel is so harshly punished comes about so arbitrarily (or at least so circumstantially) that it could happen to anyone. In fact, rather than singling her out as abnormal, even her punishment merges her with a multitude: she is maimed and disfigured by a railway accident in France that leaves her and all the other passengers in "one confused mass" (373). Compelled to watch her illegitimate child die, prematurely aged by remorse, and presumed dead by all who know her, the adulteress is left with an unrecognizable face and "a dull, apathetic indifference to all belonging to this life" (374). Her fate initially seems to echo that of Lady Dedlock in *Bleak House*, whose past sexual transgression reduces her to the status of an anonymous, abject body when she flees her husband's estate and dies of exposure in the streets. And Lady Dedlock may well be a prototype for such sensational figures as Wood's disgraced aristocratic heroine. Yet what follows for Isabel bears more resemblance to the daughter Esther Summerson's affliction— particularly, the loss of her face. Like Esther (as discussed in the previous chapter), she is disfigured, depersonalized, and thus strangely unified with a mass of other anonymous bodies.

Even in executing this spectacular form of abjection, the novel does not eradicate the figure of the redundant woman. Plucking her from the scene of mass death, it compels her to live.[12] Again like Esther, Isabel finds a strange form of protection in the erasure of all visible markers of identity. Her disfigurement ironically allows her to return incognito (under an assumed name) to England and the home she had abandoned, where she becomes governess to her children and a paid employee of her recently remarried husband. Wood requires her heroine to reenter the domestic sphere as an "interloper" in her own eyes, as "a criminal woman who had thrust herself into the house" (490).[13] After reducing the lovely Lady Isabel to the level of bare life and rendering her anonymous, *East Lynne* reaches its tragic pitch by repositioning her in the household that failed to contain her (but from which, it turns out, she cannot be excluded). What seems to exceed the limits of domesticity proves nonetheless internal to it.

Changing the Bias of Fear

It is possible to be too clamorous on behalf of a morality not endangered. Terrorism is a species of epidemic. It visits us at seasons—especially during the seasons of inactivity. Now it is Christianity that demands instant support, or it falls; now it is society that compels the elimination of certain vicious elements, or it is degraded; now it is the press that needs a more vigorous imposition of conscience, or its dignity departs. No doubt these spasms of terror are useful in their way. They compel an inquisitiveness into things that might otherwise suffer neglect. At the same time, they sometimes make great fools of us.

—"A Sermon upon Novels," *London Review* (1867)

> Turn your fear into a safeguard. Keep your dread
> fixed on the idea of increasing that remorse which is
> so bitter to you. . . . We are not always in a state of
> strong emotion, and when we are calm we can use
> our memories and gradually change the bias of our
> fear, as we do our tastes.
>
> —George Eliot, *Daniel Deronda*

Insofar as the novels of Braddon, Wood, and Collins, among others, seem to violate the domestic norms of serious fiction, it stands to reason that scholars have often read them in a constitutive tension with the realist novel. English realism of the sort exemplified in the works of Gaskell, Eliot, and Trollope was far more readily allied with domesticity than its grittier French antecedents. By Patrick Brantlinger's account, the sensation fiction of the 1860s represented "a crisis in the history of literary realism"—and some Victorian novelists and critics did in fact maintain this distinction ("What Is 'Sensational' about the Sensation Novel?" 27). Trollope, in his *Autobiography*, remarks a general impression among critics that "realistic" writing such as his own is "anti-sensational"—an opposition he himself rejects (196), and reviews of novels classified as sensational often contrasted them unfavorably with the polemically realist novels of George Eliot. For one reviewer, turning from Eliot's "works of high art" to one of Braddon's bestsellers was "like going from a fair garden to a filthy marsh, where only deadly plants and reptiles have their homes" ("Female Novelists of the Period" 232). Yet, recalling Robert Audley's trouble identifying "which is to be the one eel out of the colossal bag of snakes," Eliot's novels themselves make it somewhat difficult to distinguish her celebrated realism and high moral seriousness from the more reptilian species of fiction. After wading in the swamps of sensation fiction, readers might well wonder how to classify one particular novel whose heroine makes her first appearance "as a sort of serpent" in her gestures and the colors of her dress, menacing in her very attractiveness, and is later possessed by a "shrieking fear lest she herself had become one of the evil spirits . . . hissing around her with serpent tongues."[14] Moreover, this heroine (whose husband will eventually drown under questionable circumstances) is haunted by the "Medusa-apparition" of the woman she has displaced in a marriage that verges on bigamy (606), while the man she secretly loves turns out to be the son of an exotic princess who seems "not quite a human mother, but a Melusina" (625). The sensation novel I am describing is, of course, *Daniel Deronda*.

This name-calling may seem perverse—and certainly it would be beside the point to reclassify Eliot's novel just because its female characters adhere to the conventions of sensation fiction or to dispute its realism because its

plot involves adultery, illegitimacy, marital and parental cruelty, and a melodramatic denouement that bears a striking resemblance to spousal murder.
Nor is *Daniel Deronda* alone in its use of such character types and plot devices;
most if not all of Eliot's novels feature some element of violent crime, fraud,
blackmail, illicit passion, or domestic scandal.[15] This text, however, offers a
particularly strong case for questioning the longstanding opposition of realism and sensationalism without concluding that the former merely subsumes
and supersedes the latter.[16] *Daniel Deronda* achieves its formal objectives in
large part through its mastery of recognizably sensational techniques.[17] In
incorporating the very elements that Eliot had rejected as superfluous in her
critique of "Silly Novels by Lady Novelists" (which summarily dismissed "the
mass of feminine literature" [319]), its narrative adopts precisely what I have
called the paradigm of redundancy. The contours of the bigamy novel, notorious in the 1860s for overcrowding and destabilizing the domestic sphere,
are discernible at every level of Eliot's novel. The bourgeois home after Braddon's and Wood's fiction no longer looked like a haven from the economic
pressures and biological risks of a crowded world; in fact, it was the testing ground where those pressures and risks were revealed on a microcos-
mic level. Where *Lady Audley's Secret* plotted the failure of all attempts to
distinguish a worthy heroine from a devalued mass population or to protect
the respectable English family from the imagined excess of human material
pressing against its limits, *Daniel Deronda* is accordingly structured around a
surplus it can neither contain nor exclude.

Like the more outrageous texts of the previous decade, Eliot's novel produces and multiplies redundant women at every turn. In each case, both
their culpability and the fate they would inevitably have suffered in another
novel are registered as near misses rather than *faits accomplis*. There is Mirah
Lapidoth, whom Deronda prevents from drowning herself in the Thames to
escape the disgrace of being sold off by her father to a licentious nobleman.
There is Gwendolen Harleth, who (as her surname suggests) seems almost
to have prostituted herself in marriage to a man she does not love—a man
already informally bound to another woman—in order to spare herself the
privations of life as a governess. There are Gwendolen's sisters, merely "four
superfluous girls" in her own view, who are explicitly treated as redundant
(229). There are Lady Mallinger's daughters, widely regarded as a misfortune since Sir Hugo's marriage has yielded no male heir who can inherit
his property and title. There are the Meyrick sisters, too, whose artwork
and craft labor provide the girls and their widowed mother their modest
means of subsistence. There is Lydia Glasher, Grandcourt's former mistress
and the mother of his illegitimate children, who, having left her husband,

remains financially dependent on Grandcourt even after he rejects her in favor of Gwendolen. And the problem is evidently more than a generation old. Gwendolen's widowed mother, Fanny Davilow, can imagine no alternative to marriage and yet has been made miserable by her two past husbands and left dependent on her brother-in-law, while Deronda's mysterious mother, an opera singer who never wanted marriage, much less children, has been "living a myriad lives in one," as she puts it (626). Like Gwendolen, whose vaguely defined aim is to avoid at all costs doing "as other women do," the Princess Leonora Halm-Eberstein paradoxically speaks for all the women in Eliot's novel in attesting that she has "not felt exactly what other women feel" (628).

This question of "other women" is one that simultaneously haunts every reversal of fortune and yet curiously fails to signify in *Daniel Deronda*. While Gwendolen, per the title of Book IV, "gets her choice" of suitors (rarely an auspicious turn of events in an Eliot novel, where easy fulfillment is a recipe for regret), she does not gain but loses by her decision to profit from another woman's loss. Desire is not a zero-sum game but a virtual non-entity here; despite the premise of sexual competition between the two women, Gwendolen's marriage to Grandcourt only proves that she and Lydia are equally disposable. The lawful wife, observing her husband's disregard of the woman "destitute of acknowledged social dignity," does not triumph over her rival but is menaced by "visions of a future that might be her own" (606).[18] Rather than inviting pity or provoking resentment, the specter of the rejected mistress fills Gwendolen with a distinctly sensational terror, "as if some ghastly vision had come to her in a dream and said, 'I am a woman's life'" (152).

That any and all women's lives may become disposable is clear even at the height of animosity between the two. Eliot's heroine reveals as much in her reaction to the venomous letter Lydia sends along with the jewels Grandcourt has ordered her to return so that he may give them to her replacement. Seated before the glass and overcome by the "nervous shock" brought on by Lydia's malediction in a scene of hysteria worthy of Braddon or Collins, Gwendolen "could not see the reflections of herself then: they were like so many women petrified white" (359). Despite her "girlish dreams of being 'somebody'" and drive to prove herself exceptional among women, she is not simply doubled but multiplied in the very mirror that reflects her (357). This self-repetition becomes a simile for an imagined multitude. Gwendolen's relation to these mirror images of herself is a relation of unobserved likeness ("they were like so many women") rather than identity or mimesis, and a later scene finds her gazing at her reflection "not in admiration, but in a sad kind of companionship" (430). From the moment she reads the other woman's writing, which appears before her "legible as print" (358), she is bound not just to Lydia but also to a constantly implied crowd of others.

The reference to print in Eliot's sensationalized scene of reading is not incidental. If the simultaneous excess and devaluation of women in the sensation novel correlated with its status as a mass-produced print form, *Daniel Deronda* perpetuates this analogy—with an ironic twist. Read alongside Mansel's critique of cheap serial fiction as a "class of works which most men borrow and do not buy, and in which, therefore, they take only a transitory interest," Eliot's novel would seem to suggest that Lydia (for all the passion she once excited in Grandcourt) is the sort of woman that a man could "borrow" and not "buy" (Mansel 484). And this positions Gwendolen as the commodity most in demand. Eliot's epigraph to the chapter in which the heroine initially wins Grandcourt's preference draws an explicit analogy between the marriage market and the valuation of other manufactured goods: "The market's pulse makes index high or low, / By rule sublime," pronounces the "1st Gent." in Eliot's invented dramatic dialogue; "Our daughters must be wives, / And to be wives must be what men will choose" (99). Yet one of the repeated cruel jokes of the narrative is that the market's pulse does not beat quite as strongly as its choice of object might suggest; Grandcourt's appetite for Gwendolen too has already been exhausted long before he sends her an engagement ring and a check for five hundred pounds. Perhaps this is why Eliot's heroine—for all the "fascination of her womanhood" that stirs Deronda's sympathetic interest (324) and for all the "expectation of novelty" she initially represents for the chronically bored Grandcourt—is bound to seem strangely familiar and ultimately uncompelling (343). We have already met her in the sensation novel some ten years earlier, and she has already lost the power to excite.[19]

Excitement, indeed, is conspicuously subtracted from both sides of the equation. For Gwendolen, Grandcourt's initial appeal lies primarily in the "refined negations he presented to her" rather than in any positive expression of desire (671). Eliot is not altogether subtle in remarking that his "bearing had no rigidity [and] inclined rather to the flaccid" (111). Any subsequent thought of other admirers who might "diversify married life with the romantic stir of mystery, passion, and danger which her French reading had given her some girlish notion of" confronts this English heroine with visions of illicit pleasures that "instead of fascinating her . . . were clad in weariness and disgust" (429). Even before her marriage, "the shilling serial mistakenly written for her amusement" sours her more than usual to the avowed passion of her cousin Rex, whose love repels her (80). The stuff of so many

English novels that had merited unfavorable comparison to French tales of adultery loses its thrill in life as in art: "Many courses," the narrator remarks, "are actually pursued—follies and sins both convenient and inconvenient—without pleasure or hope of pleasure; but to solace ourselves with imagining any course beforehand, there must be some foretaste of pleasure in the shape of an appetite; and Gwendolen's appetite had sickened" (429–30). Catherine Gallagher insightfully connects the trope of declining appetites both for sex and fiction to Stanley Jevons's marginal utility theory, which she applies to Eliot's own anxieties about artistic self-similarity.[20] This concern about the waning of interest as a result of overexposure in fact has a literary precedent that predates Jevons's 1871 account of devaluation in his *Theory of Political Economy*. If Eliot worried about wearing out readers with more of the same in the 1870s, as Gallagher suggests, her worries were anticipated by the sensation novelists on whose techniques she tacitly drew.

Braddon herself plays on much the same concern when she offers a caricature of "a sensation author" in *The Doctor's Wife*—an Anglicized reworking of *Madame Bovary* (11). Describing the prolific Sigismund Smith, whose dullness and apparent lack of affect set his life in stark relief against his art, Braddon's narrator speculates, "perhaps it was that he had exhausted all that was passionate in his nature in penny numbers, and had nothing left for the affairs of real life" (13). The explanation proposed here notably treats desire (contra Malthus) as finite and exhaustible. Literary mass production, by this account, does not add to desire by investing it in fetishized objects of representation but rather empties it out and proceeds in its absence. Accordingly, in *Daniel Deronda*, the question is not why the irrepressible heroine—with her volatile temperament, bewitching attractiveness, and fierce desire for independence—commands neither the same readerly sympathy as a Maggie Tulliver nor the same disaffiliation as a Lady Audley, but simply why Eliot sees no need to kill her off or send her packing. In that Gwendolen, like the mass-produced sensation heroines of the previous decade, is both no one and a multitude of women, on what basis does she elude the abjection and critical censure that awaited her popular counterparts? On this divergence rests F. R. Leavis's attempt to extricate the better half of *Deronda* from the swamp, as we will soon see.

Judged by the standards of decency to which critics held sensation fiction, Eliot's marriage plot might well have been scandalous. Oliphant had defined this moralizing perspective in her review essays for *Blackwood's*, lauding what she regarded as the best of English literature not precisely for "what critics would call the highest development of art" but rather for "a certain sanity, wholesomeness, and cleanness" ("Novels" 172). If what was most estimable in a national literary tradition were those qualities that made the novel appropriate "family reading" and so "precious to women and unoccupied persons," then Eliot's novel would hardly seem to merit its place in such a tradition (173). Nor does its resolution, evaluated by these measures, profit by comparison with the two sensation novels previously discussed. In *East Lynne*, one might say for the sake of argument that the heroine's protracted suffering for her infidelity at least superficially enforces the norms of marriage, whereas Gwendolen, who from the first has no desire to marry, is punished cruelly for marrying Grandcourt with the misery of marriage itself. And in *Lady Audley's Secret*, the bigamist who attempts to kill her first husband fails in this scheme and winds up in an asylum; by contrast, Gwendolen—who confesses after her husband's death that she had constantly dreamed of killing him—is permitted to watch Grandcourt drown with impunity. Yet critics' objections to this novel cited neither the moral turpitude of its domestic plot nor the series of sensational "nervous shocks" to which it subjects poor Gwen. Instead, what Henry James and others called the novel's "Jewish part" proved far more disturbing to several generations of readers (987).

Without the plot that sends Deronda chasing down his previously unknown Jewish identity, thus ever farther from a match with Gwendolen, Eliot's novel would for all intents and purposes be a sensation novel. Yet more than a few critics found this other plot (that is, the main plot) superfluous. Though the book sold well both in England and abroad, a number of reviewers were bewildered by the sheer foreignness of the religious and racial identity Deronda embraces. Victorian readers complained that Mirah was improbable in her piety and could not see why Daniel should choose her over Gwendolen. They found Mordecai's Jewish mysticism obscure and tedious, and several objected that the prophetic visions and supernatural devices smacked of romance rather than of the wholesome, sober realism for which *Middlemarch* and *Adam Bede* were celebrated. Eliot's interest in Zionism continued to baffle twentieth-century critics, prompting a reviewer in the *Times Literary Supplement* of 1947 to suspect that some hidden genealogy must explain the novel's motive. More or less duplicating the racializing logic of *Daniel Deronda*'s secret-identity plot, the review speculates that Eliot's partner Lewes might have had Jewish ancestry, noting "an Hebraic look about his face."[21] And Leavis, most famously, dismissed the Jewish portions of the novel as deplorably "unreal," declaring *Daniel Deronda* an artistic failure that could be redeemed only if the "bad part" were edited out and the novel retitled *Gwendolen Harleth*. Such an altered version, he contends, would be not just "a self-sufficient and very substantial whole" but indeed a paragon of George Eliot's art "at its maturest" (*Great Tradition* 122–23). In effect, the woman who had no real interest in marriage—so troubling a figure to Greg's socioeconomic analysis and so destabilizing a presence in literature to earlier critics of sensation fiction—now appeared to Leavis and others as self-sufficient in a positive sense and demanded a novel of her own.

If the novel's Jewish element induced an unanticipated change of heart in critics, leaving them wanting more of the sensational stuff they found so objectionable in popular fiction, its narrative provoked this reaction by adapting a familiar formula. In *Daniel Deronda*, the formal imperative of incorporating and abjecting a redundant population remains constant. Rather than retaining the shape of a nondomestic woman, however, redundancy emerges here as a covertly foreign race within the English population. Eliot translates the object of the secret-identity plot from a female interloper in the house to a racially foreign English gentleman, culturally indistinguishable from the hereditary aristocracy to which he does not belong by reproductive kinship. Rather than presenting this figure as a threat to the social order, the novel awakens in Deronda "the heart and brain of a multitude" (750). And rather than treating him as a casualty of sexual and social norms gone awry, the novel gives its male hero sanction to leave the country voluntarily. In marrying not only Mirah but also her brother (who proclaims on his deathbed that the marriage of his soul with Daniel's has already begun), the foreign-born son of a Jewish singer embodies a subpopulation that becomes the imaginative basis for a new nation. Oddly enough, his final voyage to Palestine enacts something like the solution to the redundant woman problem that Greg had proposed: the mass relocation of surplus population to colonized territory.

This solution, however, seems not to have satisfied readers, many of whom would evidently have preferred a sensation novel focused on Gwendolen. While critics were inclined to treat Eliot's proto-Zionist fantasy as a failure of realism, their embrace of this novel's unseemly yet decidedly more familiar domestic plot suggests another explanation. In view of the fact that the notoriously popular subgenre of the 1860s seemed to decline after the end of the decade and had all but disappeared by the time *Daniel Deronda* came out in 1876, perhaps the key formal elements of sensation fiction had already been taken into (and reshaped) British realism. Reports of the sensation novel's death, like those of its persistent heroines, were greatly exaggerated. The interloper in the literary world had secretly become a necessary supplement to the English social novel.

Principles of Success

> In general, leave "Literature," the thing called "Literature" at present, to run through its rapid fermentations. . . . In our time it has become all the rage;

highest noblemen and dignitaries courting a new still
higher glory there; innumerable men, women, and
children rushing towards it, yearly ever more. . . .
Only wait: in fifty years, I should guess, all really serious souls will have quitted that mad province, left it
to the roaring populaces; and for any *Noble*-man or
useful person it will be a credit rather to declare,
"I never tried literature; believe me, I have not written
anything;"—and we of "Literature" by trade, we shall
sink again.

—Thomas Carlyle, "Shooting Niagara: And After?"

Given the evident inextricability of sensationalism from the novels of an
author as critically acclaimed as Eliot, the persistence of realism as a criterion of artistic merit may seem unaccountable. Yet it points back to one of
Victorian realism's defining claims: namely, that realist art represents "the
life of the People" ("The Natural History of German Life" 145). Eliot's own
earlier critical writings of the 1850s, which endorse a populist aesthetic soon
to be exemplified in *Adam Bede*, give art the social-scientific task of generalizing "the real characteristics of the working classes" (142). Whether the
population they took as their referent actually read the texts purporting to
represent them was irrelevant to Eliot's argument, but it did become a question of some interest to her generation of writers.

It is on this point that realism (or at least a certain programmatic version
of realism) met the most substantial challenge to its representational ambitions. With the expansion of literacy and an increase in the production and
circulation of affordable periodicals, reading was no longer the privilege of
a leisured class but the ordinary activity of millions.[22] Novelists and critics,
taking notice of a vast "Unknown Public" that Collins claimed to discover
in 1858, were surprised to learn that this new audience showed little interest in homely sketches of the agricultural and industrial working classes.[23]
Oliphant, in an essay that coincided exactly with Collins's, marveled to the
elite readers of *Blackwood's* that "whereas we can please ourselves with *Mary
Barton*, our poor neighbours share no such humble taste, but luxuriate in
ineffable splendours of architecture and upholstery" ("The Byways of Literature" 202). The penny miscellanies whose circulation exceeded that of
Gaskell's bestselling industrial novels, she lamented, would offer later historians no information about the life and culture of "the multitude" who were
their readers. It was not that the masses could not but rather would not represent themselves; thus, Oliphant concluded, they must be "misrepresented"
("The Byways of Literature" 202). This "everybody, who is nobody" rejected
identification with conventionally realist renderings of a national working class—and in so doing cast doubt on the very idea that what Eliot had
termed "the Natural History of social bodies" was available to representation

("The Natural History of German Life" 285). The critical moment of the sensation novel thus took on its meaning, in part, as an acknowledgment of a growing tension between the idea of the people and that of the mass. The people, understood alternately as a totalizable and self-enclosed national population or as a specific class category within the nation (broadly, those who do not own property), seemed to constitute a coherent sociological set. The more porous concept of the mass, by contrast, might encompass everyone and no one.

So too did the commercial success of cheap fiction disrupt the progress narratives of class uplift that flourished in the 1850s. For Oliphant, in 1858, the supposed intellectual and moral inferiority of the "multitude" was obviously a product of uneven development: "[I]t is only that we have got so many centuries ahead [of the working classes]," she explains to her genteel readership, "by dint of our exemption from manual labours and necessities" ("The Byways of Literature" 200). To Collins, writing in the same year (before his name became permanently linked to *The Woman in White*), it was clear that the future of English fiction rested with "the readers who rank by millions," who were only "waiting to be taught the difference between a good book and a bad" ("The Unknown Public" 216). Asserting the inevitability of cultural development, he predicted that this literate multitude "must obey the universal law of progress, and . . . learn to discriminate" (216). Yet, only four years later, the critical discourse surrounding the sensation novel suggested that bad books were multiplying at an extraordinary rate. Rather than nourishing the social body, reviews contended, these novels fed a "ravenous appetite for carrion," guided in their success by a "vulture-like instinct which smells out the newest mass of social corruption" (Mansel 502).

Even in their multiplicity and—from the perspective of critics—their overwhelming sameness, these masses of cheap print matter saturating the literary marketplace seemed to illustrate a process of decline. Sensational themes, characters, and plot devices were "destined to be repeated to infinitude," Oliphant complained, "as no successful work can apparently exist in this imitative age without creating a shoal of copyists; and with every fresh imitation the picture will take more and more objectionable shades" ("Sensational Novels" 13). Charges of plagiarism abounded (inadvertently echoing these novels' own plots of forgery and imposture), and detractors were vociferous, but sales and circulation figures showed them to be vastly outnumbered. "All our minor novelists," alleged Oliphant in 1867, "are of the school called sensational" ("Novels" 174). The *Cornhill Magazine* could not dispute the success of *Lady Audley's Secret* except by objecting that "the qualities by which the success is achieved are not literary qualities" ("Our Survey of

Literature and Science" 135). And the editors of *The Christian Remembrancer* felt obliged "to enter our protest against the form of fiction most popular in the present day, because we conceive it to fail both positively and negatively in the legitimate uses of fiction" ("Our Female Sensation Novelists" 236).

This repudiation of the popular as illegitimate marks a decisive moment in the history of criticism. In addition to breaking with the populist rhetoric of realism, it inaugurates a new discourse of mass culture. For Victorian critics, the commercial success of works of art that "fail[ed] both positively and negatively" demanded a criterion for artistic success other than popularity or sales rank. "If the test of genius were success," reasons W. Fraser Rae in the *North British Review*, "we should rank Miss Braddon very high in the list of our great novelists" (180).

The search for some other principle of selection also lent new potency to a distinctly evolutionary model of cultural preference: a model according to which the greatness of a work cannot be determined in advance according to codified rules of art.[24] Lewes, attempting to identify literature's "principles of success" in an 1865 treatise in the inaugural issue of the *Fortnightly*, would equate literary merit with fitness. With texts, as with organisms, he concludes, the only proof of worth is survival. "We may lay it down as a rule," he contends, "that no work ever succeeded, even for a day, but it deserved its success; no work failed but under conditions which made failure inevitable" (26–27). Since literature is "a delicate index of social evolution," critical judgment is moot, and there is no need to suppress the mass of published texts (19); works by writers who lack the "special aptitudes" needed for continued success will naturally disappear over time (25). The literary marketplace, here, is an ecosystem that functions in perfect autonomy; it regulates itself. Such claims show the impact of Darwin's development hypothesis on cultural criticism. Lewes treats texts as subject to processes akin to natural and sexual selection.[25] For much the same reasons Darwin would argue that a larger female population was favorable to human evolution, literary criticism proposed that a surplus of fiction was potentially advantageous, facilitating competition on a scale sufficient to promote the reproduction of the best specimens.[26]

The discourse surrounding the sensation novel thus made the analogy between cultural production and biological reproduction explicit. But simple analogy breaks down at this point; the evolutionary argument becomes most strident precisely where its plausibility evaporates. Braddon's and Wood's novels effectively implicate sexual selection in perpetuating socially aberrant tendencies that cause conventional marriages to fail—and the extraordinary appeal of these novels seemed to imply those same tendencies on the part of a new mass readership. Only a few years after the publication of *The Origin of Species*, the difficulty readers encountered was not that of thinking of both human choice and accident alike as operating at the level of species (already a familiar premise at least since Malthus) but that of believing, as Darwin did, that the conditions of selection actually promoted improvement. Darwinism had not banished the specter of degeneration that preceded it; the psychiatrist Bénédict Augustin Morel, in an 1857 treatise on what he described as the physical, mental, and moral degeneration of the human species, saw evidence of a "morbid deviation from an original type" transmitted from one generation to the next (5). To deal with this problem in the realm of fiction, Victorian critics wrote a sort of literary prologue to the eugenic theory of Francis Galton (who claimed twenty years later that the struggle for existence actually fostered degeneracy rather than selecting for what Darwin called the "favoured races").[27] They classified sensation fiction as a degenerate subrace of literature that, despite its apparent cultural unfitness, thrived and multiplied. Those who sought to isolate the worst specimens from the larger population of novels, however, were no more able to do so than Robert Audley was able to check the threat Lady Audley represented by expelling her from the household. If critics were dismayed to find scores of unfit heroines springing to life like deviant copies of each other, they clearly recognized that this was because such figures were mechanically rather than sexually reproduced.

The Mechanical Reproducibility of Life

> Surely if a machine is able to reproduce . . . we may say that it has a reproductive system.
>
> —Samuel Butler, *Erewhon*

The sensation novel thus came to represent intractable problems of reproduction not only as a narrative of female transgression but also as a self-reproducing commercial object. That the reception of art is transformed both by the expansion of audiences and by technological changes in the mode of production—one of the foundational insights of Walter Benjamin's later analysis of art's altered status in the age of its mechanical reproducibility—is, in effect, the discovery that sensation fiction's reception came to imply.[28] Equated with the frantic overproduction of human and cultural material, this popular subgenre was always metonymically linked to the industrial production of literature. While of course all fiction is mechanically reproduced, reviewers seized on sensation fiction as the consummate product of unnatural processes—the hideous progeny of the machine. The popular novel as described by its critics is so transparently manufactured, so thing-like, that the mode of production is actually perceptible in the writing: "A commercial atmosphere floats around works of this class, redolent of the manufactory and the shop," writes Mansel in the *Quarterly*. "The public want novels, and novels must be made—so many yards of printed stuff, sensation-pattern, to be ready by the beginning of the season" (483). Such reviews inaugurate a critique of commercial mass culture that extends beyond the specific texts in question. In describing an industrial system that consumes labor from masses of bodies without distinction in order to mass-produce commodities for an insatiable and undiscriminating mass market, literary critics and cultural commentators articulated a new version of the older Malthusian problem of surplus population. Together, they figured the mass as producer and product, consumer and commodity—a conflation of cause and effect that raised the threat of a homogenizing culture industry.[29]

The claim that life had come to imitate machine-made art would become a critical commonplace across the political spectrum in the twentieth century. Leavis, writing in the early 1930s, extends much the same claim to what he calls "mass civilization" as a whole—the outcome not only of demographic and sociopolitical change but also of industrialization as such:

> Mass-production, standardisation, levelling-down—these three terms convey succinctly, what has happened. Machine-technique has produced change in the ways of life at such a rate that there has been something like a breach of continuity; sanctions have decayed; and, in any case, the standards of mass-production (for mass-production conditions now govern the supply of literature) are not those of tradition. (*For Continuity* 76)

In keeping with Mansel's analysis of the sensation novel as a commodity whose technical reproducibility in itself entails a general lowering of standards, Leavis describes a "standardised civilisation" as the final victory of the machine over human life (44). His essay on "Mass Civilisation and Minority Culture" suggests that the centrality of mass production to modern society fosters a population determined more by technics than by kinship—rendering art and life alike in redundancy.

In Leavis's essay as in Greg's, the problem of redundancy does not arise from the Malthusian principle of population (the sexual impulse that geometrically increases the birth rate, checked in turn by economic scarcity) but, conversely, from disinclination toward heterosexual kinship and an overabundance of material goods. Yet the stakes of his critique are nonetheless framed as a question of life-production, as implied in his urgent call for the preservation of a "living tradition." What is left in its absence, he claims, is "academic sterility, the Humanist manipulation of the barren idea, the inability to conceive tradition as a matter of organic life" (66). Emptied out of an inherited tradition by the advent of "machine-technique" and by "mass-production conditions [that] now govern the supply of literature," modern culture is implicitly figured here as a barren womb (76). Leavis's metaphoric language in this and other essays repeatedly connects the trope of the infertile body with that of the reproducing machine. In these terms, he constructs a crisis of cultural value continuous with Victorian narratives of the end of sexual difference and of family life with the rise of industrialism.[30]

The specter of the non-procreative (or redundant) woman, coupled with that of the machine, arises in tension with the conceits of culture as living organism and of tradition as genealogy. When Leavis calls on criticism to prevent what might happen "[i]f a literary tradition does not keep itself alive here," his project relies on a biological idiom of selection for health, stressing fertility, human development, and the reduction of degenerate types (*For Continuity* 72). To guard against extinction, he makes it the responsibility of critics to identify superior literary specimens and ensure their reproduction—a task he performs by anointing George Eliot as the true standard-bearer of the Great Tradition consolidated in the novels of Jane Austen. From this standpoint, his frustration with Eliot's last novel is not surprising. Insofar as its Jewish-identity plot disrupted the coherence of national kinship (and left its English heroine single and childless), *Daniel Deronda* must have been difficult to place in a Great Tradition of English novels bound together by metaphors of filiation and intergenerational continuity.

As late as the 1970s, toward the end of his career, Leavis himself actually attempted to salvage this text and restore it to the main line of British fiction by giving Gwendolen's story an autonomous life. In the posthumously published introduction to his planned edition of *Gwendolen Harleth* (which the Bodley Head solicited but ultimately rejected), he argued that within Eliot's incoherent work was a true novel worthy of its place in a national canon: "a classic it is incumbent on us to reclaim for English literature" ("Gwendolen Harleth" 10). He had long dreamed, as he put it, of "freeing by simple surgery the living part of the immense Victorian novel from the deadweight of utterly different matter that George Eliot thought fit to make it carry" (10). Complications arose, however, when it became clear that Daniel could not simply be "eliminated" from the body of the novel, since his character remained useful "in embryo" to Gwendolen's development (10). The operation as a whole proved unsuccessful from the standpoint of publishers. Even those sympathetic to the project saw that excising a large portion of Eliot's multiplot narrative would leave gaps and discontinuities in the portion that remained.[31] But Leavis's shift in metaphor is striking in itself. While his vitalist rhetoric remains constant, his zeal to preserve an organic literary heritage here requires him to rid the English novel of the unwanted offspring it might bear.

This editorial abortion might seem an odd departure from the task of criticism set out by Matthew Arnold (always a touchstone for Leavis), but in this regard, too, the critic may turn out not to have strayed far from his Victorian predecessor. Despite some significant ideological differences between the two, Arnold's influence is unmistakable throughout Leavis's canon-building enterprise.[32] His grand vindication of culture speaks to the concerns raised by other critics of his generation who variously saw popular art as a sensuous appeal to "the animal part of our nature" or as an uncanny instance of human sense experience manufactured by industrial technology ("Our Female Sensation Novelists" 212). *Culture and Anarchy*, written in the wake of the Hyde Park riots and in a decade that constructed a peculiar triad of sexual, mechanical, and cultural reproduction in its analysis of fiction, sought to do no less than rescue humanity from both animality and machinery by instilling "the discipline by which alone man is enabled to rescue his life from thralldom to the passing moment and to his bodily senses" (210). Turning to Arnold's intervention in critical discourse, however, we find a striking illustration of the conditions for such discipline. Rather than elevate his readers above the anarchy of sensations into a loftier realm of reflection, the critic finds it necessary to descend into the depths of depravity and violence—not insignificantly, by evoking yet another scene of maternity gone awry.

"The Function of Criticism at the Present Time" models the work of criticism by responding to quotations from two political addresses: one, by Conservative MP Sir Charles Adderly, that vaunts the supremacy of "the old Anglo-Saxon race" in the context of a debate on church-rates, and one, by Radical MP John Roebuck, that boasts the perfect freedom, security, and "unrivalled happiness" of the English people in the context of an argument for extending the franchise (38–39). Arnold's startling rejoinder to both speeches, culled from "a paragraph on which [he] stumbled in a newspaper immediately after reading Mr. Roebuck," sets policy debates aside and begins with the following quotation from the *Times*: "A shocking child murder has just been committed at Nottingham. A girl named Wragg left the workhouse there on Saturday morning with her young illegitimate child. The child was soon afterwards found dead on Mapperly Hills, having been strangled. Wragg is in custody" (40).

The disruptive impact of this quotation—a sensation plot in miniature, one that powerfully reasserts the narrative logic of female redundancy—enables Arnold's defense of criticism. Its presentation is calculated to jar the nerves of readers with the sudden introduction of crime and abnormality where they are least expected. In this, the critic takes a page from Braddon, whose narrator delights in interrupting a pastoral reverie to recall that murders take place in the English countryside every day: "Brutal and treacherous murders; slow, protracted agonies from poisons administered by some kindred hand; sudden and violent deaths by cruel blows" imperceptibly blot idyllic landscapes (*Lady Audley's Secret* 91). Arnold's essay further draws on sensationalist narrative conventions in tying such unforeseen crimes and counternormative elements to the circulation of print media. Much as the unknown girl who would become Lady Audley is summoned into the novel's seemingly tranquil world by a printed advertisement in the *Times*, the female criminal here emerges from newspaper headlines to interrupt the imagined stability of a social order to which she was never really external. For reasons that by now will be clear, the cultural necessity of criticism cannot be explained without reference to this figure and her seemingly unrelated story.

Suspending his more characteristic emphasis on the selectability of superior cultural materials, Arnold uses the sordid story of this girl named Wragg to define critical practice less in terms of selection than reception. He treats the *Times* article more or less as a literary text, focusing on the newspaper's language over and above the facts of the infanticide. As a counterpoint to Adderley's celebration of "our old Anglo-Saxon breed, the best in the world," he calls attention to the suspect's name—"how much that is harsh and ill-favoured there is in this best! *Wragg!*"—and proceeds to lament "the natural growth amongst us of such hideous names" (40). Against Roebuck's jingoistic paean to "our unrivalled happiness," he contrasts that "element of grimness, bareness, and hideousness" evoked by the crime report. Embellished with his own Dickensian description of "the gloom, the smoke, the cold, the strangled illegitimate child," this imagined scene provides Arnold an occasion to discredit the self-contented nationalist rhetoric of the two MPs:

> And the final touch—short, bleak, and inhuman: *Wragg is in custody.* The sex lost in the confusion of our unrivalled happiness; or (shall I say?) the superfluous Christian name lopped off by the straightforward vigour of our old Anglo-Saxon breed! There is profit for the spirit in such contrasts as this; criticism serves the cause of perfection by establishing them. (40)

The elision of gender and of personal identity from the police blotter, as much as the sensationalism of the crime itself, makes this tale of female deviance Arnold's case in point for advancing the agenda of culture. Even in lamenting the "superfluous" status accorded to its subject, his critical performance renders the text less shocking than banal. Here too, the critic's gesture draws on such novels as *The Moonstone*, where the servant Rosanna Spearman recounts her own history, in a letter to the man she loves, as a journalistic cliché. "There is no need to tell such a common story as this, at any length," she writes of her upbringing and criminal past, summed up in a few short, declarative sentences stating the circumstances that made her a thief and her mother a prostitute: "It is told quite often enough in the newspapers" (317). If Arnold's newspaper story of child murder seems singular in the context of a belletristic essay, its significance for his purposes is likewise not that of a unique exception. On the contrary, it becomes relevant only insofar as Wragg (from her name to her journalistic representation) serves to instantiate far larger phenomena.

By injecting this devalued interloper into a political discourse that fails to anticipate her destabilizing potential, Arnold's experiment in criticism effectively does the work of the sensation novel. It compels art and politics alike to confront redundancy—the specter of a mass for which they fail to account—as the fact that must be recognized before anything meaningful can be said. What "The Function of Criticism" illustrates, then, is an unexpected lesson drawn from fiction, that the production of culture requires the perpetual reproduction of the surplus and that culture is thus structurally dependent on the very thing for which it has no place.

CHAPTER 5

"Because We Are Too Menny"

The conventions of sensation fiction outlasted their genre. In fact, as the previous chapter suggested, it was all but impossible to construct a workable marriage plot in the wake of Braddon's, Collins's, and Wood's overcrowding of domestic fiction. Thomas Hardy's *The Mayor of Casterbridge*, which opens with the sensational scene of a wife sale and closes with the death of its protagonist, produces superfluous wives and daughters as well as husbands, fathers, and workers from beginning to end. *Jude the Obscure* makes marriage a recipe for disaster, and George Gissing's *The Odd Women* explicitly finds its subject in the female surplus that *Lady Audley's Secret* and *East Lynne* had implicitly injected into their stories. Shifting focus from Monica Madden—youngest and prettiest of too many orphaned daughters, who in another sort of novel would prove her worth as heroine by marrying well—to the Madden sisters' friend Rhoda Nunn, who opposes marriage and has made it her mission to train fellow "superfluous females" for the workforce, Gissing reclaims what W. R. Greg called redundant women as a necessary force of social transformation (39). Rhoda's partner Mary Barfoot heralds "a revolution in the social order," calling for "a new type of woman, active in every sphere"—and Rhoda becomes the novel's central figure by personifying this type, choosing her feminist vocation over an unexpected offer of marriage (153–54).

It is not an exaggeration to say that the plot of *The Odd Women* makes single life the only feasible future. While Monica determines to escape from the surplus by finding a husband, her success yields no happy ending. Instead of rescuing her from a "futile" life of nondomestic labor, marriage demoralizes her and wears out her will to live. Pregnant with a child her jealous and domineering husband falsely assumes is not his, the sole married woman and would-be mother in this novel dies in childbirth; put bluntly, she dies in consequence of her choice to seek refuge in a norm that has lost its plausibility.

In turning to the 1880s and 90s and to the novels of Hardy and Gissing, this chapter looks beyond the collapse of the marriage plot to a more absolute break with the projected future that marriage had once promised. To the extent that social futurity is imaginable here, it demands to be imagined in nonreproductive terms. Hardy's and Gissing's main characters, who prove largely averse to heterosexual kinship and procreation, survive only so long as they resist these relations. Most, lacking Rhoda Nunn's conviction, are cut off from any future or are beset by fears of a future more terrible than the present. Late Victorian novels afflicted a sizeable population of protagonists with the malady of the era: an overwhelming sense of purposelessness, exhaustion, and indifference to life. Forensic and social scientists told overlapping tales of a widespread morbid tendency that William Knighton, in an 1881 *Contemporary Review* article, called "Suicidal Mania." Citing the findings of Alphonse Bertillon and others who saw a spike in suicide rates throughout Europe, Knighton sensationally declared that "Men are everywhere becoming more weary of the burden of life" (82). The self-destruction of Jude Fawley's and Sue Bridehead's children—a sign, per the grim prognosis of the novel's doctor, of a "coming universal wish not to live"—thus appears as the most extreme instance of a broader trend. Whether they perish by active suicide or sheer loss of will, the protagonists of the novels discussed in this chapter rarely make it past early adulthood, and few leave surviving offspring behind.

A different approach to demography seems to declare itself here. The previous four chapters have identified a range of fictional strategies for dealing with a population calculated to exceed the resources allotted to it. Shelley's student of natural philosophy brings to life a mass body and attempts, disastrously, to isolate life from social structure; Gaskell, setting out to sketch a demographically representative specimen of the working class, ends up calling representativeness into question as she empties her character of his characteristics; Dickens exposes a metropolitan social body to infection and transforms the novel's entire population into supernumeraries; Braddon and

Wood turn women into invaders who overrun families, making the genteel home an analogue of the city street rather than a bulwark against it. Most of these narratives entail a shift in emphasis from the individual subject to a human aggregate that surpasses its social parameters. The novels of Hardy and Gissing, read simply in terms of the mechanics of life and death, look more straightforward. They handle their populations by disposing of their main characters at a young age and curbing their reproduction—and these characters' deaths are explicitly identified as the outcome of systematic demands (alternately biological and sociological) that make them unfit to survive.

Such an approach to life often seems characteristic of naturalist fiction: a genre notorious for its unyielding conviction in the crushing force of heredity, environment, and social law. Yet this ruthless vital calculus, even or especially where it is most rhetorically explicit in these novels, does not quite add up. In the first place, there is no threat of overpopulation in Hardy's fiction that could call for such aggressive checks; his narration, on the contrary, shows rural Wessex being vacated by its inhabitants, not overburdened with life. Further, these texts disconfirm the established scientific view of human sexuality as a constant and necessarily reproductive impulse that takes its proper social form in marriage. They not only make the nuclear family unsustainable but also cast doubt on the generalized instinct to survive and multiply that Victorian fiction had previously taken as a given (and, often, as a driving force of plot). Most significantly at the level of form, these naturalist novels diverge from industrial fiction, from the multiplot city novel, and from sensation fiction in their intense focus on individual subjects—a focus that becomes discordant given their rough handling of these subjects as demographically expendable lives. To occupy what Alex Woloch calls the "space of the protagonist," for all its symbolic privilege, is a dubious honor in *Tess of the D'Urbervilles* or *Jude the Obscure*. Such novels follow the biographical conventions of the bildungsroman in plotting the course of a life from youth to adulthood, yet their plots empty these conventions of their purpose.

Naturalism, in effect, removes the developmental *telos* from the novel of development. Much as sensation fiction did away with the moral certainties of the marriage plot, Hardy's and Gissing's novels sap the bildungsroman of its vital energy and suspend its future-oriented project. Youth does not vibrate with heroic potential; coming of age carries no assurance of effective socialization, no soberly satisfactory wedding of individual autonomy to national futurity, no viable offspring. Tess Durbeyfield and Jude Fawley, among others, are thrust into adulthood without any promise that the passage of time leads anywhere other than death. These narratives stand in sharp contrast with *Jane Eyre* or *Great Expectations*, which lend themselves more readily to Franco Moretti's classic analysis of the European bildungsroman as an allegory of national progress.[1] In this respect, if not in their geographical scope, Hardy's Wessex novels share the problem Jed Esty pinpoints in such texts as Olive Schreiner's *Story of an African Farm* and Joseph Conrad's *Lord Jim*: a stalling of developmental time that registers a geopolitical crisis in the grand narrative of the nation-state.[2] Building on Moretti's account of a genre that made youth modernity's master trope and plotted the steady march of national history through its protagonists' maturation, Esty identifies a temporal rupture in the modernist coming-of-age story as it mediates the uneven and unending processes of imperial expansion and global finance capitalism. While the bildungsroman was never quite as stable or as nationally bounded as it appeared in hindsight, such tales of arrested development indeed resist the problem-solving exigencies of the form.[3]

Even as it privileges the biography of a singular character, though, the bildungsroman's social staging of its character's life makes development an uneven process from the start. If one measures the spotty careers of protagonists like Tess, Jude, Michael Henchard, and Edwin Reardon against the steady growth, education, and upward mobility of Wilhelm Meister or Jane Eyre, the disparity is plain to see. But drawing this contrast entails assuming, with Moretti, that the individual protagonist can stand as a singular personification of national destiny, her progress the sole metric of successful reconciliation and social continuity. If one reconsiders the novel's political objectives in terms of population, it becomes evident that the specter of failed development (and the quantity of redundant life onto which it mapped) had always been an underlying condition of the genre. Jane's journey from precarious youth to healthy adulthood and marriage can function as an allegory of national progress toward a neat alliance of old and new ruling classes only if one studiously ignores the corpses piling up in her wake. Nearly every bildungsroman narrates the unlikely success story of its hero against the backdrop of masses of others who do not survive—these casualties of historical development occasionally betokened by named personae like Alice Marwood in *Dombey and Son* or Jo in *Bleak House*. Hardy's and Gissing's novels, in making protagonists out of the human surplus disposed of in classic novels of formation, push an already perceptible problem out of the background and into the foreground.

In turning their full attention to figures discounted as superfluous, these late Victorian texts do more than shift focus. They change the narrative logic of population by individualizing the unknown quantity of wasted life from which earlier protagonists, by definition, had to distinguish themselves to make their life stories worth telling. The dynamic processes that shaped the lives of protagonists as such grind to a halt here. Character development and social mobility are curtailed by forces of resistance that no individual exertion can overcome. These countervailing forces find two systematic explanations that rise to prominence at the same historical moment but seem mutually exclusive: heredity, as theorized by August Weismann, who held that inherited biological defects could not be altered by life experience, and anomie, per Émile Durkheim's assessment of modern society's diminishing hold on the individual and the resulting erosion of norms. These two accounts of what hinders adaptation and stalls social advancement, enforcing inertia or propelling characters toward regression and self-destruction, collide in the novels of Hardy and Gissing. In *Jude the Obscure* in particular, hereditary biology and sociology often vie for explanatory authority.

Neither theory, however, explains the fate of characters whose stories trouble sociological as well as biological distinctions between normal and abnormal life. While Hardy's protagonists are apt to reproach themselves for violating social laws (those of marriage and kinship as well as gender and class) or for lacking the adaptability that unstable circumstances demand, their stories make them far from anomalous. In fact, they constitute a statistically registered counter-norm that challenges the universality of the laws they charge themselves with breaking. And indeed, by producing an excess of causal explanation for both models of errancy and showing how such explanation relies on figurative language to link otherwise contrary claims about failed development, these novels work as an immanent counterargument to the double bind of hereditary theory and sociology, rather than merely a reflection of it. Further, the characters' self-evaluation reveals something distinctive. These figures are marked by their voluntary subjection to newly rigorous practices of discipline—practices that generally do not work. The futility of these efforts belies the genre's old promise that stringent self-management maps out a path to success—in so doing, demonstrating not that Hardy's and Gissing's characters are bad subjects but that they have effectively been disqualified from being subjects in the first place. For perhaps the first time in fiction, we meet protagonists who (unlike Oliver Twist or Jane Eyre) are not just undervalued by the wrong people before being granted a proper place in the world but instead are stamped from birth to death as socially redundant—and recognize themselves as such. If the orphaned Jude Fawley is in good company in "feeling . . . his existence to be an undemanded one," he differs from his predecessors in yielding to this judgment, beginning in boyhood to "wish himself out of the world" and ending by fulfilling no other wish (18, 31). Hardy's narrative voice writes off the novel's subject from the start, pronouncing in terms that jarringly resist narrativity itself that the hero's life serves no purpose; Jude is merely "born to ache a good deal before the fall of the curtain upon his unnecessary life should signify that all was well with him again" (17).

Unnecessary life: this bitter recognition of disposability seems to sound a note of political defeatism. Hardy's controversial last novel, remembered for (and often reduced to) Little Father Time's suicide note, "done because we are too menny," can easily look like a literary proof of the fatal Malthusian ratio that calls a halt to any movement toward social justice or economic equality. Alternatively, or worse still, it may read as a eugenic rationale for Jude's and his children's otherwise inexplicable deaths: the ultimate thana-topolitical underside of a militant biopolitics bent on ensuring the health of populations by exterminating the unfit. Either reading points toward a totalizing imperative that subsumes all human activity and precludes resistance. The current chapter suggests otherwise, arguing that Hardy's and Gissing's novels—in forging counternarratives to the bildungsroman rather than fables of failed *Bildung*—frame a challenge to the ideologies of biological and sociological necessity they are often charged with endorsing. This entails a markedly different approach to reproduction, to organic and social development, and consequently to biopolitics. These novels indeed reveal a profound disconnect between discipline and biopower, offering up a version of the self-regulating individual rendered incompatible with all demographic calculations concerning human vital drives and yet treated (and apt to treat itself) as a residue of such calculations. Further, in refusing to functionalize characters' existence or make their deaths corroborate a set of immanent demands governing population, fiction claims a negative relation to biological life. If these novels nonetheless insist on giving form to a peculiar and destabilizing excess, they find the sources of this excess in the incalculable operation of language itself.

Figuratively Speaking

> Art is a disproportioning—(i.e., distorting, throwing out of proportion)—of realities.
>
> —Thomas Hardy, *The Life and Work of Thomas Hardy*

Read against the generic protocols of the bildungsroman, the plot of *The Mayor of Casterbridge* looks almost inverted, beginning with a climactic bang and ending with an unheard whimper. Michael Henchard is introduced on the brink of adulthood, a sturdy young man of twenty-one in the process of unlawfully terminating the marriage with which a proper story of formation would have culminated as a reward for his efforts: the first chapter finds him drunkenly auctioning off his wife Susan, who takes their infant daughter Elizabeth-Jane and willingly departs with the buyer, Newson. His subsequent struggle to better himself, make amends, and raise his status over two decades is diegetically passed over, so we encounter the self-made "man of character" again only at the start of another, slower fall extending over the last years of his life. Social mobility undoes itself; having achieved success as a grain merchant and risen to the position of mayor, Henchard loses his political authority, property, and fortune; becomes a replaceable hired hand of the man he once hired; and eventually retreats in disgrace, forgotten by the town. As he departs in his old workman's clothes with his basket on his back, the narrator remarks that he "formed at this moment much the same picture as he had presented when entering Casterbridge for the first time nearly a quarter of a century before," with the difference that the years have depleted his stamina (306–7). The intervening period of work toward mastering a profession, cultivating respectability, accumulating capital, and winning a prominent social position—the whole course of his *Bildung*—is little more than an interruption, skipped by the narrator before the protagonist sinks into nonexistence. His death, reported after the fact, is a non-event.

If this plot of decline suggests a tragedy occasioned by its central figure's inescapable flaws of character, the events composing it are driven by more impersonal forces that recharacterize personal relations and marginalize the protagonist. For all its emphasis on its unique central figure and the singular deviant act that shapes his life, a generalized logic of human fungibility is this novel's primary plot dynamic. Its long story of failure depends on the circumstantial process by which each character is supplanted. Hardy writes this process into the novel's title, which refers not to the main character personally but to an office occupied temporarily by that character before being transferred to Donald Farfrae, the friend, employee, and rival who replaces him. Employment provides the normative case of a pattern of substitution and displacement broadly echoed in sexual and familial relations. An additional, uncalled-for candidate turns up for nearly every position: not only two managers for Henchard's business (Farfrae unwittingly displacing a man named Joshua Jopp) but also two women who might claim Henchard's hand (Susan, returning as if from the dead like a classic sensation heroine, here superseding his sometime mistress Lucetta), two suitors for Lucetta (Henchard and Farfrae, the latter also taking the place of the former as proprietor of his business and owner of his house), two love interests for Farfrae

(Lucetta eclipsing Elizabeth-Jane), two fathers for Elizabeth-Jane (Henchard and Newson), two Elizabeth-Janes, and two protagonists (Henchard gradually ceding place to his adopted daughter).

Hardy's narrative handles these duplications and substitutions not merely as a plot device but as a daunting subjective problem. His characters experience it as a dissonance between contractually established obligations and the superfluity of possible subjects who might fulfill them. Farfrae's arrival is a paradigmatic instance: Henchard, on meeting the chance traveler en route to America who offers him valuable agricultural advice, is unable to conceive that his new acquaintance is not Jopp, the man who had answered his advertisement for help managing his grain business and with whom he had agreed to meet the following day. Captivated by something in Farfrae beyond his job qualifications, he struggles to channel desire into social function by identifying the stranger as the party already contracted. On being assured Farfrae had no prior appointment, Henchard insists that the person before him must be the one he encountered in writing, as there cannot be a second subject where only one was demanded: "Surely you are the man," he objects, "who arranged to come and see me?" (45). Farfrae's repeated negations are met with persistent disbelief: "And yet I could have sworn you were the man!" Henchard exclaims, though he can barely recall that man's name (46), and yet again, after further discussion, "I couldn't believe you were not the man I had engaged!" (47). There is arguably a variation on Woloch's model of character systems at work in this exchange—ironically, in a novel dominated by such an outsized central figure. Rather than create scores of minor characters vying for narrative attention or performing their minorness as a symptom, Hardy places his protagonist in the situation of readers who expect a minor character ("Jipp, Jopp, what was his name?" [44]) and are surprised to meet with a major one ready to take his place. Once the wish to keep this chance acquaintance close cannot be explained as fulfilling a contract, Henchard ultimately settles the matter by asserting equivalency: "Though you are not the young man I thought you were, what's the difference?" he pleads, "Can't ye stay just the same?" (48). This encounter, punctuated by Henchard's conclusion that it makes no difference whether the person he met today is the person he expected tomorrow, pointedly anticipates the disclosure that the Elizabeth-Jane he adopts as his daughter is not the same Elizabeth-Jane he thought she was.

This equivalential logic is enabled by, and, in turn, exacerbates a systemic condition of redundancy. The plot's persistent duplication of roles, however, cannot simply be chalked up to Malthusian causes: too much life, too little bread. While we hear Henchard lodging a classically Malthusian complaint in the opening scene (where he enters the novel as an unemployed hay-trusser struggling to support a wife and child, lamenting his "early imprudent marriage" and the poverty to which it has doomed him), it is clear that the problem besetting Hardy's characters is not the redundancy of population as such but the redundancy of social functions. *The Mayor of Casterbridge* takes a condition endemic to the instability of employment in an overstocked labor market and extends it to relationships defined by their exclusiveness. Only one person at a time can serve as wife, as mayor, as manager, as father—this much stands to reason. Yet the experience of Hardy's characters suggests that all these positions, however exclusive in theory, imply competing obligations and conflicting attachments in practice, such that they often cannot be filled by the individuals entitled to occupy them. Henchard's attempt to slot Farfrae into the job he had already offered Jopp not only displaces the first man but also assigns the second a role exceeding any job description. At the moment Donald accepts Henchard's offer, his new employer treats the handshake between them as solemnizing a bond quite different from an employment contract: "Now you are my friend!" proclaims Henchard (63). By defining their business agreement as a friendship, he renders it incompatible with contractual obligation. His every effort to legitimize relationships via contract and to assign persons to singular functional roles ends up chaotically multiplying the positions they fill.

What thwarts such efforts to contractually establish each person's standing in this novel and instead eventuates in a kind of universal redundancy is, in a peculiar sense, language itself. Hardy's narrative makes signifying systems, figures, signs, and interpretations complicit in undermining speech acts or giving them unintended outcomes. The result is a certain interpretive error at work throughout the novel that throws off any neat correspondence between persons and the social places they occupy. Henchard somewhat confusingly ascribes this error to literalism: rousing himself from a drunken stupor the morning after selling Susan, he feels "surprised and nettled that his wife had taken him so literally" when he publicly auctioned her off at a village fair and she swore her willingness to go. But the word proves imprecise, and Henchard's subsequent dealings show that the literal and figurative are never wholly separable. In a note to Susan when he hears of her return nearly twenty years later, he encloses a five-pound note supplemented by five shillings—an amount calculated to be meaningful, the narrator remarks, as "it may tacitly have said to her that he bought her back" (67). This gesture of offering the exact figure for which he sold her yields an odd synthesis of the literal and the symbolic. The very thing that made the transaction "literal" in the first place, a definite sum of money laid out in cash and coin, is repurposed here as a symbolic representation of a second agreement meant to reverse the first. Relative to Henchard's attempt to undo the past, Elizabeth-Jane becomes disconcertingly analogous to the money he uses to make amends. Susan's apologetic explanation, in a note to be read after her own death, characterizes her second daughter as a living form of compensation, an equivalent that "filled up the ache I felt at the other's loss" (123). Here, it would be incongruous to describe Henchard's mistaking Elizabeth-Jane for her namesake as the error of taking words at face value; no alternative to literalism presents itself.

There is, however, a more accurate term for what throws Henchard into confusion about the relation between verbal agreements and the subjects onto which they map: we call it realism. Whether one understands realist fiction as mimetic or formally constitutive of social structures, the dominant mode of literary narrative established the conditions for assuming that linguistic reference will hold steady within its own discursive frame. Such is the unspoken contract between novelist and reader: the novel may proliferate signifiers and multiply characters, but it cannot break the link it has forged between signifier and signified. Readers of *Bleak House*, for instance, may not know who Esther Summerson really is by birth, and even her face may change so drastically as to render her unrecognizable, but her name—whatever its origin—stands as a guarantee that it refers to the same subject, ensuring continuity across temporal gaps and uncertainties. *The Mayor of Casterbridge* violates this semiotic contract. The name Elizabeth-Jane, as we learn belatedly, does not promise consistency of reference; its repetition instead multiplies the subject to which it seems to point.

Trained to expect transparency from a third-person narrative, Hardy's readers are inveigled into the same mistake Henchard makes. The narrator, in reintroducing Susan walking down the old road to Weydon-Priors many years later with a young woman of eighteen, operates (like Susan herself) by omission rather than direct untruth in allowing the reader to assume that this daughter is the one we saw before. "A glance," Hardy's narration pronounces, "was sufficient to inform the eye that this was Susan Henchard's grown-up daughter," and indeed she is; this does not make her Michael's, though we are not disabused of the assumption any sooner than he is (19). Susan evasively describes Henchard to this daughter as "a relation by marriage," which he is in the most absolutely literal sense, and answers her inquiry, "I suppose he never knew me?" with an "uneasily" spoken but decisive "Of course not, Elizabeth-Jane"—the proper name seeming to belie this answer and falsely suturing the present addressee to the past subject whose name she shares, when in fact the mother's words are wholly true (21).

Numbers as well as names assist in perpetuating misrecognition, putting forward a count presumed to comprise all relevant facts. In a passage purporting to catch the reader up on what has transpired in the intervening years between Susan's departure and her return to the same scene, Hardy's quantitative references play almost imperceptibly on the uncertain number of subjects involved in this narrative. Susan's story, he notes, "can be told in two or three sentences"; two sentences follow, the first explaining that Newson took her to Canada and the second adding that when Elizabeth-Jane was twelve, "the three returned to England" (25). It is left to be inferred that "the three" are the original three persons who departed Weydon-Priors together. This short account, in being summed up in two sentences rather than three, omits a hypothetical third sentence that might have mentioned the death of the first Elizabeth-Jane and the birth of the second. This enumeration of sentences and of persons suggests a deceptive proportioning of units of writing to quantifiable human referents. The apparent linkage between narrative discourse and population thus points to an elemental supposition that Hardy's plot disproves: that writing, *qua* representation of some assumed social totality, promises a binding relation to a concrete demographic set.

The multiplication of human referents to which any signifier might attach is implicit even in ordinary conversation. Hardy registers this in his characters' use of pronouns. "Her 'he' was another man than her poor mother's" (56), explains the narrator, relaying an exchange in which Susan worries whether it was proper for Elizabeth-Jane to wait on Farfrae at the King of Prussia inn "for the sake of *him*" (meaning Henchard), while the daughter's reply uses similarly generic male pronouns to refer to another subject (Farfrae). Their conversation thus contains, in miniature, the plot that follows: just as Farfrae comes to occupy the referential place of the "he" that points to Henchard, so too will he occupy the social places vacated by the main character.

The truth upheld by Hardy's prose—contra Henchard's assumption that one equals one in the interchangeability of Farfrae and Jopp or that the name Elizabeth-Jane confirms that the present person is identical with the past—is that figures claim no fixed quantitative ratio with persons. Words have no fidelity to a singular referent, and signs and symbols do not mirror the objects to which they seem to attach. The climactic scene of the Skimmington ride—a form of charivari that exposes and mocks Henchard's past romantic entanglement with Lucetta, now married to Farfrae—serves to confirm that representation does not come second to life. Paraded through the streets on a donkey, the effigies of the former lovers actually take the place of the characters for which they stand. The signifier threatens to demolish the signified. When Lucetta perceives that the crude wax figure of a woman is meant to represent her, she exclaims with horror, "She's me—she's me," and dies soon after, as though supplanted by her own representation (275). Henchard too, critical of Susan for having taken things "literally," is haunted by the deadly force of figures. Seeing the shape of a body (which turns out to be his own discarded effigy) floating on the surface of a stream, he perceives "with a sense of horror that it was *himself*. Not a man resembling him, but . . . his actual double"—the lifeless figure confirming the fate on which he has already decided (293). This scene hints at the sweeping narrative import of being, as he confesses to Farfrae in the context of bookkeeping, "bad at figures" (48). Henchard is not only unable to keep track of numbers, which the novel makes difficult by masking the multiplicity of its human integers; he also cannot keep the figurative from becoming real—so much so that he hails the abandoned wax figure as an "actual double," a paradoxically literal symbol indistinct from what it symbolizes. The consequences of the Skimmington ride realize the threat that representation, rather than imitating life, might multiply it and displace its subject. This danger applies to the slipperiness of reference in general, so that the meeting of signifier and signified produces a figural surplus in itself.

Laws of Germination

> Be rather curious than anxious about your own career. . . . A naturalist's interest in the hatching of a queer egg or germ is the utmost introspective consideration you should allow yourself.
>
> —Thomas Hardy, *The Life and Work of Thomas Hardy*

The presence of superfluous figures in fiction is not new, nor is the fact that Hardy's characters end up occupying places reserved for others. Esther Summerson became the heroine of *Bleak House* by "filling a place . . . which ought to have been empty" (31), and Braddon's Lady Audley, as the previous chapter argued, compromised the security of the domestic sphere by occupying multiple positions at once. Such novels made demographic excess into a dynamic force of organic and social transformation. In Hardy's fiction, by contrast, redundancy ceases to yield progress narratives and, strikingly, ceases to correspond to the crowding of social space—not only because writing disconnects words and figures from a merely reflective relation to human numbers but also, quite simply, because population growth and ecological scarcity are not the problem. The Wessex in which most of his novels are set is almost too fertile, and its human population is shrinking. Demography remains elemental to these narratives, yet they plot the other side of the mass migration to cities that shaped the industrial era. The depopulation of the countryside is not merely the context but the substance of *Tess of the D'Urbervilles*, as Hardy suggests in placing Tess and her family among masses of small landholders and tenant farmers dislocated by the long history of land enclosure and industrialization—this "process, humorously designated by statisticians as 'the tendency of the rural population towards the large towns,'" the narrator acidly remarks, "being really the tendency of water to flow uphill when forced by machinery" (352). The resulting itinerant existence imposed on Hardy's characters is the primary manifestation of historical development, which in these narratives does not solve but causes insufficiency.

The botanical tropes that loom large in the Wessex novels provide a vocabulary for a strikingly ominous conception of growth and development. Hardy portrays organic processes from plant growth to human maturation to historical development accelerating beyond any calculable utility. As the plot of *The Mayor of Casterbridge* suggests in overshooting the mark set by the bildungsroman, tracking Henchard's rise from unemployed fieldworker to successful grain merchant and back again, maturation has no definite endpoint. When an observer at the agricultural fair in the opening scene appraises Susan as possessing "true cultivation" that only needs "a little bringing out" (10), both the idiom of breeding (with its mixed connotations of genealogy, nurture, and agricultural production) and the process of bringing out intrinsic qualities turn out to describe this novel's central problem. This chance remark begins an extended conceit linking crop cultivation to human gestation. Hardy underscores this figurative link by timing Susan's arrival in Casterbridge (in search of her former husband Henchard after Newson is presumed dead) to coincide with a local bread shortage—the consequence of Henchard's error in selling the town "grown wheat" that continues to germinate after reaching maturity and thus becomes unsuitable for baking. The moral and sexual subtext of this seedy deal is evident when a townswoman calls the resulting hypertrophic bread "unprincipled" (30). The narrative voice amplifies the echo of Henchard's matrimonial failures in his agricultural failures when it later punningly describes Casterbridge as "a representative centre of husbandry" (259).

This scenario of the grown wheat, which equates the agricultural plot with the familial plot, changes the valence of growth: it makes success contingent on arresting that process. Henchard's bad business deal in the grain trade in this way notably parallels his earlier transaction, not least of all in its irreversibility. When a townsman asks the corn-factor how he plans "to repay [the people of Casterbridge] for the past," Henchard sternly retorts,

"If anybody will tell me how to turn grown wheat into wholesome wheat, I'll take it back with pleasure. But it can't be done" (36). The grown-up daughter who accompanies Susan to Casterbridge stands as living proof that the prior deed of putting human goods into circulation has already borne fruit—a process of germination that cannot be reversed. The simultaneous arrival of Farfrae thus takes on heightened significance when he shares a technique for converting bad grain to a "wholesome" state, at least "enough to make good seconds out of it" (46). Like Henchard's subsequent attempt to redress past offenses by remarrying Susan, however, the ameliorative process may mitigate damage but cannot restore the overdeveloped crop to its former condition. "To fetch it back entirely is impossible," Donald cautions. "Nature won't stand so much as that" (47). The sprouted seed remains what it is, and the plant is salvageable only if future growth can be restrained.

Halting growth, however, proves tricky on all fronts—and the novel extends the metaphor of germination beyond its obvious associations with procreation (a double meaning that *Jude the Obscure* will make almost audible in Sue Bridehead's wish to live free of "all laws except gravitation and germination" [139]). Hardy's narrative voice in *The Mayor of Casterbridge* reveals disadvantageous development imperceptibly beginning in one place as soon as it has been curtailed in another. In tracking the relationship between the two men who collaborated on the problem of the grown wheat, the narrator metaphorizes an imminent tension between Henchard and Farfrae as a similar process of unintended germination: "the seed that was to lift the foundation of this friendship was at that moment taking root in a chink of its structure" (95). Such images of unplanned growth frame the whole career of the troubled protagonist. Henchard, whose livelihood depends on his ability to husband the growth of seeds, ultimately loses not only his friendship with Farfrae but also his claim to all his established roles—familial as well as economic and political—due to processes of growth over which he has minimal control. On a literal level, he loses his business by making another agricultural mistake: predicting that rain will spoil a coming crop, he hordes wheat that falls in value when the prophesied bad weather does not come. On a figurative level, these failed endeavors in cultivation encode his own developmental failures, as his painstaking self-cultivation veers off the course plotted by classic novels of formation.

Such imagery of sprouting seeds does similarly adverse work in *Tess of the D'Urbervilles*, even as its protagonist, compared with Henchard, seems more suited to the developmental conventions of the genre. *Tess* escorts its heroine onto the scene as a blooming girl and chronicles her maturation. Yet despite Tess Durbeyfield's youth and the story's temporal signposts of development, this novel equally resists the progressive trajectory proper to the bildungs-roman. Here too, germination and growth no longer suggest the gradual cultivation of a better self but instead figure a process that overextends and outpaces itself. Overdevelopment encodes a problem from the start. Opening in spring with a scene of May Day festivities that the narrator identifies as a local type of "Cerealia," Hardy's narrative emphasizes the hypertrophy of the land and of Tess's body at once. The young heroine, like the prodigiously fertile terrain on which she is reared, appears prematurely endowed with "a luxuriance of aspect, a fulness of growth which made her appear more of a woman than she really was"—and this early sexual development proves detrimental (42). Agricultural production furnishes the terms for the risk of untimely fertility: neighbors at the pub whisper that her mother, then scheming to send Tess to "claim kin" with the Stoke-D'Urbervilles and perhaps catch the eye of a noble suitor, should "mind that she don't get green malt in flower" (28). Forecasting the literal outcome of the ruinous plan to leverage the family name and revive its value through Tess, the narrator remarks that Joan Durbeyfield's fantasy of her daughter attracting a gentleman has "impregnated the whole family" (31). Every feature of the scenery surrounding Hardy's unfortunate heroine suggests early fecundity. The strawberries Alec D'Urberville feeds her at Trantridge have come up before their season, and the roses with which he adorns her are early to blossom: "such roses in early June!" exclaims a stranger observing Tess on her return home (44). The premature productivity of the natural world jars against the predictable rhythm of the seasons, accelerating the measured temporality of the development plot so that physical maturity and reproduction come too early, with death close on their heels.

If the imagery of early flowering makes the course of Tess's short life look like a *fait accompli*, amplifying the suggestion that her recently discovered Norman lineage has outlived its meaning, it also disrupts a certain literal chain of association between plant life and human life. What made human sexual development and fertility catastrophic, for Malthus, was the multiplication of mouths to feed over and above what the land could supply. While every aspect of Tess's life is touched by scarcity, and she herself feels a "Malthusian vexation" with her serially pregnant mother for taxing the impoverished family's resources, the novel's lush descriptions of its heroine's environment belie any Malthusian claim that the earth cannot support its population (37). The landscape in which Angel Clare courts Tess is over-ripe, "rank with juicy grass which sent up mists of pollen at a touch" (122). Talbothay's dairy and the surrounding valley flow with milk and honey all summer, when "the rush of juices could almost be heard below the hiss of fertilization" (149). Amid these eroticized scenes of wild fecundity, Angel patronizingly casts Tess as a freshly grown "daughter of the soil" ripe for the harvest (126). If this quasi-imperial fantasy of natalism without history misleads him into romanticizing Tess as an autochthonous growth of the terrain he hopes to cultivate, the metaphoric vocabulary of the seed is so tenacious that it persists even where its meaning is inverted. When the disclosure of Tess's sexual history (rather than her ancestral past) on their wedding night shatters the illusion of unspoiled produce, Angel recasts her as damaged goods but retains the same conceit; even in turning her noble lineage against her, he scorns her as "the exhausted seedling of an effete aristocracy" (232). Neither characterization is accurate. Tess is a wholly modern figure, shaped by land privatization, industrialized agriculture, a bit of national schooling, and a heavy dose of disenchantment. Yet there are other reasons why this image of the seedling remains in currency: the language of germination had been appropriated—and the metaphor bent toward a contrary meaning—by a new biological paradigm that would redefine the problem of population.

Generational Outcomes

> In her is the end of breeding.
>
> —Ezra Pound, "The Garden"

These figures of seeds and germination reveal a register of metaphor detached from the ratio of agricultural production to human reproduction. They are linked to an emerging theory that sought to explain, in the 1880s and 90s, why adaptation and development hit a dead end in certain lives: namely, August Weismann's germ plasm theory of heredity, which Hardy's fiction brings into confrontation with competing explanations provided by sociology. For this model of reproductive biology, the seed or "germ"—rather than evoking the developmental possibilities of life under formation—became the term of art for what is least changeable in organisms: "one might represent the germ-plasm," Weismann suggests, "by the metaphor of a long creeping root-stock from which plants arise at intervals, these latter representing the individuals of successive generations" (266).[4] Hereditary science provides fiction with a recognizable lexicon for explaining the success and failure of individuals as the result of inherited characteristics that cannot be altered. It is heavily thematized in *Jude the Obscure*: Jude and Sue periodically suspect that what makes them such a "weak, tremulous pair" is a compromised genetic inheritance they carry (286). Jude regards himself as a bad seed, liable either to develop beyond its usefulness, like Henchard's "grown wheat," or to remain stunted and fail to bear fruit. This feared truth of genealogy speaks as a first-person voice in Hardy's later prosopopoeic poem, "Heredity," which recasts both individual identity and generational continuity as endless repetition: "The eternal thing in man / That heeds no call to die" is not the immortal soul but the gene, leaping across the void of evolutionary time, indifferent to its carrier.

Routing Hardy's writing through Weismannism rather than Darwinism yields a notably different set of problems bound to biological and social reproduction. To account for the narrative impact of hereditary biology as well as its consequences for social theory, it is worth stressing how substantially germ plasm theory diverges from Darwin's development hypothesis. Hardy's fiction is often called Darwinian for its emphasis on the causal forces of instinct and environment, and his references to heredity can seem to later readers like the logical extension of natural selection. But while heredity came to be hailed in the twentieth century as the completing element in the modern evolutionary synthesis, it marked a dramatic departure on several fronts.[5] First, Weismannism can be understood in part as a refutation of the Lamarckian theory that an organism's adaptive use and disuse of inborn characteristics that aid its survival might alter these characteristics and, in turn, transform the species over time. Though *The Origin of Species* is sometimes treated as the corrective to Jean-Baptiste Lamarck's transmutation hypothesis, Darwin does not deny the heritability of acquired traits. He indeed speculates "that habit, use, and disuse, have, in some cases, played a considerable part in the modification of the constitution, and of the structure of various organs" (109). This view persists even when Darwin ventures a theory of inheritance in *The Variation of Animals and Plants under Domestication*, which proposes in 1868 that acquired traits too might be transmitted via the generative action of "gemmules": invisible parent particles he conjectured present in all parts of the organism. Lamarckianism lost favor after the emergence of germ plasm theory.[6] It was Weismann's contention that germ cells, or gametes, exclusively determine the heritable characteristics of progeny and that changes in the somatic cells composing the rest of the body have no hereditary outcome. Heredity, by his account, relies on "the fact that a small portion of the effective substance of the germ, the germ-plasm, remains unchanged during the development of the ovum into an organism, and that this part of the germ-plasm serves as the foundation from which the germ cells of the new organism are produced" (*Essays upon Heredity* 266). The result is an absolute "continuity of the germ-plasm from one generation to another," unmodified by the use or disuse of the soma (266).

Beyond its technical divergence from Darwinism and the skepticism it raised about natural selection, germ plasm theory substantially changes the significance of life and of history. The Darwinian world presented itself as a site of ceaseless work, adaptation, and developmental possibility—the scientific correlate, to put it reductively, of the liberal capitalist doctrine that effective competition among individuals gradually improves the condition of the group. *The Origin of Species* indeed alternates between metaphors of the employment market and metaphors of the state to describe organisms competing for a varying but always limited number of "places" in what he calls, by turns, "the economy of nature" and "the polity of nature" (346, 83). Darwin's natural history is a story of formation in which individual organisms profit by a combination of vital instinct, active struggle, and fortuitous circumstance, with time always on the side of advancement. Though importantly subject to chance, life's teleology is progressive from the standpoint of individuals and species alike; "as natural selection works solely by and for the good of each being," Darwin famously surmises, "all corporeal and mental endowments will tend to progress toward perfection" (360). Weismann's hereditary theory invalidated this progress narrative, breaking any connection between the passage of time and organic improvement. His biological model, applied to the scale of a single life, slows down evolutionary processes so radically that biographical time looks almost static. The organism, by this account, is principally a carrier of genetic material; its activity—its lifelong labor of becoming—is of little consequence apart from its transmission of the germ.

This theory was harder to reconcile with the novelistic concept of character and with the logic of plot than was Darwin's development hypothesis, which had altered the stakes of individual life experience in a different sense. The theory of natural selection valued the organism less for its uniqueness than for its capacity to survive and reproduce, passing on the traits that aided its survival within a given environment. If this left much to chance and to ecological contingency, it also lent developmental consequence to the organism's actions. Hereditary biology, by contrast, suggests not just a determinacy that minimizes individual agency but also the inconsequence of what happens during the plot of a life. Its impact, however, is evident in naturalist fiction. If the realist novel counseled that the march of history relies on unhistorical lives and that, as George Eliot puts it, "the existence of insignificant people has very important consequences in the world" (*Adam Bede* 68), the naturalist novel negates this claim. It moves its protagonists through environments in which their lives have no import before or after their early deaths; the bitter final scene of *Jude the Obscure* shows the university town of Christminster, indifferent to the novel's hero from first to last, boisterously celebrating a festival day while Jude Fawley dies alone and unmourned. And if the bildungsroman in its heyday trained readers to understand character formation as a microcosm of history, Hardy's fiction registers the insignificance of individual life from a biological perspective. However intensely individuated the novel's characters may be and however they struggle to plot their own futures, they are little more than clusters of cells—and young Jude is shaken by an early sense of the disharmonious forces of the organic world crashing against "the little cell called your life" (18).

In framing life in these terms, Hardy's fiction—classically read by Gillian Beer as the product of and response to a Darwinian universe and as valorizing the individual lifespan against the expanded scale of evolutionary time—can be seen to rework biographical form in reaction to a notably post-Darwinian moment and to formulate its conflicts in the idiom of hereditary biology.[7] Whether or not Hardy's plots corroborate the exclusive truth of heredity, Weismann's theory injects itself into the narration of his later novels. In *Tess of the D'Urbervilles*, it lies at the back of the narrator's questionable suggestion that the heroine's character and experience owe to the paternal line atavistically connecting her to her Norman ancestors. While the present drives its cart and its plow (or its gargantuan steam-powered threshing machine, in Tess's case) over the bones of the dead, an equally violent past refuses to remain buried. Stasis and change seem equally deadly, and futurity is emptied of adaptive possibility. Family history and heredity cast a similar shadow over *Jude the Obscure*, in which congenital defect enters into conscious thought and explicit discussion among characters. Jude, reared to view his family as abnormal stock, worries even before meeting his cousin Sue that a match between them would yield "a terrible intensification of unfitness" (168). When the two lose the nerve to marry, each having made that mistake once before, Jude muses that they "ought never to have been born," while Sue predicts that future generations will share their terror of life and be "afraid to reproduce" more of their kind (286, 287). By the warning of Jude's great aunt Drusilla, there is "sommat in our blood" that makes the Fawleys ill suited to marriage—and Jude is prone to suspect that some innate tendency renders all their attempts at progress abortive, all alliances futile, all contracts void, all reproduction self-destructive (70).

This novel's repeated references to blood lineage and familial anomaly, vague though they are, accordingly lent themselves to a single interpretation: to many late Victorian readers, they signaled the inescapable fact of a degraded inheritance that no character can overcome. Critics took additional hints from theories of degeneracy, which invited them to imagine the descent of man on a small scale as a story of pathological mutation rather than progressive improvement. The concept was popularized in Max

Nordau's *Degeneration*, translated into English in 1895, which expanded on Benedict-Augustin Morel's psychiatric study of "morbid deviation from an original type" (5) and applied Cesare Lombroso's anthropometric criminology to a denunciation of fin-de-siècle art. Nordau warned of "a severe mental epidemic . . . a sort of black death of degeneration and hysteria" afflicting Europe (537), finding symptoms of this biocultural scourge in everything from the deformation of earlobes to Oscar Wilde's style of dress. While raising alarm about a twentieth century populated by masochistic men, sadistic women with short hair, homosexuals, vegetarians, and members of clandestine suicide clubs, Nordau takes comfort in the conviction that nature's laws prevent such a future. "Degenerates, hysterics, and neurasthenics," he posits, "are not capable of adaptation" and are thus "fated to disappear" (540). This trendy (if incoherent) theory offered Hardy's critics a diagnostic lens through which to read his characters' fate. Edmund Gosse, who called *Jude the Obscure* a "chronicle of four unnecessary lives," detected biological deviance in the protagonists' every act. Sue displayed telltale symptoms of neurasthenia and sexual aberrance, and her story was "a terrible study in pathology" (67), while Jude's frustrated intellectual ambition was the "megalomania" of a "neurotic subject in whom hereditary degeneracy takes an idealist turn" (65). Other reviewers extended these diagnoses from characters to author, implying that the novel was itself the progeny of a diseased literary parent: *The World* titled its review "Hardy the Degenerate."

These reviews had an undeclared political impetus, effectively vindicating gender, class, and sexual norms by diagnosing abnormality in those who challenged them—and the political consequences of germ plasm theory itself were not far to seek. Weismann's account of heredity varnished the scientific authority of eugenics, enabling its proponents to champion policies that promoted or prevented the fertility of certain groups. H. G. Wells, skeptical of Francis Galton's emphasis on the selective breeding of superior human specimens, countered in 1900 that social hygiene via negative eugenics ("the sterilization of failures") was the state's best chance of beating nature to the punch. "The way of nature has always been to slay the hindmost," Wells argues, calling evolution a misnomer, "and there is still no other way, unless we can prevent those who would become the hindmost being born" (qtd. in Galton, "Eugenics" 60). Aggressive intervention in the domain of reproduction went hand in hand with a resolute policy of non-intervention in any other aspect of existence for "the hindmost." Karl Pearson, another prominent eugenicist, used hereditary biology to recommend austerity measures and argue against all extant forms of welfare. For Pearson, the continuity of the germ plasm proved that no social remediation could convert bad human specimens into "sound and healthy stock," since education, hygiene, and habits of discipline acquired during an individual's life are not genetically transmissible (26–27). Readers who applied such precepts to Hardy's last novel could persuade themselves that its protagonist's academic ambitions were futile not because they are blocked by class hegemony but because his education would die with him and carry no generational legacy. Read in line with *Jude the Obscure*, Pearson's theory resonates chillingly with the suicide of the children, which from this perspective marks the ultimate eugenic check to Jude's ambitions of generational social mobility.

If Hardy's readers were ready to take a cue from eugenics and conclude that Jude and his kin were doomed by their unfitness, his novel does not bear out any such deterministic explanation. Such a theory, in making sense of the novel's senseless tragedy, evidently appealed to Victorian critics disturbed by *Jude the Obscure*'s overt critique of the class system, the university, marriage, patriarchy, and the nuclear family. But the eugenic reading never quite suffices to make reproductive biology trump all social causes or prove that institutions cannot offset the effects of nature. Jude's view of himself as a weak specimen congeals as a strange amalgam of the normal and the abnormal: he is a bad seed because he fails to restrain the instinct marked as typical of the species and necessary to its perpetuation.

This contradiction surfaces even where Hardy's narration seems most intent on making reproductive instinct a master discourse. Jude's first encounter with Arabella presents itself as a mating scene, all signs pointing to irrepressible sexual impulses and laws of selection. At the moment when the butcher's daughter hurls that choice bit of pig flesh at Jude's head—an image that condenses sexuality's sudden ascendency with butchery and castration—we seem to witness the victory of instinct over autonomy, animal body over reasoning mind. As the narrator puts it, "the unvoiced call of woman to man . . . held Jude to the spot against his intention, almost against his will" (40). The protagonist, distracted from the syllabus of classics he is mentally devising, responds to Arabella's mating call "in commonplace obedience to conjunctive orders from headquarters, unconsciously received" (39). Yet this set piece is deceptive insofar as it appears to pit nature against culture. What is generalized as species nature at one moment gets transmuted at the next into evidence of the protagonist's unique incapacity for social mobility. When Jude first finds his dream of higher education blocked by an early marriage to Arabella, he rebukes himself with a paradoxically singular failure to resist universal instincts. That fleeting desire, heavily coded as an ordinary episode of mammalian sexual selection at the time, comes to seem so deviant to Jude in retrospect that he calls it an "erotolepsy" (98).

What sort of man, he wonders, could have allowed the prompting of a mere "transitory instinct" to cancel out "years of thought and labour" and dash his dreams of becoming a scholar—his "one opportunity of showing himself superior to the lower animals" (62)? The human-animal divide itself becomes the horizon of a sexual error in judgment that has drastic economic consequences.

It is clear, despite the suggestion that nature exerts a wild force of impulse at odds with order, that natural and social demands cannot really be divorced. Arabella relies not on the power of nature as such but on the cultural coding of natural processes to achieve her aim, declaring as she stows a bird's egg in her bosom that it is "natural for a woman to want to bring live things into the world" and entrapping Jude in marriage by alleging that their copulation has yielded such a live thing. Hardy's narration oddly conspires with her to create the impression of an irresistible procreative drive at work. Everything from Arabella's name (seeming to fuse the arable with the beautiful) to the oddly generalized biological description of her appearance ("a complete and substantial female human") points to fertility and mating, yet the pair's sexual coupling has no automatic connection to any reproductive necessity. The scene's meaning looks different once it comes to light that Arabella has faked pregnancy in order to coerce Jude into marrying her.

The novel thus contradicts the seemingly inevitable connection between sexuality and reproduction that Malthus had turned into an argument for the systematic prevention of early marriage. If what Malthus called the sexual impulse is at work in Jude's desire for Arabella, it provides no straightforward explanation in itself for what puts the brakes on his academic progress and leaves his books stained with pork grease. But the whole series of events gets corralled into a ready narrative of personal failure for the protagonist. That narrative, which the *Essay on Population* helped establish, treats poverty as the result of a deficiency of restraint. Malthus, while universalizing the sexual impulse and faulting the old Poor Laws for promoting improvidence, complained of a widespread "carelessness and want of frugality observable among the poor," an inability to plan for the future, a tendency to exhaust all savings at the alehouse (98). This version of class character, so culturally pervasive and so essentialized by the late nineteenth century that it had acquired a quasi-racial status, is familiar enough to Jude that virtually every action he takes, from drinking to sex, comes to look to him like proof of his innate inferiority to the men of Christminster. (These worthies, when Jude encounters them, turn out to be in large part a bunch of drunken college boys, different from himself mainly in their sense of entitlement and their ignorance of the Latin he has laboriously taught himself while working full-time.) Further intensifying the appearance of biological determinacy, Hardy's protagonist seeks a new form of self-evaluation in hereditary science. Its hidden truths are hinted at in ominous references to family history, which Jude treats as evidence that he descends from a doomed lineage, and raised to a fever pitch of generalization when he later laments to Sue that swearing off alcohol has not purged him of vice because he carries "the germs of every human infirmity" (266).

However heavy-handed its language of instinct and hereditary predisposition, the novel does not confirm Jude's view that nature has disqualified him from intellectual pursuits or marked him for early death by endowing him with a congenital excess of sexual desire, restlessness, improvidence, or intemperance. In fact, it consistently demonstrates the ideological reproduction of social tendencies too easily attributed to biology. This is clear, for example, in the circumstances that initiate what Jude regards as his drinking habit. When he first finds his academic plans foiled by marriage, the idea of getting drunk occurs to him as a form of self-inflicted punishment "in keeping with his present degraded position" (71). Suicide seems too heroic for him, so he chooses alcohol instead: "Of course that was it; he had forgotten. Drinking was the regular stereotyped resource of the despairing worthless," he thinks, heading for "an obscure public house" (71). The whole logic of subordination is spelled out in the thought process articulated here. What drives Jude to drink is not an innate lack of restraint, a hereditary infirmity doubly embedded in family history and class character. On the contrary, his decision to revert to the "obscure" milieu into which he is relegated is just that: a decision, at once thoroughly conscious and thoroughly overdetermined by stereotypes as well as by real economic barriers that he (as an individual acting alone) has no means to challenge. This evocation of the force of stereotype counters any hint that Jude's failures owe to degeneracy or inadequate self-control. The novel painstakingly demonstrates that virtually every adverse circumstance chalked up to inherited class characteristics, biological aberration, or unchanging laws of sexual instinct is in fact socially reproduced. To denaturalize these tropes of hereditary anomaly makes sense, and the novel makes it possible to do so by illustrating social causation.

Once one has noted that the transhistorical truths put forward by the natural sciences are shot through with historically specific demands to sanction the status quo, it feels obligatory to plunge back into the oddly cold comfort of social constructionism. Insisting on social rather than natural determination seems to hold out the prospect that existing social structures can be changed, even revolutionized (though this does not necessarily follow, as we will see). Social science in the 1890s indeed offered itself as an alternative to the prevailing theories of heredity, which plainly do not account for the blocked aspirations of Hardy's protagonist, much less justify the self-extermination of his children. Émile Durkheim, writing contemporaneously with Hardy and Gissing, contends that a sociological theory of suicide is necessitated in part by the inadequacy of biological explanations. Because humans are intrinsically social animals, he argues, their actions can never be solely dictated by instinct or physiological necessity. Countering the common assumptions that suicide was either a genetic anomaly or proof of the broader degeneration of European populations, he offered a resolutely social explanation for the maladjustment of individuals to their circumstances and a resultant weakening of the will to live.

Sociology and the Economy of Vital Forces

> Every disturbance of equilibrium, even though it
> achieves greater comfort and a heightening of general
> vitality, is an impulse to voluntary death.
>
> —Émile Durkheim, *Suicide*

What goes so hideously awry in Jude's life story looks quite different through the lens of Durkheim's sociology. It fits the trend outlined in *Suicide*: a widespread malaise and loss of stamina that novelists of the period wrote into their characters and that scientists clamored to diagnose. Challenging the biological conjectures of Bertillon and others, Durkheim cites changes in the social structure as the root cause of self-destructive behavior. His study, which breaks down suicide into four major types, correlates each type with varying degrees of excess or deficit in individuals' social integration and moral regulation. Among these, he singles out anomic suicide as the major type found in Western Europe in the late nineteenth century. Recent spikes in the suicide rate, he argues, are largely due to anomie, a condition of normlessness caused by "society's insufficient presence in individuals," which predominates at moments of social transformation (*Suicide* 258). By his reasoning, dissatisfaction and unrest are symptoms of a certain sociopolitical attenuation that impedes individuals from internalizing collective values or recognizing the moral authority of the social order. This, Durkheim argued, was the primary cause of what looked like deviant behavior in individuals.

The conflict between the two theories is clear. For hereditary biology, any attempt to improve the individual by altering his or her social conditions would be futile; conception, in effect, is destiny. For sociology, by contrast, no human tendency is fully innate. Self-destructive feelings and actions, Durkheim suggests, are never simply due to "the intrinsic nature of a person, that is, his biological constitution" (298). In analyzing patterns of suicidal behavior within kinship groups, which his contemporaries took as evidence of genetic predisposition, Durkheim finds no basis for attributing high suicide rates to heredity. Repeated patterns within a family or a so-called race, he cautions, do not prove genetic causes. Unconvinced that heredity sheds any light on group behavior, Durkheim concludes that suicide cannot be attributed to any "congenital or invariable impulse" in individuals or groups but rather to "the progressive action of social life" (102). This approach retains some of its appeal, particularly as an alternative to the militant scientific racism that was successfully entrenching itself in theories of biological degeneracy, in eugenics, and in the forensic science of anthropometry. For the sociologist, the only reality is social reality, the only law social law.

Jude the Obscure, more than any other novel of the decade, negotiates the apparent tension between sociological and hereditary explanations for an otherwise unaccountable failure to thrive. Jude himself flirts with alternately biological and sociological explanations for his discontentment. He first classifies himself as the hereditary casualty of "cross-grained . . . stock" and later as just one more "paltry victim to the spirit of mental and social restlessness" that Durkheim would call anomie (90, 327). Neither explanation is wholly plausible in the end, though the latter may sound preferable to later readers. Given the ideological foundation of eugenicists' attempts to portray social inequality as natural law, it is tempting to side with Durkheim and contend that there is nothing innately deviant in Hardy's characters—that their enervation and morbidity are structural rather than natural facts. In practice, however, the two theoretically opposed models entangle themselves even at the level of rhetoric. What looks like the sociological side of Jude's story, his relation to the class system through the institutions of work and family, is easily naturalized in the protagonist's mind as a justification for inequality. The material effects of this inequality then get codified as the cause of his social subordination and redundancy. Even in recognizing that poverty doomed his intellectual ambitions from the start, Jude reverses cause and effect: "It takes two or three generations to do what I tried to do in one," he remarks, "and my impulses—affections—vices perhaps they should be called—were too strong not to hamper a man without advantages" (326). His self-assessment conflates social mobility with evolution, instinct with deviance, affective excess with material lack.

This entanglement of theoretical causes for his failure to advance in the world owes to more than just the faulty reasoning of Hardy's protagonist. The claims of post-Darwinian biology and functionalist sociology are in fact less antithetical than they sound. Both hinge survival on fitness to existing material conditions, with the difference that Durkheim's sociology characterizes the fit between individual life and world in terms of social adjustment. "No living being can be happy or even exist," he argues, "unless his needs are sufficiently proportioned to his means" (246). Here, as in the life sciences, the axiom of scarcity remains intact. In proposing a necessary equilibrium between desire and socioeconomic status, Durkheim effectively translates the old Malthusian principle of population into an individualized economy of affective and energetic investment. Where Malthus required nation-states and parishes to proportion their populations in keeping with the existing distribution of resources, Durkheim requires personal ambition to check itself on the same basis. Where biology imagined a political economy of nature in which organisms, per Darwin, compete for a varying but always limited number of "places," sociology fashions a political economy of the subject, requiring each individual to limit his aspirations to the scope afforded by his class. Anomie arises out of the failure to submit to this calculus, with suicide as a potential outcome. Durkheim's reasoning, in linking not just contentment but also the human vital impulse to the sense of serving a defined function in the social order, makes the class status one inherits from one's family scarcely more changeable than the shape of one's skull. Given the very real barriers to mobility, this may well sound like an accurate social description—a sobering antidote to that masochistic attachment to fantasies of "the good life" that Lauren Berlant, in a contemporary context, has called "cruel optimism" (1). But Durkheim's model of society moves from the descriptive to the prescriptive in suggesting that all persons remain in the place assigned by birth and circumstance lest they lose the will to live. The premise that humans are social animals with changing desires rather than creatures beholden to purely physiological demands carries no suggestion of progress. Quite the converse, the variability of human need is a trap; discontentment and self-destructive feelings result from the fact that "human activity naturally aspires beyond assignable limits" (247–48). For this very reason, Durkheim suggests, aspiration must be kept in check.

What would a novel look like if it followed Durkheim's prescription? The classic form of the bildungsroman collides with this sociological paradigm, which turns the tireless pursuit of a new place in the world (once celebrated in bourgeois social thought as the spur to historical change) into the stuff of tragedy. The demand to accept the rightness of one's social position is antithetical to virtually every familiar account of the novel. "Leaving home, improving on the lot one was born to," per Ian Watt, "is a vital feature of the individualist pattern of life" established in the genre (65). For Durkheim, such individuation risks becoming excessive and even fatal where it clashes with social demands. One must, in order to function normally and maintain one's vital energy, fit one's ambitions to one's preordained socioeconomic circum-stances. Class, in effect, is society's reality principle, and those who resist it suffer for their maladjustment. "To pursue a goal which is by definition unat-tainable," he argues, "is to condemn oneself to a state of perpetual unhap-piness" (248). Such a formulation applies all too readily to Hardy's Jude, the stonemason walled off from the university despite his intellectual abilities and determination. Indeed, Jude perfectly exemplifies the hypothetical case Durk-heim posits of a "workman [who] is not in harmony with his social position [because] he is not convinced that he has his just deserts" (250). Since the dis-contented workman cannot reasonably expect to change his position, in Durk-heim's view, his "unsatisfied tendencies atrophy" and weaken his "impulse to live" (246). "Effort grows, just when it becomes least productive," and this frustration necessarily depletes the vitality of the person whose work yields no benefit (253). The quintessentially novelistic longing for social mobility thus becomes a morbid condition. To justify the hierarchical division of labor that this model presupposes from the start, the sociologist vacillates between imagining a meritocracy based on the natural inequality of talent (the lone form of "heredity," as he puts it, that social equality could never alter) and simply concluding that the class system, however arbitrary, is necessary.

The turn to social determination, then, does not solve the problem or banish the specter of unfitness simply by denaturalizing heredity. Rather than contesting the racial and class ideologies and material inequalities that biology so readily translated into scientific laws, it reinforces inequality pre-cisely by rendering it a social fact. Durkheim makes a virtue of necessity; fit-ting one's wishes to one's class status, he maintains, ensures the individual's harmony with the necessary constraints of society. "Besides," he reasons, by "loving what he has and not fixing his desire solely on what he lacks," a person may ensure that the "equilibrium of his happiness is secure" (250).

It is not surprising that this sociological reasoning finds its way into Hardy's last novel as the voice of institutional authority: the master of Bib-lioll College. T. Tetuphenay, who responds to Jude's request for advice on how best to pursue his academic goals with the advice that he not pursue them, speaks the language of sociology in dutifully recommending the sta-tus quo. Addressing his letter to "Mr. J. Fawley, Stone-cutter" as if to link Jude's occupation permanently to his identity, the master replies: "judging from your description of yourself as a working-man, I venture to think that you will have a much better chance of success in life by remaining in your own sphere" (117). The perverse tautology here is hard to miss: one cannot change one's social position because of one's social position. Social facts con-firm themselves. If everything remains as it stands, this discouraging advice is sound enough; regardless of Jude's aptitude in classics, he does have a "better chance of success" at the occupation he has already entered simply because it has not yet been closed to him as higher education has. Not much of a recipe for the equilibrium of happiness, the letter confirms Jude's suspicions that "his destiny lay . . . among the manual toilers in the shabby purlieu which he himself occupied, unrecognized as part of the city at all by its visitors and panegyrists, yet without whose denizens the hard readers could not read nor the high thinkers live" (116).[8]

The truth is more radical than any failed liberal fantasy of incorporating the excluded individual into the existing credentialing system would suggest. Jude, in wondering whether he is worthy to enter the university or the clergy, is asking the wrong question. (And readers, in wishing for his success, are put in the untenable position of defending his claim to be the kind of meritorious individual who should be allowed to rise above the ranks of manual labor—a story that necessarily leaves class hierarchy intact.) As Sue recognizes, neither Christminster nor the church, as presently constituted, has anything to teach him intellectually or ethically. Jude himself, however, resists questioning the legitimacy of those institutions whose ideological function it is to sustain the class system. He seeks explanations instead in his own conduct, which he analyzes in terms that equate social disadvantage with hereditary defect. His domestic failures and misdirected desires prove, in Jude's mind, that he is "as unfit, obviously, by nature, as he had been by social position," for the professions (217). This usage of the term *unfit* is a catachresis, forcing an analogy through misapplication. Hardy's phrasing makes the analogy conspicuously recursive in its proposition that nature confirms what culture had already mandated, and vice versa—the very device of comparison obscuring or inverting, in Jude's mind, the causal link between the two. Such reasoning hinges one form of inequality on another without having to prove the validity of either one.

The force of analogical reasoning itself is key to the political problem this novel exposes. While Hardy's protagonists are prone to see natural instincts and social codes colliding at one moment and conspiring at the next, the established analogies and figurative vocabularies that link the two create the apparent double bind through which the status quo declares its own necessity. What these characters are up against are neither natural nor social laws but words that have taken on determinative power in the world—gesturing toward the Nietzschean dictum that what passes for truth is a "mobile army of metaphors" that have ceased to be recognizable as such and have come to seem like hard facts rather than figures and relationships created by human language. It is more than a logical error that late nineteenth-century theories of biological and social determination, however opposed in their scientific foundations, end up reinforcing each other. Both share common premises, expressed in an intertwined pair of metaphors linking the natural to the social. Weismann's explanation of how germ cells work reveals these premises in its figurative vocabulary: his 1883 lecture "On Heredity" describes the differentiated functions of gametes and somatic cells as a "division of labour" within a "cell colony" (75). Some cells, he explains, exist for the sole purposes of seeking sustenance and performing the work of locomotion, while others serve an exclusively reproductive function undisrupted by physical activity. A recognizable model of the social organism and its self-regenerative demands takes shape in this account of reproductive biology. The body is an empire, its raw biological material a cellular population of workers with specialized tasks to perform.

Insofar as Weismann's goal is to explain why certain organisms cannot improve via adaptation during their lifetime and thus cannot breed healthy descendants, the content of his argument matches its rhetorical form. His organizing metaphor turns the theory of heredity's desired outcome into its causal basis: in showing that neither the inherent functions of cells nor the inherited properties of organisms can change, his narrative of cell biology naturalizes the capitalist division of labor and the integrated global functioning of empire by making them intrinsic to the organization of life forms. The existing forms of social organization are scarcely more alterable for Durkheim; indeed, his first book declares socially divided labor "a law of nature" as well as a moral necessity (3). The rhetoric of sociology and that of hereditary science thus forge a link between the image of divided labor and that of the organism's cellular composition. Each is summoned as a privileged metaphor for the other. Much as Weismann imagines the reproductive body as a site of divided labor, Durkheim (drawing on a well-established figure in social science) imagines society as an organism that must work as an integrated and totalized system of interdependent functions.[9] This reversible comparison, equating the facts of reproductive biology with those of the capitalist class structure so that each affirms the other, helps tie the Gordian knot of Jude's own analogical inference about his natural and socioeconomic "unfitness."

What connects sociology to the biological paradigm it disavows is not just metaphoric but methodological. Durkheim's very conception of social fact has its foundation in population science at the level of content and at the level of method. For his purposes, one can establish the facticity of social facts—those generalizable constraints on individual behavior that structure societies—only by assessing demographic data. Since a social fact must be "general over the whole of a given society," analyzing this object requires the sociologist to presume an organic cultural unity of behaviors and norms that can be statistically totalized ("What Is a Social Fact?" 27). The biopolitical foundations of Durkheim's approach are still more evident in the particular data he treats as exemplary of the collective tendencies of groups.[10] To define and concretize sociology's central concept, his essay "What Is a Social Fact?" identifies social tendencies that can be taken as unquestionably real because they measurably alter the birth rate, the marriage rate, or the suicide rate.

Sociology's attention to vital statistics as a gauge of social tendencies is far from arbitrary. In its choice of subject matter, Durkheim's research on suicide embeds biological life in the very structure of institutions and yokes vitality to the functioning of social norms. While the preface to *Suicide* provides few reasons for studying such a topic apart from a reference to its "timeliness" and an assertion that it has the advantage of being easy to define, his choice is suggestive. Viewed within the framework of nineteenth-century biopolitics, the social-scientific preoccupation with suicide is not surprising; in Foucault's view, the will to cease living was politically unsettling to the extent that death marks biopower's limit. "This determination to die, strange and yet so persistent," he observes, "was one of the first astonishments of a society in which political power had assigned itself the task of administering life" (*The History of Sexuality, Volume 1* 138–39). From this angle, it stands to reason that one of sociology's first obsessions was the relation between social incorporation and biological life and that that one of its first conjectures was that the weakening of social authority leads to a diminution of the vital drive in individuals. Without precisely explaining to what end, Durkheim's study invests the governing institutions of society with the responsibility to sustain a population's will to live.

After Discipline?

> In order to identify the social composition with the social organism in the strict sense of the term, we should be able to speak of a society's needs and norms as one speaks of an organism's vital needs and norms, that is, unambiguously. . . . But it is enough that one individual in any society question the needs and norms of this society and challenge them—a sign that these needs and norms are not those of the whole society—in order for us to understand to what extent social need is not immanent, to what extent the social norm is not internal, and finally, to what extent the society, seat of restrained dissent or latent antagonisms, is far from setting itself up as the whole.
>
> —Georges Canguilhem, *The Normal and the Pathological*

Coinciding with a generation of novels whose plots are propelled by suicidal impulses, Durkheim's study—loaded though it is—claims a certain diagnostic power. In *Jude the Obscure*, the protagonists regard themselves as individually misaligned with their socially prescribed roles, lacking in vitality, and vexed by social norms. Jude all but diagnoses himself with a case of anomie, finding himself "in a chaos of principles" with no authority beyond individual "inclinations" to govern his conduct (327). In an improvised speech to a crowd at Christminster, he describes a loss of confidence in his early moral precepts and a vague suspicion that "there is something wrong somewhere in our social formulas" (327). Positioned in discourse as a bad subject inadequately governed, he might well seem to personify a failure of Foucauldian discipline. Jude reproaches himself in these terms, as we have seen, when his efforts do not advance his academic goals; were he only able to manage himself properly, he reasons, things might be otherwise. Naturalist fiction, however, runs quite counter to a disciplinary logic of power and indeed makes discipline incoherent. What saps the life out of Hardy's protagonists can hardly be called a failure to internalize social morality and to police one's own conduct accordingly. Jude and Sue take turns accusing themselves of gross immorality, and Tess tasks herself with sins others have committed against her as though they were her own. Subordination to what Freud would later call the ego-ideal is all too present in these characters, all of whom fear the watchful eye of the community. The issue in these novels, then, is not a lack of discipline—far from it. Their plots instead illustrate how careful self-regulation fails to yield the social benefits it promises. Their characters impose on themselves new regimes of discipline that carry to an entirely different level the fantasy of a society of self-policing individuals.

These practices aim to master the body in the service of distinctive ends. They are not geared toward channeling desire into marriage, domestic economy, and measured sexual reproduction (the teleological endpoints of discipline's standard script of delayed gratification) but toward a more absolute self-denial, often expressed as abstinence and even asceticism. Rhoda Nunn, in Gissing's *The Odd Women*, shapes what might otherwise be dismissed as an individual peculiarity into a political program. She declares the need for "a widespread revolt against the sexual instinct" in the service of gender equality; like Christianity, she speculates, "this great movement for women's emancipation must also have its ascetics" (67). Sue Bridehead, less successfully, resists heteronormative sexuality and reproduction, leaving her husband Phillotson and preferring to be Jude's comrade than his conjugal mate. Jude understands his life as a long labor of self-mastery, a struggle to bring what he regards as immoderate sexual impulses and a drinking habit into subjection (even though these impulses are seldom acted upon). Against the economic myth that poverty is the penalty for improvidence, idleness, and a lack of steady application, he is shown forgoing heat and meals to buy books, studying late into the night after long days of exhausting physical labor without the supervisory prompting of any institution. Phillotson, despite his love for Sue, voluntarily gives her up and returns to his familiar bachelor life. Edwin Reardon in *New Grub Street*, who holds himself "quite free from sexual bias," likewise releases his wife of all obligations and wonders who would not forgo the miseries of love and sex if given the choice (405). Nor does his "morbid state of mind" seek relief in drinking: "I haven't that diathesis," he confesses to his friend Harold Biffen (403). Michael Henchard, attributing his past sins to intemperance, swears off drink for twenty years and apparently remains celibate through this period of self-mortification. Being "by nature something of a woman-hater," he finds it easy "to keep at a distance from the sex" (*The Mayor of Casterbridge* 76). There is no excessive animal impulse requiring social control in these novels, no ravenous appetite glutting itself, no revolutionary violence preparing to erupt. Hardy's and Gissing's main characters show little inclination to marry or reproduce but end up locked into these obligations anyway.

If the protagonists' regimes of discipline often do not work in the end, and their scrupulous efforts to monitor their own conduct fail to win them the status of lives worth protecting, this is not because desire is a "given quantity," as Malthus maintained, nor because the individuals in question are categorically abnormal or insufficiently socialized. On the contrary, it is the coerciveness of formalized social obligation that prompts these characters to take actions they recognize as inimical. Marriage is the prime example. Though it wrecks Jude's educational plans and costs him more than all he has at the time, there is no need to force his hand when Arabella claims to be pregnant; he proposes it himself, having fully internalized the principle. Sue, in turn, bows under pressure to marry Phillotson to avoid the appearance of impropriety with Jude, though she regards marriage as subjecting love to "the sordid conditions of a business contract" (286). While Jude tentatively maintains that the "intention of the contract is good" when the two again face similar demands, it is clear that social intention is beside the point (286). Any such contract, he reflects, is liable to "defeat its own ends because we are the queer sort of people we are": people, that is, who resist compulsory ties not because they cannot uphold them but because they resent the implication that their affinities require legal constraints (286). Hardy's fiction consistently shows ethical obligation and attachment arising where contractual relations have already been violated or dissolved. Sue feels more faithful to Phillotson after leaving him than in the house where she shrank from the idea of mandatory marital sexuality. Henchard recognizes an obligation to the formerly retailed wife that he evidently did not feel when married to her and discovers, belatedly, that his love for the Elizabeth-Jane who is not his daughter does not depend on biological paternity. Jude is glad to raise the child of the marriage from which he was released; voicing a Godwinian protest against the nuclear family and the "beggarly question of parentage," he contends that all children are the collective responsibility of all adults (274). His and Sue's willingness to do more than any contract requires, to care for a son for whom they have no legal responsibility once Arabella remarries, bears this out, and indeed forms a "queer" sort of family that suffers for its unofficial status.

Pressed into normative social arrangements, Hardy's characters rarely resist. Yet their submission becomes a mode of self-punishment through practices that make discipline and punishment indistinguishable. Beaten down by the traumatic consequences of all attempts to live otherwise, the formerly radical Sue acquiesces to social norms with a fanatical sense of duty to bring herself under control. "Self-abnegation is the higher road" than the pursuit of pleasure, she exclaims to Jude; taking the violent death of her children as a divine judgment, she declares, "we should mortify the flesh" (244). Returning to Phillotson, Sue seeks to bring "[her] body into complete subjection" through feverish fasting and prayer (388), and she scrubs his stairs "to discipline [her]self" and subdue her mind to "domestic duties" (393). Sue ultimately submits to conjugal relations with the lawful husband who physically repels her: "doing a penance," as she describes it to the widow Edlin (394). Neither adherence to a counternorm nor submission to the norm proves effective, since the norm is subjectively experienced as compulsory rather than automatic.

Here, the novel's disavowal of faith in the process of socialization—and thus of the bildungsroman's narrative rationale—is stark. Disconnected from the teleology that drove *Wilhelm Meister's Apprenticeship* in Georg Lukács's reading, the individual here stands no chance of finding "responses to the innermost demands of his soul in the structures of society" (*The Theory of the Novel* 133). If one understands the European bildungsroman in these terms or in Moretti's terms as affirming the "comfort of civilization" and staving off any threat of revolution by making the existing social order look personally desirable rather than coercive, *Jude the Obscure* indeed does just the opposite (*The Way of the World* 15–73). The social order, as conceived in Hardy's novels, has the ironic effect of thwarting self-regulation and bringing about the aberrations it aims to prevent. Hardy ascribes to his protagonists an intrinsic moral capacity, suppressed by the very institutions that purport to restrain vice, temper animal impulse, and ensure good conduct. "To indulge one's instinctive and uncontrolled sense of justice and right," the narrator caustically remarks, rendering Jude's thoughts in free indirect discourse, was not "permitted with impunity in an old civilization like ours" (359). Instinct, far from a bloodthirsty, self-interested drive kept in check by laws and norms, here names a tendency toward altruism and solidarity that is penalized by the social code. What prompts Phillotson, against his wishes, to release Sue from marriage is likewise described as a "humane instinct" on his part (369), the consequence of which is that he is dismissed from his teaching post for setting a bad example. Social organization seems to work in perversely contrary directions: it punishes those who need no legal compulsion to act justly while disregarding actual transgressions provided they are kept quiet. Jude and Sue court scandal when they do not conceal their circumstances—when Sue confesses to her landlady that the two are not married—the immediate repercussions being ostracism, unemployment, and eviction. Meanwhile, Hardy's plot attests that far more egregious violations of social laws (Arabella's bigamy, for example) are easily ignored so long as the pretense of respectability is maintained. Jude, who once feared that Arabella would be criminally prosecuted for her bigamous second marriage in Australia, marvels to Sue that "nobody took any interest in her—nobody inquired, nobody suspected it." This, he observes, is the mixed blessing of being "poor and obscure people like us" (258), namely, that no one much cares what they do.

Individuality as Surplus

> "Lor!" cried Mrs. Boffin. "What I say is, the world's wide enough for all of us!"
> "So it is, my dear," said Mr. Boffin, "when not literary. But when so, not so."
>
> —Charles Dickens, *Our Mutual Friend*

> April 5. London. Four million forlorn hopes!
> April 7. A woeful fact—that the human race is too extremely developed for its corporeal conditions, the nerves being evolved to an activity abnormal in such an environment. . . . It may be questioned if Nature, or what we call Nature, so far back as when she crossed the line from invertebrates to vertebrates, did not exceed her mission.
>
> —Thomas Hardy, *The Life and Work of Thomas Hardy*

In proving the world's disregard for their characters, Hardy's and Gissing's novels place readers in an anomalous position. They demand not just distant sympathy but deep affective investment in their protagonists as individuals, even while demonstrating that these figures are effectively ineligible to be treated as individuals in the novelistic sense. *Jude the Obscure* expresses this dilemma in its title; the epithet turns the title character's social positioning into his defining existential condition, thus paradoxically marking him as too peripheral to be the hero of a novel. Obscurity is the essential social characteristic of all these texts' central figures. Their lives pass unseen, and the large scale of historical (let alone evolutionary or geological) time is necessarily indifferent to their existence. Yet, even as the inexorable logic of plot moves forward at these characters' expense, the novels just as insistently cast their lot with those who are written off from the start. Gissing, in one of his narratorial interjections in *New Grub Street*, pleads on behalf of Reardon and Biffen as personalities "wholly unfitted for the rough and tumble of the world's labour-market" (462). Anticipating impatience with their "failure to get on . . . push and bustle, welcome kicks so long as halfpence follow," the narrator speculates that readers will be conditioned to blame the two beleaguered writers' lack of success on their lack of grit (462). Easy though it is to dismiss them as "unequal to the coarse demands of life," he contends that, if viewed "in possible relation to a humane order of society" (unlike that of late Victorian capitalism), they will prove "admirable citizens" (462). Reardon, who can imagine no such humane order, nonetheless reflects that he and his similarly impoverished friend are model citizens even by the inhumane terms of the existing social order: "Doesn't it strike you that you and I are very respectable persons? We really have no vices," he remarks to Biffen. "Put us on a social pedestal, and we should be shining lights of morality. I sometimes wonder at our inoffensiveness. Why don't we run amuck against law and order? Why, at the least, don't we become savage revolutionists, and harangue in Regent's Park of a Sunday?" (405, 403). "Because," replies Biffen, "we are passive beings, and were meant to enjoy life very quietly. As we can't enjoy, we just suffer quietly, that's all" (403).

This overwhelming sense of human passivity on one side and of society's antagonism or cruel indifference on the other has earned naturalist fiction a reputation for political bad faith and even ideological complicity. Lukács—most famously in "Narrate or Describe?"—accuses Gustave Flaubert and Émile Zola, among others, of validating a cynical viewpoint from which "the final victory of capitalist inhumanity is always anticipated," and the disillusionment and slow destruction of the individual can only be relayed with a resigned shrug (146). Yet what most radically distinguishes these narratives of blocked mobility, exhaustion, and early death lies less in the suggestion that their characters are isolated individuals at odds with a hopelessly inhumane society than in the suggestion that they are statistics. To put it differently, individuality and statistical aggregation cease to be opposed; the very traits that define the protagonists' identities render them both generalizable and redundant. In this, Gissing's and Hardy's characters anticipate Virginia Woolf's Septimus Smith, that later autodidact and aspiring writer who makes his way into the indifferent metropolis unaware that "London had swallowed up many millions of young men called Smith" (82). This sense of redundancy extends to the most seemingly subjective aspects of characters' experience: Hardy's Tess is counted among "not a few millions of others" for whom "birth itself was an ordeal of degrading personal compulsion" (441), joining a demographic depressed by its own existence. Such quantitative generalization of characters' lives is not restricted to the narrative voice. It passes into the consciousness of protagonists, who recognize themselves as redundant—a nearly unprecedented form of demographic self-perception in the novel, for all its concern with population.

If earlier Victorian fiction crowded its plots with multitudes of lives that compromised the primacy of the individual, these later novels make their subjects excessive in their very individuality. Jude behaves like a good protagonist, applying himself diligently to the work of self-improvement, preparing for the future, fulfilling his obligations, and dreaming of social mobility. Yet the qualities that distinguish him as a worthy individual ironically equate him with masses of unknown others. Even before he has met anyone like himself, Jude "sometimes felt that by caring for books he was not escaping commonplace nor gaining rare ideas, every working-man being of that taste now" (66). Gissing's Reardon, brooding on his own exhausted ambition, similarly surmises that his mistake in aiming to make his unique mark on the literary world "was that of numberless men nowadays" (*New Grub Street* 474). At the very moments when these characters strive to be exceptional, they glimpse their reflections in the mirror of statistics: "There were thousands of young men," Jude imagines, "on the same self-seeking track" (129). Sue, revered for her intellectual originality, likewise balks at adding to the sum of a superabundant type: "I hate to be what is called a clever girl," she complains, as if anticipating her critical reception as an instance of the New Woman. "[T]here are too many of that sort now!" (107).[11] Sue and Jude extend this sense of their own excessiveness to a collective future. Borrowing a line from Percy Shelley, Sue predicts that future generations will shrink from the thought of "shapes like our own selves hideously multiplied" by human reproduction (287).

Given this novel's brutal dispatching of its protagonist and his children, these characters' subjective sense of their own redundancy might seem to confirm their objective status as surplus population—hence the critical consensus that *Jude the Obscure* is a "Malthusian tragedy."[12] To be sure, Hardy's narrative thematizes the principle of population in the most heavy-handed terms. Jude's marriage to Arabella at nineteen is just the sort of premature union Malthus aimed to prevent. Sue, despite her near asexuality and reluctance to "bring beings into the world" (312), ends up bearing two children in rapid succession and is pregnant with another—an outcome she attributes to the "law of nature"—when they find themselves unemployed and evicted from their lodgings (333). The characters' language persistently echoes the *Essay on Population* in suggesting that life comes about inadvertently—"not quite on purpose," as Sue apologizes when Little Father Time blames her for her pregnancy—while death is programmatic (334). Time's notorious suicide note, its sparse syntax rationalizing the voluntary self-extermination of "too menny" offspring, reads as the most bluntly Malthusian formula for the dreaded positive check. The children's suicide, from this standpoint, carries population control to an unprecedented extreme: the poor, rather than needing to be restrained from reproducing or thrown in the workhouse, can be counted on to dispose of themselves. But the Malthusian rhetoric of demographic excess, overdetermined as it is in the characters' resigned sense of being too many for the social categories to which they add, returns with a vengeance in the context of a problem it fails to explain. There is no way to reconcile the precarious lives and untimely deaths of Hardy's characters with political economy's mandate to check creaturely nature's excesses. The circumstances that make their existence unsustainable are not due to a procreative sex drive geometrically swelling the birth rate and depleting the world's food supply. Rather than a mass population lacking individual restraint, what is declared superfluous in this novel is precisely the self-regulating individual.

If it seems inconceivable that an individual could become at once too individuated and too numerous in the social differentiation that constitutes its identity, it bears remarking that the term *individual* is more ontologically tenuous than its common usage suggests. Its etymology links its definition to a process of division that has reached a point beyond which it cannot continue and thus, as Canguilhem notes, "negates the concept 'individual.' The individual is a being at the limit of nonbeing, since it is what cannot be further fragmented without losing its proper characteristics. It is a minimum of being" (*Knowledge of Life* 49). In the context of late nineteenth-century biopolitics, perhaps it is no wonder that individuation, restraint, self-cultivation, and depth psychology cannot valorize the lives of Hardy's characters. The concept of the individual has slipped out of alignment with that of the disciplinary subject or self-contained social unit. Here, too, natural and social science are strikingly consonant. For Durkheim, one of the dominant pathologies of industrialized societies is the cult of the individual—a cancerous overdevelopment of personality that deviates from group identity.

Hereditary biology charges individual life with a parallel tendency toward excessive development at the cellular level: Weismann credits Ernst Haeckel with redefining reproduction as an "overgrowth of the individual" through excessive cell division (qtd. in *On Heredity* 72). Rather than a necessary drive to regenerate a biologically varied and progressively differentiating species, reproduction comes to signify a peculiar error in the singular organism's growth process: a failure to die.

Hardy's fiction gives personal shape to this cellular conception of individuation and reproduction as interconnected forms of excess. Sue's resistance both to propagating life and to adding her cultivated identity to a large statistical set accords with a view of individuality and of procreation as overdevelopment. The underlying suggestion of this and other late Victorian novels' fatal outcomes is not really that nature slays the hindmost in a brute struggle for existence. They instead relentlessly hint at a stranger possibility that Freud would later hypothesize: rather than an individual pathology, the death drive is a universal fact. The emerging symptom of modernity that the novel's doctor (quoted by Jude) diagnoses as a "coming universal wish not to live" will become, for Freud, the most primitive and historically unchanged characteristic of organisms.

"A Sort of Shuddering": Fiction's Death Drive

> And a thousand thousand slimy things
> Lived on; and so did I.
>
> —Samuel Taylor Coleridge, *The Rime of the Ancient Mariner*
>
> There was an embrace in death.
>
> —Virginia Woolf, *Mrs. Dalloway*

Through its dramatically revised theory of instinct, *Beyond the Pleasure Principle* twenty-five years later would alter the most basic premises of the life sciences and, by extension, of biopolitics. Darwin had preserved from Malthus the anchoring concepts of an automatic reproductive impulse and a struggle for existence among individual organisms, with the crucial difference that the development hypothesis turned this struggle into an optimal condition for change rather than a prescription for stasis. In either case, populations were agonistic formations, fluctuating with the competitive vital energy of multiplying organisms driven to satisfy natural needs and instincts. Freud's research on traumatic neurosis after the First World War, in positing a death drive that seeks to relieve tension and restore equilibrium by shielding against disturbing stimuli, inverts the accepted biological view that links instinct to self-preservation. He redefines it as "an urge inherent in living organic matter impelling it toward the reinstatement of an earlier condition," namely, the primal state of inanimacy that preceded its chemical disruption by life (43). Contra the Darwinian model, which by Freud's account gives instincts the "deceptive appearance of being forces tending toward change and progress" (45), life betrays a tendency toward inertia— an essentially "conservative" rather than developmental nature (43). This thesis resonates with the earlier psychological claims of Lombroso, who coined the term *misoneism* to describe a similarly generalized natural aversion to any change of state in individuals and institutions, ensuring that bodies at rest remain at rest: "Like the plant, the animal, and the stone," Lombroso contends, "man remains motionless, unless a disturbance of his state occurs through other forces, and through the law of inertia itself" ("Innovation and Inertia" 357).[13] So much for that restless striving that lent natural history and individual life their epic character. Freud takes the law of inertia one step further. Rather than pleasure, adaptation, or perfection, he submits, "the aim of all life is death" (46). What motivates much of organic activity is simply a demand to relieve the tension of being alive in the first place.

Sexuality, further, is not at odds with this cellular will toward death—and thus what Foucault regards as an invention and key target of biopower takes on a markedly different status, ceasing to correspond either to individual desire or to the health and reproduction of populations. Freud would indeed decouple eros from reproduction, and reproduction from any organic instinct to perpetuate life. This rethinking of the libido has a Victorian precursor in the work of Edward Wilson Carpenter, who argued that the "the prime object of Sex" is not progeny but "union" (27). That "generation" can result from specific forms of sexual relation, he reasoned, does not prove this outcome to be the motive force (27). *Love's Coming of Age*, published a year after *Jude the Obscure*, analyzes sexuality in terms adapted from microbiology: "If we go to the lowest material expressions of Sex—as among the protozoic cells," Carpenter notes, "we find that they, the cells, unite together, two into one; and that, as a result of the nutrition that ensues, this joint cell after a time (but not always) breaks up by fission into a number of progeny cells" (28). This union, he proposes, rather than procreation, is the morphological aim of so-called sex and, more importantly, of love at every level of its material expression. Carpenter's cellular model of erotic instinct thus anticipates Freud's reconsideration of sexuality, which draws similarly on microbiology and on Weismann's morphological study of the germ-plasm. Via a surprising combination of science and myth, *Beyond the Pleasure Principle* attributes the sex drive to the instinct of cells to reunite—like divided bodies longing to merge back into a whole, per Aristophanes' mythic explanation of love's origin in Plato's *Symposium*—and thus return to a primordial state prior to their division. For Freud, however, the primal condition to which organic matter seeks to return is not prelapsarian unity but biological nonbeing. The sex drive and the death drive are thus one and the same. While a version of this theory has been taken up by Lee Edelman in order to side with the death drive against an oppressive cultural investment in reproductive futurism, it is worth stressing that, for Freud, the impetus behind reproduction is inseparable from the organism's unconscious will toward death.

Reconsidered in the terms Freud would develop, the entire narrative of Jude Fawley's life looks less like a Malthusian conflict between the sexual compulsions of nature and the ideals of culture or a Darwinian struggle to survive and multiply in a competitive ecosystem than a gradual movement toward realizing a morbid tendency operative from the start. A resistance to organic growth and even to continued existence is evident in Jude from boyhood; "seized with a sort of shuddering" at the felt discord of natural life, the child determines that he "[does] not want to be a man" (18). A pretext of development conceals (or sublimates, in the form of intellectual longing) this urge to halt the process of becoming. The dogged pursuit of an ideal that constantly recedes from fulfillment, the burst of sexual maturation disguised as a competing impulse, the repetition compulsion that drags the protagonist back to Christminster to torture himself by revisiting the scene of his rejection, and the dream of generational progress all end up looking less like future-oriented activity and more like the scenic route to death. These seemingly opposed motives are allied even in Jude's reproductive fantasy of fulfilling his own educational goals vicariously through the morose son who uncannily repeats, almost verbatim, his father's childhood wish that he had never been born. Little Father Time's horrific act of violence—a more direct enactment of his father's latent suicidal tendency—cruelly ironizes Jude's former expression of hope for the future by proving his words true in quite a different sense: "What I couldn't accomplish in my own person perhaps I can carry out through him?" (278). Hardy drives home the similitude between the two figures when his narrative voice calls the unnamed boy "Little Jude" at the moment the murder-suicide is discovered, as if to confirm that Little Father Time is not just his father's son but, more unnervingly, the "Little Father" himself (335). What comes in the guise of a different reproductive future is a repetition of the past. Rather than an icon of life's renewal and developmental possibility, the child in Hardy's last novel becomes a personification of the death drive.

There could be no greater nullification of the bildungsroman than that of unmasking the child as a monstrous incarnation of a collective death wish. The dead end that biographical narrative thus reaches, from Edelman's standpoint, might seem a consummation devoutly to be wished: a refusal to perpetuate the social order though an endless reproductive cycle or sacralize a nation's future in the figure of the child. From a Lukácsian perspective, by contrast, the collapse of the bildungsroman looks consistent with the general ideological bent of naturalism: an antipolitical "fatalism," amounting to total "capitulation before capitalist inhumanity," was to blame for "the absence of development in [Flaubert's and Zola's] 'novels of development'" ("Narrate or Describe?" 146). Yet the critic's insistence on the desirability of development calls on an organicist vocabulary that makes political struggle and historical process conceivable only in terms of a vital drive. Lukács disparages novels of disillusionment as lacking "the vitality of continuous development" and indeed as populated by the undead; rather than narrating the life and death of a fully alive human being, as he memorably puts it, they track "a corpse in passage through still lives becoming increasingly aware of being dead" (146). While there is certainly no future for these subjects, perhaps there is something to be said for naturalist fiction's resistance to the very notion of continuous development and to the political energetics Lukács found wanting. Contra Lukács, it is possible to understand the social dynamism and vitality of classic realist fiction as affirming capital's own endless *Bildung* of expansion, accumulation, and inexhaustible productive energy.[14] Hardy's fiction may indeed be understood as plotting in opposition to a master narrative of organic continuity and growth—as refusing the fantasy of incorporation through which *Middlemarch*, for example, projected a developmental future that clears away all obstructions, a "growing good of the world" that triumphantly subsumes every unhistorical life. Perhaps, then, this negation of futurity and of organic continuity, rather than signifying an antipolitical stance that Lukács would lament and Edelman would welcome, points toward another politics: one that divests biological life of its presumed economic value and refuses its totalization.

Not Quite on Purpose: Hardy and the Intentional Fallacy

> Life is not governed by will or intention. Life is a question of nerves, and fibres, and slowly built-up cells in which thought hides itself and passion has its dreams.
>
> —Oscar Wilde, *The Picture of Dorian Gray*

Little Father Time's strange agency attests that there are forces at work in fiction's worlds that override individual intention or, at times, are enacted through what are felt to be conscious personal choices. Hardy seems to have grasped what this meant for the novel. Fiction's very form, for all its confidence in the potential to make a sequence of events signify, can no longer be understood as the work of a single, mastering intention that moves narrative toward a desired end. The novelist thus disowns something broader than a particular political agenda when he calls *Jude* a novel without a "purpose."[15] A certain severing of words from intentions is written into the paradox of Time's suicide note, with its chillingly impersonal syntax of cause and effect. The violent deed is simply marked as "done," no subject affixed to the bare participle. A personal pronoun appears only in the subordinate clause that purports to explain why: "we are too menny." What looks like an incontestable formula—the letter of the law—is thrown into confusion by the contingency of its reference. If the "we" seems plainly to refer to the three small bodies strung up on clothesline, the verb tense throws off the correspondence between these words and those bodies.

Further, its syntax, through the present-tense "we are," obliges the active verb to outlast the now-past moment at which the impersonal voice counts the existing set of lives as excessive. In so doing, it calls the temporal parameters of this set into question. It does not say "we were too menny," meaning either the present children now detracted from the count or the entire family prior to the deaths that dissolve it altogether; neither does it say "we would have been too menny," counting the projected increase after another expected birth. The mismatch of verb tenses, no less than the implied root "men" in the misspelled "menny," is crucial here. Against the stark finality of the past participle, the active verb states—unintentionally, to be sure, and this is just the point—a present and ongoing condition. We are too many.[16] In its hypotactic structure, the note verbalizes a contradiction between what is "done" (the self-imposed check) and the systematic purpose it serves (to limit demands on a group that persistently includes those who eliminate themselves from it). The text's most economical sentence, with its rigid insistence on proportioning life to means rather than redistributing the means of life, thus violates its own economy of reference by yielding meanings in excess of words. Far from forcing art to imitate the calculated management of life, Hardy's novel allows writing to exhaust the object of its grim actuarial calculation, translating suicidal and homicidal impulses—ironically enough—into an obscure claim of community.

Jude and Sue, not surprisingly, are inclined to take the act (rather than the note) as a text to be read, drawing conclusions that render it definitively intentional. Yet interpretations proliferate, and words stray from denotation even in the most apparently stringent biological, sociological, and economic prescriptions to which the narrator and characters give voice. What we are left with, in the attempt to close the appalling gap between meaning and event, word and world, is a statement that withdraws the ground of its own intentionalism. To put it differently, what we are left with is a scrap of writing—discarded words oddly intruding in the visual frame of the gory scene so impassively described here, rendered objectlike yet utterly abstract, alongside these discarded bodies that appear before Jude and Sue as flesh and before us as text. This scrap of writing is the device by which the novel implicates itself in the deaths it demands. It is precisely writing, the world-making power invested in words, that brings about the event that unravels all predetermined meaning. Hence the novel's Pauline epigraph, "the letter killeth": not just the letter of the law, the regime of literalism embodied in Little Time, but the written word as such makes life its own to dispose of. Hardy's protagonist, in mastering dead languages and chasing the promise of something transcendent that beguiles him in the form of books, is fatally caught in his longing to enter a locked realm of letters, with the maddening irony that he has already entered it by being in a novel. But hence also the gesture that closes Hardy's defense of this, his last novel, which implicitly opposes the letter of literature to the letter of the law. His postscript to the Wessex edition observes (in response to critics who read *Jude the Obscure* as a feminist polemic), "no doubt there can be more in a book than the author consciously puts there, which will help either to its profit or to its disadvantage as the case may be" (468). Hardy thus speculatively invents what the New Criticism fifty years later would term the intentional fallacy. Disavowing interpretative authority, the novelist anticipates a surplus of meaning that escapes the autonomy of any fixed intention. That surplus of meaning is present, as I have suggested, even in the indeterminate reference of the note that appears to declare the most literal accounting of the ratio of bodies to words and of lives to social functions.

This makes superfluity a literary condition, an effect of the accumulation of signs that have no binding relation to any fixed referent. Here, as in *The Mayor of Casterbridge*, it would be inapt to approach this proliferation of meanings and subjects, this flight from denotation, as a resistance to literalism. When Sue blames her words for Time's actions ("I said it would be better to be out of life than in it at this price, and he took me literally"), her lament is not that figurative language has been mistaken for literal meaning—the lethal letter of the law—but that words (in the other sense of the letter) have found their way into life. The case recalls Henchard's complaint that Susan took the wife-sale "literally"; in both instances, a crisis ensues when words conduce to events rather than remaining only words, safely cordoned off from a world of objects, bodies, and acts toward which they ambiguously point. In loosening intention's grip on meaning and repeatedly narrating a loss of control over signification, these novels yield a strange kind of lexical crowding. It hangs in the air even in the most banal exchanges: in the indefinite reference of pronouns spoken between Elizabeth-Jane and Susan in *The Mayor of Casterbridge*, where the simple fact that "he" can refer to two different subjects has the effect of conjuring two people out of one signifier (just as those two people will occupy the same places in the world that they occupy in discourse). It extends to the name Elizabeth-Jane, which misleads Henchard and breaks the semiotic contract between novel and reader by multiplying subjects under the sign of a proper name that appears to guarantee a single human referent. It is entailed in the unsettling "we" of Little Time's note, which corrals readers into its potentially endless circuit of reference that threatens to count us, too, among the discounted—the unspecified we who will always be too many so long as the existing socioeconomic order is not enough. This is where fiction splits most definitively from the calculus of biopolitics at the very moment when it seems to announce that there is no escape from its economic reasoning. The novel's dilemma is not how to handle too many characters for one story, too large a population for one nation, too many lives for too few social functions, but how to contest the very premises of natural or social scarcity by making every sign contain multitudes.

Conclusion

> The need has been increasingly felt of the *vue d'ensemble*, of the synthetic mode of regarding organisms, men, and institutions, not as single things, self-contained and complete in themselves, but as merely nodes or meeting points of all the forces of the world acting and reacting in unlimited time and space.
>
> —William McDougall, *The Group Mind*
>
> I hazard the guess that man will ultimately be known for a mere polity of multifarious, incongruous and independent denizens.
>
> —Robert Louis Stevenson, *The Strange Case of Dr. Jekyll and Mr. Hyde*

The advent of modernism—anticipated in Hardy's later novels—marks a pivot point in the literary politics of population, hence my concluding with the end of the nineteenth century. *Tess of the D'Urbervilles*, avowing that "the world is only a psychological phenomenon," leans toward a subjectivism that Virginia Woolf will make programmatic; "there is no such place as 'the world,'" she contends, "no such life as 'life as it is'" ("Novels of George Gissing" 360). The call to "look within," per Woolf's 1925 anti-realist polemic "Modern Fiction," relocates literary truth from outward social expression to psychological subjectivity (160). Such appeals to inwardness moved to dismiss the very possibility of a coherent social world that plot can order or disorder. In this respect, the literary strategies tracked in the previous chapters, which aimed at giving narrative order to collective life, would seem to lose their exigency as interiority comes to the fore.

Clearly, however, the biopolitical demand to regulate human numbers remains in force at the turn of the century. What motivated Mrs. Jellyby's pet project of settling England's "superabundant home population" in African colonies, in Dickens's parody of imperialism's sham "telescopic philanthropy," lent its rationale to the European powers' rabid Scramble for Africa in the 1880s and 1890s—a rationale that resurfaces in the narration of *Heart of Darkness*. For all Charles Marlow's faith in the uniqueness of Kurtz's experience and his own, his account both of the system of forced labor in King

Leopold's Congo and of his own ostensible reasons for going there implicitly confirms Hannah Arendt's claim that imperialism relied on a vast global reserve of "superfluous men" (189). At one end, as his vague description of the work overseen by the unidentified Company attests, empire amasses colonized populations and harnesses their labor to extract raw materials, leaving them to die as soon as they become "inefficient" (17); at the other, it uses territorial expansion to reduce crowding and unemployment in the metropole. A certain oblique recognition of his own fungibility surrounds Marlow's perplexed pursuit of some more deliberate intent than he finds in himself. While the storyteller is compelled to devise a personalized motive for venturing out to the colonial frontier by tracing it back to a youthful curiosity to fill in what were never really "blank spaces" on the map (8), his self-deprecating recollections of anxious effort to cease "loafing about" make it clear that he goes for lack of any other occupation (7). Always partly audible behind drumbeats, as Michael Sayeau's reading aptly suggests, are the more fitful rhythms of modern work and unemployment—a distinct temporal pressure that makes itself felt in Marlow's perpetual restless waiting to be occupied.[1] Men as unspecified as Marlow and as dangerously overspecified as Kurtz (or the actual ivory trader Arthur Hodister, whose enemies in the 1891–94 Congo Arab war reportedly stuck his head on a pole, or the journalist Henry Morton Stanley, known for his 1871 expedition to Tanzania to find the missionary David Livingstone and notorious for his brutality, or the Belgian colonial station commander Léon Rom, reported to have decorated his garden at Stanley Falls with the severed heads of Congolese people, among many possible colonial warlord prototypes), per Arendt, "had not stepped out of society but had been spat out by it"; rather than exceptional individuals, they became "living abstractions," "shadows of events" in which their real role was merely functional (189).[2] Even in high modernist fiction, the premise of surplus population persists. *Mrs. Dalloway* shows it to be the focus of regulatory attention, whether in Sir William Bradshaw's eugenic mandate to prevent his psychiatric patients from reproducing or in Lady Bruton's scheme of promoting emigration to Canada to limit "the superfluous youth of our ever-increasing population" (107). Woolf eerily personifies this demographic excess in Septimus Smith, that walking war casualty regarded by his doctors as a social burden and in truth already written off as redundant life—one more Smith among millions engulfed by an indifferent London, as the narration attests—even before he was sent to the trenches.

Modernism, to be sure, brings markedly different aesthetic and formal techniques to bear on the phenomena of mass life. What happens to the novel's experiments in aggregation involves a notably psychologizing turn.

Yet population does not vanish from the narrative horizon with the shift from society to consciousness as the novel's primary object. Indeed, fiction's intensified psychologism—rather than divorcing the individual subject from social context, as Lukács would argue in "The Ideology of Modernism"—is itself a means of managing the human aggregate. Turning briefly to two transitional texts, *The Strange Case of Dr. Jekyll and Mr. Hyde* and *Heart of Darkness*, both of which seem to revolve around the horror of what lies buried within the isolated individual, I suggest that these novellas participated in an effort to theorize masses and crowds in the new idiom of psychological processes. If nineteenth-century fiction, as the previous five chapters have argued, enacts a certain narrative consciousness of demography, what emerges at the edges of modernism looks more like a demography of consciousness. These texts thus intersect with a model of mass behavior conceived in the 1880s and 1890s by Gabriel Tarde and Gustave Le Bon, later refined by Wilfred Trotter and William McDougall—all key interlocutors for Freud's account of the ego.[3] Finally, revisiting the psychoanalytic paradigm conventionally applied to Robert Louis Stevenson's and Joseph Conrad's novellas, I approach Freud's own story of the formation and ongoing struggle of the ego not as a hermeneutic explanation of these literary texts but as a variation on the narrative strategies through which they reconstituted surplus population in the realm of the unconscious.

Even before Tarde's and Le Bon's theories of a group mind gain currency, the story they tell about crowds finds a precursor in *Dr. Jekyll and Mr. Hyde*, a text that claims the fittingly dual identity of a "shilling shocker" and a philosophically serious work. Julia Wedgewood praised it in *The Contemporary Review* for "investigat[ing] the meaning of the word self" (595), and the hidden deviance it uncovered left John Addington Symonds doubting, as he wrote to Stevenson, "whether a man has a right so to scrutinize the 'abysmal deeps of personality'" (139). But even as the tale shades toward the vanishing point of interiority, Henry Jekyll's solitary experiment exposes something more than a second self. Rather than a fable of divided consciousness, *Dr. Jekyll and Mr. Hyde* recounts the discovery of a multitude within. The political metaphors that enter Jekyll's confession suggest as much, linking consciousness to statecraft and describing a state of "perennial war among [his] members"; if he initially hypothesizes that "man is not truly one but truly two," Jekyll's prediction is that the human being will be properly understood in the future as an entire "polity" of heterogeneous and disconnected subjects (55, 56).

Encounters with Hyde bear out this suggestion of an ungovernable *demos* at the core of the ego, such that even two is a crowd. The created double enters the frame less as a projection of individual depravity than as an incarnation of all the anonymous features of mass behavior. What renders him terrifying, in appearance and deed, is so impersonal that it nearly beggars description. Eyewitnesses can isolate no distinguishing marks of identity in the villain; Enfield, wishing to ascribe to him some unique deformity, cannot "specify the point" and "really can name nothing out of the way" (10). Their testimony of Hyde's crimes, further, recounts actions more characteristic of a mob than of a single person: his sociopathic violence, whatever its euphemistic suggestiveness, takes the peculiar form of "trampling" (7).

Le Bon will in fact sketch something strikingly akin to Hyde in *The Crowd: A Study of the Popular Mind* (as it was translated into English in 1896). This quasi-scientific work offers its own Gothic conception of crowds spontaneously springing into being, surging through city streets under the sway of the unconscious, endowed with a superhuman energy that overtakes personal identity and dissolves all ordinary forms of reason and impulse control. The differences among individuals, by Le Bon's account, evaporate as they congregate, as do the accumulated effects of culture and historical development. A man, he declares, "descends several rungs in the ladder of civilization" as soon as he enters a crowd. However "cultivated" in private life (like Jekyll, with his comically long string of professional titles), he becomes "a barbarian . . . a creature acting by instinct"—all the conscious elements of personality engulfed by unconscious forces of suggestion and social contagion (52). Here, Le Bon extends Hippolyte Taine's earlier claim that the individual in a state of "spontaneous anarchy" instantly "catches the fever from those who are fevered" (52). So too is Le Bon's account of regression indebted to Taine's conjectures concerning mass behavior during the French Revolution: "from the peasant, the labourer, and the bourgeois," Taine submits, "we see all of a sudden spring forth the barbarian, and still worse, the primitive animal" (53).

Such accounts of regression to a primitive state differ from the forms of atavism and individual degeneracy readers often detect in Jekyll's narrative of becoming Hyde: his decreasing stature and the growth of dark hair on his hands, coincident with his lapse into antisocial violence. These bodily signs of difference are often attributed to biological determinism and theories of innate criminality.[4] By contrast, Le Bon's story of sudden descent down the evolutionary or cultural ladder disconnects social tendencies from human types—a point to which I will return shortly. This free-floating potential for regression, for throwing off the constraints of civilization, is one of the threads that runs from Stevenson's tale to *Heart of Darkness*, that more overtly geopolitical saga of norms undone. While the genres of the urban Gothic and imperial romance obviously differ, both texts can be understood

to link the specter of metropolitan mass-political unrest with that of imperial violence as counterpart scenes of the limits of sovereignty.[5] (Indeed, the
discourse of mass population and that of empire have long been figuratively
held together—for example, in De Quincey's impressions of East London as
an internal *terra incognita* doubling an imperial "East," or in Dickens's portrayal of Jo as a homegrown "savage" occluded by telescopic philanthropy,
or in the Salvation Army's missionary rhetoric of "Darkest England"—albeit
often in a mystified manner, as though the two were analogous but mutually
exclusive concerns.) Conrad's novella, coming a decade after Stevenson's,
moves its audience from metropole to colony—symbolic spaces that prove
almost explicitly, if surprisingly, reversible. Yet it shares with *Dr. Jekyll and
Mr. Hyde* a concern with the anomie that follows from "utter solitude, without a policeman," as Marlow puts it, and a certain dread of what tendencies
might erupt from within the solitary subject (49). For that reason, it too has
been read as a psychological parable of sorts.

"Utter solitude," however, is not all that solitary in the scenes Conrad
evokes. Despite the text's concern with psychic isolation and solipsism, dis-
tilled in its storyteller's fear that the tale cannot even be told because "we live,
as we dream—alone" (27), it is in dialogue with crowd psychology that Marlow's equivocal effort to account for Kurtz takes on its weight. While he casts
this specter of empire as a lone individual who exits society and consequently
loses "restraint," his narration places Kurtz at the epicenter of a social world
and aligns his deviance with mass behavior. The spectacle that greets Marlow
on his arrival at the Inner Station, estranged as it is, registers predominantly
as an image of demographic aggregation: when Kurtz is borne in, Marlow's
first view is not of him but of "streams of human beings" forming a crowd
of thousands (59). What looms before the imperial functionary's fascinated
gaze is a coordinated "mass of human bodies" in motion (67). The ostensibly structureless wilderness of the Congo evoked in this narrative is not the
converse of the metropole, a space outside institutional regulation, a cultural
vacuum where civilization cannot take root. As envisioned here, it is a site of
mass sociality rendered fearful in part because of its population density and
synchronized human activity.

Even in describing the expedition upriver as a return to prehistory and
equating the central African interior with the deep strata of the unconscious,
Heart of Darkness notably parallels the claims of mass psychology regarding the disinhibiting effects of social aggregation. There, too, internal and
external causes are not at odds. Le Bon treats crowds as an external stimulus
capable of changing individual behavior, but one that works on something
internal to the individual: a half-buried human race memory shared among

any spontaneously assembled group. He posits an inherited unconscious filled with mnemic vestiges of "savage, destructive instincts . . . left dormant in us from the primitive ages"—instincts always ready to be called into action by the power of numbers (41). Marlow echoes this hypothesis when he speculates that Kurtz's environment has transformed him "by the awakening of forgotten and brutal instincts, by the memory of gratified and monstrous passions" (65). If such language bears out Chinua Achebe's charge that *Heart of Darkness* is less an exposé of empire than a warning to "keep away from Africa," it draws on a theory of group behavior applied to European cities— not least of all London, that dark heart of empire where Marlow's tale is told.

Conrad's tendency to collapse geographical difference in just this way has provoked critique, and understandably so. For historicist and especially postcolonial critics, his subjectivism and emphasis on the psyche risk befogging the reality of imperial violence, transforming Marlow's dilatory tour of the Congo Free State into a journey to the center of the id. Conrad's "will to style," per Fredric Jameson, blurs historical substance with impressionistic aesthetics, shrouding events in dreamlike unreality and settings in symbolic ambiguity.[6] And the elements of psychological allegory in this novella do indeed loosen it from context; *Heart of Darkness* chases its narrative material into the submerged depths of interiority, eclipsing historical and geographic signposts as it goes. By some readings, notably Achebe's and Edward Said's, ideology wins out through these subjectivizing tendencies. The text's psychological undertow seems to pull Marlow's tale away from any definite ground and toward the vagaries of the individual mind (Kurtz's or his own, if the two are distinct) or toward universalized reflection on man's inner darkness— in either case making the voyage to the Inner Station a chronotope for the unconscious, which by Freud's account has no history. For Achebe, indeed, Conrad's supposed demystification of empire masks the actual hegemonic tactics of colonial depredation behind a veil of incomprehension and metaphysical abstraction while performing its own implicit parable of European mastery.[7] Its specious universalism makes the entire continent of Africa, as he memorably puts it, into "a set of props for the break-up of one petty European mind" (12). But here, while acknowledging the text's production of a generalized Africa as a symbolic space for the fantasies and crises of European subjects, it may be necessary to revise a false antithesis, one that sets the psychological at odds with all sociopolitical content. *Heart of Darkness*, even as its narrative voices sound the depths of alienation and dislocation, situates the psyche at the center of a debate on collective behavior. The implicit stakes of that debate were the meaning of historical development and the durability of social order.

The psychological theories with which Conrad's fiction coincides indeed set their sights on the comparative analysis of political formations, and did so with a definite political agenda. Broadening a project that might be seen to begin with Taine's analysis of the French Revolution, written in the wake of the Paris Commune, Le Bon's study of crowd behavior aimed not merely to describe a generalizable phenomenon in social psychology—a spontaneously constituted "popular mind"—but to make prescriptive claims on that basis against socialism, democracy, and popular sovereignty. He joins a long line of writers in presaging a new "era of crowds," and his book begins in a monitory tone: "To-day the claims of the masses . . . amount to nothing less than a determination to utterly destroy society as it now exists"; by Le Bon's inference, demands for limits on labor hours, the nationalization of railways and factories, and economic equality evince a popular will to reinstate a "primitive communism which was the normal condition of all human groups before the dawn of civilization" (xvii). This description bears out Foucault's account of a theory of social war that, as we saw in earlier chapters, came to predominate nineteenth-century political thought; his lectures in *"Society Must Be Defended"* describe a danger to the social body imagined to come from within rather than outside it. Le Bon conceives of "the masses" along just these lines. Surveying populist movements since the 1870s, he conjures a threat to society itself as the occasion for studying mass behavior. But the historical and political conjuncture is quickly eclipsed by universal claims about the character of crowds. "Little adapted to reasoning," he generalizes, "crowds . . . are quick to act. As the result of their present organisation their strength has become immense," such that "[t]he divine right of the masses is about to replace the divine right of kings" (xvii).

The tendentiousness of Le Bon's project will be plain to later readers: beyond its anti-socialist polemics and the obvious fear of the masses it channels, it relies on facile distinctions between modern and primitive societies, founds universal claims about human behavior on scant evidence, and consigns all rationality to the individual while peddling sexist, racist, and classist stereotypes to characterize the irrationality of crowds. Competing theories would complicate Le Bon's simple opposition of individual and collective by distinguishing crowds from other formations (in Tarde's case, publics; in McDougall's, organized social groups), though largely without altering the negative connotations attached to the crowd.[8] The paradigm of mass psychology, however, had some unexpected effects—most remarkably, its covertly de-essentializing logic. Diverging from the methods of criminal anthropology that prevailed in the 1880s, theorists of a group mind ascribed social danger not to any pathological typology (like Lombroso's "born criminal") but to the ambient force of social context, mutable from one moment to the next by the proximity of bodies and capable of altering seemingly fixed identity characteristics.[9] This meant that, however Le Bon might disparage "the masses" as though this term indexed a permanent social category, mass psychology became a transitory and ductile phenomenon ready to absorb anyone. For much the same reason, this theory eroded the foundational status of the individual on which he wished to insist—enabling Freud, later, to counter that individual psychology is always already social psychology. Le Bon's ironic contribution to psychology is thus that, in granting all reason to the cultivated, elite individual, he takes it away with the other hand by subjecting it to the variable features of social environment and demography. Further, by linking demographic aggregation (a feature of everyday city life) to the periodic reactivation of a collective unconscious that depersonalizes subjects and alters power relations, his psychological model makes the processes of modern political organization surprisingly circumstantial, tenuous, and at times reversible.

It is just this sense of the tenuousness of political structures and the frailty of individual self-discipline that the figure of Kurtz alarmingly illustrates for Marlow. While critics justly charge *Heart of Darkness* with dehistoricizing empire, this is, paradoxically, the very ground of its resistance to empire. To the extent that it can be read as a critique of imperialism, its critique lies in a disavowal of the difference history makes. This holds true for the same reason Marlow and Kurtz, like Jekyll, Hyde, & co., cannot be treated as atavistic exceptions, unique specimens of degeneracy to be purged from national space. Both narratives, in concert with Le Bon's, effectively belie any permanent distinction between the cultivated individual and the degenerate or the savage.

Like the studies of mass psychology with which it coincides, *Heart of Darkness* is deeply skeptical of sociality itself. For this very reason, Conrad's novella does not chronicle an escape from civilization, which, however hollow its pieties, proves necessary to repress the savagery of solitary individuals like Kurtz. Contra Marlow, there is no solitude, no blank space beyond social order; the Kurtz he encounters indeed personifies the process of sociopolitical formation. Here, *Heart of Darkness* arguably comes closer to anticipating Freud's account of group psychology, which diverges from Le Bon's in suggesting that "restraint" itself is a vestige of inherited memory and that aggressive and libidinal impulses are not the antithesis of civilization but its very basis.[10] This paradigm entails a different temporality—in effect, a nondevelopmental social history—so that regression no longer suffices to explain the continuous presence of id. Indeed, rather than a modern figure who has regressed to some anterior state, Kurtz becomes, in Marlow's own mythology, a prototype of the primal father whose death Freud would place at the symbolic foundation of social collectivity. By retroactively transforming the demonic patriarch into a "remarkable man" (70), a disembodied voice lingering in the guilty conscience of the living, Conrad's storyteller finds the stuff of the superego and the id in the same place. His narrative implies, in so doing, that neither he nor Kurtz has ventured outside civilization; quite the contrary, Kurtz's treatise on the imperial civilizing mission, punctuated with the scrawled postscript "exterminate all the brutes!" (49), exposes the lack of distinction between so-called civilization and the death drive. This is the essence of Conrad's critique of empire—a reactionary if not simply nihilistic critique, but a critique nonetheless.

Yet even as *Heart of Darkness* invalidates imperialism's moral pretenses and doubts its capacity to subdue the world's population by any higher means than enslavement, massacre, rape, and plunder, its narrative attempts something new with regard to fiction's techniques for managing a human aggregate. Rather than handle demography as an objective datum external to the subject, it transforms the imagined demographic surplus—all the human waste products of empire—into a global multitude untethered from history that can then be subsumed within individual consciousness. Marlow's subjective response to the stimuli of human activity in the Congo, his pulse answering the beat of drums, becomes evidence, for his purposes, that the external social world refers to something internal to himself: "The mind of man is capable of anything," he speculates, "because everything is in it, all the past as well as all the future" (36). Reasoning thus, he makes the population that surrounds him into the primordial material of his own unconscious. Marlow's unsettling images of Congolese masses distill an altered conception of population and of the subject: a Dark Continent within, a repressed primal horde and unknown other at the core of the self.

The novella's form, with its multiply framed and layered narrative, structurally reiterates this layering of miscellaneous human material within the subject—a formal feature it shares with *Dr. Jekyll and Mr. Hyde*. Both texts offer one man's narration of another man's narration of yet another man's story, seized on vicariously at the moment of his death or of his ego's dissolution. Each subject thus becomes one psyche containing masses of others. *Heart of Darkness* formally embeds the primal horde around Kurtz and the mass of drives inside him within the memory of Marlow within that of the unnamed first-person speaker, to whom Marlow too becomes, as Kurtz was to him, "no more . . . than a voice," the tale told in the dark seeming "to shape itself without human lips" (27), much as *Dr. Jekyll and Mr. Hyde* embeds the mob that is Hyde within the narrative of the late Jekyll within that of Enfield and Lanyon within that of Utterson, introduced by some unknown impersonal narrator who vanishes: subject within subject, voice within disembodied voice.

It is easy to see why *Dr. Jekyll and Mr. Hyde* and *Heart of Darkness* have invited psychoanalytic interpretations—why both have at times been read as allegories of repression, of the ego's struggle to master the id and appease the superego, or (in pre-Freudian terms that recall Buffon's *Homo duplex*) of the duality of human nature, with its competing rational and animal tendencies.[11] Freud is indeed pertinent here, though not as decoder of universal truths of consciousness in literary narrative. Instead, looking at his interconnected stories of social organization in *Totem and Taboo* and *Group Psychology and the Analysis of the Ego* and of the personality's formation in *The Ego and the Id*, I would suggest that these works themselves constitute a modernist experiment in the crowding of consciousness. Freud hypothesizes the origins of social groups in the form of the primal horde or band of brothers ruled over despotically by the Kurtz-like totemic father they unite to overthrow. He conceptualizes a Hyde-like force of id within the psyche as a plurality of inherited experience bridging the apparent gap between individual and species. His tripartite model of the psyche casts consciousness as an amalgam of parts, turning subjectivity into a site of fragmentation and internal struggle. In so doing, his similarly homosocial narrative of the making of political community and of the self offers up another version of the same plot, one that transfigures global mass population into the dark matter of depth psychology.

The psychological subject is neither primary nor unitary in this story. Freud locates the seat of personality in the undifferentiated mass of drives from which the ego works to distinguish itself through repression and identification with an ego-ideal. The individual ego, by his account, is not the opposite of primal community but the product of its heterogeneous remnants. Indeed, it is simply "a specially differentiated part of the id," that inherited portion of the psyche that accumulates, retains, and biologically transmits "residues of the existences of countless egos" (*The Ego and the Id* 28). The id, from which the ego springs, appears eerily populated with masses of other selves, libidinal remains of prior human groups. Psychoanalysis thus creates a model of the individual that contains the human aggregate of out of which it emerges.[12] For this reason, Eric Santner is quite right to credit Freud with the discovery that "individual psychology and the theory of the libido are always . . . *a theory of masses*"; both are readable as models of the dissolution of sovereign power rendered within the individual and threatening "to 'crowd' out the self from within" (*The Royal Remains* 96).

It should now be possible to observe that the psychoanalytic account of personality and the biopolitical analysis of population are less disparate than they appear. In fact, Freud's agonistic model of the ego's formation takes its terms from a recognizably biopolitical framework. It lodges a dehistoricized mass of life—the inherited unconscious drives of a global human aggregate— within the subject. On the terrain of the unconscious, it stages a war between the ego and an accretion of biological and psychological impulse, which draws new energy as the superego presents a new foe: "The struggle which once raged in the deepest strata of the mind," Freud conjectures, with the introduction of the superego, "is now continued in a higher region" (*The Ego and the Id* 29). In so doing, it rewrites the biopolitical plot of ceaseless struggle within populations—so essential to nineteenth-century theories of society and species—as a conflict internal to the psyche. The organizing metaphor is the same as Stevenson's: human consciousness, the object of Jekyll's scientific inquiry, becomes the site of "perennial war among [its] members" (*Dr. Jekyll and Mr. Hyde* 55). The mass of humanity that once swarmed the streets of the city novel and threatened to riot in industrial fiction does not vanish with the rise of psychology; it becomes the very stuff of subjectivity.

Psychoanalysis, rather than presupposing an individual subject set at a remove from social bodies, makes group psychology the most elemental form of consciousness. Further, Freud attributes political principles to libidinal motives that can be expressed only by reference to population. This is most evident in his psychoanalytic explanation for the moral premise of equality in democratic codes of political justice. *Group Psychology and the Analysis of the Ego* locates the basis for egalitarian ethics in a form of conscience best exemplified, Freud suggests, in persons afflicted with venereal disease. The democratic "demand for equality," he notes, "reveals itself unexpectedly in the syphilitic's dread of infecting other people"—a dread he reads as the correlate of infected persons' "violent struggles against the unconscious wish to spread their infection on to other people; for why should they alone be infected and cut off from so much?" (67).

The standard anthropological emphasis on exogamy as the foundational social principle, affirmed in *Totem and Taboo*, is here set aside. Political communities, Freud argues, are constituted not only by the binding force of the libido but also, and above all, by the secret wish to expose other bodies to the ailments afflicting one's own.[13] This theory could be read as a peculiar spin on the logic by which Mary Shelley's *The Last Man*, as we saw in chapter 1, makes a plague the condition for universal equality. In the context of contemporary theories of biopower, so too might it invert the immunitary paradigm of modern sovereignty that Roberto Esposito reads into *Dr. Jekyll and Mr. Hyde,* among other texts. Stevenson's novella, like Conrad's after it, indeed anticipates Freud in this regard too. Both texts incline toward a suspicion that society, rather than giving order to biological life and immunizing human populations against the risks of disease, scarcity, and war, is itself a formalized system built on life's internally aggressive tendencies, but one from which no retreat into the depths of interiority or out to the edges of empire is possible. In this sense, they gesture toward the thesis of *Civilization and Its Discontents.* Yet they arrive at this perspective by binding political organization to the imagined excessiveness of human life, and thus they, like previous works of fiction, find their narrative task in the contrary objects of biopolitics.

So this, I have suggested, is what happens to the concept of population and to the novel form at the century's end: both, in effect, are psychologized. And this psychological turn, oddly enough, makes the unconscious the site of political collectivity and of species-being. In unearthing a multitude within the self, Freud repeats the strategy of Conrad's imperial romance and Stevenson's urban Gothic tale; psychoanalysis too enables the crowd outside to be absorbed as the crowd within. Repression, then, starts to look like the new narrative device for imagining population management: if not a political allegory, then at least a master trope through which human life and human numbers can be subjected to social regulation—whether that repressed material appears as industrial or colonial labor force, anticolonial resistance, or revolutionary masses assembling in the streets of London or Paris. Psychoanalysis thus takes up what had long been the project of fiction as it turned to the life of the species: to narrate the possibility of giving political order to a human aggregate that necessarily exceeds and thus challenges the finality of any existing society.

It makes sense that contemporary political theorists, particularly as they turn to questions of biopower and concepts of the *demos* even under the altered circumstances of the twentieth and twenty-first centuries, often find their most arresting instances in nineteenth-century fiction. The literary techniques tracked throughout this book show how elemental Victorian novels were to conceptualizing a politics activated by population. Given the exemplary function that Esposito, Gilles Deleuze, Giorgio Agamben, Jacques Rancière, and Michael Hardt and Antonio Negri have assigned to certain works of fiction as illustrations of the political problem of life or of politics as such, it seems worth reflecting on the novel's particular uses for theories of the political. The turn to literature, of course, is hardly new; it was not just novelist-critics like George Eliot and Margaret Oliphant who insisted on the political truth-producing function of art but also Victorian social scientists who cited the novels of Charlotte Brontë, Gaskell, Dickens, and others as agents in and evidence of political phenomena. In other theoretical discourses, psychoanalysis perhaps above all, literary texts have similarly provided a narrative vocabulary of conceptual models. In this sense, theory finds in literature what literary criticism has at times sought in theory: explanations born of particulars yet independent of them and ready to operate at the level of abstraction.

Such appeals to the explanatory power of the luminous example in the service of theoretical abstraction are not always at odds with historicization: witness Esposito's brief assessments of *Dr. Jekyll and Mr. Hyde*, *Dracula*, and *The Picture of Dorian Gray*, which do not stray from historicist criticism in thematizing the scourge of degeneracy that critics often read as the prime mover in these Gothic tales of internal differentiation. By Esposito's account, all three fin-de-siècle texts—in their efforts to split apart "health and sickness," "norm and abnormality," within the individual and to project a feared degeneracy outside the self onto some separable body or object—instantiate fantasies of racial purification that eugenics will try to make real (124–27). This claim is not unusual; it was to earlier versions of this symptomatic reading that Stephen Arata responded in his analysis of Stevenson's conscious play on the bourgeoisie's discursive construction of degeneracy in *Dr. Jekyll and Mr. Hyde*. Yet the dream of killing death that Esposito identifies in this text and in *The Picture of Dorian Gray* finds a new theorization within the framework of biopolitics, which helps explain the political drive to shield life from itself. It also extends the problematic of these texts beyond the contextual particularity of a concept like degeneracy. We might, after all, see the dream of killing death as harking back to Victor Frankenstein's project and perhaps carrying forward to such recent dystopian novels as Margaret Atwood's *Oryx and Crake* and Kazuo Ishiguro's *Never Let Me Go*, both of which reveal the specter of disposability lurking behind the longstanding fantasy of optimizing health and longevity. If the valences of population are historically variable, the literary-historical scope of the novel's concern with the political and economic uses of life attests to its persistent engagement with biopolitics.

What appears as a warning in all these texts is not merely symptomatic. While Esposito aptly identifies a wish to manage species life that lingers, as I have suggested, even in late Victorian narratives that seem consumed with individual psychology, his readings implicitly treat texts like *The Picture of Dorian Gray* as mythology rather than literature—that is to say, as explanatory devices for culture's ordering logic. Does literature operate this way? Without

proclaiming the absolute autonomy of art, we might nonetheless place fiction at a remove from any strictly functional imperative to explain and justify
political order. (Rancière, for whom literature itself is a key object to be
theorized along with and in relation to the political rather than a free-floating
source of illustrations thereof, diverges from other political philosophers in
recognizing this; indeed, he sets literature's aesthetic character against all
principles of hierarchy and defines politics as a disordering of existing divisions of space, time, and value.) So too might it be worthwhile to question
the theoretical premise that "bare life," animate existence deprived of form,
comes forth as a narrative object in fiction. This claim has been a mainstay of
Agamben's and Esposito's analyses of *Our Mutual Friend*—both concluding
that Dickens, in temporarily reducing Rogue Riderhood to what Agamben
calls a "cipher of bare biological life," glances ahead to the Nazi camp, and
that the "outer husk" of the unconscious rogue, per Esposito, "has not a little
to do with the 'empty shells' and 'life unworthy of life' . . . with Treblinka's
flesh of the ovens" (194). Such a reading recalls Arendt's fatalist account of
modern politics, and it makes fiction a mirror of the state's darkest fantasies.
Could we not, however, see a different configuration of biopolitics written
into the conditions of narrative itself, and conjecture that the novel's demand
to make life narratable, to give it particularity, form, heterogeneity, and temporal sequence—qualities theoretically denied to bare life—suggests just the
opposite? The previous chapters should attest that the surplus of human
material generated by fiction is never merely a tragic remnant of biological existence exiled from political space and bereft of meaning. Instead of
confirming life's fatal capture by totalizing power, the sheer excessiveness of
the novel's subjects runs over the edges of any social body, state, empire, or
valorizing structure that aims to encompass the species. In so doing, it makes
the possibility of resistance immanent to fiction's biopolitical imagination.

Notes

Introduction. The Biopolitical Imagination

1. See especially *Spectator* 69, which describes the bustling cosmopolitan scene of the Royal Exchange and relates the Spectator's enjoyment in mixing with crowds from around the world, relishing the variety of the "busie Multitude of People" (294). See also Stow, who credits the effects of "liv[ing] in the eyes of others" for city-dwellers' virtues (201).

2. On debates concerning the causes of historical population growth in England, particularly whether and how significantly fertility increased in the late eighteenth and early nineteenth centuries and the relative weight of fluctuations in fertility compared with the effects of a generally declining mortality rate, see Wrigley and Shofield 229–36.

3. Wrigley and Shofield, by looking at historical price indexes and showing how the longstanding "link between population growth and price rise was broken" starting around 1800, in fact conclude that Malthus ironically warned of an economic "issue that haunted most pre-industrial societies" at almost the precise moment when it was ceasing to be a national problem (404). On the history of the census and the economic and demographic assumptions that variously informed and followed from it, see Levitan, who argues that "the notion of surplus population arose alongside and in dialogue with the development of the census" (47). It relied not simply on raw numbers but on the concept of unproductive lives (47–72).

4. See, for instance, Petty's *Another Essay in Political Arithmetick, concerning the Growth of the City of London*, which predicted in 1682 that the metropolis could double its population in forty years; Petty (despite Jonathan Swift's satire of his political arithmetic in *A Modest Proposal*) found no cause for alarm that such an increase would outstrip the limits of subsistence. European political thinkers at least as early as the mid-sixteenth century, including Jean Bodin and Giovanni Botero, indeed argued that the power and wealth of kingdoms depend centrally on human numbers for labor and military might—an assumption that was nearly indisputable by the eighteenth century. On the rise of expansionist population theory in the early modern period, see Federici 87.

5. See Colley, *Britons* 240–41 and *Captives* 308–10. French philosophers and physiocrats, including Montesquieu and Mirabeau, were likewise convinced that the population of France and of Europe as a whole had declined precipitously in consequence of bad policies that discouraged childbearing; see Cole 28–29.

6. Wallace reasons that "a nation shall be more populous in proportion as good morals . . . prevail" and that agricultural development is crucial because it serves "to render the earth as populous as possible" (19). On similar grounds, Franklin calls

policies that encourage the export of goods "generative Laws," since they "strengthen a Country, doubly, by increasing its own People and diminishing its Neighbors" (10).

7. Foucault, in his earlier work, credits Bichat with relativizing death and taking away its absoluteness; the fear of death no longer haunts medicine after Bichat, and what was once a "decisive, irrecoverable event" becomes a "distributed" phenomenon that coexists with and suffuses life (*The Birth of the Clinic* 144).

8. Collings is thus correct to argue, counter to Foucault's emphasis on panopticism as the shape of modern power in *Discipline and Punish*, that "it is Malthus, rather than Bentham, who most ruthlessly attempts to displace the king" (185).

9. While Foucault rightly notes a tension between the concept of the people and that of population (see *Security, Territory, Population* 43–44), the two figures of aggregation share a common genealogy.

10. Foucault's account of the relations among sovereignty, discipline, and biopower changes over the course of his lectures. In *"Society Must Be Defended,"* he identifies disciplinary power, whose emergence he dates to the seventeenth and eighteenth centuries, as "absolutely incompatible with relations of sovereignty" (35), and biopower, which emerges in late eighteenth century, as "a new technology of power" that is "not disciplinary" (242). In *Security, Territory, Population*, by contrast, he suggests that the three (now renamed "law," "discipline," and "security") are not sequential but interrelated and sometimes simultaneous, the latter two constituting dual elements of a larger phenomenon called governmentality.

11. Durkheim's sociology of religion offers similar insight; he argues (in reference to totemic objects rather than figures of the popular body, though similarly citing "the scenes, either sublime or savage, of the French Revolution") that modern states imbue society with the properties of the divine and the immortal (*The Elementary Forms of Religious Life* 211).

12. On the history and changing uses of the term "literature," see Williams, *Marxism and Literature* 46–48.

13. See Frankel 9, Hacking 3.

14. See "The Natural History of German Life" 418–22.

15. Cf. *The Political Unconscious* 151–84; see also Moretti, *The Way of the World*.

16. See Woloch; Plotz; Levine, *Forms*. On population and species, see also Gallagher, *The Body Economic*, and McLane, which have importantly brought Malthus into dialogue with his literary interlocutors. McLane credits Romantic poetry with shaping modern humanism via an anthropological discourse of the species to which Malthus contributed. Gallagher positions nineteenth-century literature and Malthusian political economy as competing forms of organicism, both of which defined value in terms of life and bodily sensation rather than financial abstraction. For a different account of how quantitative generalization suffuses and overtakes even the most seemingly qualitative dimensions of individual experience, see Jaffe; *The Affective Life of the Average Man* brings the history of statistics to bear on a conception of character and of emotion shaped by Quetelet's idea of averageness. On demography's centrality to nineteenth-century national politics, see also Levitan's history of the census, Schweber's study of vital statistics, Cole's historiographic analysis of the politics of large numbers in France, and Frankel's account of "print statism." Daly, too, has recently posited demographic growth as the theme of several literary genres. And considerations of the masses and of social aggregation have been a

fixture of Victorian cultural studies from the start; see Williams, *Culture and Society* 297–312; Briggs, "The Human Aggregate"; and Poovey, *Making a Social Body*.

17. For engagements with deep time in humanistic scholarship, see esp. Chakrabarty, Dimock, Morton, and McGurl.

18. See esp. *The Politics of Literature* 3–30.

19. On the emergence of fictionality in the eighteenth century and its essentially non-referential status, see Gallagher, "The Rise of Fictionality."

20. See *The Politics of Literature* 49–71.

21. On the use of masses and crowds to promote privacy and psychological interiority, see, for instance, Plotz 154–93 and Poovey, *Making a Social Body* 132–54. Daly takes a similar tack (or perhaps takes interiority and privacy somewhat for granted) in focusing on instances of demographic consciousness from an implicitly private-individualistic and agoraphobic perspective; his book treats the fact of demographic growth itself—the reality of crowding—as an evident cause of the representations he considers. Cf. Lynch's account of the emergence of character as depersonalized rather than further individuated by crowded public spaces; Frances Burney's characters, Lynch suggests, "would have the best chance of remaining characters— rather than fading into the background . . . rather than being reduced to anonymous types—if they stayed still" and remained safely enclosed in domestic space (175).

22. On the ways in which character is forged out of generality, see Jaffe, who understands George Eliot's subjects and audience alike as taking on the properties of an aggregate: "like the characters he or she reads about," Jaffe observes, "the reader is a mass character, the ground for an ungrounded identity" (36.)

23. Raymond Williams is right to recognize the ideological baggage of the term without categorically dismissing it: "In most of its uses masses is a cant word" and a term of contempt, he acknowledges, "but the problems of large societies and of collective action and reaction to which [such words] are addressed, are real enough and have to be continually spoken about" (*Keywords* 32). To dispense with such terminology would preclude describing aggregate social realities.

24. Laclau argues rigorously that an "empty signifier is something more than the image of a pre-given totality: it is what *constitutes* that totality, thus adding a qualitative new dimension" (162). Concerned primarily with the process of identification with a given collective that he treats as the basis of politics, Laclau proposes that the people as an empty signifier "can operate as a point of identification only because it represents an equivalential chain" of possible referents (162). My account of the mass, by contrast, suggests that this form remains potent in part because it defers identification.

25. Santner, as previously noted, reconsiders the link between popular sovereignty and biopolitics from another angle; see *The Royal Remains*.

26. On the underspecified meanings of *life* and the terms describing it in biopolitical theory, see Mills, who notes the slippage among Agamben's terms; since Agamben never defines the *natural* in "natural life," or defines it only "negatively as the nonpolitical," it becomes impossible to conceptualize it other than through its politicization (87).

27. For Deleuze, the answer is more decisive: life stands as a force of pure potentiality against all efforts to control it; "Life becomes resistance to power when power takes life as its object" (*Foucault* 92).

28. See *Security, Territory, Population*. See also Esposito, for whom the problem with biopower is not depoliticization but that fact that "it is precisely politics that is awarded the responsibility for saving life" (59).

29. In addition to presupposing a reified concept of life as though it preceded the social formations that invest it with value, Bazzicalupo and Clò's suggestion that survival has become the only political goal actually distorts a central element of biopolitics. Modern biopower's distinctive character, per Foucault, is that it makes survival a problem of the past and focuses on optimizing life, extending longevity, and enhancing health; its aim is "doing better than just living" in the interest of developing the state's forces (*Security, Territory, Population* 327).

30. Dubreuil, like Derrida, rejects Agamben's premise of an originary distinction between *bios* and *zōē* that founds Aristotle's city-state; by the reasoning of the *Politics*, he argues, "full human life exists only *in* the polis, *through* politics. . . . Only the city may lend constituency to *bios* and *zōē*" (95). For Dubreuil, however, that Aristotle's conception of ethical existence (the goal of living well, with its correlates not only of justice but also friendship and pleasure) depends on political existence may itself be problematically totalizing. He ultimately reads the *Politics* and *Nichomachean Ethics* against such apparently totalizing claims, suggesting that friendship and ethics, insofar as they exceed the immediate aims of governance, "contradict the grandeur of the political hold"; even while Aristotle celebrates a polis that "governs all life, and all of life," he indicates a field beyond this totality: "a space where life exceeds life" (96).

31. A conception of vital phenomena as distinct from mechanical phenomena can be found in Bichat's observations on physiology and pathology. Unlike such constants of the inorganic world as the acceleration of gravity, he argues, "all the vital functions are susceptible of numerous variations. They are frequently out of their natural state; they defy every kind of calculation. . . . It is impossible to foresee, predict, or calculate, any thing with regard to their phenomena" (qtd. in Hacking 14). While the causes of vital phenomena are scientifically explicable and not random, changes of state in any organism cannot be determined in advance. This unpredictability, for Bichat, is the stamp of animate existence.

32. While I hesitate to give form intrinsic political agency as Levine does, I share her conviction that literary forms can have "a destabilizing relation to social formations, often colliding with social hierarchies rather than reflecting or foreshadowing them" ("Strategic Formalism" 626).

1. Populating Solitude

1. See Waterman; McKusick; and Becker et al. For readings of Malthus and the Romantics that challenge this opposition, see Ferguson, McLane, Connell, and Gallagher, *The Body Economic*.

2. "I could almost eat my litter," declares one of the starving multitude of talking pigs in Shelley's *Oedipus Tyrannus*—a satire on public responses to Queen Caroline's trial and a heavy-handed anti-Malthusian allegory (392).

3. On Romantic writers' efforts to identify literature (or poetry) with human nature, see McLane 9–42. On the changing connotations of the word "literature" in the eighteenth and nineteenth centuries, see Williams, *Marxism and Literature* 46–48.

4. Aristotle distinguishes man as "the most imitative of living creatures," and Godwin follows him in calling man "an imitative animal" (*The Enquirer* 358). Aristotle adds, intriguingly, that among the representations from which man derives pleasure (as opposed to the pain of perceiving the objects themselves) are "the forms of the most ignoble animals and of dead bodies" (*Poetics* 1:4). Mimesis thus seems not simply to separate humans from other animals but also to enable aesthetic reflection on animality itself: the intermittent horror and pleasure of perceiving embodied life and mortality.

5. Derrida reads the *Critique of Judgment* along these lines in "Economimesis," noting that, for Kant, "art is not nature," since nature implies "mechanical necessity," as opposed to "the play of freedom" (4). He argues, however, that the analogy between art and nature nullifies the opposition between the two; the concept of genius becomes "the means by which art receives its rules from nature," permitting nature (via mimesis) to "reflect . . . itself through art" (4).

6. Santner, in a compelling reading of the creaturely status of humans in Kafka's fiction and Benjamin's criticism, finds it possible to understand human beings as "in some sense *more creaturely* than other creatures by virtue of an excess that is produced in the space of the political and that, paradoxically, accounts for their 'humanity'" (*On Creaturely Life* 26).

7. See Buffon, *Natural History* 5:55–56.

8. "It remains to be seen," Southey notes, "whether we are to complain of the folly of man, or of the will of God" in making humans increase and multiply or in rendering countries populous; "*Wilt thou condemn me that thou mayest be righteous*, said the Lord: who is he that will dare answer the question in Mr. Malthus's behalf?" (297).

9. On these points, Godwin echoes the arguments of his partner, Mary Wollstonecraft, who had maintained that "[l]ove, considered as an animal appetite, cannot long feed on itself without expiring" (167).

10. In a debate in which the rhetoric of virile masculinity would become a strategic line of defense, Malthus ridiculed this response in the *Edinburgh Review* as a feeble and "old-womanish performance" (qtd. in P. James 381).

11. Contra Kant's view, Santner turns to Freud for the insight that sexuality, "that dimension of human life where we seem to be utterly reduced to animality, is actually the point at which our difference from animals is in some sense most radical," since it deviates from the teleology of instinct that supposedly drives animal mating (*On Creaturely Life* 30).

12. See *The Body Economic* 15.

13. As Gallagher does well to note, Shelley's characterization of Malthus as asexual ironically echoes Malthus's own jabs at Godwin (*The Body Economic* 15). In response to the claim in *An Enquiry concerning Political Justice* that intellectual pleasures are superior to sensuality—and against Godwin's "conjecture concerning the future extinction of the passion between the sexes" in a more perfect social state—Malthus derisively remarks, "[t]hose who from coldness of constitutional temperament have never felt what love is, will surely be . . . very incompetent judges with regard to the power of this passion" (146).

14. This claim is underscored in *Oedipus Tyrannus*, where Malthus makes an allegorical appearance as "Moses the Sow-gelder." (The phrase is likely borrowed from Coleridge's annotation of Malthus's 1806 *Appendix*. Responding to the proposal that

parish clergymen read a prescribed statement reminding wedding couples of their obligation to provide for future children, Coleridge scribbled in the margin: "Clergyman! Mr. M. you must send for the Sow-gelder" [qtd. in P. James 131].) In this persona, Malthus is called upon by the King of Thebes to "spay those Sows / That load the earth with Pigs" (392)—a satirical literalization of Burke's epithet, "the swinish multitude," who serve as Shelley's Greek chorus.

15. Christopher Herbert is thus quite right to remark that, for Malthus, "'[b]odily cravings' are not vile and animalistic after all, nor could they be successfully repressed without inflicting grievous harm on society," the peculiar irony of the *Essay* being that Malthus "writes as a champion of desire against its adversaries such as Godwin, even as he proclaims the potentially catastrophic results of mankind's reproductive impulse" (111–12).

16. As a Fellow of Jesus College in 1793 (unrelated to the positions he held in the Anglican Church before and after), Malthus was required not to marry during his tenure at Cambridge; he resigned his fellowship in 1804 when he married Harriet Eckersall, with whom he fathered three children (P. James 161–63).

17. Fogarty, Introduction (n.p.).

18. See, for example, *Grundrisse* 605 and *Capital* 766n.

19. For other readings of *Frankenstein*'s connection to Malthus, see Collings and McLane.

20. McLane reads *Frankenstein* similarly, observing that "Victor's thought follows and parodies the inexorable logic of the principle of population. He cannot imagine his creature *not* reproducing" (103).

21. See also Arendt, who offers a different but pertinent account of a modern political situation in which "[d]eadly danger to any civilization is no longer likely to come from without" (302). While the context of her assessment is twentieth-century totalitarianism, the paradigm of race war remains operative. The perceived political "danger arising from the existence of people forced to live outside the common world" in the case of the dispossessed and the stateless, she suggests, "is that they are thrown back . . . on their natural givenness, on their mere differentiation" (302).

22. See Kant, *Toward Perpetual Peace* 88.

23. See, for example, Sterrenburg.

24. See *The Sexual Contract*, esp. 1–19 and 39–77.

25. See McLane 90–92; Spivak 135; and Marshall 178–227.

26. Rights, per Agamben, "are attributed to man . . . solely to the extent that man is the immediately vanishing ground . . . of the citizen" (*Homo Sacer* 128). See also Arendt, who posits that the concept of universal and inalienable human rights (supposed to precede the constitutional rights of the citizen) breaks down when it encounters the exact creature and the exact situation for which these rights were imagined: the politically unspecified "human being as such" (299). On the relation between kinship and citizenship, see also Jacqueline Stevens, who argues that Lockean social contract theory has strangely masked the kinship rules on which all political societies' laws of membership rely (50–101).

27. Rousseau recounts his petty household theft of a ribbon during childhood and his false accusation of Marion, which resulted in her expulsion (86–89). The memory of this incident and the desire to relieve his own guilty conscience, he suggests, "greatly contributed to my resolution of writing these *Confessions*" (88).

28. See Moretti and Baldick, who also read *Frankenstein* as an allegory of proletarianization (Moretti, *Signs Taken for Wonders* 87; Baldick 54).

29. See McLane 100.

30. On cosmopolitan hospitality in *Frankenstein*, see Armstrong, *How Novels Think* 70–71.

31. Kant's later *Anthropology from a Pragmatic Point of View* suggests that man's divided species-nature at once challenges the project of universal peace and renders global citizenship all the more necessary: "even under a civil constitution," he notes, "*animality* manifests itself earlier and, at bottom, more powerfully than pure *humanity*" (188). At the same time, he maintains, the "character of the species" can only be understood "collectively . . . [as] a multitude of persons" compelled by nature to produce "a coalition in a cosmopolitan society . . . which, though constantly threatened by dissension, makes progress on the whole" (191). Kant concludes that perpetual peace can be achieved "only by a progressive organization of citizens of the earth into and towards the species, as a system held together by cosmopolitan bonds" (193). The species, then, is not merely a problem; it is the paradoxical yet necessary form of human futurity.

32. On the history of the opium trade and its transmutation in De Quincey's *Confessions*, see Krishnan.

33. For a compelling reading of the process of psychological displacement and self-inoculation by which De Quincey condenses imperialist anxieties with a desire to supervise the working class, see Barrell (8). In Barrell's reading, *Confessions* narrates the means by which the opium eater "inoculates himself" (as De Quincey describes his method of increasing his tolerance for opium) against foreignness by "taking something of the East into himself, and projecting whatever he could not acknowledge as his out into a further East [i.e., China], an East *beyond* the East" (16).

34. These visions of infinite scale corroborate Janowitz's account of an urban sublime (primarily in poetry); see 246–60.

35. Notably, the projection that population could double every twenty-five years is not drawn from British parish registers but from Franklin's 1751 estimate of the colonial American birth rate in *Observations concerning the Increase of Mankind* (which drew its conclusions by correlating land use with demography) and Adam Smith's calculations concerning China's population in *The Wealth of Nations*.

36. Similar poetic visions of the fall of the British Empire appear in Anna Barbauld's "Eighteen Hundred and Eleven," Percy Shelley's *Queen Mab*, and Horace Smith's less celebrated "Ozymandias" sonnet, written together with Shelley's.

37. Feminist critics, including Mellor, have sometimes read this novel as an anti-Godwinian or anti-Shelleyan vindication of the family, domesticity, and local community (as against the ostensibly separate sphere of Romantic individualism and masculine political conflict), espousing an "ethic of care" (65–69). As *The Last Man*'s plot demonstrates, however, kinship sanctions the ethical exclusions that undercut universalism; the vain desire to care for the nuclear family—the social form through which conservatives going back to Robert Filmer had naturalized the state—causes a disastrous failure of fidelity to a larger human "family" and thus fails to sustain social obligation.

38. See Aristotle's *Politics*, which understands the *polis* as organizing social life in the interest of justice rather than mere self-preservation: "while it comes into

existence for the sake of mere life, it exists for the sake of a good life" (1252^{b}27). Foucault frames the rift between classical and modern politics in just these terms: "For millennia, man remained what he was for Aristotle: a living animal with the additional capacity for a political existence; modern man is an animal whose politics place his existence as a living being in question" (*The History of Sexuality* 143). Cf. Agamben, who argues that the process by which "bare life . . . begins to coincide with the political realm" is already in motion at the moment of Aristotle's distinction between *"zōē"* and *"bíos"* and in the premise that the exclusion of the former enables the functioning of the latter (*Homo Sacer* 9). "In Western politics," Agamben argues, "bare life has the peculiar privilege of being that whose exclusion founds the city of men" (7). Yet he distinguishes modernity by "the entry of *zōē* into the sphere of the *polis*—the politicization of bare life as such" (4). This claim draws on Benjamin's analysis of "the dogma of the sacredness of life," defined in the "Critique of Violence" as a teleological reversal; Benjamin argues that the "idea of man's sacredness," insofar as it corresponds to "mere life" or to the body's vulnerability, suggests that "what is here pronounced sacred was, according to ancient mythic thought, the marked bearer of guilt: life itself" (251).

39. See esp. Sterrenburg, Paley, and Løkke.

40. See Allard 64.

41. Qtd. in Nicoll 70.

42. See also Rancière, who reads other instances of this conceit in similarly affirmative terms; writing of the pathologies with which realist and naturalist fiction later became obsessed, he submits that "this great disease" of the modern social body "is called democracy" (*The Politics of Literature* 67).

43. See "On the Jewish Question" 33.

44. On global mobility, see Sussman's "'Islanded in the World,'" which links *The Last Man* to contemporaneous debates on emigration. My reading concurs both in emphasizing the pressures Shelley's plot brings to bear on the nation and in understanding this novel as focused on population. However, where Sussman treats the plague as the spur to human mobility, resulting in depopulation and a tragic loss of national community and history, I read their correlation the other way around: Mass migrations are not just a state policy for handling population crises but a de facto outcome of global commerce, empire, and war, and the novel shows these conditions to precede and enable pandemic.

45. Derrida's reading of the *pharmakon*—the essential non-substance that appears as a poison but is also the cure and "harbor[s] within itself [the] complicity of contrary values"—is an apt model for the logic by which Verney is inoculated against difference ("Plato's Pharmacy" 125). This, together with Derrida's later reflections on autoimmunity in *Rogues*, notably informs Esposito's immunitary paradigm.

46. On the immunitary mechanism and individuality, see Esposito 58–61.

47. These lines distinctly echo Frankenstein's solitary musings before the sublimity of Mont Blanc: "Alas! why does man boast of sensibilities superior to those apparent in the brute; it only renders them more necessary beings. If our impulses were confined to hunger, thirst, and desire, we might be nearly free"; instead, he laments, humans are prey to "a chance word or scene that that word may convey to us" (64). The trap, in other words, is not bodily need but consciousness.

48. This is similarly formulated in Kant's late work, which posits that "the one property that distinguishes man from all other animals" is the faculty of "*self-consciousness* by virtue of which he is a *rational* animal" ("Announcement" 84). Yet he acknowledges that in the absence of a "middle term" enabling comparison of the experientially known and unknown, "the problem of indicating the character of the human species is quite insoluble" (*Anthropology from a Pragmatic Point of View* 183). Heidegger would later confront this problem by treating the animal as a middle term rather than the opposite of the human, mediating between the "having of world" that defines humanity and the worldlessness of a stone (176–200).

49. Language and self-consciousness, classically understood as distinctive of the human species, are linked here to a Romantic concern with the human inability to subordinate the mind to sensuous experience. Keats's "Ode to a Nightingale" perfectly exemplifies what Pippin identifies as Romanticism's tendency "to see . . . alienation . . . or nonidentification wherever one can detect the presence of self-consciousness and reflection alone, as if such reflection . . . is inherently doubling and so alienating" (592).

50. See Barbara Johnson, who argues that *The Last Man* voices Romanticism's end: "Mary Shelley does more than give a universal vision of her mourning [for those she has lost]; she mourns for a certain type of universal vision" (263). See also Bennett, who suggests that this novel is not a disavowal of Romanticism but a testament of "the fears and hopes of 'the last Romantic,' who like Verney was setting out in search of other survivors" (152).

2. Political Animals

1. Mill and Carlyle, widely as they differ in their approaches to industrialized society, draw on the same figural vocabulary to link social organization to human vitality and to equate dissidence with pathology. Anticipating the universal "laws of health" on which Mill's *System of Logic* would base social science, Carlyle metaphorizes the Swing Riots and Chartist meetings as "so many symptoms on the surface" of the human body, which would be treated to no purpose if the underlying "virulent humour festers deep within; poisoning the sources of life" ("Chartism" 37).

2. James Phillips Kay, concerned though he was to monitor the sexuality of the working class, did not hesitate to link its multiplication to industrial expansion and the consequent need for a large labor force: "the rapid progress of our physical civilisation," he explains, "has occasioned the growth of masses of manufacturing population" (202). Engels would put the same view more critically by attributing relative surplus population to capitalism's demand for an expendable "unemployed reserve army of workers" (*The Condition of the Working Class* 119). Marx would elaborate this claim in *Capital*, arguing that industrial capitalism is responsible for what appear to be natural laws of population: "if a surplus population of workers is a necessary product of accumulation or of the development of wealth on a capitalist basis," he reasons, "this surplus population also becomes, conversely, the lever of capitalist accumulation, indeed it becomes a condition for the existence of the capitalist mode of production." This system breeds offspring necessarily in excess of its own demands for labor: "a disposable industrial reserve army . . . a mass of human material always ready for exploitation" (784).

3. On the history of the British census, see Levitan; on "print statism" and demographic reportage, see Frankel.

4. Critics and historians of Victorian social science, notably Poovey and Joyce, have understandably linked this corporeal view of the city to a liberal philosophy of government. Reformers like Kay and Chadwick, in forging a popular body that could be diagnosed and treated, indeed enshrined a recognizably liberal understanding of society as a self-regulating natural entity. However, the process of fashioning the complexity of industrialized societies into an organic assemblage does not always correspond neatly with the embedded bourgeois class interests of liberalism or with the political ambitions of the nation-state. If Kay used the discourse of social anatomy, as Poovey suggests, to indemnify English national identity against risks ascribed to foreign bodies within (notably, the Irish [*Making a Social Body* 55–72]), Engels—as this chapter will show—bends the same technique toward contesting nationality.

5. See Murphet 262, Poovey, *Making* 133, and Anderson 25.

6. The making of masses, whether through social anatomy, statistical analysis, or fiction, thus does not simply reduce an already existing class of individuals to a "passive aggregate"; it arguably makes class analysis possible in the first place, while revealing why class cannot function as an identity category (cf. Poovey, *Making* 74). Even the concerted effort of industrial capitalist social organization to attribute shared characteristics to a population of workers, and thus to naturalize their status as such—as Balibar's analysis of class racism aptly suggests—owes both its ideological urgency and its ultimate implausibility to the market itself, which ensures that the workforce is always in flux (209). Statistical social analysis, often viewed as a regime of reductive generalization, might alternatively be seen to resist "essentialism, or the idea that an individual case can reflect its kind," proving instead "a variation within kind" (Gagnier 119), much as the census may be used to assert the existence and rights of subjugated groups (Levitan 6).

7. The term would pass into currency as a verb later in the century, as Koven describes in his study of "slumming": a practice of cross-class exploration, encompassing a range of "activities undertaken by people of wealth, social standing, or education in urban spaces inhabited by the poor," and characterized by the disavowal of those engaged in it (9).

8. See *Race, Nation, Class* 212.

9. Levitan too sees an implicit link between domestic and political subversion—a suspicion among sanitary reformers that "if people were not living in families, they were potentially associating in far more dangerous combinations" (112).

10. For this reason, Benjamin is right to suggest that "Engels's description of these masses in his early writings may be regarded as a prelude . . . to one of Marx's themes," since Marx indeed "recognized it as his task to forge the amorphous mass . . . into the iron of the proletariat" ("On Some Motifs in Baudelaire" 166).

11. See Marx, *The Poverty of Philosophy* 189. Balibar notes that the term *mass* alternately describes "a social *condition*, in which the 'communal bonds' of traditional societies are collapsing and a radical isolation of individuals is emerging," and a *"movement*, in which the diversity of conditions is covered over by a common 'consciousness' . . . which aims at transforming the existing order" (145).

12. On Engels's relationship with Mary Burns, see Marcus 98–100.

13. See *The History of Sexuality*, in which Foucault argues that "[c]onflicts were necessary (in particular, conflicts over urban space: cohabitation, proximity, contamination, epidemics, such as the cholera outbreak of 1832, or . . . prostitution and venereal diseases) in order for the proletariat to be granted a body and a sexuality; economic emergencies had to arise" before, finally, "an entire administrative and technical machinery made it possible to safely import the deployment of sexuality into the exploited class" (126). Though Engels does not serve this administrative machinery, his descriptions of the deformities and abnormal physiologies of working people (symptoms of malnutrition and exhaustion, overwork, exposure to disease and contamination, and unregulated sexual exchanges) illustrate the process Foucault describes.

14. Foucault makes much of the point that Marx, in letters to Engels and to Joseph Weydemeyer, locates the sources of class analysis "in the work of the French historians who talked about the race struggle": namely, Augustin Thierry, François Guizot, and François-Auguste Mignet (*"Society Must Be Defended"* 79). This seems to be Foucault's modification of passages likely cited from memory; Marx does not use the phrase "race struggle," though one of his letters to Engels does name Thierry "the father of the 'class struggle' in French historiography" (qtd. in *"Society Must Be Defended"* 85). The remark, further, is taken out of context; Marx bestows this distinction on Thierry not in order to avow indebtedness to his methods but to mock him for conflating the French bourgeoisie and proletariat within a falsely unified Third Estate.

15. Marx, similarly concerned by the declining level of subsistence, treats its causes as systemic rather than cultural. Political economy, he argues, enforces a state of needlessness in workers "[b]y counting the lowest possible level of life (existence) as the standard, indeed as the general standard—general because it is applicable to the mass of men" (*Economic and Philosophical Manuscripts of 1844* 95). It is possible, however, to see a disconnect within capitalism itself between the motive to maximize profits by driving down wages to the level of mere "existence" and the fantasy of maximizing life's productive potential.

16. See Stallybrass and White, whose reading of Chadwick's *Sanitary Report* shows how "metonymic associations" between filth (for which the state initially appears responsible) and disease are "displaced by a metaphoric language in which filth stands in for the slum-dweller" rather than attesting to a social injury inflicted on him or her (131). See also Poovey, who makes a similar claim about the "implied parallels between prostitutes and waste" in William Acton's prostitution studies (*Making a Social Body* 93).

17. In contrast with Marx, Fanon identifies "the people of shanty towns and the lumpenproletariat" in *The Wretched of the Earth* as "one of the most spontaneously and radically revolutionary forces of a colonized people" (80). On the role of the lumpenproletariat in anticolonial movements, including in Kenya and the Congo, see Fanon 66–83.

18. See *The Country and the City* 220.

19. Even Williams takes this relational approach for granted when he describes *Mary Barton* as "a story less of the poor and the outcast than of starving working men and their families who are beginning to realise their common condition and to unite to amend it" (*The Country and the City* 219). Women, whom this phrasing implicitly

collapses along with children into the category of men's families, are appended to the true subject ("working men") by a conjunction and a possessive pronoun. While Williams rightly discerns Gaskell's attention to class consciousness, the distinction he draws here between texts that sentimentalize "the poor and the outcast" and those that recognize class struggle thus seems to hinge class identity not only on occupation but also on maleness.

20. On the relationship between gender and class, see especially Joan Wallach Scott, who argues that the formation of class concepts depended on the naturalization of gendered positions (48). On the long historical process that yielded the "definition of women as non-workers" starting in the early modern period, see Federici 61–132.

21. The dignity of labor is typically vindicated in utilitarian terms. See, for example, Cassell's *The Working Man's Friend and Family Instructor*, in which an umbrella-maker named W. G. Denham argues that "[t]rue dignity consists . . . in being useful; for, certainly, a useless being cannot be a dignified one" (Denham 12). Such claims pick up a key theme of Chartism in celebrating "the diligent worker who earns his bread by the sweat of his brow" while deriding the idle rich (12). This affirmation of manual labor, though intended to combat stereotypes of a class debased by toil, effectively reinforces the existing division of labor—encouraging workers to take pride in being "useful" and keep up the good work. In so doing, further, it bases respectability on physical ability. What looks like a criticism of the leisured class is also, by implication, a means of discrediting the nonworking poor and those who are not able-bodied as "useless beings." Such was the status even of the "deserving poor"—the elderly or impaired—from the vantage point of policymakers. Jelinger C. Symons opposed mass emigration to the colonies on the basis that it depleted Great Britain's strength and increased the proportion of "[t]he sickly, the infirm, the aged and the disabled," with whom the country is "overburdened enough" and who, he exclaims, "constitute our weakness!" (213). Insofar as it adopts this logic, the industrial novel reveals how bodies deprived of stamina or not engaged in recognized forms of work are socially divested of all "use."

22. For Lucas, the contrast between the two homes illustrates a local knowledge of differences within the working class that makes Gaskell a more authoritative observer of Manchester life than Engels, who sees only filthy slums; see *The Literature of Change* 55. While it may well be true that *Mary Barton* more accurately depicts the range of domestic scenes to be found in Manchester in the 1830s and 1840s, my reading suggests that the novel unsettles such distinctions (too easily treated as proof of moral character) by first appealing to middle-class preferences for a certain version of domesticity and then showing the impossibility of sustaining it against the vicissitudes of the industrial economy.

23. Mayhew, though he valorizes productive energy and exertion, notably differs from Mill and other Victorian political economists in extending the term *workers* to "all those who do *anything* for their living . . . without regard to the question whether such labourers tend to add to or decrease the aggregate wealth of the community" (4:9).

24. See Williams, who dismisses Mary's story as a capitulation to "the familiar and orthodox plot of the Victorian novel of sentiment" (*Culture and Society* 89); see

also Lucas, who criticizes this plot along similar lines in "Mrs. Gaskell and Brotherhood," and Bodenheimer, who argues that the novel's domestic and sentimental aspects displace "attention from political issues to individual acts" (204).

25. Gaskell expresses reluctance about retitling the novel formerly called *John Barton*. Her letters identify the working-class radical unequivocally as "my hero, *the* person with whom all my sympathies went," thrust aside by "a London thought coming through the publisher [Chapman]" that a love story centered on Mary would be more palatable (*The Letters of Mrs. Gaskell* 75, 70).

26. See Schor 13–44; see also Flint, *Elizabeth Gaskell* 11–28.

27. Notably, this very scene hints at a different division of household labor than Jane Wilson's remarks suggest; the narrator mentions Mary's observation of the late George Wilson's houseplants, his "pride and especial care," languishing after his death (118). Gaskell's novel accords less starkly gendered roles to its working-class characters than bourgeois fiction would typically prescribe, often portraying men as caregivers. On the novel's complex account of working-class masculinity and its intersection with a Chartist discourse of male familial responsibility, see Surridge.

3. Dickens's Supernumeraries

1. In the first of his Barsetshire Chronicles, Trollope caricatures the Dickensian project of "radical reform" through fiction. Parodying the formula of the study-in-contrasts, he describes a novel (ripped from the headlines on the minor scandal that predominates his own novel's plot) in which "the conversation of . . . eight starved old men in their dormitory shamed that of the clergyman's family in his rich drawing room" (137).

2. See Rose 197–232.

3. See esp. Stallybrass and White 125–48; Lougy 488–91; and Gilbert 133–54.

4. Eagleton's *Criticism and Ideology* exemplifies the Marxist tradition Miller rejects—though Miller's claim that Eagleton recurs to a bourgeois fantasy of the artist as transcending "social tensions" and "invariably on the right side of the struggle" mischaracterizes Eagleton's readings of Dickens (65n). Indeed, Eagleton's claim that Dickens's late work makes the very institutions that appear as objects of his criticism (Chancery, the Circumlocution Office, the structures of finance capitalism) into the "protagonists" and centers of symbolic coherence is not drastically different from Miller's own argument about the institutional work of *Bleak House*; see Eagleton 129–30. As for poststructuralist readings, J. Hillis Miller's classic account of the endless proliferation of texts and interpretations in *Bleak House* errs, in D. A. Miller's view, in treating the incoherence of this novel's world as an effect of signification rather than a strategy for creating coherence by other means.

5. See, for example, Morris, Anderson, and Goodlad.

6. Morris, in reading *Bleak House* as a critique of new "form[s] of power as sinister panopticon knowledge" rather than an instance thereof (118), and Goodlad, in contending that Dickens's fiction bespeaks an "acute distrust of modern agency" and aims to plot the limitations of bureaucratic power (106), effectively disregard Miller's claim that the novel is ideally situated to disavow policing because "it has already reinvented it, *in the very practice of novelistic representation*" (20).

7. Cf. Hadley for a somewhat different account of liberalism that expresses irritation with the pervasiveness of the term *liberal subject*. Hadley's emphasis on cognition and "political opinion" as constitutive of the notion of individual character anchoring liberalism notably makes Dickens uninteresting to her, since opinion and interiority are apparently of minimal interest to him (33–34).

8. Goodlad is one of the few Victorianist scholars who identifies Foucault's work on governmentality as a more pertinent model than disciplinary power—a view I share. Her analysis, however, equates governmentality with a distinctly Victorian liberalism that she opposes to discipline and to administrative power. I would suggest, by contrast, that liberalism and discipline can be understood as complementary (and have been treated as complementary by Miller, Armstrong, Poovey, and others). The emphasis Victorian political discourse placed on self-government and individual freedom, which Goodlad invokes against Miller's panoptic reading of *Bleak House*, is compatible with the objectives of surveillance, which aimed to create self-monitoring individuals precisely in order to make state intervention unnecessary. More importantly for the argument of the present chapter, I would emphasize that Foucault's account of "security" as the overriding technique of governmentality actually departs from a version of liberalism centered on the individual subject's capacities and liberties and turns its attention to population as a probabilistic object. Here, however, it is also worth noting that Foucault's own terminology becomes unstable in the 1978 lectures as the terms *governmentality* and *security* alternately supplant the term *biopower*. Governmentality eventually comes to embrace discipline and biopower, and at times sovereignty too, as part of a total system (a totalization that, as I have stressed in this chapter and elsewhere, is less coherent than Foucault suggests).

9. On the split (at times, less decisive than it seems) between omniscient and first-person narration and its relation to subjectivity, see esp. Jaffe, *Vanishing Points* 114–21.

10. For a reading of *Bleak House* that treats Jo as a crucial node of disparate 'networks,' see Levine, *Forms* 122–31. Though our conceptual frameworks differ, one commonality between Levine's approach and mine is her claim that Dickens's novel reworks character as a function of transpersonal forces rather than an autonomous or irreplaceable subject.

11. Cf. Stout for a bold reading of Dickens's revolutionary "decapitation" of character in *A Tale of Two Cities*—a novel often read, like *Hard Times*, as a reaction to the horror of reducing individuals to numbers.

12. Deleuze seizes on something elemental to Dickens's fiction when he reads it as an art of impersonal life: "a haecceity no longer of individuation but of singularization" (28–29).

13. Cf. *Capital* 138–77.

14. See esp. Jakobson 25 and J. Hillis Miller 100; see also Elaine Freedgood's metonymic readings of realism's object matter in *The Ideas in Things*.

15. Gallagher's reading of *Our Mutual Friend* is relevant here; Gallagher argues persuasively that death, in that novel, is "portrayed as a sanitizing process . . . in which a pure potential called 'Life' is released" (*The Body Economic* 93).

16. Gilbert 148.

17. Cf. Gilbert, who suggests that *Bleak House* favors "a healthy social body [that] promotes the closure, separation, and containment of individual bodies and selves" (149).

18. On the publishing market for statistical social research, see Frankel, who additionally notes that the British and U.S. governments drew on literary strategies and formats like serialization to enhance the appeal of their reports (9).

4. The Sensation Novel and the Redundant Woman Question

1. Greg's use of the term *redundant*, though borrowed from Malthus, represents a revised account of political economy, of class, of sexuality, and of species nature. Where Malthus posited an essentially static model of humanity and of society based on a system of checks, Greg—echoing Herbert Spencer, among others—posits a dynamic model based on the adaptability not only of organisms but also of institutions and systems of production. Where Malthus understood the demographic problem of surplus population in class terms, Greg reformulates it as a question of gender. Moreover, where Malthus identified marriage and sexual reproduction as the source of a "redundant population" exceeding the resources needed to sustain it (*Essay on Population* 115), Greg attributes his particular demographic surplus to a decline in marriage and maternity rather than a geometrically increasing birthrate; to conditions of material luxury rather than scarcity; and to cultural variables rather than Nature's grinding laws of necessity.

2. Though the perceived rise in employment and decline in marriage among women in situations of class privilege appeared to be recent developments, commentary on this trend extends back to earlier discussions of working-class women. Engels, as noted in chapter 2, had suggested nearly twenty years earlier that the entry of women and girls into the factory system not only increased competition for scarce employment but also did violence to the gender norms and family structures he presupposed. The relative autonomy of women in the workforce and their lack of incentive to marry, Engels argued, effectively "unsexes the man and takes from the woman all true womanliness without being able to bestow upon the man true womanliness, or the woman true manliness" and thus "degrades in the most shameful way both sexes, and, through them, humanity" (*The Condition of the Working Class in England* 168). Cf. Bythell, who argues that it is actually "remarkable how little many of the basic characteristics of women's work changed between 1750 and 1850" and that fears of the saturation of the labor market and of women displacing men were exaggerated (50).

3. Greg specifically suggests, among other measures, that "the removal of 500,000 women from the mother-country, where they are redundant, to the colonies, where they are needed" will have the added benefit that "those who remain at home will rise in value, will be more sought, will be better rewarded" ("Why Are Women Redundant?" 38).

4. See Oliphant, "Novels" 174.

5. See Armstrong, *Desire and Domestic Fiction* 8.

6. Cf. Poovey, who cites Greg's essay as a case in point in her discussion of gender ideology; see *Uneven Developments* 1–6.

7. On feminist uses of the 1851 census, see Levitan 123–46; on feminism's relation to eugenics, see Richardson 27–39.

8. See Eliot, "Silly Novels by Lady Novelists" 296–321. Eliot's criticism suggests that this redundancy is replicated stylistically in the novels' language. She reasons that if fiction, for these hack writers, were truly a means of "getting their bread,"

then their "vacillating syntax and improbable incident" would have "a certain pathos for us, like the extremely supererogatory pincushions and ill-devised nightcaps that are offered for sale by a blind man. We felt the commodity to be a nuisance, but we were glad to think that the money went to relieve the necessitous" (297–98). Economic need, she suspects, can hardly be the driving motive for the production of most of the popular literature to which she objects. Dismissing the sentimental image of "lonely women struggling for a maintenance," Eliot submits that these novelists' "frothy" style, elevated diction, and aristocratic bias in their choice of subject matter suggest a different milieu: "It is clear that they write in elegant boudoirs with violet-covered ink and a ruby pen" and must be "inexperienced in any form of poverty except poverty of brains" (298). Though sardonically acknowledging a "want of verisimilitude in their representations of the high society in which they seem to live," she insists that the writers "betray no closer acquaintance with any other form of life" (298). Where verisimilitude is applied as a criterion, Eliot's mockery of these novels' inauthenticity carries an implicit irony; insofar as "silly novels" enjoyed commercial success, they succeeded by massively reproducing a relatively consistent simulation of life in "fashionable society" that needs no external referent (298).

9. See esp. D. A. Miller 146–91. In his elegant reading of *The Woman in White*, Miller argues that the sensation novel "is profoundly about enclosing and secluding the woman in . . . institutions like marriage and madhouses," controlling not only the woman but also the dangers represented as the "woman inside" of the sexed male body (155–56). While this carceral theme is certainly elemental to sensation fiction, the claim that the novel is "profoundly about" containment does not explain what such about-ness would imply. I argue, by contrast, that the novels of Braddon, Collins, and others more often illustrate the failure to enclose social dangers either in bodies or within institutions of "supralegal modern discipline" (D. A. Miller 157).

10. In a notable passage from Braddon's novel, Lady Audley suggests that Phoebe could easily become her double with "a bottle of hair dye, such as we see advertised in the papers, and a pot of rouge" (95), despite the narrator's observation that the resemblance between the two women is "not a striking likeness" (138). Commenting on this scene, Rubery notes that "[t]he ease with which Phoebe could potentially transform her life through the advertisements tacitly undermines the comfortable distance by which the exceptional Lady Audley is set apart from the novel's other, more virtuous female characters including Alicia Audley and Clara Talboys" (72). The dissemination of print—whether in advertisements for cosmetics, anonymous messages, and fraudulent death notices circulating in the *Times*, and perhaps even in a serial novel that dangerously invites imitation—seems to allow anyone to become someone else.

11. In this respect, as in others, the sensation novel's not just multiple but multiplying identities differ markedly from the feminine Gothic trope of the secret double (or the "madwoman in the attic").

12. Given the prevalence of falsified or misreported death notices in sensation plots, Rubery does well to observe that "[d]eath is no longer a climax in sensation novels as it would have been for the vast majority of novels published [earlier in the century]. It is instead the starting point for narratives about a second life" (72). This "second life," I would add, significantly counteracts the determinacy of natural life in the Victorian novel.

13. Viewed from the perspective of later nineteenth-century fiction, the female "interloper" seems to anticipate the trope of "woman as an invader" in the defiant speech given by Gissing's Mary Barfoot; see *The Odd Women* 151–54. Though *East Lynne* does not explicitly suggest (as *Lady Audley's Secret* does, in Robert Audley's semi-ironic meditations on "petticoat government" [228–29]) the possibility of women "invading" the sphere of conventionally male occupation, its presentation of the heroine from beginning to end as an "interloper" in her own home effectively makes the same argument: that domestic life provides no solution to the problems that follow from redundancy. Gissing's novel, discussed in the next chapter, makes a similar case in illustrating the fate of Monica Madden, who is morally compromised and ultimately destroyed by marriage and maternity rather than by the working life she rejects.

14. *Daniel Deronda* 12, 762.

15. To wit, George Sala's defense of sensation fiction (commissioned by Braddon to respond to attacks from *Blackwood's* and the *Quarterly Review*) argued that, by the standards of recent critics, even so celebrated a novel as "*Adam Bede* . . . is clearly 'sensational'" in exposing readers to seduction and infanticide ("The Cant of Modern Criticism" 1:201). Not to be outdone by the Blakean proverb, "sooner murder an infant in its cradle than nurse unacted desires," this prototypically realist novel has Hetty Sorrel do both. *Middlemarch* makes much of Lydgate's susceptibility to the fatal attractions of such women as the French actress who murders her husband; this sensational episode anticipates the less theatrical but similarly destructive impact of his marriage to Rosamond. And *Felix Holt*, with its blackmail plot and backstory of adultery and illegitimacy, was explicitly equated with sensation fiction by a reviewer for *The Contemporary*, H. A. Page, who identified Eliot's sympathy for Mrs. Transome's moral "weakness" as a point at which "we regret to say, Miss Braddon and George Eliot join hands, Lady Audley and Mrs. Transome being true twin-sisters of fiction" (178). On sensation fiction's actual or imputed influence on Eliot, see esp. Hughes 171–72.

16. The most strenuous objections to the so-called sensation school were not made on behalf of realism as such but on behalf of a certain conventional moralism. As Oliphant put it, Braddon's and Collins's fiction—though unquestionably "genuine in its way"—offends against "[t]hat sublime respect for sentimental morality and poetic justice which distinguishes the British public" ("Novels" 178, 177). It bears remarking, further, that the value of realism had already come under question by the 1860s. Lewes, who had embraced the term a decade earlier, almost anticipates Lukács's critique of naturalism when he charges contemporary realism with "detailism" and argues that "[t]he rage for realism, which is healthy in as far as it insists on truth, has become unhealthy, in as far as it confounds truth with familiarity, and the predominance of unessential details" (83–84).

17. Trodd suggests that *Daniel Deronda* draws strategically, and somewhat ironically, on sensational conventions; she argues that the novel's opening raises classically sensational questions about the ambiguity of good and evil in its unsettling description of Gwendolen and, further, that the heroine "sees herself as potentially a character in a sensation novel"—particularly in the scene in which her multiple reflections appear "like so many women petrified white" (124–25). See also Cvetkovich, who similarly compares the mystery of Gwendolen's character to the aura of secrecy surrounding the sensation heroine (130).

18. Here, one might track the complications of romantic prehistory in Eliot's marriage plot back to earlier domestic novels, including *Pamela*. Sussman argues that Richardson's novel offers the backstory of Sally Godfrey's seduction as a counterpoint to the marriage plot, "allow[ing] the text to include not only Pamela's happy ending but also the extremely unhappy ending to which a different plot twist would have led her" ("Poor Miss Sally Godfrey" 97). The presence of Mr. B's abandoned former lover and the mother of his illegitimate child, Sussman suggests, attests to "the extremely precarious nature of Pamela's 'happiness'" (97). What separates Eliot's novel from Richardson's, however, is the erosion of any permanent distinction in status between the married woman and the single woman, both in terms of the sexual morality ascribed to her and in terms of the security of her position. This is evident even in the verb tense in which Gwendolen's apprehensions are expressed; whereas Sussman finds Sally personifying another ending "to which a different plot twist *would have* led" Richardson's heroine (emphasis added), this concern moves out of the conditional past when Eliot's married heroine dreads the shunned single woman as a specter of "a future that might be her own."

19. Gallagher, along similar lines, suggestively observes that "Eliot repeatedly creates scenarios in which a 'consumer,' for example Grandcourt, has no real appetite for what he purchases," notably Gwendolen (*The Body Economic* 131). She reads this scenario as arising out of the novelist's own anxiety that her artistic success had outworn its welcome; the analogy between sexual desire and consumer interest—particularly readerly interest—expresses a fear that her novels are becoming more of the same and merely adding to what Eliot called "the 'too much' of literature" (*The Body Economic* 118).

20. See Gallagher, *The Body Economic* 118–55.

21. Qtd. in Johnson 208.

22. Loesberg reads the Victorian sensation novel (particularly its thematization of identity loss) as a narrative of the transgression of class boundaries. He locates the genre's primary political significance in the debates surrounding the Second Reform Act; see 115–38.

23. See Collins, "The Unknown Public" 207–16.

24. This logic persists today in the methods of distant reading. Moretti's *Graphs, Maps, Trees* figures literary history as an evolutionary landscape governed by universal laws of adaptation, selection, and morphological variation. Darwin's model of natural selection, for Moretti, best conveys the ruthless competition that decides the fate of any literary form. For him, as for Lewes, fitness to existing conditions is the only predictor that a work will become part of a repeatable genre.

25. On the influence of the theory of sexual selection on fiction after Darwin's *The Descent of Man*, see Beer 196–219.

26. That Victorian novel criticism becomes one of the first articulations of the Spencerian doctrine of "the survival of the fittest" is clear even in Mansel's essay, which hypothesizes that literature might benefit from "an increased struggle for existence, under the pressure of which weaker writers would give way, and the stronger would be improved by the stimulus of effective competition" (Spencer, *Principles of Biology* 1:444; Mansel 513).

27. Bernstein suggests that the sensation novel's reception is shaped by cultural anxieties about Darwinism and the ambiguous boundary between humans and (other) animals; see 250–71. This concern is certainly present in critical responses to sensation fiction's supposed address to "the animal part of our nature" or to its implied "degradation of the human into the animal or brutal, on the call of strong emotion" ("Our Female Sensation Novelists" 212). I would argue, however, that negative reviews of Braddon and others are divided between those that ultimately imply a positive end to evolution and those that point, contra Darwin, toward theories of degeneration that would regain popularity toward the end of the century. Such theories recognize a struggle for existence, yet they deny that this struggle favors improvement. Greg adopts this viewpoint in an essay called "Non-Survival of the Fittest," advocating proto-eugenic programs: "Every damaged or inferior temperament might be eliminated, and every special or superior one be selected and enthroned, till the human race, both in its manhood and its womanhood, become one glorious fellowship of saints, sages, and athletes" (*Enigmas of Life* 112). On the relation between Collins's novels and theories of evolution and of degeneracy, see Bourne Taylor 63–70, 207–42.

28. Describing the mass as "a matrix from which all traditional behavior toward works of art issues today in a new form," Benjamin contends that "[t]he greatly increased mass of participants has produced a change in the mode of participation" ("The Work of Art in the Age of Mechanical Reproduction" 239). His emphasis on the situation of "reception . . . in a state of distraction" (239) recalls Mansel's analysis of the railway novel as an accommodation of literature to a crowded social world in which attention is scarce and the "shock effect" paradoxically ordinary (238; cf. Mansel 489). While his conclusions are decidedly different, Benjamin's analysis of aesthetic effects on the masses and their basis in the mass reproduction and reception of art finds an unlikely precedent in nineteenth-century criticism.

29. On the culture industry, see Horkheimer and Adorno 120–67. Building implicitly on concerns about mass culture established in nineteenth-century criticism, Horkheimer and Adorno theorize the culture industry as replacing high art with an endless supply of commercially manufactured entertainment that is aesthetically and ideologically redundant in its essence. By their account (which notably echoes Victorian criticism of sensation fiction as an imitative form both in substance and in mode of production), it ensures the triumph of "the inferior work of art [that] has always relied on its similarity with others"; through its technologies of mass production, the regime of "imitation finally becomes absolute" (131). They describe its products as coercive, designed to elicit unconscious consent to the ideology of the market.

30. See, for example, Engels, *The Condition of the Working Class in England* 168.

31. For a detailed account of the failed attempt to publish *Gwendolen Harleth*, see Storer 40–49. Leavis was invited by the Bodley Head in 1973 to edit the abridged version of the novel he had conceived years earlier as *Gwendolen Harleth*. James Mitchie, the editor who proposed the project, ultimately abandoned it for several reasons, including the resistance of external manuscript readers. Another sympathetic publisher rejected the idea as impractical for formal reasons: "While there are two stories

in *Daniel Deronda*," he wrote, "they are so closely intermingled that in one's attempt to cut one, a lot of the other is lost" (45). That plot elements are not reducible to the individual characters they most centrally concern seems obvious enough in all of Eliot's novels, but it is particularly significant in the case of *Daniel Deronda* that the novel's structure precludes the removal of what Leavis viewed as the unwelcome or unnecessary element. While Daniel may choose to leave England, removing him forcibly from the text would do violence to the narrative.

32. Leavis does in fact differ markedly from Arnold on some counts. His aggressive defense of an intellectual minority culture in particular diverges from Arnold's project of raising up "the masses" by transmitting "from one end of society to the other, the best knowledge, the best ideas of [the] time" (*Culture and Anarchy* 79). From Leavis's perspective, drastic measures are required at a moment when the "enemies" of culture are "now, to a degree that Arnold can hardly have foreseen, invested with power and conscious of virtue" (*For Continuity* 77).

5. "Because We Are Too Menny"

1. See Moretti, *The Way of the World*.

2. For readings of colonial novels that key their characters' developmental lags to their imperial setting and to the collapse of allegories of progress, see Esty 71–100.

3. Among possible counterexamples, consider *Great Expectations*, which founds its hero's growth and social mobility on self-delusion, shame, dirty money, colonial labor, and misplaced desire. And *Jane Eyre*, even as it secures its heroine's place in society, exposes a disquieting recognition of what its own fantasy of social incorporation requires. Its resolution (if settling a restless protagonist in a dank house off the map to nurse a maimed and emasculated husband she calls "master" counts as a resolution) is conspicuously balanced on the back of empire. Brontë's plot makes it hard to miss the point that everything set forth as nationally desirable and socially respectable is achieved through extraordinary feats of repression and explosions of violence. Cf. Buzard and Esty, who read *Jane Eyre* as a narrative of national closure (see Buzard 165; Esty 51).

4. Galton would use similar metaphors to frame a eugenic program of cultivating good genetic stock: eugenicists, he suggests, should take interest in "families of civic worth" and "should regard such families as an eager horticulturalist regards beds of seedlings of some rare variety of plant" (*Essays in Eugenics* 119).

5. The evolutionary biologist Julian Huxley coined this phrase in his 1942 book *Evolution: The Modern Synthesis*.

6. Weismann's theory was nonetheless debated throughout the 1880s and 90s—Lombroso and Spencer, for example, continuing to offer evidence that acquired traits could be passed down; see esp. Lombroso, "The Heredity of Acquired Characteristics" 200–208.

7. Beer argues that, despite the diminished importance of individual life from a Darwinian standpoint, "Hardy in his emplotment opposes this perception and does so by adopting . . . the single life span as his scale," noting that his novels "pay homage to human scale by ceasing as the hero or heroine dies" (222–23). While the point is well taken, the current chapter suggests that Hardy's novels match their scope to that of an individual life in order to ironize the gap between their narrative focus

and the disposability (and decisively end-stopped mortality) of their subject matter. I obviously differ from Beer, too, in emphasizing the ascendency of heredity, which drastically curtails Darwinian optimism.

8. One might draw a stark contrast here between Hardy's Jude and Eliot's earlier autodidact, Adam Bede, who, the narrator remarks, is bound to leave only anonymous traces of his existence. Eliot ranks Adam with a class of "peasant artisans" whose "lives have no discernible echo beyond the neighborhood where they dwelt," reassuringly adding that such obscure existences have utility: "you are almost sure to find some good piece of road, some building" attributable to their efforts (213). For Jude, contributing a piece of road or a building is simply subordination, and the edifices on which he works—crumbling facades of archaic institutions—seem liable to disappear.

9. *The Division of Labor in Society* turns to natural history and morphology to locate the origins of labor division in the origins of life on earth, suggesting that functional specialization is "no mere social institution . . . but a general biological phenomenon of organic matter" and that the evolution of organisms is analogous to the evolution of social bodies in tending toward increasing specialization (3).

10. For a somewhat different account of Durkheim's relation to biopolitics, see Hacking, who makes much of Durkheim's use of the metaphor of "contagion" to describe the repetition of suicidal behavior (171–92); such language, I would suggest, diverges substantially from the eugenic account of suicide as hereditary. Yet I agree, for different reasons explained in this section, that Durkheim's analysis of suicide and his entire conception of "social fact" have biopolitical foundations.

11. Hardy's 1912 postscript to the Wessex edition remarks on Sue's reception as an instance of this prevalent new type. He paraphrases the opinion of a German reviewer that Sue was "the first delineation in fiction of the woman who was coming into notice in her thousands every year—the woman of the feminist movement—the slight, pale 'bachelor' girl—the intellectualized, emancipated bundle of nerves that modern conditions were producing" (468).

12. See Beer, who calls *Jude the Obscure* a "late-Malthusian tragedy" (240), and Gallagher, who reads Hardy's plot as an instance of "literary Malthusianism" at its bleakest (*The Body Economic* 183–84). See also Gagnier, who identifies "Hardy's terms" in *Jude* as "those of political economy: production, reproduction, and the [laboring] body" and adds that these terms are "specifically Malthusian in the body's reproductive capacity" (129).

13. On other anthropological theories of inertia developed in the 1890s and 1900s and on the process by which inertia was dissociated from pathological fatigue and normalized as a mechanism for conserving energy, see Rabinbach 172–78.

14. Esty finds a comparable negativity and a pertinent critique of "permanent capitalist transition" in modernist tales of "frozen youth": "by autonomizing youth into a trope with no fixed destination," he argues, fiction can "bring the force of modernist critique to bear on the *mythos* of development, exposing it as a more or less eternal logic of deferral" (210).

15. See Hardy's letter to a correspondent, qtd. in *The Life and Work of Thomas Hardy* 297.

16. In this, it echoes Wordsworth's "We Are Seven," where the child's refrain stubbornly counts her dead siblings in the present tense as part of a continuous "we."

Conclusion

1. See Sayeau. This staging of late-capitalist conditions of unemployment in the Belgian Congo is one of several ways in which Conrad's tale might support Stoler's analysis of colonies as "laboratories of modernity" (15).

2. On the multitude of potential models for Kurtz, see esp. Brantlinger, "*Heart of Darkness*: Anti-Imperialism, Racism, or Impressionism?"

3. See Le Bon, *The Crowd* (1895); Tarde, "The Public and the Crowd" (1897); Trotter, "Herd Instinct and its Bearing on the Psychology of Civilized Man" (1908); and McDougall, *The Group Mind* (1920). See also Freud, *Group Psychology and the Analysis of the Ego* (1921).

4. See Pick and Lawler; cf. Arrata, who argues that Stevenson's story, rather than ratifying the theory of regression to savagery or degeneracy and the class connotations attached to these concepts, at once reveals their discursive construction and "turns the discourses centered on degeneration, atavism, and criminality back on the professional classes that produced them, linking gentlemanliness and bourgeois virtue to various forms of depravity" (244).

5. For a reading of *Dr. Jekyll and Mr. Hyde* as a narrative of imperial decline, see Hensley. Emphasizing both material signs of decay in the story's metropolitan architecture and dates that align Jekyll's transformation with a concrete geopolitical history (the transition to the more militant closing phase of British imperial power from 1875 to the 1885 Berlin Conference), Hensley suggests that, through these details, "Stevenson plots the emergence of open violence on a similar timeline" (282). The tale, as he reads it, chronicles "how a civilized body might 'come to itself' as brute violence" (281). My reading diverges from his in suggesting that the historico-political dimensions of this text (like Conrad's after it), rather than standing opposed to the psychological, precisely enable the imagined lapse into an apparently ahistorical state of consciousness, much as Le Bon's analysis of contemporary politics will entail a dehistoricizing account of crowds.

6. See *The Political Unconscious* 225. Though Jameson focuses on *Lord Jim*, his analysis of Conrad's impressionistic style in relation to reification is pertinent to *Heart of Darkness*. See also Brantlinger, who applies Jameson's description of Conrad's impressionism to the misty haloes enveloping Marlow's story. Brantlinger too sees ideological ambivalence in Conrad's aesthetics but concludes more decisively that his "critique of empire is never strictly anti-imperialist" ("*Heart of Darkness*: Anti-Imperialism, Racism, or Impressionism?" 382).

7. Said, while admiring Conrad's formal self-awareness and the attention it draws to the constructedness of the imperial worldview (including its narrator's), finds that the text in the end offers no alternative: "Neither Conrad nor Marlow gives us a full view of what is outside the world-conquering attitudes" it challenges, he notes, concluding that "*Heart of Darkness* works so effectively because its aesthetics and politics are imperialist" (24).

8. On Tarde's and McDougall's contributions to group psychology, see Laclau 40–52.

9. On the decline of criminological and pathological models of mass psychology (which initially drew on Lombroso's work) and on relevant debates in French psychiatry between the Salpêtrière and Nancy schools, see Laclau 35–39.

10. Freud conjectures that the superego "originated from the experiences that led to totemism," those processes through which "primitive man" acquired the father complex, and with it, religion and moral restraint (*The Ego and the Id* 28). On the primal father and the emergence of totemism, see also *Group Psychology and the Analysis of the Ego* 69–77.

11. For a Freudian reading of Conrad, see, for example, Guerard; for psychoanalytic and metaphysical readings of Stevenson, see, for example, Miyoshi and K. Miller.

12. See esp. *Group Psychology and the Analysis of the Ego* 69. See also *Totem and Taboo*, where Freud—working from Darwin's conjectures concerning early forms of society and, in part, from Frazer's *Totem and Exogamy*—first addresses the myth of the band of brothers killing the primal father and posits the resulting collective guilt as the origin of religious and social laws (125–32).

13. This hypothesis contrasts with Esposito's reading of the individual's biopolitical function for modern sovereignty as a form of autoimmune inoculation against the perceived viral contagion of community; see Esposito 57–63.

Bibliography

Abelove, Henry. "Some Speculations on the History of Sexual Intercourse during the Long Eighteenth Century in England." *Genders* 6 (Fall 1989): 125–30.

Achebe, Chinua. "An Image of Africa: Racism in Conrad's *Heart of Darkness*." In *Hopes and Impediments: Selected Essays*. New York: Doubleday, 1989.

Addison, Joseph, Richard Steele, et al. *The Spectator*. Ed. Henry Morley. 3 vols. London: Routledge, 1891.

Adorno, Theodor. *The Culture Industry*. Ed. J. M. Bernstein. London: Routledge, 1991.

Agamben, Giorgio. "Absolute Immanence." In *Potentialities*. Ed. and trans. Daniel Heller-Roazen. Stanford: Stanford UP, 1999. 220–39.

——. *Homo Sacer: Sovereign Power and Bare Life*. Trans. Daniel Heller-Roazen. Stanford: Stanford UP, 1998.

——. *The Open: Man and Animal*. Trans. Kevin Attell. Stanford: Stanford UP, 2004.

Alison, Archibald. *The Principles of Population, and Their Connection with Human Happiness*. Edinburgh: Blackwood, 1840.

Allard, James Robert. *Romanticism, Medicine, and the Poet's Body*. Aldershot: Ashgate, 2007.

Anderson, Amanda. *The Powers of Distance: Cosmopolitanism and the Cultivation of Detachment*. Princeton: Princeton UP, 2001.

Arendt, Hannah. *The Origins of Totalitarianism*. San Diego: Harcourt, 1976.

Armstrong, Nancy. *Desire and Domestic Fiction: A Political History of the Novel*. New York: Oxford UP, 1987.

——. *How Novels Think: The Limits of British Individualism from 1719–1900*. New York: Columbia UP, 2005.

Arnold, Matthew. *Culture and Anarchy: An Essay in Political and Social Criticism*. Ed. Stefan Collini. Cambridge: Cambridge UP, 1993.

——. "The Function of Criticism at the Present Time." In *Culture and Anarchy*. Ed. Stefan Collini. Cambridge: Cambridge UP, 1993. 26–51.

Arrata, Stephen. "The Sedulous Ape: Atavism, Professionalism, and Stevenson's *Jekyll and Hyde*." *Criticism* 37 (1995): 233–59.

Auerbach, Erich. *Mimesis: The Representation of Reality in Western Literature*. Trans. Willard T. Trask. Princeton: Princeton UP, 1953.

Austin, Alfred. "Our Novels: The Sensational School." *Temple Bar* 29 (1870): 410–24.

Baldick, Chris. *In Frankenstein's Shadow: Myth, Monstrosity, and Nineteenth-Century Writing*. Oxford: Clarendon, 1987.

Balibar, Etienne. *Masses, Classes, Ideas: Studies on Politics and Philosophy before and after Marx*. Trans. James Swenson. New York: Routledge, 1994.

Balibar, Etienne, and Immanuel Wallerstein. *Race, Nation, Class: Ambiguous Identities*. Trans. Chris Turner. London: Verso, 1991.

Barrell, John. *The Infection of Thomas De Quincey: A Psychopathology of Imperialism.* New Haven: Yale UP, 1991.

Baudelaire, Charles. *Le Spleen de Paris: Petits poèmes en prose.* Ed. Robert Kopp. Paris: Gallimard, 2006.

Bauman, Zygmunt. *Wasted Lives: Modernity and Its Outcasts.* Cambridge: Polity, 2004.

Bazzicalupo, Laura, and Clarissa Clò. "The Ambivalences of Biopolitics." *diacritics* 36 (2006): 109–16.

Becker, Christine, Malte Faber, Kirsten Hirtel, and Reiner Manstetten. "Malthus vs. Wordsworth: Perspectives on Humankind, Nature, and Economy." *Ecological Economics* 53 (2005) 299–310.

Beer, Gillian. *Darwin's Plots: Evolutionary Narrative in Darwin, George Eliot, and Nineteenth-Century Fiction.* Cambridge: Cambridge UP, 2000.

Benjamin, Walter. "Critique of Violence." Trans. Edmund Jephcott. In *Walter Benjamin: Selected Writings, Vol. 1: 1913–1926.* Ed. Marcus Bullock and Michael W. Jennings. Cambridge: Belknap, 1996. 236–52.

——. "On Some Motifs in Baudelaire." In *Illuminations.* Ed. Hannah Arendt. Trans. Harry Zohn. New York: Schocken, 1968. 155–200.

——. "The Work of Art in the Age of Mechanical Reproduction." In *Illuminations.* Ed. Hannah Arendt. Trans. Harry Zohn. New York: Schocken, 1968. 217–51.

Bennett, Betty T. "Radical Imaginings: Mary Shelley's *The Last Man.*" *The Wordsworth Circle* 26.3 (1995): 147–52.

Berlant, Lauren. *Cruel Optimism.* Durham: Duke UP, 2011.

Bernasconi, Robert. "Perpetual Peace and the Invention of Total War." In *Philosophy and the Return of Violence.* Ed. Nathan Eckstrand. New York: Continuum, 2011. 44–60.

Bernstein, Susan David. "Ape Anxiety: Sensation Fiction, Evolution, and the Genre Question." *Journal of Victorian Culture* 6 (2001): 250–71.

Bichat, Marie-François Xavier. *General Anatomy, Applied to Physiology and the Practice of Medicine.* Trans. Constant Coffyn and George Calvert. London: Shackell, 1824.

——. *Physiological Researches upon Life and Death.* Trans. Tobias Watkins. Philadelphia: Smith, 1809.

Blanc, Louis. *Organization of Work.* Trans. Marie Paula Dickoré. In *University of Cincinnati Studies.* Ed. Louis T. More, John M. Burman, and Henry G. Hartman. Vol. 2. Cincinnati: U of Cincinnati P, 1911.

Bodenheimer, Rosemarie. "Private Grief and Public Acts in *Mary Barton.*" *Dickens Studies Annual* 9 (1981): 195–216.

Booth, William. *In Darkest England; And the Way Out.* Montclair, NJ: Patterson Smith, 1975.

Bourne Taylor, Jenny. *In the Secret Theatre of Home: Wilkie Collins, Sensation Narrative, and Nineteenth-Century Psychology.* London: Routledge, 1988.

Boyle, Thomas. *Black Swine in the Sewers of Hampstead: Beneath the Surface of Victorian Sensationalism.* New York: Viking, 1989.

Braddon, Mary Elizabeth. *The Doctor's Wife.* Ed. Lyn Pyckett. Oxford: Oxford UP, 1998.

——. *Lady Audley's Secret*. Ed. Natalie M. Houston. Peterborough, Ontario: Broadview, 2003.

Brantlinger, Patrick. *"Heart of Darkness*: Anti-Imperialism, Racism, or Impressionism?" *Criticism* 27 (1985): 363–85.

——. *The Reading Lesson: The Threat of Mass Literacy in Nineteenth-Century British Fiction*. Bloomington: Indiana UP, 1998.

——. "What Is 'Sensational' about the Sensation Novel?" *Nineteenth-Century Fiction* 37 (1989): 1–28.

Briggs, Asa. "The Human Aggregate." In *The Victorian City: Images and Realities*. Ed. H. J. Dyos and Michael Wolff. London: Routledge, 1973. 83–104.

Brimley, George. Review of *Bleak House*. *The Spectator* (24 Sept. 1853). Reprinted in *Charles Dickens: The Critical Heritage*. Ed. Philip Collins. London: Routledge, 1995. 283–89.

Brontë, Charlotte. *Jane Eyre*. Ed. Stevie Davies. London: Penguin, 2006.

Buffon, Georges-Louis Leclerc. *Natural History, containing A Theory of the Earth, a General History of Man, of the Brute Creation, and Vegetables, Minerals, &c.* Vol. 5. London: Barr, 1792.

Burke, Edmund. *Reflections on the Revolution in France*. Ed. J. G. A. Pocock. Indianapolis: Hackett, 1987.

Butler, Josephine. *An Appeal to the People of England on the Recognition and Superintendence of Prostitution by Governments*. 2nd ed. Nottingham: Frederick Banks, 1870.

Buzard, James. *Disorienting Fiction: The Autoethnographic Work of Nineteenth-Century British Novels*. Princeton: Princeton UP, 2005.

Byron, George Gordon [Baron]. "Darkness." In *The Works of Lord Byron*. Vol. 4. Ed. Ernest Hartley Coleridge. London: Murray, 1901. 42–45.

——. *Don Juan*. Ed. T. G. Steffan, E. Steffan, and W. W. Pratt. London: Penguin, 1982.

Bythell, Duncan. "Women in the Workforce." In *The Industrial Revolution and British Society*. Ed. Patrick O'Brien and Roland Quinault. Cambridge: Cambridge UP, 1993.

Canetti, Elias. *Crowds and Power*. Trans. Carol Stewart. New York: Farrar, 1973.

Canguilhem, Georges. *Knowledge of Life*. Ed. Paola Marrati and Todd Meyers. Trans. Stefanos Geroulanos and Daniela Ginsburg. New York: Fordham UP, 2008.

——. *The Normal and the Pathological*. Trans. Carolyn R. Fawcett. New York: Zone, 1991.

Carlyle, Thomas. "Characteristics." In *Critical and Miscellaneous Essays*. Boston: Munroe, 1839.

——. "Chartism." *Critical and Miscellaneous Essays by Thomas Carlyle*. Vol. 4. New York: International Book Company, 1869. 36–117.

——. *Past and Present*. Ed. Chris R. Vanden Bossche, Joel J. Brattin, and D. J. Trela. Berkeley: U of California P, 2005.

——. "Shooting Niagara: And After?" *Macmillan's* 16 (Apr. 1867): n.p.

Carpenter, Edward. *Civilisation: Its Cause and Cure*. London: Swan Sonnenschein, 1895.

——. *Love's Coming of Age*. New York: Modern Library, 1911.

Chadwick, Edwin. *Report on the Sanitary Condition of the Labouring Population of Great Britain*. Ed. M. W. Flinn. Edinburgh: Edinburgh UP, 1965.

Chakrabarty, Dipesh. "The Climate of History: Four Theses." *Critical Inquiry* 35.2 (2009): 197–222.

Chesterton, G. K. *Criticisms and Appreciations of the Works of Charles Dickens*. New York: Haskell House, 1970.

——. *The Victorian Age in Literature*. New York: Holt, 1913.

Cole, Joshua. *The Power of Large Numbers: Population, Politics, and Gender in Nineteenth-Century France*. Ithaca: Cornell UP, 2000.

Coleridge, Samuel Taylor. "Fears in Solitude." In *Samuel Taylor Coleridge: The Major Works*. Ed. H. L. Jackson. Oxford: Oxford UP, 1985. 92–98.

——. "Religious Musings." In *Samuel Taylor Coleridge: The Major Works*. Ed. H. L. Jackson. Oxford: Oxford UP, 1985. 13–23.

Colley, Linda. *Britons: Forging the Nation, 1707–1837*. 2nd ed. New Haven: Yale UP, 2005.

——. *Captives: Britain, Empire, and the World, 1600–1850*. New York: Anchor, 2002.

Collings, David. *Monstrous Society: Reciprocity, Discipline, and the Political Uncanny*. Lewisburg, PA: Bucknell UP, 2009.

Collins, Wilkie. *The Moonstone*. Ed. Sandra Kemp. London: Penguin, 1998.

——. "The Unknown Public." *Household Words* 18 (Aug. 1858): 217–22. Reprinted in *Victorian Print Media*. Ed. Andrew King and John Plunkett. Oxford: Oxford UP, 2005. 207–16.

——. *The Woman in White*. Ed. Matthew Sweet. London: Penguin, 1999.

Commissioners of Inquiry into the State of Large Towns and Populous Districts. *Reports of the Commissioners for Inquiring into the State of Large Towns and Populous Districts*. London: Clowes, 1844–45.

Condorcet, Marie-Jean-Antoine-Nicolas de Caritat [Marquis de]. *Sketch for a Historical Picture of the Progress of the Human Mind*. Trans. June Barraclough. Westport, CT: Hyperion, 1979.

Connell, Philip. *Romanticism, Economics, and the Question of "Culture."* Oxford: Oxford UP, 2001.

Conrad, Joseph. *Heart of Darkness*. Ed. Paul B. Armstrong. New York: Norton, 2006.

Cooke-Taylor, Richard Whately. *Introduction to a History of the Factory System*. London: Bentley, 1886.

Cooper, Melinda. *Life as Surplus: Biotechnology and Capitalism in the Neoliberal Era*. Seattle: U of Washington P. 2008.

Cvetkovich, Ann. *Mixed Feelings: Feminism, Mass Culture, and Victorian Sensationalism*. New Brunswick, NJ: Rutgers UP, 1992.

Dallas, E. S. *The Gay Science*. London: Chapman, 1866.

Daly, Nicholas. *The Demographic Imagination and the Nineteenth-Century City: Paris, London, New York*. Cambridge: Cambridge UP, 2015.

Darwin, Charles. *On the Origin of Species by Means of Natural Selection*. Ed. Gillian Beer. Oxford: Oxford UP, 1996.

——. *The Descent of Man, and Selection in Relation to Sex*. Ed. James Moore and Adrian Desmond. London: Penguin, 2004.

Deleuze, Gilles. *Foucault*. Ed. and trans. Séan Hand. Minneapolis: U of Minnesota P, 1988.

——. "Immanence: A Life." In *Pure Immanence: Essays on a Life*. Trans. Anne Boyman. New York: Zone, 2001.

De Quincey, Thomas. *Confessions of an English Opium-Eater*. Ed. Althea Hayter. London: Penguin, 1971.

Denham, W. G. "The Dignity of Labour." *The Working Man's Friend and Family Instructor* 1 (1850): 12–14.

Denning, Michael. "Wageless Life." *New Left Review* 66 (2010): 79–97.

Derrida, Jacques. *The Beast and the Sovereign*. Ed. Michel Lisse, Marie-Louise Mallet, and Ginette Michaud. Trans. Geoffrey Bennington. Chicago: U of Chicago P, 2009.

——. "Economimesis." Trans. Richard Klein. *Diacritics* 11 (1981): 3–15.

——. "Plato's Pharmacy." In *Dissemination*. Trans. Barbara Johnson. Chicago: U of Chicago P, 1981. 61–84.

——. *Rogues: Two Essays on Reason*. Trans. Pascale-Anne Brault and Michael Naas. Stanford: Stanford UP, 2005.

Dickens, Charles. *Bleak House*. Ed. Nicola Bradbury. London: Penguin, 2003.

——. *A Christmas Carol*. In *A Christmas Carol and Other Christmas Writings*. Ed. Michael Slater. London: Penguin, 2003. 27–118.

——. *Great Expectations*. Ed. Charlotte Mitchell. London: Penguin, 1996.

——. *Hard Times*. Ed. Kate Flint. London: Penguin, 2003.

——. *Little Dorrit*. Ed. Helen Small and Stephen Wall. London: Penguin, 2004.

——. "Nobody's Story." In *Christmas Stories*. Oxford: Oxford UP, 1996. 59–66.

——. "On Duty with Inspector Field." *Household Words* (14 Jun. 1851). Reprinted in *Charles Dickens: Selected Journalism, 1850–1870*. Ed. David Pascoe. London: Penguin, 1997. 306–17.

——. *Our Mutual Friend*. Ed. Adrian Poole. London: Penguin, 1997.

——. *A Tale of Two Cities*. Ed. Richard Maxwell. London: Penguin, 2003.

——. "To Working Men." *Household Words* (7 Oct. 1854). Reprinted in *"Gone Astray" and Other Papers from* Household Words, *1851–59*. Ed. Michael Slater. Columbus: Ohio State UP, 1999. 225–29.

Dimock, Wai Chee. *Through Other Continents: American Literature across Deep Time*. Princeton: Princeton UP, 2006.

Disraeli, Benjamin. *Sybil, or The Two Nations*. Ed. Thom Braun. Harmondsworth: Penguin, 1980.

Douglas, Mary. *Purity and Danger: An Analysis of the Concepts of Pollution and Taboo*. London: Routledge, 1996.

Driver, Felix. *Geography Militant: Cultures of Exploration and Empire*. Oxford: Blackwell, 2001.

Dubreuil, Laurent. "Leaving Politics: Bios, Zōē, Life." *Diacritics* 36.2 (2006): 83–98.

Duncan, Ian. "We Were Never Human: Monstrous Forms of Nineteenth-Century Fiction." In *Victorian Transformations: Genre, Nationalism, and Desire in Nineteenth-Century Literature*. Ed. Bianca Tredennick. Surrey: Ashgate, 2011.

Durkheim, Émile. *The Division of Labor in Society*. Trans. George Simpson. Glencoe, IL: Free Press, 1933.

——. *The Elementary Forms of Religious Life*. Trans. Joseph Ward Swain. London: Allen, 1915.

——. *Suicide: A Study in Sociology*. Ed. George Simpson. Trans. John A. Spaulding and George Simpson. New York: Free Press, 1951.

——. "What Is a Social Fact?" *The Rules of Sociological Method*. Trans. W. D. Halls. New York: Free Press, 1982. 20–28.

Eagles, John. "Civilization—the Census." *Blackwood's Edinburgh Magazine* (Oct. 1854). Reprinted in *Essays Contributed to Blackwood's Magazine by the Reverend John Eagles*. Edinburgh: Blackwood, 1857. 304–56.

Eagleton, Terry. *Criticism and Ideology*. London: Verso, 1976.

——. Preface. *Bleak House*. Ed. Nicola Bradbury. London: Penguin, 2003. vii–xii.

Ebbatson, Roger. *The Evolutionary Self: Hardy, Forster, Lawrence*. Sussex: Harvester Press, 1982.

Edelman, Lee. *No Future: Queer Theory and the Death Drive*. Durham: Duke UP, 2004.

Eliot, George. *Adam Bede*. Ed. Stephen Gill. London: Penguin, 1980.

——. *Daniel Deronda*. Ed. Terence Cave. London: Penguin, 1995.

——. *Middlemarch: A Study of Provincial Life*. Ed. Rosemary Ashton. London: Penguin, 1994.

——. *The Mill on the Floss*. Ed. A. S. Byatt. London: Penguin, 1979.

——. "The Natural History of German Life." In *George Eliot: Selected Critical Writings*. Ed. Rosemary Ashton. Oxford: Oxford UP, 1992. 260–95.

——. "Silly Novels by Lady Novelists." In *George Eliot: Selected Critical Writings*. Ed. Rosemary Ashton. Oxford: Oxford UP, 1992. 296–321.

Elmer, Jonathan. *On Lingering and Being Last: Race and Sovereignty in the New World*. New York: Fordham UP, 2008.

Engels, Friedrich. *The Condition of the Working Class in England*. Ed. Victor Kiernan. Trans. Florence Wischnewetzky. London: Penguin, 1987.

——. "Outlines of a Critique of Political Economy." In *Marx and Engels: Collected Works*. Trans. Richard Dixon et al. Vol. 3. New York: International, 1975–2005. 418–43.

Esposito, Roberto. *Bios: Biopolitics and Philosophy*. Trans. Timothy C. Campbell. Minneapolis: U of Minnesota P, 2008.

Esty, Jed. *Unseasonable Youth: Modernism, Colonialism, and the Fiction of Development*. Oxford: Oxford UP, 2011.

Fanon, Frantz. *The Wretched of the Earth*. Trans. Richard Philcox. New York: Grove, 2004.

Federici, Silvia. *Caliban and the Witch*. Brooklyn: Autonomedia, 2004.

"Female Novelists of the Period." *The Period* (22 Jan. 1870): 99. Reprinted in *Varieties of Women's Sensation Fiction: 1855–1890*. Vol. 1: Sensationalism and the Sensation Debate. Ed. Andrew Maunder. London: Pickering, 2004. 231–33.

Ferguson, Frances. *Solitude and the Sublime: Romanticism and the Aesthetics of Individuation*. New York: Routledge, 1992.

Flint, Kate. *Elizabeth Gaskell*. Plymouth: Northcote, 1995.

Forster, E. M. *Aspects of the Novel*. San Diego: Harcourt, 1955.

Foucault, Michael. *The Birth of the Clinic: An Archaeology of Medical Perception*. Trans. A. M. Sheridan Smith. New York: Vintage, 1974.

——. *The History of Sexuality, Volume 1: An Introduction*. Trans. Robert Hurley. New York: Vintage, 1990.

——. "Life: Experience and Science." In *Aesthetics, Method, and Epistemology*. Ed. James D. Faubion. New York: New Press, 1998. 465–78.

——. *The Order of Things: An Archaeology of the Human Sciences*. New York: Vintage, 1994.

——. *Security, Territory, Population: Lectures at the Collège de France, 1977–78*. Ed. Michel Senellart. Trans. Graham Burchell. Basingstoke: Palgrave, 2007.

——. *"Society Must Be Defended": Lectures at the Collège de France, 1975–76*. Ed. Mauro Bertani and Alessandro Fontana. Trans. David Macey. New York: Picador, 2003.

Frankel, Oz. *States of Inquiry*. Baltimore: Johns Hopkins UP, 2006.

"Frankenstein." Rev. of *Frankenstein*, by Mary Shelley. *The British Critic* (Apr. 1818): 432–38.

"Frankenstein." Rev. of *Frankenstein*, by Mary Shelley. *The Quarterly Review* (Jan. 1818): 379–85.

Franklin, Benjamin. *Observations concerning the Increase of Mankind*. Boston: Kneeland, 1755.

Freud, Sigmund. *Beyond the Pleasure Principle*. Ed and trans. James Strachey. New York: Norton, 1961.

——. *The Ego and the Id*. Ed. James Strachey. Trans. Joan Riviere. New York: Norton, 1960.

——. *Group Psychology and the Analysis of the Ego*. Ed. and trans. James Strachey. New York: Norton, 1959.

——. *Totem and Taboo*. Trans. James Strachey. New York: Norton, 1950.

Gagnier, Regenia. *The Insatiability of Human Wants: Economics and Aesthetics in Market Society*. Chicago: U of Chicago P, 2000.

——. "Methodology and New Historicism." *Journal of Victorian Culture* 4 (1999): 116–22.

Gallagher, Catherine. *The Body Economic: Life, Death, and Sensation in Political Economy and the Victorian Novel*. Princeton: Princeton UP, 2006.

——. *The Industrial Reformation of English Fiction: Social Discourse and Narrative Form, 1832–1867*. Chicago: U of Chicago P, 1985.

——. "The Rise of Fictionality." *The Novel*, vol. 1: History, Geography, and Culture. Ed. Franco Moretti. Princeton: Princeton UP, 2006. 336–63.

Galton, Francis. *Essays in Eugenics*. In *The World's Greatest Books*, vol. 15: Science. Ed. Lord Northcliffe and S. S. McClure. [New York]: McKinlay, 1910. 111–22.

Galton, Francis et al. "Eugenics: Its Definition, Scope, and Aims." In *Sociological Papers*. London: Macmillan, 1905. 45–99.

Gaskell, Elizabeth. *The Letters of Mrs. Gaskell*. Manchester: Manchester UP, 1997.

——. *Mary Barton: A Tale of Manchester Life*. Ed. Macdonald Daly. London: Penguin, 1996.

——. *North and South*. Ed. Patricia Ingham. London: Penguin, 1995.

Gilbert, Pamela K. *The Citizen's Body: Desire, Health, and the Social in Victorian England*. Columbus: Ohio State UP, 2007.

Gissing, George. *The Immortal Dickens*. New York: Palmer, 1925.

——. *New Grub Street*. Ed. Bernard Berganzi. London: Penguin, 1976.

——. *The Odd Women*. Ed. Elaine Showalter. London: Penguin, 1983.

Glendening, John. *The Evolutionary Imagination in Late-Victorian Novels*. Aldershot: Ashgate, 2007.

Godwin, William. *The Enquirer: Reflections on Education, Manners, and Literature*. 1st ed. London: Robinson, 1797.

——. *An Enquiry concerning Political Justice and Its Influence on Morals and Happiness*. 3 vols. Ed. F. E. L. Priestley. Toronto: U of Toronto P, 1946.

——. *Of Population: An Enquiry concerning the Power of Increase in the Numbers of Mankind.* London: Longman, 1820.

Goodlad, Lauren M. E. *Victorian Literature and the Victorian State: Character and Governance in a Liberal Society.* Baltimore: Johns Hopkins UP, 2003.

Greenslade, William P. *Degeneration, Culture, and the Novel: 1880–1940.* Cambridge: Cambridge UP, 2010.

Greenwood, James. *The Seven Curses of London.* London: Rivers, 1869.

Greg, William Rathbone. *Enigmas of Life.* Freeport, NY: Libraries Press, 1972.

——. "Mary Barton." In *Mistaken Aims and Attainable Ideals of the Artizan Class.* London: Trübner, 1876. 111–73.

——. "The Relation between Employers and Employed." *Westminster Review* 57 (1852): 61–95.

——. "Why Are Women Redundant?" *National Review* 4 (Apr. 1862): 434–60. Reprinted in *Literary and Social Judgments.* Vol. 2. London: Trübner, 1877. 44–90.

Grosz, Elizabeth. *Becoming Undone: Darwinian Reflections on Life, Politics, and Art.* Durham: Duke UP, 2011.

——. *The Nick of Time: Politics, Evolution, and the Untimely.* Durham: Duke UP, 2004.

Guerard, Albert J. *Conrad the Novelist.* Cambridge: Harvard UP, 1958.

Hacking, Ian. *The Taming of Chance.* Cambridge: Cambridge UP, 1990.

Hadley, Elaine. *Living Liberalism: Practical Citizenship in Mid-Victorian Britain.* Chicago: U of Chicago P, 2010.

Hamacher, Werner, and Kirk Wetters. "The Right to Have Rights (Four-and-a-Half Remarks)." *South Atlantic Quarterly* 103 (2004): 343–56.

Hardt, Michael, and Antonio Negri. *Multitude: War and Democracy in the Age of Empire.* London: Penguin, 2004.

Hardy, Thomas. *Jude the Obscure.* Ed. Dennis Taylor. London: Penguin, 1998.

——. *The Life and Work of Thomas Hardy.* Ed. Michael Millgate. Athens: U of Georgia P, 1985.

——. *The Mayor of Casterbridge.* Ed. Keith Wilson. London: Penguin, 1997.

——. *Tess of the D'Urbervilles.* Ed. David Skilton. London: Penguin, 1985.

Hazlitt, William. *A Reply to the "Essay on Population" by the Rev. T. R. Malthus, in a Series of Letters.* London: Longman, 1807.

Heidegger, Martin. *The Fundamental Concepts of Metaphysics.* Bloomington: Indiana UP, 1995.

Hensley, Nathan. "Allegories of the Contemporary." *Novel: A Forum on Fiction* 45 (2012): 276–300.

Herbert, Christopher. *Culture and Anomie: Ethnographic Imagination in the Nineteenth Century.* Chicago: U of Chicago P, 1991.

Hobbes, Thomas. *Leviathan; or, The Matter, Forme, & Power of a Common-Wealth, Ecclesiasticall and Civill.* Ed. C. B. Macpherson. London: Penguin, 1985.

Hollingshead, John. *Ragged London in 1861.* New York: Garland, 1985.

——. *Underground London.* London: Groombridge, 1862.

Hood, Thomas. "The Song of the Shirt." In *Selected Poems of Thomas Hood.* Ed. Susan J. Wolfson and Peter J. Manning. Pittsburgh: U of Pittsburgh P, 2000. 141–43.

Horkheimer, Max, and Theodor W. Adorno. *Dialectic of Enlightenment.* Trans. John Cumming. New York: Continuum, 1972.

Hughes, Winifred. *The Maniac in the Cellar: Sensation Novels of the 1860s.* Princeton: Princeton UP, 1980.

Hume, David. "Of the Populousness of Ancient Nations." In *Essays and Treatises on Several Subjects.* Vol. 1. Edinburgh: Bell, 1817. 373–443.

Huxley, Thomas. "The Struggle for Existence in Human Society." In *Evolution and Ethics, and Other Essays.* London: Macmillan, 1895.

Jaffe, Audrey. *The Affective Life of the Average Man: The Victorian Novel and the Stock-Market Graph.* Columbus: Ohio State UP, 2010.

——. *Vanishing Points: Dickens, Narrative, and the Subject of Omniscience.* Berkeley: U of California P, 1991.

Jakobson, Roman. "On Realism in Art." In *Language in Literature.* Ed. Krystyna Pomorska and Stephen Rudy. Cambridge, MA: Belknap, 1987.

James, Henry. "*Daniel Deronda*: A Conversation." *Literary Criticism.* Vol. 1. New York: Library of America, 1984. 974–92.

James, Patricia. *Population Malthus: His Life and Times.* London: Routledge, 1979.

Jameson, Fredric. *The Political Unconscious: Narrative as a Socially Symbolic Act.* Ithaca: Cornell UP, 1981.

Janowitz, Anne. "The Artifactual Sublime: Making London Poetry." In *Romantic Metropolis: The Urban Scene of British Culture, 1780–1840.* Ed. James Chandler and Kevin Gilmartin. Cambridge: Cambridge UP, 2005. 246–60.

Johnson, Barbara. "*The Last Man.*" In *The Other Mary Shelley: Beyond Frankenstein.* Ed. Audrey Fisch, Anne Mellor, and Esther Schor. New York: Oxford UP, 1993. 258–66.

Johnson, Claudia. "F. R. Leavis: The 'Great Tradition' of the English Novel and the Jewish Part." *Nineteenth-Century Literature* 56 (2001): 198–227.

Jones, Gareth Stedman. *Outcast London: A Study in the Relations between Classes in Victorian Society.* New York: Pantheon, 1984.

Joyce, Patrick. *The Rule of Freedom: Liberalism and the Modern City.* London: Verso, 2003.

Kant, Immanuel. "Announcement of the Near Conclusion of a Treaty of Eternal Peace in Philosophy." In *Raising the Tone of Philosophy: Late Essays by Immanuel Kant, Transformative Critique by Jacques Derrida.* Ed. Peter Fenves. Baltimore: Johns Hopkins UP, 1993. 83–100.

——. *Anthropology from a Pragmatic Point of View.* Trans. Mary J. Gregor. The Hague: Nijhoff, 1974.

——. "Duties towards the Body in Respect of Sexual Impulse." In *Lectures on Ethics.* Trans. Louis Infield. Indianapolis: Hackett, 1963. 162–68.

——. *Toward Perpetual Peace.* Ed. Pauline Kleingeld. Trans. David L. Colclasure. New Haven: Yale UP, 2006.

Kay-Shuttleworth, James Phillips. "The Moral and Physical Condition of the Working Classes of Manchester in 1832." In *Four Periods of Public Education.* London: Longman, 1862. 3–84.

Keating, Peter, ed. *Into Unknown England, 1866–1913: Selections from the Social Explorers.* Manchester: Manchester UP, 1976.

King, Andrew, and John Plunkett, eds. *Victorian Print Media.* Oxford: Oxford UP, 2005.

Kingsley, Charles. *Alton Locke: Tailor and Poet.* London: Macmillan, 1890.

——. "Cheap Clothes and Nasty." In *Alton Locke: Tailor and Poet*. London: Macmillan, 1890.

——. "Recent Novels." *Fraser's Magazine* 39 (1849): 417–32.

Knighton, William. "Suicidal Mania." *Contemporary Review* 39 (1881): 81–90.

Knox, Robert. *The Races of Men: A Fragment*. Philadelphia: Lea, 1850.

Koven, Seth. *Slumming: Sexual and Social Politics in Victorian London*. Princeton: Princeton UP, 2004.

Krishnan, Sanjay. "Opium and Empire: The Transports of Thomas De Quincey." *boundary 2* 33 (2006): 203–34.

Laclau, Ernesto. *On Populist Reason*. London: Verso, 2007.

"Lady Audley's Secret." Rev. of *Lady Audley's Secret*, by Mary Braddon. *The Spectator* 35 (1862): 1196–97.

Laplace, Pierre Simon. *A Philosophical Essay on Probabilities*. Trans. Frederick Wilson Truscott and Frederick Lincoln Emory. New York: Dover, 1951.

"The Last Man." Rev. of *The Last Man*, by Mary Shelley. *The Monthly Review, or Literary Journal* (Mar. 1826): 333–35.

"*The Last Man*. By the Author of 'Frankenstein.'" Rev. of *The Last Man*, by Mary Shelley. *The Literary Gazette and Journal of Belles Lettres, Arts, Sciences, &c.* (18 Feb. 1826): 102–3.

"The Last Man, by the Author of Frankenstein." Rev. of *The Last Man*, by Mary Shelley. *The Panoramic Miscellany* (Mar. 1826): 380–86.

Lawler, Donald. "Reframing *Jekyll and Hyde*: Robert Louis Stevenson and the Strange Case of Gothic Science Fiction." In *Dr. Jekyll and Mr. Hyde After One Hundred Years*. Ed. William Veeder and Gordon Hirsch. Chicago, U of Chicago P, 1988. 247–61.

Leavis, F. R. *For Continuity*. Freeport, NY: Libraries Press, 1933.

——. *The Great Tradition: George Eliot, Henry James, Joseph Conrad*. London: Chatto, 1948.

——. "Gwendolen Harleth." Reprinted in *The London Review of Books* 4:1 (1982).

Leavis, Q. D. *Fiction and the Reading Public*. London: Chatto, 1939.

Le Bon, Gustave. *The Crowd: A Study of the Popular Mind*. London: Benn, 1930.

Levine, Caroline. *Forms: Whole, Rhythm, Hierarchy, Network*. Princeton: Princeton UP, 2015.

——. "Strategic Formalism: Toward a New Method in Cultural Studies." *Victorian Studies* 48 (2006): 625–57.

Levitan, Kathrin. *A Cultural History of the British Census*. New York: Palgrave, 2011.

Lewes, G. H. *Principles of Success in Literature*. Ed. Fred N. Scott. 3rd ed. Boston: Allyn, 1891.

Loesberg, Jonathan. "The Ideology of Narrative Form in Sensation Fiction." *Representations* 13 (1986): 115–38.

Løkke, Kari. "The Last Man." *The Cambridge Companion to Mary Shelley*. Ed. Esther Schor. Cambridge: Cambridge UP, 2003. 116–34.

Lombroso, Cesare. *Criminal Man*. Trans. Mary Gibson and Nicole Hahn Rafter. Durham: Duke UP, 2006.

——. "The Heredity of Acquired Characteristics." *The Forum* 24 (Oct. 1897): 200–208.

——. "Innovation and Inertia in the World of Psychology." *The Monist* 1 (Apr. 1891): 344–61.

Lougy, "Filth, Liminality, and Abjection in Charles Dickens's *Bleak House*." *English Literary History* 69 (2002): 488–91.

Lucas, John. *The Literature of Change: Studies in the Nineteenth-Century Provincial Novel.* Hassocks: Harvester, 1980.

——. "Mrs. Gaskell and Brotherhood." In *Tradition and Tolerance in Nineteenth Century Fiction.* Ed. D. Howard, J. Lucas, and J. Goode. London: Routledge, 1966. 141–205.

Lukács, Georg. "Narrate or Describe?" *Writer and Critic and Other Essays.* Ed. and trans. Arthur D. Kahn. New York: Grosset, 1970. 110–48.

——. *The Theory of the Novel.* Trans. Anna Bostock. Cambridge: MIT Press, 1971.

Lynch, Deidre Shauna. *The Economy of Character: Novels, Market Culture, and the Business of Inner Meaning.* Chicago: U of Chicago P, 1998.

Maistre, Joseph Marie [Comte de]. *Considerations on France.* Ed. and trans. Richard A. Lebrun. Cambridge: Cambridge UP, 1994.

Malthus, Thomas. *An Essay on the Principle of Population.* Ed. Anthony Flew. London: Penguin, 1970.

[Mansel, H. L.] "Sensation Novels." *Quarterly Review* 113 (Apr. 1963): 481–514. Reprinted in *Varieties of Women's Sensation Fiction: 1855–1890.* Vol. 1: Sensationalism and the Sensation Debate. Ed. Andrew Maunder. London: Pickering, 2004. 32–56.

Marcus, Stephen. *Engels, Manchester, and the Working Class.* New York: Norton, 1985.

Marshall, David. *The Surprising Effects of Sympathy.* Chicago: U of Chicago P, 1988.

Marx, Karl. *Capital: A Critique of Political Economy.* Trans. Ben Fowkes. London: Penguin, 1976.

——. *Economic and Philosophical Manuscripts of 1844. The Marx-Engels Reader.* 2nd ed. Ed. Robert C. Tucker. New York: Norton, 1978. 66–125.

——. "The English Middle Class." In *Marx and Engels on Literature and Art: A Selection of Writings.* Ed. Lee Baxandall and Stefan Morawski. New York: International, 1973. 106.

——. *The German Ideology.* In *The Marx-Engels Reader.* 2nd ed. Ed. Robert C. Tucker. New York: Norton, 1978. 146–200.

——. *Grundrisse: Foundations of the Critique of Political Economy.* Trans. Martin Nicolaus. London: Penguin, 1973.

——. "On the Jewish Question." In *The Marx-Engels Reader.* 2nd ed. Ed. Robert C. Tucker. New York: Norton, 1978. 26–52.

——. *The Poverty of Philosophy.* Trans. H. Quelch. Amherst, NY: Prometheus, 1995.

——. "Wage Labor and Capital." In *The Marx-Engels Reader.* 2nd ed. Ed. Robert C. Tucker. New York: Norton, 1978. 203–17.

Marx, Karl, and Friedrich Engels. *The Holy Family, or, Critique of Critical Critique.* Moscow: Foreign Languages Publishing House, 1956.

——. "Theses on Feuerbach." In *The Marx-Engels Reader.* 2nd ed. Ed. Robert C. Tucker. New York: Norton, 1978. 143–45.

Matz, Aaron. "Terminal Satire and *Jude the Obscure*." *English Literary History* 73 (2006): 519–47.

Maudsley, Henry. *Body and Mind.* London: Macmillan, 1873.

Maunder, Andrew, ed. *Varieties of Women's Sensation Fiction: 1855–1890.* Vol. 1: Sensationalism and the Sensation Debate. Ed. Andrew Maunder. London: Pickering, 2004.

Mayhew, Henry. *London Labour and the London Poor.* 4 vols. London: Griffin, 1861.

McDougall, William. *The Group Mind: A Sketch of the Principles of Collective Psychology.* New York: Putnam, 1920.

McGurl, Mark. "The Posthuman Comedy." *Critical Inquiry* 38.3 (2012): 533–53.

McKusick, James. *Green Writing: Romanticism and Ecology.* New York: St. Martin's, 2000.

McLane, Maureen N. *Romanticism and the Human Sciences: Poetry, Population, and the Discourse of the Species.* Cambridge: Cambridge UP, 2000.

Mellor, Anne K. *Romanticism and Gender.* New York: Routledge, 1993.

Mill, John Stuart. "Civilization." *London and Westminster Review* (Apr. 1836). Reprinted in *J. S. Mill on Civilization and Barbarism.* Ed. Michael Levin. London: Routledge, 2004.

——. *Principles of Political Economy.* Ed. Jonathan Riley. Oxford: Oxford UP, 1994.

——. *A System of Logic, Ratiocinative and Inductive: Being a Connected View of the Principles of Evidence and the Methods of Scientific Investigation.* London: Longmans, 1872.

Miller, D. A. *The Novel and the Police.* Berkeley: U of California P, 1988.

Miller, J. Hillis. "The Fiction of Realism: *Sketches by Boz, Oliver Twist,* and Cruikshank's Illustrations." In *Dickens Centennial Essays.* Ed. Ada Nisbet and Blake Nevius. Berkeley: U of California P, 1971. 85–126.

——. "Interpretation in *Bleak House.*" In *Victorian Subjects.* Durham: Duke UP, 1991. 179–200.

Miller, Karl. *Doubles: Studies in Literary History.* New York: Oxford UP, 1985.

Mills, Catherine. "Biopolitics and the Concept of Life." In *Biopower: Foucault and Beyond.* Ed. Vernon W. Cisney and Nicolae Morar. Chicago: U of Chicago P, 2016. 82–101.

Miyoshi, Masao. *The Divided Self: A Perspective on the Literature of the Victorians.* New York: New York UP, 1969.

Morel, Bénédict Auguste. *Traité des Dégénérescenes Physiques, Intellectuelles et Morales de l'Espèce Humaine.* Paris: Baillière, 1857.

Moretti, Franco. *Graphs, Maps, Trees: Abstract Models for Literary History.* London: Verso, 2007.

——. *Signs Taken for Wonders: Essays in the Sociology of Literary Forms.* Revised ed. Trans. Susan Fischer, David Forgacs, and David Miller. London: Verso, 1988.

——. *The Way of the World: The Bildungsroman in European Culture.* London: Verso, 2000.

Morris, Pam. *Imagining Inclusive Society in Nineteenth-Century Novels: The Code of Sincerity in the Public Sphere.* Baltimore: Johns Hopkins UP, 2004.

Morton, Peter. *The Vital Science: Biology and the Literary Imagination, 1860–1900.* London: Unwin, 1984.

Morton, Timothy. *Hyperobjects: Philosophy and Ecology after the End of the World.* Minneapolis: U of Minnesota P, 2013.

Murphet, Julian. "The Mole and the Multiple: A Chiasmus of Character." *New Literary History* 42 (2011): 255–76.

Nicoll, Henry James. *Great Orators: Burke, Fox, Sheridan, Pitt.* Edinburgh: MacNiven, 1880.

Nordau, Max. *Degeneration.* 7th ed. Trans. from 2nd German ed. New York: Appleton, 1895.

[Oliphant, Margaret.] "The Byways of Literature: Reading for the Million." *Black-wood's Edinburgh Magazine* 84 (Aug. 1858): 200–215. Reprinted in Andrew King and John Plunkett, eds., *Victorian Print Media*. Oxford: Oxford UP, 2005. 196–206.

——. "Novels." *Blackwood's Edinburgh Magazine* 102 (Sept. 1867): 257–80. Reprinted in Andrew Maunder, ed., *Varieties of Women's Sensation Fiction: 1855–1890*. Vol. 1: Sensationalism and the Sensation Debate. Ed. Andrew Maunder. London: Pickering, 2004. 171–90.

——. "Sensational Novels." *Blackwood's Edinburgh Magazine* 91 (May 1862): 564–80. Reprinted in Andrew Maunder, ed., *Varieties of Women's Sensation Fiction: 1855–1890*. Vol. 1: Sensationalism and the Sensation Debate. Ed. Andrew Maunder. London: Pickering, 2004. 8–15.

"Our Female Sensation Novelists." *Christian Remembrancer* 46 (Jul. 1864): 209–36.

"Our Survey of Literature and Science." *The Cornhill Magazine* 7 (1863): 132–44.

Owen, Robert. *A New View of Society: Essays on the Formation of Character*. London: Dent, 1927.

Page, H. A. "The Morality of Literary Art." *The Contemporary Review* 5 (1867): 161–89.

Paley, Morton. "*The Last Man*: Apocalypse without Millennium." *Keats-Shelley Review* 4 (1989): 1–25.

Parry, Benita. *Conrad and Imperialism*. London: Macmillan, 1983.

Pateman, Carole. *The Sexual Contract*. Stanford: Stanford UP, 1988.

Petty, William. *Another Essay in Political Arithmetick, concerning the Growth of the City of London: with the Measures, Periods, Causes, and Consequences Thereof*. London: Pardoe, 1683.

Pick, Daniel. *Faces of Degeneration: A European Disorder, 1848–1918*. Cambridge: Cambridge UP, 1989.

Pippin, Robert. "Authenticity in Painting: Remarks on Michael Fried's Art History." *Critical Inquiry* 31 (2005): 575–98.

Plotz, John. *The Crowd: British Literature and Public Politics*. Berkeley: U of California P, 2000.

Poe, Edgar Allan. "The Man of the Crowd." In *Edgar Allan Poe: Poetry, Tales, and Essays*. Ed. Patrick F. Quinn and G. R. Thompson. New York: Library of America, 1996. 388–96.

Poovey, Mary. *Making a Social Body: British Cultural Formation, 1830–1864*. Chicago: U of Chicago P, 1995.

——. *Uneven Developments: The Ideological Work of Gender in Mid-Victorian England*. Chicago: U of Chicago P, 1988.

Rabinbach, Anson. *The Human Motor: Energy, Fatigue, and the Origins of Modernity*. Berkeley: U of California P, 1992.

[Rae, W. Fraser.] "Sensation Novelists: Miss Braddon." *The North British Review* 43 (1865): 180–204.

Rancière, Jacques. *The Politics of Literature*. Trans. Julie Rose. Cambridge: Polity, 2011.

——. *Proletarian Nights: The Workers' Dream in Nineteenth-Century France*. Trans. John Drury. New York: Verso, 2012.

——. "Ten Theses on Politics." In *Dissensus: On Politics and Aesthetics*. Ed. and trans. Steven Corcoran. London: Continuum, 2010. 27–44.

——. "Who Is the Subject of the Rights of Man?" *South Atlantic Quarterly* 103 (2004): 297–310.

Reynolds, G. W. M. *The Mysteries of London.* First series. London: Vickers, 1845.

Richardson, Alan. "*The Last Man* and the Plague of Empire." Romantic Circles MOO Conference. 13 Sept. 1997. Available at www.rc.umd.edu/villa/vc97/richard son.html.

Richardson, Angelique. *Love and Eugenics in the Late Nineteenth Century: Rational Reproduction and the New Woman.* Oxford: Oxford UP, 2003.

Robbins, Bruce. "Cruelty Is Bad: Banality and Proximity in *Never Let Me Go*." *Novel: A Forum on Fiction* 40 (2007): 289–302.

——. "Telescopic Philanthropy: Professionalism and Responsibility in *Bleak House*." In *Bleak House: Charles Dickens.* Ed. Jeremy Tambling. New York: St. Martin's, 1998. 139–62.

Rose, Nikolas S. *Powers of Freedom: Reframing Political Thought.* New York: Cambridge UP, 1999.

Rousseau, Jean-Jacques. *The Confessions of Jean-Jacques Rousseau.* Ed. and trans. J. M. Cohen. London: Penguin, 1953.

Rubery, Matthew. *The Novelty of Newspapers.* Oxford: Oxford UP, 2009.

Ruskin, John. "Fiction, Fair and Foul." Part 1. *The Nineteenth Century* 7 (Jun. 1880): 944–46. Rpt. in *The Works of John Ruskin.* Ed. E. T. Cook and Alexander Wedderburn. Vol. 34. London: Allen, 1908. 265–302.

——. "Fiction, Fair and Foul." Part 5. *The Nineteenth Century* 10 (Oct. 1880): 520–21. Rpt. in *The Works of John Ruskin.* Ed. E. T. Cook and Alexander Wedderburn. Vol. 34. London: Allen, 1908. 370–94.

——. *The Stones of Venice.* New York: Alden, 1885.

——. *Unto This Last.* Ed. Clive Wilmer. London: Penguin, 1985.

Said, Edward W. *Culture and Imperialism.* New York: Vintage, 1993.

Sala, George Augustus. "The Cant of Modern Criticism." *Belgravia* 4 (Nov. 1867): 45–55. Reprinted in Andrew Maunder, ed., *Varieties of Women's Sensation Fiction: 1855–1890.* Vol. 1: Sensationalism and the Sensation Debate. Ed. Andrew Maunder. London: Pickering, 2004. 194–209.

——. "On the Sensational in Literature and Art." *Belgravia* 4 (1868): 455.

Santner, Eric L. *On Creaturely Life: Rilke, Benjamin, Sebald.* Chicago: U of Chicago P, 2006.

——. *The Royal Remains: The People's Two Bodies and the Endgames of Sovereignty.* Chicago: U of Chicago P, 2011.

Sayeau, Michael. "Work, Unemployment, and the Exhaustion of Fiction in *Heart of Darkness*." *Novel: A Forum on Fiction* 39 (2006): 337–60.

Schmitt, Carl. *The Concept of the Political.* Trans. George Schwab. Chicago: U of Chicago P, 1996.

Schor, Hilary M. *Scheherezade in the Marketplace: Elizabeth Gaskell and the Victorian Novel.* Oxford: Oxford UP, 1992.

Schweber, Libby. *Disciplining Statistics: Demography and Vital Statistics in France and England, 1830–1885.* Durham: Duke UP, 2006.

Scott, Joan Wallach. *Gender and the Politics of History.* New York: Columbia UP, 1999.

"The Sensational Williams." *All the Year Round* (Feb. 1864): 14–17. Reprinted in Andrew Maunder, ed., *Varieties of Women's Sensation Fiction: 1855–1890*. Vol. 1: Sensationalism and the Sensation Debate. Ed. Andrew Maunder. London: Pickering, 2004. 97–103.

"A Sermon Upon Novels." *London Review* (Sept. 1867): 293–94. Reprinted in Andrew Maunder, ed., *Varieties of Women's Sensation Fiction: 1855–1890*. Vol. 1: Sensationalism and the Sensation Debate. Ed. Andrew Maunder. London: Pickering, 2004. 191–93.

Shelley, Mary. *Frankenstein; or, The Modern Prometheus*. Ed. J. Paul Hunter. New York: Norton, 1996.

——. *The Last Man*. Ed. Morton D. Paley. Oxford: Oxford UP, 2008.

Shelley, Percy Bysshe. *A Defence of Poetry*. *Shelley's Poetry and Prose*. Ed. Donald H. Reiman and Neil Fraistat. New York: Norton, 2002. 509–35.

——. *Oedipus Tyrannus; or, Swellfoot the Tyrant*. *The Complete Poetical Works of Percy Bysshe Shelley*. Ed. Thomas Hutchinson. London: Oxford UP, 1905. 430–51.

——. "On *Frankenstein*." *The Athenaeum Journal of Literature, Science, and the Fine Arts* 10 Nov. 1832. Reprinted in *Frankenstein*. By Mary Shelley. Ed. J. Paul Hunter. New York: Norton, 1996. 185–86.

——. *A Philosophical View of Reform*. Ed. T. W. Rolleston. London: Oxford UP, 1920.

——. *The Revolt of Islam*. *The Complete Poetical Works of Percy Bysshe Shelley*. Ed. Thomas Hutchinson. London: Oxford UP, 1905. 31–156.

Simmel, Georg. "The Metropolis and Mental Life." In *The Sociology of Georg Simmel*. Ed. and trans. Kurt H. Wolff. New York: Free Press, 1950. 409–24.

Smith, Adam. *An Enquiry into the Nature and Causes of the Wealth of Nations*. Ed. Kathryn Sutherland. Oxford: Oxford UP, 1998.

——. *The Theory of Moral Sentiments*. Ed. Knud Haakonssen. Cambridge: Cambridge UP, 2002.

Smith, Thomas Southwood. *The Philosophy of Health; or, An Exposition on the Physical and Mental Constitution of Man, with a View to the Promotion of Human Longevity and Happiness*. 3rd ed. London: Cox, 1847.

Southey, Robert. Review of *An Essay on the Principle of Population*, by T. R. Malthus. *The Annual Review, and History of Literature; for 1803*. Vol. 2. London: Longman, 1804. 292–301.

Spencer, Herbert. *Principles of Biology*. 2 vols. New York: Appleton, 1910.

——. *Social Statics*. New York: Schalkenbach, 1954.

——. "A Theory of Population, Deduced from the General Law of Animal Fertility." *Westminster Review* 57 (1852): 250–68.

Spivak, Gayatri Chakravorty. *A Critique of Postcolonial Reason: Toward a History of the Vanishing Present*. Cambridge: Harvard UP, 1999.

Stallybrass, Peter, and Allon White. *The Politics and Poetics of Transgression*. Ithaca: Cornell UP, 1986.

Sterrenburg, Lee. "Mary Shelley's Monster: Politics and Psyche in *Frankenstein*." In *The Endurance of Frankenstein: Essays on Mary Shelley's Novel*. Ed. George Levine and U. C. Knoepflmacher. Berkeley: U of California P, 1979. 143–71.

Stevens, Jacqueline. *Reproducing the State*. Princeton: Princeton UP, 1999.

Stevenson, Robert Louis. *The Strange Case of Dr. Jekyll and Mr. Hyde.* Ed. Robert Mighall. London: Penguin, 2002.

Stoler, Ann Laura. *Race and the Education of Desire: Foucault's* History of Sexuality *and the Colonial Order of Things.* Durham: Duke UP, 1995.

Storer, Richard. "F. R. Leavis and 'Gwendolen Harleth.'" In *F. R. Leavis: Essays and Documents.* Ed. Ian Mackillop and Richard Storer. London: Continuum, 2005. 40–49.

Storey, Mark. *The Problem of Poetry in the Romantic Period.* New York: St. Martin's, 2000.

Stout, Daniel. "Nothing Personal: The Decapitation of Character in *A Tale of Two Cities.*" *Novel: A Forum on Fiction* 41 (2007): 29–52.

Stow, John. *A Survey of London, Written in the Year 1598.* Ed. William J. Thoms. London: Whittaker, 1842.

Surridge, Lisa. "Working-Class Masculinities in *Mary Barton.*" *Victorian Literature and Culture* 28 (2000): 331–43.

Sussman, Charlotte. "'Islanded in the World': Cultural Memory and Human Mobility in *The Last Man.*" *PMLA* 118 (2003): 286–301.

———. "'I Wonder Whether Poor Miss Sally Godfrey Be Living or Dead': The Married Woman and the Rise of the Novel." *diacritics* 20 (1990): 88–102.

Symons, Jelinger C. *Tactics for the Times: As Regards the Condition and Treatment of the Dangerous Classes.* London: Ollivier, 1849.

Taine, Hippolyte. *The Origins of Contemporary France, Vol. I: The French Revolution.* Trans. John Durand. New York: Holt, 1878.

Tarde, Gabriel. "Human Aggregation and Crime." *Popular Science Monthly* 45 (1894): 447–59.

———. *The Laws of Imitation.* Trans. Elise Clews Parsons. Gloucester, MA: Smith, 1962.

———. "The Public and the Crowd." *Gabriel Tarde on Communication and Social Influence.* Ed Terry Clark. Chicago: U of Chicago P, 1969. 277–96.

Taylor, William Cooke. *The Natural History of Society in the Barbarous and Civilised State.* London: Longman, 1840.

Tocqueville, Alexis Charles Henri Maurice Clerel de. *Memoir on Pauperism.* Trans. Seymour Drescher. Chicago: Dee, 1997.

Trodd, Anthea. *Domestic Crime in the Victorian Novel.* New York: St. Martin's, 1989.

Trollope, Anthony. *Autobiography of Anthony Trollope.* New York: Dodd, 1912.

———. *The Warden.* 1855. Ed. Robin Gilmour. London: Penguin, 1986.

Trotter, Wilfred. "Herd Instinct and Its Bearing on the Psychology of Civilized Man." Rpt. in *Instincts of the Herd in Peace and War.* London: Unwin, 1917.

Vaughan, Robert. *The Age of Great Cities; or, Modern Society Viewed in its Relation to Intelligence, Morals, and Religion.* London: Jackson, 1843.

Wallace, Robert. *A Dissertation on the Numbers of Mankind in Ancient and Modern Times.* Edinburgh: Constable, 1809.

Waterman, A. M. C. "'The Bitter Argument between Economists and Human Beings': The Reception of Malthus's *Essay on Population.*" *Research in the History of Economic Thought and Methodology* 20.1 (2002): 261–70.

Watt, Ian. *The Rise of the Novel.* 2nd American ed. Berkeley: U of California P, 2001.

Wedgwood, Julia. "Contemporary Records I.: Fiction" *The Contemporary Review* 49 (1886): 590–98.

Weismann, August. *Essays upon Heredity.* London: Oxford: Clarendon, 1889.

Williams, Raymond. *The Country and the City.* New York: Oxford UP, 1973.

———. *Culture and Society: Coleridge to Orwell.* London: Hogarth, 1990.

———. *Keywords: A Vocabulary of Culture and Society.* New York: Oxford UP, 1983.

———. *Marxism and Literature.* Oxford: Oxford UP, 1977.

Wilson, Elizabeth. *The Sphinx in the City: Urban Life, the Control of Disorder, and Women.* Berkeley: U of California P, 1991.

Wohl, Anthony S. *Endangered Lives: Public Health in Victorian Britain.* Cambridge: Harvard UP, 1983.

Wollstonecraft, Mary. *A Vindication of the Rights of Woman.* Ed. Miriam Brody. Harmondsworth: Penguin, 1986.

Woloch, Alex. *The One vs. the Many: Minor Characters and the Space of the Protagonist in the Novel.* Princeton: Princeton UP, 2003.

Wood, Ellen. *East Lynne.* Ed. Andrew Maunder. Peterborough, Ontario: Broadview, 2000.

Woolf, Virginia. "Modern Fiction." *The Essays of Virginia Woolf.* Ed. Andrew McNeillie. Vol. 4. London: Hogarth, 1984.

———. *Mrs. Dalloway.* Orlando: Harcourt, 2005.

———. "The Novels of George Gissing." *The Essays of Virginia Woolf.* Ed. Andrew McNeillie. Vol. 1. San Diego: Harcourt, 1986. 355–62.

Wordsworth, William. "The Old Cumberland Beggar." In *Lyrical Ballads, and Other Poems, 1797–1800.* Ed. James Butler and Karen Green. Ithaca: Cornell UP, 1992. 228–34.

———. Preface. *Lyrical Ballads, and Other Poems.* Ed. James Butler and Karen Green. Ithaca: Cornell UP, 1992. 741–60.

———. *The Prelude, or Growth of a Poet's Mind.* Ed. Ernest de Selincourt. Oxford: Oxford UP, 1970.

———. "We Are Seven." *Lyrical Ballads, and Other Poems, 1797–1800.* Ed. James Butler and Karen Green. Ithaca: Cornell UP, 1992. 73–75.

Wrigley, E. A., and R. S. Shofield. *The Population History of England, 1541–1871: A Reconstruction.* Cambridge: Harvard UP, 1981.

Yeazell, Ruth Bernard. "Why Political Novels Have Heroines." *Novel: A Forum on Fiction* 18 (1985): 126–44.

Index

Abelove, Henry, 44

abjection, 19, 27, 57, 69, 93, 94, 134, 149, 154; and contamination, 111; in Malthus, 59; of redundant population, 142, 156; and social crisis, 91–92, 121; and unemployment, 100

Achebe, Chinua, 215

Acton, William, 23, 235n16

Agamben, Giorgio, 221; bare life, 25, 65, 67, 86–87, 223, 227n26, 231n38; and biopower, 24, 116; definitions of the human, 26, 54, 71, 228n30, 230n26, 231n38; on sovereignty, 23–24; on surplus life, 87

Adderley, Sir Charles, 163–164

Addison, Joseph, 2

aggregation, 2, 10, 15, 30, 76, 82, 115, 124, 212, 217, 226n9, 227n23, 234n6; Gothic, 129; language of, 22; and mass life, 18, 21–23, 31, 38, 118–119, 214; narratives of, 77–78, 142, 168, 211, 218; and otherness, 45, 49; politics of, 28, 55, 85; pressures of, 3, 12, 18, 76; and psychoanalysis, 219–221; and statistics, 13, 75–76, 93, 115, 136, 200. *See also* crowds and crowding; population; demography; masses; statistics

alienation, 2, 25, 82, 215, 233n49

Althusser, Louis, 105

Anderson, Amanda, 13–14, 234n5

Anderson, Benedict, 76

anomie. *See* Durkheim, Émile

anthropometry, 185, 190. *See also* criminology

anthropology, 40, 59, 81, 89, 226n16, 231n31, 233n48, 245n13; criminal, 216; and exogamy, 220; philosophical, 36, 38, 46, 59; and population management, 76

anti-bildungsroman, 28, 33, 171, 178, 180, 198, 206

Arendt, Hannah: on human rights, 9, 33, 66–67, 230n26; on imperialism and surplus population, 33, 211; on totalitarianism, 223, 230n21

Aristotle: on human as political animal, 25, 64, 228n30, 231n38; mere life vs. the good life, 25; mimesis as innate human tendency, 37, 229n4; on the nature of life, 24–26

Armstrong, Nancy, 13–14, 117–118, 140

Arnold, Matthew, 44, 163, 165, 244n32; sensationalism and criticism, 163–165

Atwood, Margaret, 222

Austen, Jane, 143, 162

autobiography, 38

Balibar, Etienne, 81, 92, 102, 104, 234n6, 234n10

bare life (mere life), 9, 36, 64, 87, 93–94, 231n38, 235n15; degradation of, 25, 59, 86–87; *homo sacer*, 24, 54, 230n26; and political domination, 24, 27, 67, 87; reduction to, 86, 61, 86, 223; vs. good life, 25–26. *See also* Agamben, Giorgio; Benjamin, Walter; poverty

Bauman, Zygmunt, 4, 9

Bazzicalupo, Laura, 25, 228n29

Beer, Gillian, 184, 244n7, 245n12

Benjamin, Walter, 24, 160, 229n6, 231n38, 234n10, 243n28

Berlant, Laurent, 191

Bertillon, Alphonse, 167, 189

Bichat, Marie-François Xavier, 5–6, 24, 226n7, 228n31

bildungsroman, 11, 32, 168–169, 171, 180, 191, 198; collapse of, 206; as microcosm of history, 184; and national destiny, 169. *See also* anti-bildungsroman

Binny, John, 94

biocracy, 6

bioeconomics, 15, 87

biology and the life sciences, 5–7, 24, 39, 170, 181–183, 185, 190–194, 203, 204

biopolitics, 5, 8–14, 20, 23, 27–28, 40, 47, 65, 70, 203, 220, 227nn25–30; the biopolitical imagination, 3, 10, 45, 223; and economic